Psychophysiological Aspects of Reading and Learning

MONOGRAPHS IN PSYCHOBIOLOGY: AN INTEGRATED APPROACH

Edited by Samuel A. Corson
Department of Educational Theory and Practice
Ohio State University
Columbus, Ohio, U.S.A.

VOLUME 1 PSYCHOPHYSIOLOGICAL ASPECTS OF READING AND LEARNING
Edited by Victor M. Rentel, Samuel A. Corson, and Bruce R. Dunn

Other volumes in preparation

ISSN 0749-1190

The publisher will accept continuation orders for this series, which may be cancelled at any time and which provide for the automatic billing and shipping of each title in the series upon publication. Please write for details.

Psychophysiological Aspects of Reading and Learning

Edited by

Victor M. Rentel
Ohio State University
Columbus, Ohio

Samuel A. Corson
Ohio State University
Columbus, Ohio

Bruce R. Dunn
University of West Florida
Pensacola, Florida

Gordon and Breach Science Publishers
New York • London • Paris • Montreux • Tokyo

Published under license by OPA Ltd. for Gordon and Breach Science Publishers S.A.

Gordon and Breach Science Publishers

P.O. Box 786
Cooper Station
New York, New York 10276
United States of America

P.O. Box 197
London WC2E 9XP
England

58, rue Lhomond
75005 Paris
France

P.O. Box 161
1820 Montreux 2
Switzerland

14-9 Okubo 3-chome
Shinjuku-ku
Tokyo 160
Japan

Library of Congress Cataloging in Publication Data
Main entry under title:

Psychophysiological aspects of reading.

(Monographs in psychobiology, ISSN 0749-1190; v. 1)
Includes bibliographies.
1. Reading—Physiological aspects. 2. Reading—Psychology of. 3. Neurolinguistics. 4. Psycholinguistics. 5. Metalanguage. I. Rentel, Victor M. II. Corson, Samuel Abraham, 1909-. III. Dunn, Bruce R. IV. Series. [DNLM: 1. Psychophysiology. 2. Reading. 3. Cognition—physiology. 4. Psycholinguistics. W1 M0568NS v. 1/BF456.R2 P974]
QP399.P793 1985 153.6 84-21149

ISBN 2-88124-000-3 (cloth), 2-88124-025-9 (paper).

Printed in Great Britain by Bell and Bain Ltd., Glasgow.

CONTENTS

Series Editor's Preface

The guiding principles underlying this series of monographs can perhaps be best epitomized by a quip from a distinguished American neurophysiologist, the late Ralph W. Gerard, to the effect that "wherever there is a crooked thought, there must be a corresponding crooked molecule." The reverse in some situations is also true; that is, biological molecules can in turn be "twisted" by "crooked" thoughts and by psychosocial events.

During the past several decades, biomedical and behavioral scientists and clinicians have come to recognize the limitations of mechanistic behaviorism, on the one hand, and of the traditional reductionist biomedical model of health and disease, on the other.

The inadequacies of these reductionist models can be ascribed to:

1. the lingering illusion of mind-body dualism and the consequent fractionation in research, diagnosis, and treatment of physical, emotional, and mental health problems;
2. emphasis on the treatment of biomedical and behavioral disorders and insufficient attention to disease prevention and optimal health maintenance;
3. excessive reliance on medical technology, pharmacotherapy, and surgical intervention;
4. the inadequate attention that the biomedical and behavioral sciences have paid to the interaction of pyschosocial, emotional, and biological factors in health maintenance and in educational practices;
5. insufficient attention to constitutional differences in physiologic and behavioral reactions of living organisms.

This is not to disparage reductionism *per se* or fractional-analytic methods in biomedical and biobehavioral research. Such analytic studies have made and will continue to make important contributions to biomedical and behavioral sciences. The argument is that: a) the functioning of living organisms cannot be understood merely by studying the individual components of the living machinery, since living organisms operate as integrated dynamic systems designed to maintain physiologic homeostasis and adaptive behavior, and b) mechanisms of sexual reproduction are such as to lead to differences in psychophysiologic and behavioral adaptive patterns.

The object of this series is to offer a forum for the publication of systems-oriented experimental and theoretical studies and critical scholarly discussions of integrative approaches to the solution of biomedical, biobehavioral, and educational problems and studies of the interaction of genetic, developmental, and psychosocial factors in pyschophysiologic and biobehavioral adaptation.

Samuel A. Corson

Introduction

Bruce R. Dunn
University of West Florida

The chapters contained in this volume cover many topics, ranging from linguistics to neurophysiology. Although somewhat diverse, they share many common threads. The most important of these are a call for the use of neurophysiological and linguistic theory and measurement in cognitive and educational research, and an argument for the use of integrative rather than dichotomous (e.g., left vs. right hemisphere) models of brain functioning as a basis for studying cognitive phenomena. It is interesting to note that such models are currently gaining favor in the neurophysiological literature (e.g., Goldberg and Costa 1981; Sergent 1982a, 1982b; Sergent and Bindra 1981; Sperry 1982).

Other important books have been published previously that overlap, in part, with the topics covered in this volume (e.g., Fillmore et al. 1979; Pirozzolo and Wittrock 1981). What makes this volume unique, however, are the various views expressed throughout concerning the study of reading comprehension and general cognition. These views appear to fall into the following four major categories, which will serve as an outline for this introduction: (1) the use of neurophysiological theory and measurement in research on cognition and reading, (2) the implications of recent advances in linguistics for neurolinguistic and reading research, (3) the importance of individual differences for cognitive and neurolinguistic theory, and (4) the implications of recent interactive brain models for educational practice.

The Use of Neurophysiological Theory and Measurement in Research on Cognition and Reading

Several excellent comprehensive reviews of neurophysiological research and its relation to cognitive processing and reading comprehension are provided in this volume. Chapter 4, by Rentel et al., is completely devoted to this topic. These authors have reviewed the various physiological techniques which appear to be potentially useful in research on cognition and reading. They have included discussions of the following physiological measurements: electrical brain activity (EEG), heart rate (HR), event related (ERP) and evoked potentials (EP), eye movements, contingent negative variation (CNV), brain tomography (BT), pupillometrics (PM), and regional blood flow to the brain (rCBF).

Rentel et al. suggest that current neurocognitive research argues against the simplistic hemispheric model of cerebral functioning. This general theme, that both hemispheres of the brain interact in a complex manner while an individual is reading or engaging in other complex cognitive activities, was also expressed by other authors throughout this book (Dunn, Chapter 2; Languis and Kraft, Chapter 8; Kraft, Chapter 6; Sandman and Walker, Chapter 3; Zutell, Chapter 1).

Kraft's chapter is notable for her ontogenetic model of brain specialization and its correlation with cognitive development. Among other things, Kraft demonstrates clear parallels between the development of reading skills and brain development, particularly in terms of the sequence of myelinization of subcortical and cortical areas of the brain. Of particular interest is her review of the myelinization process and its relation to the onset of Piaget's stages of cognitive development.

Not only did Kraft assert that both hemispheres are highly involved in reading and other complex tasks, but she also argued that subcortical areas may be involved. The latter notion concerning the positive role of the subcortical areas was also expressed in other reviews (e.g., Dunn, Chapter 2; Zutell, Chapter 1).

Zutell, in a highly speculative but well-reasoned treatise, argued that, even though several sequential functions of language may be lateralized in the left hemisphere, the majority of language functions, as well as other cognitive processes, may be diffusely distributed in the brain. Furthermore, many of these functions may be under the direct or indirect control of the subcortical areas. In short, Zutell stated that a "whole brain" approach to neurocognitive research should be pursued. He also pointed out that most neurophysiological researchers view language much too narrowly. As a consequence of the choice of research tasks and simple stimuli (words and, at best, concrete sentences) results supporting language lateralization have been obtained. Although he never stated this, Zutell seemed to imply that many early neuroscientists overgeneralized their results to encompass all areas of language production and comprehension. I will return to this topic later in this introduction.

Sandman and Walker (Chapter 3) took a different tack in developing an integrative brain model. In fact, they argued against a totally "centralist position," i.e., that the brain (including its subcortical areas) is the *sole* determiner of attention and cognition. They marshalled evidence, including some of their own, that partially supports the noncentralist view of William James, who assumed that emotional functioning is primarily controlled by visceral and autonomic input to the brain. Based on their review of the literature, Sandman and Walker presented an interactionist theory that states that emotion and cognition are at least partially affected and controlled by autonomic and visceral input (noncentralist) as well as the converse (centralist).

Advances in Linguistics and Their Implications for Neurolinguistic Research

The chapters by Pepinsky (Chapter 7), Zutell (Chapter 1), and Dunn (Chapter 2) contain in-depth reviews of recent theory and research in linguistics and psycholinguistics. The Dunn and Zutell chapters also focus, in different ways, on how these advances could have a favorable impact on neurophysiologically based reading research.

Pepinsky's chapter is extremely important, although it is not directly related to the physiological aspects of reading. In the first half, Pepinsky presents his own theory of language and language use called the *metalanguage of text*. Briefly, his theory holds that speech and language have evolved to become the primary, but not exclusive, means of communicating meaning by humans. It suggests further that human language cannot be truly understood without including the context, especially the social and cultural context, in which it is produced or understood. Pepinsky's view that natural language is a form of communication implies an intention on the part of the speaker/writer to convey a meaning to another.

In the second half of his chapter, Pepinsky elaborates on his theory by extending its use to the description of social policy (see also Corson and Corson, Chapter 5). He also explains the nature of the Computer Assisted Language Analysis System (CALAS) which he and his colleagues have developed, which is based on the principles of his metalanguage theory. Although currently limited to the analysis of microlevels of text (basically clauses and sentences), CALAS is an extremely powerful language parsing system that could be modified to analyze macrolevels of text. (In written text, macrolevels would correspond to relations among large chunks like paragraphs.)

Zutell (Chapter 1) not only stresses the importance of the social context and intention for understanding language use, as does Pepinsky, but also provides an excellent historical overview of linguistic and psycholinguistic theory and research. This review includes the structuralist (behaviorist) position concerning language and the challenge to structuralist theory by the syntacticists led by Chomsky. This is followed by a discussion of generative semantic theory, which differs from syntactic theory in its emphasis on the underlying meaning of a text regardless of the text's syntactic form. Zutell ends his historical review by giving an overview of sociolinguistics and several text analysis systems.

Dunn (Chapter 2) is much more pragmatic than Pepinsky and Zutell in that he reviews several text analysis systems that can be used in reading research. He also points out that neurophysiological research related to reading must use more complex texts if it is ever to be capable of adequately assessing the cognitive and neurological processes underlying reading.

One clear theme inherent in the above chapters, particularly the ones by Pepinsky and Zutell, is that language is a very complex and rich medium. It cannot be regarded in a trivial manner if research on human cognition, reading, and neurolinguistics is to have much application to education. Few readers would dispute that most neurolinguistic studies have tended to view language naively; this is evidenced by the typical use of linguistic stimuli having little complexity.

The Importance of Individual Differences in Cognitive and Neurolinguistic Research

Many authors stress the importance of studying cognitive style as well as nervous system differences in order to account for learning phenomena. Several authors (Dunn, Chapter 2; Kraft, Chapter 6) report on their own coauthored studies, which specifically address the issue of individual differences using on-line monitoring of reading and cognitive processing. Corson and Corson (Chapter 5) argue that there are behavioral and psychophysiological differences among individuals and that these differences can have a major effect on their learning.

In his chapter, Dunn reports on several studies in which he and his colleagues investigated differences in the semantic recall of expository texts between students hypothesized to have either a high analytic or a low analytic (holistic) style. The results showed that when text is tightly structured, high analytics (those producing relatively less bilateral alpha than holistics) recalled more of the logically or semantically important information than holistics. Holistics, on the other hand, recalled superordinate and subordinate information at approximately the same rate. More impressive still were results showing that holistics were more likely to recall text read when they were producing *greater* than their average reading alpha levels. Further, much of the holistics' recall occurred at the more subordinate levels of the text's semantic heirarchy than at the more superordinate levels. In sharp contrast, analytics tended to recall more of the superordinate information from text when they produced *less* than their mean alpha generated while reading that information. With both the EEG and recall data showing opposite patterns for analytics and holistics, these findings argue for clear qualitative as well as mere quantitative differences in comprehension style.

Kraft (Chapter 6) reports the results of a study in which she and her coworkers monitored children's EEG activity while performing reading comprehension and Piagetian conservation tasks. Briefly, their results showed greater *right-hemisphere* involvement across subjects during the silent reading of a narrative text, which shifted to greater *left-hemisphere* involvement when the subjects answered comprehension questions about the passage. Poor comprehenders (those who answered relatively few comprehension questions) actually showed more left-hemispheric activation when answering the questions than did good comprehenders. Kraft postulates that both hemispheres are used during acquisition and that an integrated balance between them is needed, especially at retrieval. Thus, the good comprehenders showed less left-hemispheric activation than poor comprehenders because the former were using a more integrated, more bilateral retrieval strategy than the latter. Highly similar results were found with their conservation performance data.

It is interesting to note that the data provided by Kraft et al. parallel those of Dunn and his colleagues, who indicate more right- than left-hemisphere utilization during the reading of expository texts. Although more research is needed using different tasks, populations, and recording sites in order to test the robustness of these findings, it is clear from both studies that reading and other complex cognitive tasks are not solely left-hemisphere dominant processes. In fact, both lend credence to a "whole brain'' approach to the study of language and cognition.

The Corsons' chapter (Chapter 5) focuses on individual differences, but does so from the perspective of differential reactions to stress and learning. They argue eloquently that most learning and psychosomatic behavioral disorders are a function of innate, constitutional differences in the nervous systems individuals possess, as well as the interaction of those differing systems with the environment.

More generally, Corson and Corson argue that we must begin a systematic study of individual differences in the behavioral and biological sciences (preferably integrating the two) because the present stress on investigating *average* behavior (i.e., cognitive and biological universals) has produced theories which are distorted and which have very little predictive power for intra- and inter-individual behavior.

The Implications of Brain Research for Educational Practice

Many authors report specific implications of neurophysiological theory and research for educational practice. The review by Languis and Kraft (Chapter 8), however, specifically addresses these issues and thus will serve as the focus for this section. Many implications are given by these authors, but the major ones concern curriculum development and individual differences in learning style. Languis and Kraft assert that the curriculum of the typical American school stresses analytic and logical prowess and neglects, in large part, the development of holistic, visuospatial, and intuitive skills. They suggest, as do Sandman and Walker (Chapter 3), that more emphasis be placed on teaching various modes of thought.

More specifically, they stress the necessity for developing curricula and teaching methods that cause the brain's hemispheres and subcortical structures to work in an integrated fashion. Furthermore, such development should take other variables into account, such as the response mode needed to perform the task, the instructions given, the student's neural organization (e.g., cross-dominance), etc. Such a reorientation of education, based on neurophysiological research, would, in Languis and Kraft's view, promote a higher level of problem solving and creative thinking abilities.

The second major implication for education reported concerns the use of neurophysiological measures to assess individual differences in cognitive processing. Languis and Kraft suggest that a more accurate picture of a person's particular cognitive style will emerge through the use of these indices and that, eventually, a curriculum could be developed to match that person's unique style.

Although the literature using complex tasks and stimuli is sparse, the reports of Dunn (Chapter 2), Kraft (Chapter 6), and Rentel et al. (Chapter 4), as well as the work of E. Roy John and his colleagues (which uses neurometrics to assess learning disabilities and other sources of individual variation (John 1977)), attest to the potential of neurophysiological measurement for a diagnosis of one's processing style. It remains to be determined if something as complex as a curriculum can be written to match a given style—and, if so, whether such matching will produce a major improvement in students' knowledge acquisition.

Summary

Clearly, the majority opinion of the present authors is that a more integrative, or whole-brain, model of reading and general cognition needs to be developed. The work of Kraft and others in this volume (e.g., Dunn; Languis and Kraft) suggests that, when experimental tasks become more complex—for instance, reading extended expository and narrative texts or performing difficult visuospatial conservation tasks—the brain's hemispheres and subcortical structures work in complex integrated patterns. No doubt it will take many years of intensive research to unravel these patterns, but the evidence thus far suggests that this route needs to be explored.

The broad and rich definitions of language presented by many of the present authors, most notably Pepinsky and Zutell, suggest that language is full of affect, purpose, and intention, and is highly influenced by the social context (including experimental situations) under which it is produced or observed. The obvious implication for neurolinguistic and reading researchers is that factors like context and intent should be treated as variables in future investigations and theoretical accounts if such work is to have much import for applied educational problems.

Most authors also stress the importance of identifying consistent individual differences in cognitive strategies using neurophysiological and behavioral indices. In fact, a major conclusion is that no adequate theory of learning, reading (Dunn; Corson and Corson; Kraft) development (Kraft), or curricula (Languis and Kraft; Sandman and Walker; Zutell) can be produced without taking these stylistic differences into account.

Many of these chapters will be highly controversial and should provide an impetus to scholarly debate. The themes inherent in this volume are, we hope, harbingers of new directions that will be taken in future investigations of the neurophysiological aspects of reading and cognition.

Acknowledgments

The authors would like to express their deepest appreciation to Mary Armentrout, Debbie Kins, and Mildred Otis for typing, correcting, and proofing the many drafts of the chapters represented in this volume. Gratitude is expressed to Dr. Frank Wittwer, Director of the Educational Research and Development Center of the University of West Florida, for providing secretarial as well as graphics and photographic support. A special note of thanks is given to Rebecca VanCleave, a graduate student in psychology at the University of West Florida, for her heroic efforts in helping us meet our publishing deadline.

References

Fillmore, C.J.; Kempler, D.; and Wang, W.S., eds. 1979. *Individual differences in language ability and language behavior.* New York: Academic Press.

Goldberg, E., and Costa, L.D. 1981. Hemisphere differences in the acquisition and use of descriptive systems. *Brain and Language* 14:144–173.

John, E.R. 1977. *Neurometrics.* Hillsdale, NJ: John Wiley & Sons.

Pirozzolo, F.J., and Wittrock, M.C., eds. 1981. *Neuropsychological and cognitive processes in reading.* New York: Academic Press.

Sergent, J. 1982a. About face: Left-hemisphere involvement in processing physiognomies. *Journal of Experimental Psychology:* Human Perception and Performance 8:1–14.

________. 1982b. The cerebral balance of power: Confrontation or cooperation? *Journal of Experimental Psychology: Human Perception and Performance* 8:253–272.

Sergent, J., and Bindra, D. 1981. Differential hemisphere processing of faces: Methodological considerations and reinterpretation. *Psychological Bulletin* 89:541–554.

Sperry, R. 1982. Some effects of disconnecting the cerebral hemispheres. *Science* 217(24): 1223–1227.

List of Contributors

Samuel A. Corson is professor emeritus, Department of Psychiatry and Department of Educational Theory and Practice at the Ohio State University in Columbus, Ohio.

Elizabeth O'Leary Corson was a Research Associate in the Laboratory of Cerebrovisceral Physiology, Department of Psychiatry, Ohio State University and is currently associated with the Psychobiologic Stress Research Center, Columbus, Ohio.

Bruce R. Dunn is professor of psychology in the Department of Psychology at the University of West Florida in Pensacola, Florida.

R. Harter-Kraft is associate professor of Child Development in the Department of Applied Behavior Sciences at the University of California, Davis.

Marlin L. Languis is professor of early and middle childhood education in the Department of Educational Theory and Practice at the Ohio State University in Columbus, Ohio.

Christine Pappas is assistant professor of education in the Division of Teacher Education at the University of Oregon, Eugene.

Harold B. Pepinsky is professor of psychology in the Department of Psychology at the Ohio State University in Columbus, Ohio.

Barbara Pettegrew is adjunct assistant professor of reading education director of the Reading Clinic at Otterbein College in Westerville, Ohio, and language consultant in the Communications Disorders Institute, St. Anthony Hospital, Columbus, Ohio.

Victor M. Rentel is professor of english education and of literature, language, and reading in the Department of Educational Theory and Practice at the Ohio State University in Columbus, Ohio.

Curt A. Sandman is professor of psychiatry and human behavior in the Department of Psychiatry and Human Behavior at the University of California, Irvine, and director of research at Fairview Hospital, University of California Irvine Medical Center.

Barbara B. Walker is assistant professor of psychology in the Psychology Department, Walter S. Hunter Laboratory of Psychology, Brown University in Providence, Rhode Island.

Jerry Zutell is associate professor of early and middle childhood education in the Department of Educational Theory and Practice at the Ohio State University in Columbus, Ohio.

Chapter 1

Linguistic and Psycholinguistic Perspectives on Brain Mechanisms and Language

by Jerry Zutell

INTRODUCTION

During the past decade various developments in neurological research have greatly increased our understanding of how the brain and central nervous system (CNS) mechanisms organize and control human behavior. Given science's abiding interest in language as one of man's most unique and complex activities, it is not surprising that much of this work has been directed toward understanding the neurological mechanisms underlying language learning and use. And, in fact, recent brain research has greatly contributed to our understanding of the neurological correlates of linguistic activity. (See bibliography and other papers in this volume.)

However, such investigations provide usable information about language only to the degree that they conform to an acceptable linguistic research paradigm, as well as to a biological one. Yet, at present there is no single universally received research paradigm for the study of language comparable to those established for the physical sciences (Kuhn 1970). In fact, the direction of linguistic, psycholinguistic and sociolinguistic research has changed markedly over the last decade and continues to change even now. There is, for example, much debate about 1) what constitutes a realistic yet analyzable seg nent of language, 2) which proposed linguistic units and dimensions have psychological reality, and 3) what analytic techniques provide fruitful insights into language structure, use and acquisition. Until such major issues are resolved, it will be difficult to determine what neurological investigations using rather traditional definitions of language tell us about neurolinguistic processes.

On the other hand, it would be absurd to halt neurolinguistic investigations until a broader and more universally accepted language research paradigm has been established. The current state of research and research paradigms available in the various language disciplines, however, suggests that a review of current neurolinguistic findings in the context of related developments in linguistic theory and psycholinguistic research may yield both new and more refined interpretations of the literature in neurolinguistics; thus the goal and topic of the present chapter.

I will begin with a historical perspective on changing linguistic and psycholinguistic models including a discussion of some of the major questions currently under debate and then discuss some recent investigations of perception, information storage and information processing that bear directly on our understanding of how language is learned and used. Next, neurolinguistic studies will be interpreted in light of this work. What emerges will be a perspective on language and brain mechanisms which stresses the integrative 'whole brain' nature of language activities and their related brain mechanisms. Finally, a section will be devoted to the specific implications of this view for understanding the reading process and how children learn to read.

LINGUISTIC PERSPECTIVES

Language scholars generally identify two major periods or movements in the history of twentieth century American linguistics: the Structuralist[1] movement which dominated linguistic theory until approximately midcentury (Lyons 1970) and Syntacticism (Chafe 1970) which began with Chomsky's development of generative transformational grammar (Chomsky 1957, 1965). Each of these movements has been marked by its own characteristic way of thinking about language and by its relationship with prevailing contemporary psychological theory, especially in terms of models of perceiving and learning (i.e., Structuralism to Behaviorism and Syntacticism to Cognitive Psychology). Thus each period is characterized by its own unique perspectives on or 'biases' toward the nature of linguistic inquiry and toward the way language is structured, learned and used. A brief review of the perspectives of each will provide a context for understanding neurolinguistic methodology and research.

In an effort to make linguistics a more 'scientific' discipline, modeled on the empirical methods of the physical sciences, linguists during the Structuralist period focused their attention on observing and describing the surface features of languages—their sounds. While it was never denied that meaning is a crucial element of language, semantics received little attention because it was neither easily nor 'objectively' measurable. Thus fundamental units were derived from and described in terms of slices of *sounds* (e.g., the phoneme). Similarly, analytic techniques based on introspection and judgments of well-formedness, given their somewhat 'subjective' nature, were dismissed as 'unscientific' and their results as empirically unverifiable.

Language learning and use were discussed in behavioristic terms of habit formation and stimulus-response bonds. Environmental influences thus became critical elements in verbal learning, differing environments leading to differing language structures, with the long-term use of such structures ultimately leading to different ways of organizing and responding to the physical world. (Strong form of the Whorfian Hypothesis, see Hormann 1971.)

Although Syntacticism has inherited many of its concepts and techniques from Structuralism, its *direction* has been quite different. Chomsky in particular (see esp. Chomsky 1968) has adhered to a rationalist and nativistic position on the crucial issues involving language and mental phenomena, as opposed to a behavioristic one. His distinctions between *competence* and *performance* and *deep* and *surface structures* highlight these differences.

Competence refers to the native speaker's idealized ability to use the rules of grammar consistently and acceptably, while *performance* refers to the application of these rules to specific situations. Errors in language *use* are thus errors in performance, which is affected by environmental factors, but the speaker's competence generally remains unchanged (Lyons 1970).

Transformationalists use the concepts of *deep* and *surface structures* to explain how sentences with very different sequences of sound (*surface structure*) could be interpreted as having similar if not identical meanings, while other sequences of sounds could each be interpreted in two or more meaningful ways (e.g., the ambiguous sentence, "Flying planes can be dangers.", see Chafe 1970, 2). Chomsky posited an underlying set of rules or a syntax that maps basic propositions or 'kernel sentences' (*deep structures*) into various acceptable *surface structures*.

These distinctions illustrate some basic tenets of Syntacticism: Language is creative, not merely imitative. Native speakers use a finite number of rules (many of which are recursive, i.e. repeatable within the same structure) and a finite number of known lexical items to generate infinitely varying and appropriate language patterns. Both distinctions also indicate a willingness to go beyond the immediate physical aspects of language to a 'deeper' inferred set of rules and structures which map *deep structure* to *surface structure*.

The creative nature of language and the relative ease with which children learn its rule system with rather sparse, fragmented environmental data require more than mere conditioning as an adequate explanation. Hence Syntacticism tends to emphasize the genetic component of language learning (e.g., the notion of a Language Acquisition Device, Chomsky's Appendix to Lenneberg 1967). Human infants are especially prewired or *programmed* to learn language irrespective of the specific language or race of the child (See also the neurolinguistic concept of a language center below). Consequently there is a shift in focus, from one emphasizing language *differences* to one stressing language *universals* and various attempts to specify general principles common to all languages and language learning situations (Slobin 1973).

In summary, then, we may broadly characterize the Structuralist perspective as emphasizing phonetics, the surface or observable aspects of language, description, Behavioristic theory as a learning model, the environment and language differences. In contrast, Syntacticism has stressed formal abstract rules, logical analysis as an investigative technique, creativity in language production and learning, the genetic character of language, and language universals as opposed to their differences.

CURRENT ISSUES: SYNTAX AND SEMANTICS

While one of the major contributions of generative grammar has been to move the focus of linguistic investigation beyond the description of surface structure phenomena, recently many linguists have asserted that it has not gone far enough. Generative semanticists (e.g., Chafe 1970; Fillmore 1968; Grimes 1975) have argued that it is highly unlikely that any grammar can work independently of meaning. Language is not a closed system, unrelated to other aspects of thought. Rather it does depend on underlying thought processes that are not necessarily linguistic (Smith 1975). Thus a syntactic deep structure composed of 'kernel sentences' or propositions that can be transformed into various surface structures is not 'deep' at all since its existence must be preceded by symbolization processes based on semantic and 'real world' knowledge and beliefs, processes that both Structuralism and Syntacticism have for the most part ignored.

To illustrate this crucial difference we might briefly contrast Syntactic and Semantic approaches to the formulation of adequate explanations of well formed sentences. Syntactic explanations begin with 'kernel sentences' that are transformed by the application of appropriate syntactic rules prescribing which word order and what possible function words (e.g., prepositions, modal verbs) will be available in the surface structure. The analysis thus *begins* with a form like:

$$\text{(Sentence} \rightarrow \text{Noun Phrase} + \text{Verb Phrase.)}$$

Notice the terms involved are those describing syntactic units—nouns, verbs, etc.

In contrast, semantic analyses like Fillmore's Case Grammar (1968) begin with the positing of order-free 'real world' or case relationships which can later be mapped into a variety of acceptably ordered surface structure representations, e.g.:

$$\text{Sentence} \rightarrow \text{Action, Agent, Instrument, Dative.}$$

Notice the terms involved here describe 'real world,' semantic relations.

One significant advantage of case descriptions is that they differentiate between sentences that have similar syntactic structures but very different meanings, differentiations that purely syntactic descriptions are unable to provide. Contrast, for example, the following sentences:

1. John killed Harry.
2. Harry was killed by John.
3. The knife killed Harry.
4. Someone killed Harry with a knife.

While strictly syntactic analyses can adequately and simply explain the relationship between sentences 1 and 2 by a set of transformational rules governing the formation of passive constructions, they are unable to account for the very different meanings in sentences 1 and 3 which have similar syntactic organizations. A case grammar, using terms like Agent (John, someone), Instrument (knife), Dative (Harry), Action (killed) to which syntactic rules can later be applied can more adequately account for the differences and similarities between all four sentences.

Winograd's (1972) computer program simulating natural language comprehension provides a concrete illustration of the need for consistent interaction and feedback between the syntactic, semantic and logico-mathematical systems involved in linguistic communication. Though his program is highly sophisticated, the world of Winograd's system is a small and very specific one. It consists simply of a three-dimensional grid, several geometric objects occupying space on that grid and a "robot" capable of manipulating these objects. Yet within the limits of this world and the vocabulary with which it is equipped to deal, the robot under the control of this system can (1) receive messages written in no special code but in what we may loosely call "standard English", (2) reduce these messages by means of syntactic and semantic analyses to basic logico-mathematical propositions, and (3) respond to these propositions as their nature requires (i.e., judge their truth or falsity, carry out the manipulations they request, provide the information about its world they ask for, etc.). Furthermore, the system can detect ambiguity in the messages submitted and decide on the most probable meaning intended or request clarification. It can also add to its lexicon when provided with new words and definitions and understand these words in later communications.

Thus Winograd's system does not depend upon precise and restricted sentence structures, nor does it use the trick of seizing on key words and producing a standard response to them. Theoretically it can handle an infinite variety of semantic and syntactic input as long as such input is confined to relationships within the boundaries of the machine's limited environment.

The critical feature that makes Winograd's system so effective is its flexibility. Semantic, syntactic and logico-mathematical analyses are not carried on separately, but they interact at all stages of the analysis in order to produce the best possible interpretation. Thus the system can be responsive to changing states in its environment and incorporate that information into subsequent linguistic communications.

One questionable feature of Winograd's model is the obviously limited nature of its world and relationships it can handle. This may cast some doubt on its usefulness as a model of how human beings deal with language. On the other hand, it would seem to make sense to suppose that the more complex the interrelationships involved, the more flexible and interactive the system would have to be. Thus it seems reasonable to assert that the success of Winograd's system in simulating natural language can be attributed to its highly integrative characteristics.

SOCIOLINGUISTIC PERSPECTIVES

Chafe (1970) terms Syntacticism's failure to deal with symbolization processes a 'phonetic bias', that is, a basic orientation toward surface structure as opposed to semantic structure. He asserts that such an approach must see language as *bidirectional:*

Production = meaning → semantic and postsemantic

processes → phonological processes → phonetic structure

Comprehension = phonetic structure → phonological processes

postsemantic and semantic processes → meaning

He argues that such a view is grossly mistaken. Language is fundamentally *undirectional:*

> Meaning and sound do not play balanced roles in the act of speech. Meaning is at both the beginning and the end of such an act, whereas sound occupies a position in the middle. The speaker creates a semantic structure and converts it into meaning. Normally the hearer assumes that the sound which he hears has a meaning underlying it, already produced by the speaker. Presumably the hearer retrieves that meaning by applying the phonological, symbolization, and postsemantic processes of his language in reverse, but he applies them to something which has already been produced by these processes during their original application. It is the speaker who "generates" the semantic structure in the first place, and it is the semantic structure that determines what comes after. The hearer's role is a matter of recovering what the speaker began with, a second-hand role at best. (p. 59)

Such a focus on meaning has required new ways of looking at language and new techniques for collecting and analyzing linguistic data in terms of its meaning.

First, many linguists have asserted that in order to construct a truly comprehensive theory of language we must broaden the base of investigation to include the interrelationships between language use and the context of the situation. In dealing with issues in the philosophy of language,

Searle (1969) suggests that a theory of language must be a theory of action in which the linguistic unit cannot be divorced from the action it is intended to perform. Speech acts are thus directly related to both *intention* and *convention*. Convention here refers not only to rules of sentence structure but more broadly to the constitutive rules that describe the ways in which utterance X counts as act Y (e.g., utterances of the form, "Would you . . . " usually, but not always, count as requests). Thus it is evident that a comprehensive understanding of language requires understanding of the intention of the speaker, his relationship to the listener and the cultural, social, linguistic and even idiosyncratic constitutive rules of language use operating between the two.

Grice analyzes the relationship between speaker and listener in terms of adherence to a cooperative principle. In being cooperative speakers try to satisfy four maxims: quantity (providing an efficient amount of information), quality (truthfulness), relation (relevance to the conversation) and manner (clarity). However, speakers can perform special linguistic acts by violating one of the maxims in ways that are obvious to the listener. Sarcasm, for example, usually involves a blatant violation of the maxim of quality (Clark and Clark 1977, 122–24). More to the point, how and when maxims are adhered to and violated may depend on cultural and social conventions as well as linguistic ones.

Following in the tradition of the earlier Prague Circle, Hymes (1974) argues that "one cannot take linguistic form, a given code, or even speech itself, as a limiting frame of reference. One must take as context a community, or network of persons, investigating its communicative capacities as a whole, so that any use of channel and code takes its place as part of the resources upon which the members draw." (p. 4) Thus the context of language must include: "form and content of text, setting, participants, ends (intent and effect), key, medium, genre and interactional norms" (Halliday and Hasan 1976, 22).

From such a sociolinguistic perspective, several traditional linguistic concepts require critical revision. Chomsky's definition of competence as the speaker's idealized knowledge of grammar is overly restrictive and Syntacticism's derogative connotations for 'mere' performance unwarranted. Sociolinguists like Hymes have replaced this narrow understanding of *linguistic competence* with the broader concept of *communicative competence*—a member of a speech community's knowledge of when to speak and when to remain silent, which code to use, when, where and how, as manifested in his verbal and nonverbal behavior. (Sinclair and Coulthard 1975).

Concurrently the concept of linguistic well-formedness has also undergone serious revision. The emphasis on syntactic acceptability has been replaced by one on semantic usefulness: "If a speaker wishes to, however, he can use any role sets that he thinks will get him understood" (Grimes 1975, 198).

Finally, it is quite evident that a focus on words or even the sentence as the basic unit of linguistic analysis is often inappropriate in sociolinguistic investigations. In understanding the nature of speech acts sentences must be viewed in the larger contexts of meaning as they are woven through a series of language exchanges. These exchanges themselves may vary widely in terms of grammatical units, length and semantic and/or social unity (Halliday and Hasan 1976).

In order to better understand how situational variables influence language use and effective communication sociolinguists have recently begun to borrow and adapt investigative techniques from anthropology and sociology. The result has been a growing number of "ethnographies of speaking" (Hymes 1974).

Ethnographies differ from traditional linguistic investigations in several important respects (Delamont and Hamilton 1976; Mehan 1979; Sarup 1978):

1) A holistic framework is employed; language is observed in its larger cultural context with emphasis on overal effects rather than on minute slices of linguistic data.
2) The focus is on routine, everyday events and the implicit organizing structures used in such circumstances.
3) Investigators do not separate themselves from the situation they are observing, but attempt to become accepted participating members in order to maximize the naturalness of the situation and to heighten their own sensitivity to the structures in operation.
4) Categories of classification are not rigidly imposed, but remain flexible so that new ones develop as they emerge from the data itself. Structures and structuring are interwoven throughout the study.
5) Data collection remains open ended and a variety of sources may be used—field notes, videotapes, case studies, reports of informants, etc. The focus of data collection is on description as opposed to manipulation and on each individual as opposed to an average.

The aim of such studies has been to detail the ability to communicate by describing what a person needs to know in order to make sense as a talking and listening member of a particular community. In doing ethnographies investigators attempt to examine what people are doing to and with each other with their speech (McDermott 1977).

Classroom settings provide especially fruitful environments for ethnographic research. They furnish easily available 'microcultures' whose temporal and spatial boundaries are clearly marked. More importantly, schools often require that children learn different procedures and rules for using language than those that apply in the home environment. Under such circumstances cultural differences between teachers and children can lead to communication breakdowns that serve to reveal essential aspects of language in use which may otherwise go unnoticed. Recent classroom ethnographies have provided such insights.

For example, several investigators have noted that for native Hawaiian (Boggs 1972) and American Indian (Dumont 1972; John 1972; Phillips 1972) children's individual public performances (e.g., the teacher questions-child answers format so prevalent in American classrooms), run counter to already established cultural ways of interacting with adults. In such situations children often talk out of turn, volunteering unwanted information, or remain silent. Dumont points out that these same quiet children are bold, curious, daring and noisy away from school. In parallel, the work of Labov (1969) and others has helped to destroy the myth of wholesale language deficiencies among urban Black children by contrasting school performance with the sophisticated language games of Black adolescents and the prestige associated with oral language performance within the Black community.

The point is that traditional linguistic paradigms which focus on the literal interpretation of isolated sentences in terms of their phonological, syntactic and even semantic structure may ignore the very factors which determine the successful use of language in real life situations. Conversely, neurological studies using such paradigms also run the dual risk of ignoring critical aspects of language behavior (e.g., turn taking) while possibly labeling cultural differences as neurologically based deficits (McDermott 1974). In either case a somewhat distorted neurological perspective on language functioning can result.

TEXT ANALYSIS

Halliday and Hasan (1976) point out that a text, or passage of discourse, should cohere, or hang together, in *two* regards: externally in terms of its context and internally in terms of its own organization. Thus a second focus for recent linguistic and psycholinguistic studies has been *Text Analysis*, which may be defined as the study of various properties of extended discourse which give it texture, i.e., enable it to function as a unity with respect to itself and its environment. (See Halliday and Hasan 1976, 2.) There are three components which help create texture: macrostructure, cohesion and textual structure within each sentence.

The macrostructure of a text refers to an overall pattern of organization that establishes it as a well or poorly developed text of a particular kind. Each of the many genres of text has its own discourse structure. This includes both formal and informal, spoken and written discourse.

For example, Sacks, Schegloff and Jefferson (1974), have shown that even informal conversation depends on some highly structured principles for turn-taking. Also, Sinclair and Coulthard (1975) have begun the investigation of classroom lessons in terms of their discourse structures. Using a rank scale for their descriptive model, they have suggested a hierarchical organization consisting of lessons, transactions, exchanges, moves and acts (from the top down). Each rank is composed of a combination of elements at the next lower rank. Lessons consist of patterns of transactions, transactions of a set of exchanges, etc.

Using Bartlett's (1932) classic work on remembering as a starting point, many pyscholinguists have recently explored the organization and comprehension of simple narratives. Such studies begin with a story which is analyzed in terms of its structure into a setting and a series of episodes, each of which may consist of an initiating event, internal response, attempted consquence and/or reaction. Episodes are connected either causally, temporally or additively. (See Stein 1978 for further elaboration.) A subject's recall is scored for amount of structure present in the text, subject's expectations regarding content, and/or developmental differences. In general these studies indicate that: 1) given identical content, "well-organized" stories result in a higher number of propositions being recalled; 2) propositions higher in the structural hierarchy are better recalled than those further down; 3) causally related propositions are better recalled than temporally related or optional ones; 4) changing the subject's perspective on a story (for example from a burglar to a real estate agent when the text describes a house) affects how and what propositions are remembered; 5) though there are some developmental differences, children and adults use the same general strategies in comprehending; and 6) as stories are retold over longer time periods, subjects' retellings come to more closely approximate some ideal or stereotypic story structure based on subjects' past experience. (See especially Anderson and Pichert 1977; Frederickson 1975; King and Rentel 1979; Mandler and Johnson 1977; Thorndyke 1977). These studies demonstrate that all speakers and listeners use macrostructural features or schemas in processing and retrieving information about narrative texts.

At another level cohesive features of texts also play an important role in the creation and understanding of extended discourse. Halliday and Hasan (1976) characterize *cohesion* as the linguistic means by which a text can function as a single meaningful unit. It includes the set of semantic resources available for linking a sentence or clause with what has gone on before. These are systematic grammatical (e.g., references) and lexical (e.g., synonyms) resources built into the language itself.

Cohesion involves both a referring item and a referent. If the referent is outside the text itself, in the context of the situation, cohesion is said to be exophoric. If, on the other hand, the referent is within the text itself, cohesion is endophoric. A single instance of cohesion is called a *tie*. Thus any segment of text can be characterized in terms of the number and kinds of ties present and the distance between them.

It is evident that situational constraints—the relationships between speakers and listeners, the immediate physical environment, etc.—will influence the kind of cohesion used and its effectiveness. For example, language-in-action and language among close knit social groups is characterized by a higher proportion of exophoric reference than would be approrpriate in other contexts (Halliday and Hasan 1976). Also, patterns of lexical cohesion between speakers may be used to establish specific orientations: "By choosing to repeat the vocabulary of a previous speaker one signals a willingness to negotiate in his terms; by using synonyms or paraphrase, one signals the opposite. Words of reference like pronouns, and elliptical syntax (e.g., one word answers to questions) realize other selections of orientation." (Halliday and Hasan 1976, 292).

In addition to the properties that create unity across sentences for the text as a whole, there are also textual structures at the sentential level that add to this unity. Halliday and Hasan (1976) specify two major components: the *theme* systems and the *information* systems.

The theme systems are concerned with the sentence as a message structured in terms of a topic (theme) and a comment on that topic (rheme). Though these often take the syntactic forms of noun phrase and verb phrase in a constituative analysis of sentence structure, they are *semantic* structures. A wide range of semantic variation is possible within the theme systems. For example, in any given event the agent, beneficiary, instrument or the action itself may be designated as the topic. (Contrast: John/killed Harry with a knife; The knife,/John killed Harry with it; and Kill Harry with a knife/was what John did).

In contrast, information systems are structured in terms of what the speaker supposes is presently recoverable by the hearer from other sources, e.g., the immediate environment and/or the preceding text (*given* information) and what is not (*new* information). In English this relationship is expressed by intonation patterns within tone groups and thus can only partially be represented in print by punctuation, italics, etc. Given the interaction of these two systems (in the above examples, stress could fall in a variety of places), the speaker has a wide range of combinations available for meshing his own topical concerns (theme system) and his listener's present capacity for relating them to what information is presently available to him.

While a text can be analyzed separately in terms of each of these aspects—context of the situation, discourse structure, cohesion, theme and information systems—it is quite evident that the production and comprehension of effective language communication requires a complex integration of all of these.

Grimes (1975) analyzes some specific aspects of this interaction. First, he has shown that in high information blocks (higher proportion of *new* information) renaming is more useful as a cohesive device than reference. Second, in at least one language (Oksapmin of Popua New Guinea) and possibly others, the main verb of a sentence is inflected differently for marked and unmarked information centers. Verbs are typically uninflected until a marked center is reached. Then the inflection of the verb carries tense and mode information which applies to the string of medial clauses as well as the final clause itself. Thus, there is a direct connection between the grammatical form used and the speaker's construction of an appropriate information structure.

Chafe (1972) also touches on this interaction in his discussion of foregrounding. An item is 'foregrounded' when it is assumed to be in hearer's consciousness. In referring to such items we often use pronominalization (e.g., "Vic told a joke. *It* wasn't very funny."). We are also 'permitted' to use definite articles in referring to specific features of that item. (e.g., "Kathy and Jerry bought a house. The bathroom is rather small." Which bathroom? The one we *assume* is part of the house.) There are several characteristics about the use of these devices that are particularly interesting: Foregrounded items are consistently pronounced with lower volume and pitch in contrast to new information being presented with them. There is no formal boundary which indicates when material is no longer foregrounded. Rather the boundary depends on the speaker's intuitive sense of what is in the listener's immediate consciousness. Finally, those features which can be treated as 'definite' without foregrounding (and without drawing special attention) will change over time and situation, depending upon the predictable semantic relationships available to both listener and speaker.

Several other investigators (e.g., Halliday and Hasan 1976; Rumelhart 1978) along with Chafe and Grimes have used camera and scene based images in describing textual processes. Characters and events move in and out of focus, on or off stage, in accordance with the author's intentions, his understanding of the context of the situation and his intuitive and conscious estimation of the knowledge and limitations of his particular audience. Given the complex nature of these various text elements and their interaction, a bottom up, word-sentence-paragraph model would be inadequate. It would seem that effective communication must involve some conceptual, holistic, gestalt-like processes as well as sentential and syntactic ones.

SUMMARY

Linguistic theory, language research and the investigative techniques used in such research have all changed quite markedly during this century. Methodologically, though Structuralists did tend to use observational data, their analyses rarely went beyond phonetic transcriptions and surface analyses. In contrast, Syntacticists have focused their investigations on the discovery of rule systems underlying idealized notions of grammaticality. Their methods and models have been logical rather than empirical. Currently, however, the focus of linguistic attention has shifted toward closer examination of texts and contexts, the aim being to discover those universal and context-specific principles governing language-in-use.

Essentially then, the focus has consistently moved both 'deeper' and 'broader', that is, from sounds to syntactic structures to meaning and conceptual relations underlying meaning, and thus, concurrently, from words to sentences to texts and the situations and intentions governing the creation of texts. Three crucial findings seem to emerge consistently from recent investigations: 1) the importance of situational and intentional variables for effective linguistic communication, 2) the inadequacy of linguistic models that treat phonology and syntax as separate systems, analyzable independently of their relationship to semantics and knowledge of the real world, and 3) the great skill of the language user as he implicitly integrates a variety of linguistic dimensions in understanding others and in making himself understood.

PSYCHOLOGICAL MODELS AND NEUROLOGICAL MECHANISMS

Although at times language has been treated as a highly unique phenomenon, it is, of course, one aspect of the more general human mental activities of perceiving, learning and remembering. Thus, to be more fully adequate and parsimonious a linguistic theory should have some close ties with contemporary theories of psychological processes and the neurological mechanisms underlying them. On the other hand, language studies have generated important insights and questions affecting psychological models of perception, learning and memory. These influences combined with contemporary technological and theoretical advances within psychology and neurology themselves have, of course, resulted in changing, growing models of how human beings process information.

There are some fundamental issues at the heart of such models which remain as on-going topics of discussion and debate. These focus on: 1) the relative contributions of environmental, genetic and individual factors to learning and remembering and 2) whether processing can be broken down into discrete, sequential, linear stages (bottom-up models) or whether it also involves more holistic activities (top-down models). In terms of neurology, corresponding issues involve the nature of the mechanisms that would carry out sequential and/or holistic processing activities and their location and relative autonomy within the central nervous system.

Historically the prevailing processing models have been linear, sequential, part-to-whole ones. Behaviorist research and theory focussed on the role of external conditions in determining animal and human responses. The organism was viewed as basically passive, a *tabula rasa*, which could be conditioned to act in certain ways through the manipulation of stimulation-response and reinforcement contingencies. This model is linear in that habits and associations are built up gradually over time through repetition and reward strength. Learning is viewed as a matter of appropriate conditioning (either experimentally or naturally) and memory as the recall and/or performance of particular habits in response to external stimuli. Learning is also treated as a bottom-up process since more complex tasks are typically analyzed into smaller components or skills, each of which is taught separately and in isolation.

Questioning the adequacy of associative bond models to explain complex human activities, especially language, cognitive psychologists began close examinations of memorial, retrieval and categorizing processes (See Brewer 1974; Hormann 1971; and especially Chomsky's (1959) review of Skinner's *Verbal Behavior*). Current cognitive models have been particularly affected by three developments in this area: the discovery of stages of memory with particular processing characteristics, rapid advances in computer technology and the application of Syntactic questions, principles and paradigms to psycholinguistic investigation.

The discovery of iconic, short-term and long-term memory components and their different characteristics, especially the limited capacity of short-term memory (Miller 1967; Sperling 1960) has shaped recent models of information processing. First, it suggests the importance of sequential as well as parallel components in the storage processes since information must work its way time-wise through the memory system. Second, the limitations of the system imply that the processor must *actively* decide what to pay attention to, selectively sampling the environment for relevant information, and using previously acquired information to 'fill in the gaps' as the stimulus is, in some sense, 'reconstructed' by the mind (However, for a criticism of constructivist interpretations see E. Gibson 1977).

The development of computer technology over the last three decades has also added a significant new dimension to information processing and psycholinguistic research. Attempts to create artificial intelligence and language simulation programs have served a heuristic function. Investigators have been forced to carefully examine the properties and highly complex organizational problems inherent in effective and efficient storage and retrieval systems and program languages.

Computer simulations have been attractive models for a variety of reasons. The binary nature of digital computers (electrical current is either on or off) suggested a neat parallel with neuronal firings within the CNS and with distinctive feature theories of both perceptual and semantic category formation (Katz and Fodor 1963; Selfridge 1959). Whether a feature is present or not can simply be represented by a single on-off circuit or firing. Thus, any particular field could be described in terms of a set of particular relevant features, and instances of specific members could be represented by a unique binary pattern or bits of information. Letters, for example, may be described in terms of lines vs. curves, open vs. closed forms, diagional vs. non-diagional elements, etc. Each letter can thus be identified in terms of a specific feature pattern. 'O', for example, would be plus curved, plus closed and minus everything else.

The compatibility of computer approaches with the Syntactic paradigm is well worth noting. Logical analysis and the specification of formal rule systems are at the heart of both types of investigations. Language simulation programs have also provided a means of operationalizing and testing hypothesized Syntactic principles. But as the previous description of Winograd's program suggests (see above, p. 798) such approaches require constant interaction between lexical, syntactic and 'real world' systems. Furthermore, the 'real world' facts themselves must be simple and explicit enough to be easily encoded into logical propositions.

The issue remains, however, whether current processing and neurological models differ from earlier assocation and reflex-arc models *in kind* or *in degree*. While more complex networks of relationships like current schema structure models have replaced simplistic S-R bond models, and while complex modular theories of cortical structure (Popper and Eccles 1977) have replaced the reflex-arc, it can be argued that many of these models are still linear, sequential, hierarchical, localistic, propositional (digital) and bottom-up in nature. Certainly a vast psychological and neurological literature supports many of the concepts and principles underlying such models. At the same time there is a growing research base which criticizes the conditions and procedures under which such research has been conducted and which argues for the importance of different kinds of processing and memory: parallel, holistic, distributive, analogic and top-down.

A major criticism of the prevailing research paradigm for investigating perception, memory and concept formation is that laboratory situations and controlled manipulation of variables have little ecological validity. For example, Rosch (1973, 1975a, 1975b, etc.) has criticized studies on the nature of category formation (e.g., Bruner, Goodnow and Austin 1956) on precisely these grounds. In such experiments, the category itself is arbitrarily established (e.g., all red squares). It is a logically bounded entity whose membership is defined by a simple set of criterial features, and all instances of the category have equal membership. Rosch points out that many natural categories (e.g., color, names), violate these principles. Instead, she proposes a prototype or analog model of category structure in which best examples or clearest cases of a category serve as reference points, with other members being various distances from the prototype. (A robin, for instance, is a better example of a bird than a penguin.) Her own research, including examination of the use of hedges (verb phrases like 'kind of', 'almost', etc.), judgments of category membership, and cross cultural studies of color and shape categories support this model.

Some other aspects of Rosch's model are particularly relevant to the current topic:

1) Natural categories have an internal structure or pattern as opposed to discrete and equal membership. This structure is complex, and probably based on laws of central tendency, similar to principles of multivariate analysis. Furthermore, since natural, unrelated features are not necessarily orthogonal, that is, they may *both* tend to occur in natural settings, attributes may contribute to a pattern even when they are formally irrelevant.

2) The organism is not simply a passive recipient of sensory information, however. It seems that we *actively* engage in the construction of prototypes. In fact, subjects think that typical instances and events are more frequent than they really are (Rosch 1975b).

3) Finally, some prototypes may be 'biologically given'. Rosch argues that cross cultural differences have been distorted by emphasis on category boundaries while focal instances have been ignored. In fact, focal colors are more easily learned and remembered. Symmetrical

shapes (e.g., squares, circles, equilateral triangles) also seem to function as universal prototypes (Rosch 1975b).

In presenting his own perceptual theory J. J. Gibson (1977) also takes issue with models of perception which fail to incorporate an ecological perspective. Several aspects of Gibsonian theory seem particularly relevant to our questions about the nature of perception and information processing.

Gibson stresses the importance of environmental space and surfaces and of the human being in that environment to the perceiving process. The whole body can be and is mobilized in the interests of visual exploration and, for Gibson, when it is being used in this way it is as much a part of the visual system as the eyeball itself (Mace 1977). Furthermore, what we perceive when we view an object are not its qualities, per se, but its affordances, which may be defined as the useful features of objects in the context of 'human-in-environment'. Thus, to fully understand perception we must be able to specify the physical features of the environment as well as the uses or affordances which that object permits. From this perspective, perception involves abstracting relevant invariant features from the flowing texture of the visual display. As Gibson (1977) says:

> If this is true for the adult, what about the young child? There is now a great deal of evidence to show that the infant does not begin by first discriminating the qualities of objects and then learning the combination of qualities that specify the objects themselves. Phenomenal objects are not built up of qualities. It is quite the other way around. Objects, more exactly the affordances of objects, are what the infant begins by noticing. *The meanings are observed before the substances and surfaces are.* Affordances are invariant combinations of variables. And it is only reasonable to suppose that it is easier to perceive an invariant combination than it is to perceive all the variables separately. (p. 75, emphasis author's)

Gibson's focus on the primacy of meaning and environment in perception is supported by several perceptual experiments. For example, McGuinness and Pribram (1978) report an unpublished study by Biggs in which subjects were presented word lists below perceptual threshold followed by a masking stimulus. They were then asked to make several judgments regarding the words in the list. The results showed that meaning was processed earlier and more accurately than any other characteristic. Biggs concluded that word recognition is at least partially a sequential task in which meaning is extracted first following by physical characteristics and finally by recognition and naming in conscious awareness.

In Gibson's model there is a strong rejection of constructivist, stepwise approaches. Instead, perception is seen as analytic *and* holistic. And it is active and immediate as well. This perspective is most compatible with what has been termed a motor theory of perception (Turvey 1974). According to this model, the classical distinction between sensory and motor neurons underlying the Sherrington reflex arc is simplistic and misleading. First, evidence indicates that motor neurons are directly involved in the perceiving process. In fact, one third of the motor fibers leaving the spinal cord for muscle tissue influence receptors independently of changes in the muscles (Weimer 1974). Conversely, integrated movement must involve information from muscle receptors as well as motor neutrons. Collectively, a variety of experiments suggest that:

> . . . a profound reorganization of the spinal cord precedes movement. There are both nonspecific and specific components of this reorganization and the latter have been shown to include the mechanisms of reciprocal inhibition in addition to servomechanisms regulating agonist activity. Moreover, the reorganization of the interaction among neural mechanisms at the spinal level follows the pattern of being initially diffuse becoming more localized the closer in time to the manifestation of the desired movement. (Turvey 1974, 239)

From this perspective a hierarchial model of perceiving, acting and knowing which highlights the role of an 'executive command center' must be revised to include *coalitions* of complex, interactional structures, neuronal pools and feedback and feedforward loops located away from the cerebral cortex which permit direct adjustments in actions without executive involvement.

Two important features of such a model are its capacity for holistic, diffuse and direct memory storage and the importance of subcortical systems for perceiving and remembering.

Pribram (Pribram 1971, 1977; Pribram, Nuwer and Baron 1974) has provided a description of the neurological mechanisms that allow for such processing through a comparison of neurological structures and recently developed optical information processing devices, holograms:

> When a piece of film is exposed to coherent light that is reflected and scattered by objects in the visual field, there is no ordinary image produced on the film. In fact, the film becomes so blurred that there is no resemblance whatever between the pattern that is stored on the film and the visual field itself. However, when properly il-

luminated, the film reconstructs the wavefronts of light that were presented when the exposure was made. As a result, if an observer looks toward the film, it appears as if the entire visual scene were present behind it. The reconstructed image appears exactly as it did during the exposure, complete in every detail and in three dimensions! The light waves from each point of the visual field had interacted to produce an interference pattern at the film, and it is this interference pattern that was stored throughout the film. (Pribram, et. al. 1974, 420)

Moreover, the storage of the information on the film is not local and point by point, but diffuse. That is, the whole image can be reconstructed from any section of the photographic plate.

As Pribram points out, interference patterns give rise to these remarkable characteristics of optical information storage. He proposes that the sheets of horizontally connected neurons that exist at every cell station in the optic pathway in a plane perpendicular to the parallel fiber system also give rise to interference patterns through the structural arrangements of slow graded potentials generated in the fine fibered connectivity of the visual system. These tuned resonance patterns account for a variety perceptual phenomena.

The relative importance placed on these micropotential fields at neuronal junctures in Pribram's model has met with some criticism. Eccles argues that this theory involves too much information loss and that these fields have negligible influence because of the small amount of current generated (Popper and Eccles 1977). Yet Eccles' own model of neuronal organization also allows for a holographic processing interpretation.

Eccles (Popper and Eccles 1977) summarizes a variety of evidence supporting a columnar or modular theory of cortex organization: "There are more or less well defined groups of cells, perhaps up to 10,000, which are locked together by mutual connectivities, and which have as a consequence some unitary existence, building up power within themselves and inhibiting the cells of columns nearby" (p. 242). He speculates that there are perhaps one to two million such columns arranged orthogonally to the cortical surface. Columns are also horizontally laminated into five layers. A crucial functional property is that there appear to be two levels of performance. Layers 3, 4, and 5 are more concerned with localized action and the build-up of power within the module; layers 1 and 2 are zones of mild diffuse excitory action and major connections with other columns, both near and distant. All in all,

> The operation of a module can be imagined as a complex of circuits in parallel with summation of hundreds of convergent lines onto its constituent neurons in addition to a mesh of feedforward and feedback excitatory and inhibitory lines. . . . Thus we have to envision levels of complexity in the operation of a module far beyond anything yet conceived, and of a totally different order from any integrated microcircuits of electronics, the analogous systems mentioned earlier. (Popper and Eccles 1977, 241)

Recently Anderson (1977) has elaborated on the mathematical compatibility of this neurological model with a distributive or holographic memory system and with current perspectives on categorization and search strategies. In particular, he demonstrates how such a model fits nicely with Rosch's prototype model discussed earlier. As Anderson points out, language use is an activity that requires direct and large searches of memory, an activity best served by a holographic system. Anderson's final hybrid model is based on a cascading filter system in which one analogic process begins before the previous one has finished. In this way he attempts to integrate both holistic and sequential models. This analysis is a highly viable one if, adding the 'ecological' focus of Gibson and Rosch, we recognize that the initial filter must be based on the usefulness or affordance which the event serves.

A distributive, holographic memory system helps to account for a consistent and puzzling neurophysiological finding: large sections of associative cortex can be removed without visibly affecting specific memories as long as the remaining tissue is functioning normally. (Lashley 1950; Penfield and Roberts 1959). Another approach to this enigma has been to investigate subcortical involvement in memorial processes.

Meyer and Meyer (1977; forthcoming) review the neuropsychological literature on the memories of habits. In this research paradigm animals are trained on specific tasks, cortical tissue is removed and testing, retraining and/or drug treatment follow. Meyer and Meyer reach some important conclusions for our understanding of memory: 1) Memories are formed rapidly and directly; they are stable, very difficult to destroy, and unlikely to undergo significant changes as a function of time. 2) Engrams are not stored cortically, but subcortically. Most memory impairments are the result of injuries affecting retrieval, not storage, and cortical injuries that suppress memories do so only indirectly by affecting engram retrieval. 3) Differences in recall of recent versus older memories in traumatic amnesias are not dependent on the age of the memories;

rather they are functions of the *numbers of contexts* in which they are recalled. Thus, the richer and more varied the environment surrounding learning and remembering, the more permanent the engram. 4) The cortex acts not as a place of storage, but as an aggregate of routes to and from the deep structures of the cerebrum and other neural mechanisms.

Chafe (1977) offers a more direct linguistic perspective on the nature of memory storage. First, using and supporting Rosch's concept of prototypes, he argues that some events are more or less 'codable' than others. Using his own analysis he shows that codability is directly reflected in linguistic and psycholinguistic phenomena—in situations of low codability, where there is less consistency and agreement in categorization, people are more likely to hesitate and to use more modifying linguistic structures. Second, Chafe points out that while recall protocols can be analyzed according to their propositional structure, this structure can vary quite markedly over several retellings by the same person, depending upon a variety of situational factors:

> In sum, none of the arrows in Figs. 7, 8, and 9 (semantic structure diagrams) need in principle represent what is known about this event, but only decisions as to how to verbalize it. What is known must be of such a nature as to allow multiple interpretations of these kinds. *The most attractive conclusion, I think, is that what is known is not necessarily in a propositional format at all, but that it is in many cases in some analogic format that allows various propositional interpretations to be given to it.*
>
> The implication for linguistics is that there cannot be any such thing as a well defined or autonomous semantic structure underlying a discourse (or a sentence). Talking is a creative process by which an underlying knowledge, to a large extent analogic in nature, is crystallized into propositional and linguistic structures. (p. 245, emphasis author's)

In summary, while computer-like processing has been used as a powerful theoretical metaphor for human processing, we should approach this model with some skepticism and caution. A good deal of converging theory and research from a variety of sources—perceptual, psychological, neurophysiological and linguistic—suggest that holistic, parallel activities distributed throughout the central nervous system are also involved in perceiving, learning and remembering. Significantly, recent sociolinguistic focus on the importance of context is complemented by the perspectives developed in the work of Rosch, Gibson, Meyer and Meyer, and Chafe. Distributive, holographic storage is based on the intercorrelation of a variety of 'traces'. The establishment of analogic patterns in the devlopment of prototypes requires a rich and varied environment, a large number of different contexts, from which invariant patterns can be detected.

LANGUAGE AND THE BRAIN

One of the most persistent issues in the history of human neurological investigation has involved the cortical localization of language. Such investigations have certainly demonstrated an obvious relationship between the left hemisphere and *certain aspects* of linguistic processing. However, in many respects the case for localization has been overstated as an all or none opposition. In keeping with the theme of this paper, this section will provide a brief summary of the neurological evidence supporting a more integrative model of brain functioning in general and linguistic communication in particular.

Relying on the obvious physical and morphological symmetry of the brain, early investigators customarily supposed that brain *function* is symmetrical as well. Thus, each hemisphere was viewed as a distinct entity complete in itself. During the second half of the nineteenth century, however, the findings of Broca (1865), Wernicke (1874), and others challenged such theories. Through mostly post-mortem examinations of patients with language disorders, obvious brain injury, or both, they showed that in the large majority of cases disturbances in language function (aphasias) were related to injuries to specific areas of the left cerebral hemisphere, while, in general, right-hemispheric lesions were not highly correlated with such disturbances. This rather striking discovery suggested an assymetry in brain function: the left hemisphere controls linguistic processing. Since it was also generally accepted that language is instrumental in shaping human thinking processes, the non-language hemisphere was considered automatic in function or 'mute.' Thus developed the notion of 'cerebral dominance.' Though prominent neurologists (Jackson 1932) expressed strong reservations about such localization theories, suggesting more integrative models, the major-minor hemisphere approach prevaded neurological theory until only recently.

However, with the advent of the commissurotomy technique (i.e., the cutting of the corpus callosum, the major communication network between the two hemispheres) for decreasing and even eliminating epileptic seizures, neurologists generated a pool of subjects whose cerebral hemispheres were essentially isolated from each other. These investigators developed techniques for testing the relative strengths, weaknesses, and specialized functions of each hemisphere. The most important findings of these 'split-brain' experiments were the previously unsuspected strengths and specializations of the right hemisphere, suggesting a general paradigm in which the left hemisphere controls time ordered, analytic, propositional functioning, including language, while the right hemisphere is superior on tasks requiring spatial, synthetic, 'gestalt-like' processing (Wittrock, 1975).

As with earlier investigations, the data are far from perfect and do not preclude other less dichotomy-oriented explanations. Several investigators (Dimond 1972; Pribram 1971, 1975) have cautioned strongly against all-none hemispheric oppositions, suggesting more integrative theories. In these models, each hemisphere does seem to have control over certain kinds of processing. But at the same time, both interhemispheric communication and the ability of one hemisphere to compensate in some measure for injury or loss of functioning of the other also play essential roles in the efficient processing of and responding to information.

There are several sources of evidence which together offer convincing support for this point of view. The very existence of the corpus callosum, the largest nerve tract in the brain, indicates that interhemispheric communication or 'cross-talk' is an important component of efficient brain functioning. Not surprisingly, processing capacity increases when information is available to both hemispheres or can be shared through 'cross-talk' as compared to when each hemisphere must analyze the information independently, without any communication with the other. Furthermore, the constructive-visual process necessary for the perceptions of three dimensional space *requires* the integration of 'conflicting' visual information, that is, information that includes two disparate visual perspectives (Dimond 1972).

In regard to language, two factors in particular cast some doubt on strong localistic interpretations of the data. First, most of the evidence supporting specific locations for language processing comes from patients with severe neurological trauma induced by brain injury (especially in war victims) or stroke. In both cases, the extensiveness of damage and/or the reduction of blood flow through the cerebral arterial system limit the certainty that only specific areas have been injured.

Second, neurologists have generally taken a rather narrow view of language functioning. Measurement instruments typically involve artificial, syntactically oriented tasks in a formalized, 'decontextualized' setting. Language is thus operationally defined in terms of Chomsky's notion of *linguistic* competence as opposed to Hymes' definition of *communicative* competence. Also, right hemisphere lesions may cause a change in the relationship between the patient and his environment. Though such injuries are often diagnosed as causing deficits in spatial orientation, they may affect the way one uses language to express perceptual relationships (Weinstein 1964). (See also the discussion of Winograd 1972 above.) Thus, rather arbitrary differentiations between linguistic and non-linguistic disturbances have led to apparent inconsistences in results summarized across investigators.

Furthermore, there are several findings which suggest right hemisphere participation. Dimond (1972) reports that scalp command potentials provide evidence that the right hemisphere sensory-motor region produces cortical activity immediately preceding speech. In their study of cortical blood flow during differential cognitive activities, Lassen, Ingvar and Skinhoj (1978) note that they were impressed to find that both right and left hemispheres become active in the same manner during speech processes, including oral and silent reading. Kraft (1976) used EEGs to examine cortical functioning of six to eight year olds during silent reading and comprehension tasks. She found that the reading task itself elicited right hemispheric activity, and while the response or comprehension task elicited primarily left hemispheric activity, high performers tended to show functioning in both hemispheres.

Conversely, while aphasic, brain-injured subjects do significantly worse on language tasks than nonaphasic (often right hemisphere injured) subjects, *both* consistently do worse than controls (Gosnave 1977). Dimond (1972) also reports that in one study "about 50 percent of the right hemisphere patients showed some difficulty in generating grammatically correct phases beyond three or four words in length, as well as the more symbolic aspects of reading and writing." (p. 172)

Lenneberg (1976) has synthesized significant evidence which shows that at least until puberty the non-language hemisphere has the ability to compensate for injuries to the language hemisphere by assuming control of linguistic processing. Children who are subject to such injuries eventually regain normal language facility. The data thus indicate the active involvement of both hemispheres at the earliest and most intense periods of language development.

In their comprehensive review of bilingualism and brain function, Albert and Obler (1978) reach several conclusions which support a more dynamic, integrative model. First, studies of bilinguals demonstrate a major right-hemispheric contribution to language, especially in the learning of a second language. Second, hemispheric dominance is in fact influenced by particular demands of the language being learned. "Particularly strong is the evidence that different orthographic systems (e.g., phonemic versus logographic, left-to-right, versus right-to-left) may encourage different cerebral organization." (p. 253). Contrary to the traditional concept of cerebral dominance, their evidence suggests that " . . . the brain is seen to be a plastic, dynamically changing organ which may be modified by the process of learning. The brain does not have a rigid, predetermined neuropsychological destiny. The learning of a second language may alter patterns of cerebral organization even for the first learned langauge." (p. 243).

A final source of support for a more interactive model of neurological organization is the evidence that subcortical areas are also somewhat involved in language functioning. There is evidence, for example, that children discriminate speech sounds before the development of the auditory cortex, implying the relevant mechanisms could well be at the brain stem level. Cerebellar disorders have also been shown to affect the articulatory movements and prosodic features involved in speech (Selnes and Whitaker 1977). Considering that stress placement is closely related to information structure (see above, p. 17), such disorders may directly affect subtle but potentially crucial aspects of effective communication.

Several authors have suggested that subcortical mechanisms affect language through their relation to attention. In one study, patients' language performance varied considerably with their degree of alertness which, in turn, was related to a malfunction of thalamically related arousal mechanisms (Mohr, Walters and Duncan 1975). McGuinness and Pribram (1978) show that there are some major inconsistencies in the current trend to attribute sex differences in processing, including language functioning, to differences in hemispheric functioning. They argue that a better explanation would be in terms of hormonal differences between males and females in the arousal system.

Penfield (Penfield 1975; Penfield and Roberts 1959) has consistently maintained that the subdivisions of the cortex are best viewed as extensions or projections of some area of gray matter in the older brain stem, and that this approach is in many ways a surer guide to the prediction of functional subdivision than cyto-architectonic maps (Penfield and Roberts 1959, 23). He argues for a centrecephalic coordinating system as integrator of cortical and subcortical speech mechanisms. Penfield and Roberts also point out that only tumors involving the thalamus *alone* have been found in some aphasic patients. In one case, a small hemorrhagic lesion of the pulvinar in the dominant hemisphere without the involvement of the cerebral cortex caused severe aphasia. The hypothesis that a thalamic center serves an organizing role may make it easier to understand the clinical findings of recovery of speech function following aphasia without displacement to the other hemisphere, notably after partial lesion of the posterior speech cortex or the destruction of the anterior or superior speech areas. "It suggests that the thalamic speech center can be employed for the ideational mechanisms of speech with the assistance of changing (or previously unemployed) areas of the cortex in the same hemisphere" (Penfield and Roberts 1959, 216).

THE RESULTING MODEL

Undoubtedly, some general regions of the left hemisphere (Broca's area, Wernicke's area, the posterior speech cortex, the supramarginal and angular gyri) organize important aspects of language function. These seem particularly concerned with the planning and execution of the sequential aspects of language, aspects primarily involving phonological and syntactic processes. And, depending on the region(s) involved, dysfunction may well affect comprehension, production, or both. Thus, cerebral lateralization and some specificity of function are necessary for the overall coordination of language activities.

But it would be inappropriate to conclude that language is somehow specifically 'located' in these regions, that linguistic functions and memories are 'stored' there, or that other areas of the brain do not participate in language processes. The research and models reviewed in this paper show that both memories and functions are, to some degree, more widely distributed throughout the brain and even other parts of the central nervous system. Very often the plasticity and dynamic nature of brain functions allows for recovery of language abilities when these regions have been seriously injured (Chall and Mirsky 1978; Penfield and Roberts 1959). Moreover, recent psychological and linguistic perspectives suggest that real world facts, the semantic base and attentional and perceptual mechanisms play critical roles in determining how language is used, organized and understood. In a very real sense, language is a 'whole brain,' not 'split brain' process.

READING IN WHOLE BRAIN PERSPECTIVE

Reading is primarily a means of communicating through written language. As such, it is best understood as a 'whole brain' activity. While the disconnection of particular cortical regions may disrupt reading ability in some cases (Benson 1976; Geschwind 1974), effective reading requires the integration of both sequential and parallel, holistic processes (See especially Kraft 1976, this volume and Lassen et. al. 1978 cited above).

Consequently, fluent reading and learning to read are activities which depend on perceptual and conceptual relationships. They are best accomplished when author and reader, teacher and learner, share, at least tacitly, some basic assumptions about the purpose of the activity and the cultural, social, linguistic and even idiosyncratic constitutive rules of language use operating between them. Methodologies which stress isolated structural components like word frequency and word repetition *at the expense* of a meaningful relationship between instructional material and the perceptual-conceptual-semantic-cultural world of the child deprive him of the comparative, interhemispheric and subcortical information essential for efficient processing.

In contrast, the work of Chafe, Gibson, Meyer and Meyer, Rosch and others suggests that, given the analogic and synergistic properties of the perceptual and memorial systems, categories, memories and skills are best established and refined through the convergence of many rich and meaningful experiences rather than through direct instruction in restrictive, tightly controlled, decontextualized settings. A 'whole brain' model would seem to imply that effective instructional practice should utilize a conceptual framework readily available to the learner. One source of such a framework would be the purposeful construction of a shared context for learning to read through children's literature and shared book experiences. Another is the child's own personal experience as it is filtered through and mirrored in his own oral and written language.

If a shared context and a rich and varied supportive linguistic environment are important for success in learning to read, they are essential for the child who is having difficulty. Historically, the trend has been to view severe reading disability in terms of psychological or neurological deficits with comparatively little attention given to the match between the educational environment and the world of the child. The focus in diagnosis has been on locating specific deficits within the child, and the educational prescription has often been more intensive and isolated drill on specific skills. This is particularly disturbing in light of the large proportions of poor and minority children among the growing number labeled as problem readers.

A 'whole brain' perspective on reading suggests a biologically more conservative but sociologically and educationally more radical approach to disability on several counts. Undoubtedly, there are children and adults who appear normal in every other respect but, because of some unknown neurological or psychological processing difficulty, are unable to learn to read. These we might call 'true dyslexics.' But the number of 'true dyslexics' is probably very much smaller than the number haphazardly and arbitrarily given the 'dyslexic' or 'reading disabled' labels. The dynamic and flexible nature of neural organization and the brain's remarkable potential for recovery argue against specific biological explanations. Certain neurological and psychological indices may correlate with reading difficulty, but individual differences are great enough that some successful readers often show the same trait while other problem readers do not. Overall adaptability is often more important than and can compensate for particular processing weaknesses.

Furthermore, there is a growing body of evidence that points to cultural and environmental factors that may directly affect what seem to be neurological or psychological processing deficiencies. For example, McDermott (1974) argues that " . . . a significant number of what are usually described as reading disabilities represent situationally induced inattention patterns which make sense in terms of the politics of the interethnic classroom." (p. 390).

Ryan (1977) offers a somewhat similar perspective on the language development of mongoloids. While there is little concrete neurological or linguistic evidence supporting brain mechanism defects as explanations for their retardation, psychologists persist in describing their alleged defects in neurobiological terms. On the other hand, few studies have been done on how normal adults behave to subnormal people. What evidence there is suggests that we provide them with restricted linguistic environments. Large institutions are unsuited for language acquisition, and there are case studies showing regression of verbal behavior *after* admission. Subnormals feel normals 'talk down' to them, creating lower self-concepts and expectations which lead to lower performance. Research suggests that adults do adjust their speech, using excessive yes-no answer type questions, with mothers using patterns requiring only single word responses. The mismatch between physical maturation and language development may also result in a nonsupportive environment. Older, slower children are unlikely to get the physical contact at the onset of language that younger, normal children do. In sum, we may very well create contexts where it is almost impossible for these people to reach their full language potential.

The techniques used with problem readers and 'disadvantaged' beginning readers are often similarly restrictive. Useless derogatory labels lead to lower expectations and lower performance. Increased time spent on isolated skills takes time away from exploring and/or reading books, from listening to stories and thus from developing appropriate story schemas and concepts of print. From the 'whole brain' perspective presented in this chapter the larger shared contexts must be established first, for they are the sources from which skillfulness in reading is most readily developed.

ENDNOTES

[1] Not to be confused with the European tradition of structural linguistics which includes the work of Roman Jakobson and other members of the Prague Circle.

REFERENCES

Albert, M., and Obler, L. 1978. *The bilingual brain.* New York: Academic Press.

Anderson, J. 1977. Neural models with cognitive implications. In *Basic processes in reading,* eds. D. LaBerge and S. Samuels. Hillsdale, NJ: Lawrence Erlbaum Associates.

Anderson, R., and Pichert, J. 1977. *Recall of previously unrecallable information following a shift in perspective* (Tech. Rep. No. 41). University of Illinois, Center for the Study of Reading.

Bartlett, F. 1932. *Remembering.* Cambridge, England: Cambridge University Press.

Benson, D. 1976. Alexia. In *Aspects of reading acquisition,* ed. J. Guthrie. Baltimore: Johns Hopkins University Press.

Boggs, S. 1972. The meaning of questions and narratives to Hawaiian children. In *Functions of language in the classroom,* eds. C. Cazden, V. John, and D. Hymes. New York: Teachers College Press.

Brewer, W. 1974. There is no convincing evidence for operant classical conditioning in adult humans. In *Cognition and the symbolic processes,* eds. W. Weimer, and D. Palermo. Hillsdale, NJ: Lawrence Erlbaum Associates.

Broca, P. 1865. Sur le faculte du langue articule. *Bul. Soc. Antrhropol* 6:462-465.

Bruner, J.; Goodnow, J.; and Austin, G. 1956. *A study of thinking*. New York: John Wiley and Sons.

Cazden, C.; John, V.; and Hymes, D. 1972. *Functions of language in the classroom*. New York: Teachers College Press.

Chafe, W. 1970. *Meaning and the structure of language*. Chicago: University of Chicago Press.

________. 1972. Discourse structure and human knowledge. In *Language comprehension and the acquisition of knowledge*, eds. R. Freedle and J. Carroll. New York: John Wiley and Sons.

________. 1973. Language and memory. *Language* 49(2): 261–281.

________. 1974. Language and consciousness. *Language* 50(1): 111–133.

________. 1977 The recall and verbalization of past experience. In *Current issues in linguistic theory*, ed. R. Cole. Bloomington: Indiana Press.

Chall, J., and Mirsky, A. 1978. Implications for education. In *Education and the brain*. NSSE Yearbook, Part 2.

Chomsky, N. 1957. *Syntactic structures*. The Hague: Mouton Press.

________. 1959. Review of B.F. Skinner's *Verbal behavior*. *Language* 35(1): 26–58.

________. 1965. *Aspects of the theory of syntax*. Cambridge, MA: M.I.T. Press.

________. 1968. *Language and mind*. New York: Harcourt Brace Jovanovich, Inc.

Clark, H., and Clark, E. 1977. *Psychology and language*. New York: Harcourt Brace Jovanovich, Inc.

Delmont, S., and Hamilton, D. 1976. Classroom research: a critique and a new approach. In *Explorations in classroom observation*, eds. M. Stubbs, and S. Delamont. London: John Wiley and Sons.

Dimond, S. 1972. *The double brain*. London: Churchill Livingstone.

Dumont, R. 1972. Learning English and how to be silent: Studies in Sioux and Cherokee classrooms. In *Functions of language in the classroom*, eds. C. Cazden, V. John, and D. Hymes. New York: Teachers College Press.

Fillmore, C. 1968. The case for case. In *Universals in linguistic theory*, eds. E. Bach and R. Harms. New York: Holt, Rinehart and Winston.

Franks, J. 1974. Toward understanding understanding. In *Cognition and the symbolic processes*. Hillsdale, NJ: Lawrence Erlbaum Associates.

Frederickson, C. 1975. Acquisition of semantic information from discourse. *Journal of Verbal Learning and Verbal Behavior* 14:158–169.

Geschwind, N. 1974. *Selected papers on language and the brain*. Boston Studies in the Philosophy of Science, Vol. 16. Boston: D. Reidel Publishing Co.

Gibson, E. 1977. How perception really develops: A vew from outside the network. In *Basic processes in reading*, eds. D. LaBerge and S. Samuels. Hillsdale, NJ: Lawrence Erlbaum Associates.

Gibson, J. 1977. The theory of affordances. In *Perceiving, acting and knowing*, eds. R. Shaw and J. Bransford. Hillsdale, NJ: Lawrence Erlbaum Associates.

Gosnave, G. 1977. Sentence production test in sensory aphasic patients. In *Sentence production: Developments in research and theory*, ed. S. Rosenberg. Hillsdale, NJ: Lawrence Erlbaum Associates.

Grimes, J. 1975. *The tread of discourse*. The Hague: Mouton Press.

Halliday, M., and Hasan, R. 1976. *Cohesion in English*. London: Longman.

Hormann, H. 1971. *Psycholinguistics*. New York: Springer-Verlag.

Hymes, D. 1972. Introduction. In *Functions of language in the classroom*, eds. C. Cazden, V. John, and D. Hymes. New York: Teachers College Press.
________. 1974. *Foundations in sociolinguistics.* Philadelphia: University of Pennsylvania Press.
Jackson, J. 1932. On the duality of the brain. *Selected writings of John Hughlings Jackson*, ed. J. Taylor. London: Hodder and Stoughton.
John, V. 1972. Styles of learning—styles of teaching: Reflections on the education of Navajo children. In *Functions of language in the classroom*, eds. C. Cazden, V. John, and D. Hymes. New York: Teachers College Press.
Katz, J., and Fodor, J. 1963. The structure of a semantic theory. *Language* 39:170–211.
King, M., and Rentel, V. 1979. Toward a theory of early writing development. *Research in the Teaching of English* 13(3): 243–254.
Kraft, R. 1976. An EEG study: Hemispheric brain functioning of six to eight year old children during piagetian and curriculum tasks with variation of presentation mode. Ph.D. Diss., The Ohio State University.
Kuhn, T. 1962. *The structure of scientific revolutions.* International Encyclopedia of Unified Science, vol. 2, #2. Chicago: University of Chicago Press.
LaBerge, D., and Samuels, S. 1977. *Basic processes in reading.* Hillsdale, NJ: Lawrence Erlbaum Associates.
Labov, W. 1969. The logic of non-standard English. In *Linguistics and the teaching of standard English*, ed. J. Alatis. Mongraph Series on Languages and Linguistics, #22. Washington, DC: Georgetown University Press.
Lashley, K. 1950. In search of the engram. Symposium for the society of experimental biology, #4. New York: Cambridge University Press.
Lassen, N.; Ingvar, D.; and Skinhoj, E. 1978. Brain function and blood flow. *Scientific American* 239:62–71.
Lenneberg, E. 1964. Language disorders in childhood. *Harvard Education Review* 34(2): 152–177.
________. 1967. *Biological foundations of language.* New York: John Wiley and Sons, Inc.
Lyons, J. 1970. *Noam Chomsky.* New York: The Viking Press.
Mace, W. 1974. Ecologically stimulating cognitive psychology: Gibsonian perspectives. In *Cognition and the symbolic processes*, eds. W. Weimer and D. Palermo. Hillsdale, NJ: Lawrence Erlbaum Associates.
________. 1977. James J. Gibson's strategy for perceiving: Ask not what's inside your head, but what your head's inside of. In *Perceiving, acting and knowing*, eds. R. Shaw and J. Bransford. Hillsdale, NJ: Lawrence Erlbaum Associates.
Mandler, J., and Johnson, N. 1977. Remembrance of things parsed: Story structure and recall. *Cognitive Psychology* 9:111–151.
McDermott, R. 1974. Achieving school failure: An anthropological approach to illiteracy and social stratification. In *Education and the cultural process: Toward an anthropology of education*, ed. G. Spindler. New York: Holt, Rinehart and Winston.
________. 1977. The ethnography of speaking and reading. In *Linguistic theory: What can it say about reading*, ed. R. Shuy. Newark, DE: International Reading Association.
McGuinness, D., and Pribram, K. 1978. The origin of sensory bias in the development of gender differences in perception and cognition. In *Cognitive growth and develop-*

ment: Essays in honor of Herbert G. Birch, ed. Bontuer. New York: Bruner Mazil.

Mehan, H. 1979. *Learning lessons: Social organization in the classroom.* Cambridge, MA; Harvard University Press.

Meyer, D., and Meyer, P. 1977. Dynamics and bases of recoveries of functions after injuries to the cerebral cortex. *Physiological Psychology* 5(2): 133-165.

________, n.d. Inductions of recoveries from amnesias. To appear in *Learning and memory*, eds. J. McGaugh and R. Thompson. New York: Plenum Press. Forthcoming.

Miller, G. 1967. *The psychology of communication.* Baltimore: Penguin Books.

Mohr, J.; Walters, W.; and Duncan, G. 1975. Thalamic hemorrhage and aphasia. *Brain and Language* 2:3-17.

Penfield, W. 1975. *The mystery of the mind.* Princeton, NJ: Princeton University Press.

Penfield, W., and Roberts, L. 1959. *Speech and brain mechanisms*, Princeton, NJ: Princeton University Press.

Phillips, S. 1972. Participant structures and communicative competence: Warm Springs children in community and classroom. In *Functions of language in the classroom*, eds. C. Cazden, V. John, and D. Hymes. New York: Teachers College Press.

Popper, K., and Eccles, J. 1977. *The self and its brain.* Berlin: Springer Internationnal.

Pribram, K. 1971. *Language of the brain.* Englewood Cliffs, NJ: Prenctice-Hall, Inc.

________. 1975. Neurolinguistics: The study of brain organization in grammar and meaning. *Totus Homo* 6:20-30.

________. 1977. Some comments on the nature of the perceived universe. In *Perceiving, acting and knowing*, eds. R. Shaw and J. Bransford. Hillsdale, NJ: Lawrence Erlbaum Associates.

Pribram, K.; Nuwer, M.; and Baron, R. 1974. The holographic hypothesis of memory structure in brain function and perception. In *Measurement, psychophysics, and neural information processing*, eds. D. Krantz, R. Atkinson, D. Luce, and P. Suppes. San Francisco: W.H. Freeman and Company.

Rosch, E. 1973. On the internal structure of perceptual and semantic categories. In *Cognitive development and the acquisition of language*, ed. T. Moore. New York: Academic Press.

________. 1975a. Cognitive reference points. *Cognitive Psychology* 1:532-547.

________. 1975b. Universals and cultural specifics in human categorization. In *Cross cultural perspectives on learnings*, eds. R. Brislen, S. Bochner, and J. Lonnen. New York: John Wiley and Sons.

Rumelhart, D. 1978. *Schemata: The building blocks of cognition* (Tech. Rep. No. 79). San Diego: University of California, Center for Human Information Processing.

Ryan, J. 1977. The silence of stupidity. In *Psycholinguistics: Development and pathological*, eds. J. Morton and J. Marshall.

Sacks, H.; Schegloff, E.; and Jefferson, G. 1974. A simplest systematics for the analysis of turn-taking in conversation. *Language* 50.

Sarup, M. 1978. *Marxism and education.* London: Routledge and K. Paul Ltd.

Searle, J. 1969. *Speech acts.* Cambridge, England: Cambridge University Press.

Selfridge, O. 1959. Pandemonium: A paradigm for learning. In *Symposium on the mechanism of thought processes.* London: H.M. Stationery Office.

Selnes, O., and Whitaker, H. 1977. Neurological substrates of language and speech production. In *Sentence production: Developments in research and theory*, ed. S.

Rosenberg. Hillsdale, NJ: Lawrence Erlbaum Associates.

Shaw, R., and Bransford, J., eds. 1977. *Perceiving, acting and knowing.* Hillsdale, NJ: Lawrence Erlbaum Associates.

Sinclair, J., and Goulthard, R. 1975. *Toward an analysis of discourse.* London: Oxford University Press.

Slobin, D. 1973. Cognitive prerequisites for the development of a grammar. In *Studies of child language development*, eds. C. Ferguson and D. Slobin: New York: Holt, Rinehart and Winston.

Smith, F. 1975. *Comprehension and learning.* New York: Holt, Rinehart and Winston.

Sperling, G. 1960. The information available in brief visual presentations. *Psychological Monographs* 74(11).

Stein, N. 1978. *How children understand stories: A developmental analysis* (Tech. Rep. No. 69). University of Illinois, Center for the Study of Reading.

Thorndyke, P. Cognitive structures in comprehension and memory of narrative discourse. *Cognitive Psychology* 9:77–110.

Turvey, M. 1974. Constructive theory, perceptual systems, and tacit knowledge. In *Cognition and the symbolic processes*, eds. W. Weimer and D. Palermo. Hillsdale, NJ: Lawrence Erlbaum Associates.

Weimer, W. 1974. Overview of a cognitive conspiracy: Reflections on the volume. In *Cognition and the symbolic processes*, eds. W. Weimer and D. Palermo. Hillsdale, NJ: Lawrence Erlbaum Associates.

Weimer, W., and Palermo, D., eds. *Cognition and the symbolic processes.* Hillsdale, NJ: Lawrence Erlbaum Associates.

Weinstein, S. 1964. Deficits concomitant with aphasia or lesions of either cerebral hemisphere. *Cortex* 1(2): 154–167.

Wernicke, C. 1874. *Der aphasische Symptomencomplex. Eine psychologische Studie auf anatomischer Basis.* Breslau: Cohn and Weigert.

Winograd, T. 1972. Understanding natural language. *Cognitive Psychology* 3(1).

Wittrock, M., ed. 1975. Education and the hemispheric process of the brain. *U.C.L.A. Educator* 17(2).

Chapter 2

Bimodal Processing and Memory From Text

by Bruce R. Dunn

INTRODUCTION

In recent years, one of the major research interests of various cognitive psychologists and neuroscientists has been the encoding and retrieval of information from long-term memory. Although many studies of memory have been conducted independently in these fields, few, if any, have systematically investigated hypotheses from the research results or the theoretical approaches of both. Two theories, in particular, appear to have important implications for studying long-term memory of connected discourse.

The first theory, greatly influenced by research in the neurosciences, suggests that the two hemispheres of the brain have specialized and somewhat different functions in terms of perceptual and semantic processing (Bogen and Gazzaniga 1965; Levy-Agresti and Sperry 1968). This theory, which will be termed *bimodal theory*, argues that the representation of information contained in memory is highly dependent on the mode of conscious processing used in encoding the information. Over the years, various investigators have given differing names to the two modes of consciousness. Most, however, have emphasized that one mode is predominantly analytical and logical in its processing, while the other processes information in a more holistic or gestalt manner (see Bogen 1969, for a review). For the purposes of this chapter, the terms *analytical* and *holistic* will be used to describe these differing modes of consciousness. It is interesting to note that these ideas are similar to those proposed by Paivo (1975a) in his dual-coding theory of memory.

The second theory, from the cognitive and psycholinguistic areas of psychology, suggests that most complex verbal information stored in long-term memory is coded into logically related semantic structures. These structures are assumed to be used later as the basis for retrieval (Frederiksen 1975a, 1977b; Kintsch 1977; Mandler 1967, 1970; Meyer 1977a, 1977b; Rumelhart and Ortony 1977).

After providing an extensive review of relevant theory and research concerning these two positions, this chapter concludes with recent exploratory research that attempts to integrate aspects of both theories of memory for complex information. Specifically, this study investigated how recall is affected by conscious processing modes during the encoding of expository text.

Lengthy reviews of both bimodal and semantic theories should both aid in grasping the rationale for our research, and provide the unitiated reader an opportunity to gain a basic understanding of theory and research underlying each area. The reviews are given separately as a convenience to experienced investigators who may skip this familiar information.

In the bimodal theory section, recent physiological and psychological research is reviewed which indicates that: 1) at least two modes of conscious processing exist that differentially process information; 2) the relation between bimodal processing and hemispheric processing is *not* as direct as originally assumed; and 3) by using electrophysiological measurements (primarily EEG), individuals who are relatively more analytical in their general processing style can be distinguished from those who are less analytical and perhaps even "holistic" in their processing.

The section concerning semantic theory and prose grammars deals with *schema-based* and *text-based* approaches to discourse analysis. Special emphasis will be placed on a semantic grammar for text, developed by Bonnie Meyer (1975), and on how it can be used to identify the *microstructure* and *macrostructure* levels of written expository text. Briefly, and somewhat arbitrarily, the use of *microstructure* will describe the semantic relations contained within sentences, whereas the term *macrostructure* will be limited to descriptions of between-sentence and between-paragraph semantic relations. However, since Pepinsky (this volume) has adequately described micro-levels of written and oral discourse, this chapter will focus on the use of these grammars to describe a text's macro-level or higher-order stimulus properties.

BIMODAL PROCESSING THEORY

Beginning with Jackson's seminal work in 1864, several researchers suggested that two different, yet coexisting, modes of conscious processing are available to the individual (Bogen 1969). These two modes are specialized for specific types of experiences and cognitive processes (Bogen 1969; Deikman 1971; Galin 1974; Levy-Agresti and Sperry 1968; Ornstein 1973, 1977).

Recently, bimodal theory attracted serious attention in the neurosciences, psychology, and psychiatry, taking several related forms. Because of the extensive coverage of basic research literature underlying bimodal theory by others in this volume, I will address only those aspects which have particular relevance for our research. But, even this restricted task cannot be meaningfully accomplished without at least a brief historical overview.

Early manifestations of bimodal theory (e.g., Ornstein 1973) gained scientific credibility and support in the neurophysiological literature suggesting that the two hemispheres of the human brain have specialized functions in terms of perceptual and verbal processing. Studies of split-brain subjects indicated that the right hemisphere is superior for visual-spatial tranformations (e.g., Bogen and Gazzaniga 1965, Nebes 1971), as well as for recognizing complex visual patterns (Levy, Trevarthen and Sperry 1972). In contrast, the left hemisphere appears to be superior for speech and calculation (Sperry, Gazzaniga and Bogen 1969).

Although generalizations about normal functioning from neurologically deficient populations is questionable, hemispheric specialization has received considerable additional support from a large body of studies using normal subjects (Galin 1974). Much of this literature has used rapid visual half-field presentations and dichotic listening tasks to the capacities of the two cerebral hemispheres.

DICHOTIC AUDITORY RESEARCH

The dichotic listening task, which presents different information to both ears simultaneously, has become an important tool in neuropsycholinguistic research because of earlier research showing a right ear superiority for verbal material, and a left ear superiority for nonverbal sounds such as musical phrases (Kimura 1964). It is assumed by researchers utilizing this task that for right-handed people, the right ear (RE) projects primarily to the contralateral left-hemisphere (LH), whereas the left ear (LE) projects to the right hemisphere (RH), although the exact neuroanatomical basis for this assumption is far from clear (see Haaland 1974). Thus the RE advantage for linguistic material was originally assumed to be a function of LH domance, and the LE advantage for nonverbal sounds was attributed to RH dominance.

The dichotic task and its underlying assumptions of specific hemispheric specialization have increasingly been criticized. Freides (1977), for example, points out that if the left hemisphere in the normal right-hander was specialized for processing verbal items, then one would expect large hemispheric differences in recall. The data, however, when they do occur in the expected direction, often account for only 2%–6% of the total variance. Freides also points out that lateral differences often have not been found in well-controlled studies where one would clearly expect them (e.g., Bryden 1963, Repp 1975, 1976). It appears, then, that recall of linguistic and non-linguistic sound patterns is not a simple function of "specialized" cerebral hemispheres.

A dichotic listening study which casts further doubt on the "specialization" hypothesis has been reported by Heeschen and Jürgens(1977). These researchers presented sequences of three words to subjects using a dichotic presentation with three-word strings having either underlying semantic-pragmatic relationships or syntactic relationships. Although the results showed a general RE/LH advantage overall, they also indicated that the left hemisphere is solely responsive to syntactic relationships, while the two hemispheres appear to be equally responsive to semantic-pragmatic relationships. This suggests that hemispheric specialization is not completely related to different types of information processed by the two hemispheres, and that language processing may be due to an interaction of both.

VISUAL HALF-FIELD RESEARCH

Parallel and almost identical to the dichotic listening research is the literature describing the use of rapid visual half-field presentation of stimuli for assessing the specialization of the two cerebral hemispheres. Early research had indicated that tachistoscopic word recognition was faster in the right visual field (RVF) which projects to the left hemisphere (LH) (e.g., Barton, Goodglass, and Shai 1965; Bryden 1965; Kimura 1966; McKeever and Huling 1970). In contrast, the left visual field-right hemisphere (LVF-RH) superiority for nonverbal functions also has been demonstrated in several investigations (e.g., Geffin, Bradshaw, and Wallace 1971; Kimura 1966, 1969). Recent critical analysis, however, has challenged the interpretation of these findings.

Although it has become popular to assume that the left hemisphere is specialized for processing language and the right hemisphere for processing visuospatial stimuli, the literature using visual half-field presentation, like the dichotic listening literature, is far from conclusive. In a recent study, Hardyck, Tzeng and Wang (1978) obtained results that question much of the data showing cerebral specialization of function by indicating that earlier results may be procedural artifacts. The possibility that procedures rather than hemispheric specialization might account for observed processing differences rested initially on findings from a few well-controlled studies indicating no hemispheric effects for comparisons where such effects were predictable (Dimond, Gibson and Gazzaniga 1972). The crucial difference between this latter work and that research indicating hemispheric specialization for verbal tasks (Davis and Schmit 1973; Geffin, Bradshaw and Wallace 1971) and for non-verbal tasks (Geffin et al. 1971; Rizzolati, Umilta and Berlucchi 1971) was that in those studies where specialization effects were obtained, subjects were confronted by a restricted stimulus set over a great many trials, a procedure that permitted subjects to memorize or store the entire stimulus set, while in Dimond et al. (1972), new stimuli were presented on each trial, a procedure that prevented subjects from storing a stimulus set. These procedural differences respectively implicated memory, or in controlling for memory, processing. With memory left uncontrolled, differences in response latencies, the criterion employed in all cases, could have been interpreted as storage differences as readily as processing differences. Where subjects were prevented or, at least discouraged, from storing a set, findings could be interpreted presumably as processing differences.

To settle the issue, Hardyck et al. (1978) conducted four experiments alternately controlling in several ways for processing differences but eliminating memory as a confounding factor. Visual half-field tachistoscopic presentations of Chinese characters and their equivalent English words were given to fluent Chinese-English bilinguals (exps. 1 and 2) as well as monolingual English-speaking subjects (exps. 3 and 4).

The use of these particular stimuli permitted comparison reaction times for semantic judgments of same-different which would not be confounded by visual similarities between the English words and Chinese characters. In addition, Chinese-Chinese and English-English word pairs were tested.

In their first two studies new information was presented on each trial and the results clearly showed that subjects' mean reaction times did not differ systematically with visual field presentation. Experiment 3 was identical to the first two experiments except that English-speaking monolingual subjects were used. If lateralized processing differences existed, there should have been a clear RVF-LH advantage for English words and a LVF-RH advantage for Chinese characters with these subjects, for whom the Chinese characters were novel, nonverbal stimuli. The results again showed that when new information is presented on each trial, there were no significant visual half-field differences. In their final experiment, Hardyck et al. replicated the procedure of previous experimenters, namely the use of restricted stimulus sets (eight stimulus pairs) presented over many trials (200), allowing the subjects to become familiar with each stimulus pair. Typical visual field differences were found.

Based on their results, these investigators argued that lateralization effects, as reported in previous studies, are not a function of immediate cognitive *processes* which differ in the two cerebral hemispheres; rather, they reflect differences in memory storage locations. That is, when a subject has to evaluate new information on each trial, reaction times do not vary systematically with visual field presentation. This suggests that initial evaluation or processing of information is *not* dependent on hemisphere locations. When subjects are exposed to few stimuli for many trials, however, they probably retain all possible response alternatives in memory, thereby causing retrieval to become a matter of simple matching rather than problem solving. Thus, although immediate cognitive processing may not be lateralized, memory for language may be highly lateralized in the left hemisphere and, correspondingly, visuospatial and pattern storage may be located in the right hemisphere. Regardless of the final outcome of this somewhat controversial memory lateralization hypothesis, the results of the Hardyck et al. as well as other related studies (e.g., Cohen 1975; Freides 1977) question simplistic approaches to specific lateralized information processing.

This research, coupled with the large body of literature showing the linguistic capability of the right hemisphere, (see Searleman 1977 for an extensive review) and the left hemisphere for finer aspects of facial recognition (see Sergent 1982a and Sergent and Bindra 1981) has led to recent and relatively more sophisticated bimodal processing theories that stress different cognitive processing styles of the cerebral hemispheres.

BIMODAL PROCESSING REVISITED

Galin (1974), as well as others (Levy-Agresti and Sperry 1968; Ornstein 1973, 1977; Patterson and Bradshaw 1975), emphasized that the major characteristic of the hemispheres is not that they are specialized to work with different types of material, but that each hemisphere is specialized for a different cognitive or processing style. The left hemisphere appears to operate in an analytical, logical mode for which words are an excellent tool. It processes information in a linear, serial, or sequential manner. In contrast, the right hemisphere seems to operate in a holistic, gestalt mode, which is particularly suitable for spatial relations, as well as music, and appears to process information in a more simultaneous or parallel manner.

A recent model by Goldberg and Costa (1981) provides a modification of this view. They argue that the anatomical differences between the right and the left hemisphere suggest that the right hemisphere is more adept at peforming intermodal integration and at processing novel stimuli and events. In contrast, the left hemisphere is better at unimodal integration and motor processing as well as storing and utilizing compact, routine codes. Although the main focus of the Goldberg and Costa model is novelty, their view that the right hemisphere is superior at intermodal integration and the left at unimodal processing, nicely parallels the earlier notions above, namely that information is processed by the right hemisphere holistically and the left analytically.

Other evidence, however, indicates that both hemispheres may possess both analytical and holistic processing capability (e.g., Cohen 1975; White and White 1975). These studies, as well as an increasing number of others (Basso, Bisiach, and Capitani 1977; Freides 1977; Hardyck, Tzeng and Wang 1978; Heeschen and Jürgens 1977; Levy and Trevarthen 1976; Sergent 1982b), suggest that analytical and holistic processing styles are best viewed as unique products caused by different "mixtures" or interactions of the cerebral hemispheres, rather than as separate functions of each.

In fact, many investigators have stressed the need for an integrative approach to hemispheric processing (Ben-Dov and Carmon 1976; Broadbent 1974; Hellige and Cox 1976; Levy and Trevarthen 1976; Luria and Simernitskaya 1977; Sergent 1982b; Trevarthen 1978). For example, Sergent and her colleagues (Sergent 1982a, 1982b; Sergent and Bindra 1981) have argued that both hemispheres can process verbal and visuospatial information and both can process that information analytically and holistically. The major difference between them appears to be a function of the level of sensorimotor resolution required for processing the stimulus information presented. If the information is degraded, has relatively few subcomponents and/or has low spatial frequency, then the right hemisphere shows a processing advantage. If, however, the information has high resolution (or the task imposed requires a high resolution output), has many components and/or consists of units having high spatial frequency, a left hemisphere processing advantage occurs.

The results of a study by Levy and Trevarthen (1976) led them to conclude that information processing is organized by a *metacontrol* system which regulates hemispheric processing (also see Kraft and Zutell this volume). They argue that cerebral lateral specializations pertain not just to the ability and manifest behavioral differences between the two sides of the brain, but also to the expectations of the metacontrol system and their implications for processing requirements. Further, the metacontrol system makes its decision *prior* to actual information processing, and the chosen hemipshere remains in control even if as a consequence of that decision, performance declines. This notion was used by Levy and Trevarthen to account for numerous dissociations between hemispheric specialization and matching task performance exhibited by their commissurized patients. The dispositions of the metacontrol system to act are independent of, though usually correlated to some extent with, differential aptitudes of the hemispheres.

Of crucial importance for our research, Levy and Trevarthen concluded by stressing that not only is perception (encoding) and active, constructive process, but it is also highly dependent on the *internal* state of the subject, which in turn depends on constraints imposed by learned values, expectations, knowledge, and intentions. This view nicely parallels other bimodal theories (e.g., Deikman 1971, reported below), and suggests that the metacontrol system of a given individual can be biased towards a particular mode because of past learning, culture, etc. This of course does not preclude the shifting of modal balance in an individual because of an unsuccessful outcome or because of varying external constraints on processing (e.g., Hymes, Dunn, Gould, and Harris 1977; Levy and Trevarthen 1976).

It is not simply that the metacontrol system merely engages either the left hemisphere as an exclusive analytical processing system, or the right hemisphere as a sole holistic analyzer. For example, even thought the left hemisphere has a dominant analytical style, analysis is not completely the left's domain (e.g., Cohen 1975; Sergent 1982b). Nor is the left hemisphere the sole processor of linguistic information (Searleman 1977). These sentiments are echoed by Trevarthen (1978) who states " . . . the mature hemispheres must certainly act together in complimentary ways—the left does not replace or supersede the right in any sense. Without a right hemisphere the left chatters and lacks a sense of proportion, just like the discipline of science does when divorced from cultural perspective and the humanities" (p. 119).

Deikman (1971) has proposed a less specific but similar bimodal theory of consciousness, which he utilizes to clarify a number of phenomena in the fields of attention, mystical perception, hallucinogenic drugs, and psychosis. His model has the advantage of suggesting certain electrophysiological correlates by which two modes, an action and a receptive mode, can be identified. The action mode (referred to hereafter as the active mode) is a state used to organize and manipulate the environment, and enables us to categorize and analyze the environment primarily via language. "The principal psychological manifestations of this state are focal attention, object-based logic, heightened boundary perception, and the dominance of formal characteristics over the sensory; shapes and meanings have a preference over colors and textures" (p. 480). When an individual is in the active mode the EEG is characterized by beta activity (> 13Hz), and baseline muscle tension is increased. In contrast, the receptive mode is described as a state organized around maximizing the intake of the environment, rather than manipulating it, and is primarily sensory in nature. This mode is associated with ineffable experience. "Other attributes of the receptive mode are diffuse attending, paralogical thought processes, decreased boundary perception, and the dominance of the sensory over the formal" (p. 481). The physiological correlates accompanying this state are increased alpha activity (8–13Hz) of the brain and lower baseline muscle tension.

Deikman argues that, although different, the active and receptive modes are complementary and simultaneously coexist in each of us. The active and receptive modes do not ordinarily occur in their pure states. Typically, there is a modal balance or mixture, the characteristics of which depend on the extent of dominance of a particular mode. Thus, in most receptive mode conditions, an active relationship with the environment occurs to some degree. Furthermore, within both modes the attributes or components are interrelated to form a system, so that a shift in any one component can affect the others. As a result, a shift from active to receptive mode dominance can be induced by meditation, alpha feedback, and relaxation techniques, among other means. Similar points have been made by Das (1973), and are implied by the work of others (Levy and Trevarthen 1976; Trevarthen 1978).

Some have argued (e.g., Ornstein 1973) that the specialized functions of Deikman's two modes of consciousness are quite similar to the cognitive processes attributed to the two cerebral hemispheres. It is of primary importance for later discussion, however, for the reader to note that Deikman does not specifically argue that his two modes are hemispheric dependent; thus, his theory appears to have an integrative flavor.

The notions of bimodal conscious processing presented thus far are also quite similar to Paivio's dual-coding process theory of memory (Paivio 1971, 1975a, 1975b), particularly since Paivio does not directly relate this theory to hemispheric processing. Paivio argues that there are two distinct but interconnected and interacting memory systems; the imaginal and the verbal. The imaginal system is assumed to be specialized for processing non-verbal information and storing that information in a rather direct analog form called images. The verbal system, on the other hand, is specialized for dealing with abstract, linguistic units, which are sequentially arranged, and only indirectly and arbitrarily related to actual things.[1]

Information is processed by the imaginal system in a synchronous (similar to holistic) manner, in contrast to the verbal system which processes material in a sequential, analytical, logical manner. Thus, the verbal system is seen as the abstract logical mode of thinking, whereas the imaginal system is seen as the concrete alogical mode. The interesting point is that Paivio's system was developed from a different area of research, verbal learning, in contrast to the physiological and perceptual areas reported above.

Although studies using split-brain patients (e.g., Levy and Trevarthen 1976; Zaidel 1977) and normal subjects using visual half-field presentation (e.g., Hines 1976) are highly important basic research studies, they have certain major limitations, particularly when applied to natural reading research. First, in most of this research simple words or pictures were used as stimuli, rather than prose or text materials (e.g., Pirozzolo and Rayner 1977). Perhaps even more important is the fact that the processing styles of each cerebral hemisphere have been the primary focus in these studies. Given the apparent organizational complexity of the hemispheres as suggested by the new and highly interactive bimodal theories just discussed, this may turn out to be an extremely difficult, and perhaps even a fruitless research strategy when applied to reading. Few researchers have focused on the comprehension of text material in which the reader uses both visual fields, and where some simultaneous assessment of brain functioning is taken. Therefore, it could be argued that to be more ecologically valid, psychophysiological research related to reading needs to utilize broader methods. These should allow subjects opportunity to read more than can be shown using rapid visual half-field presentations, while still providing a means to measure some possibly related aspect of cerebral functioning. One method which appears to have particular promise employs the electroencephalograph (EEG) to bilaterally record subjects' brain activity during complex tasks including reading.

EEG CORRELATES OF COGNITIVE PROCESSING

There is mounting evidence that the EEG can be used to show differential hemispheric activity during various cognitive tasks (e.g., Doyle, Ornstein and Galin 1974; Ornstein and Galin 1976). Doyle et al. gave 10 adult right-handed subjects various cognitive tasks including letter writing, serial arithmetic and modified Kohs Block Design, while their EEG was being bilaterally recorded from two temporal and two parietal regions of the cortex. These records were subjected to discrete Fourier transforms, and power ratios from homologous leads were computed in the conventional frequency bands. The results showed that these ratios (right hemisphere/left hemisphere) were significantly greater during verbal and arithmetical tasks than during spatial tasks primarily in the alpha (8–13Hz) band. That is, the left hemisphere produced less alpha during analytical tasks (high ratio) and more alpha during spatial or holistic tasks (low ratio). Further, the beta (above 13 Hz) and theta bands (4–7 Hz) showed the same effect but less consistently. Delta activity (1-3 Hz) showed no systematic relationship with the various cognitive tasks. Other researchers have also found the alpha band to be particularly sensitive in showing differential activity during complex tasks (Bennett and Trinder 1977; Doktor and Bloom 1977; McLeod and Peacock 1977; Osborne and Gale 1976); thus the alpha band appears to be a powerful physiological correlate of information processing.

Osborne and Gale (1976) state that although past research has shown that the ratio of right to left hemisphere EEG amplitude tends to be greater for verbal than for spatial tasks, ratio scores only show that the left side of the brain is more activated (less alpha) than the right during processing of verbal material. No conclusions can be drawn from ratio scores concerning the effects of spatial material on the right hemisphere, since ratio differences could be due to changes in the absolute level of EEG activity in either or both hemispheres. Therefore, they suggest that besides ratio scores, alpha abundance scores from each hemisphere should be used to measure EEG during performance of cognitive tasks. Unlike ratio scores, alpha abundance scores allow comparisons to be made *within* each hemisphere for different tasks, assuming of course that task time is held constant.

The results of the studies reported above suggest that the magnitude of alpha activity, used in a ratio or alone, is an important correlate of cognitive activity. It also appears to be sensitive to possible processing differences attributed to the two cerebral hemispheres. Due to our interest in relating physiological brain correlates to the encoding and recall of text, bilateral recording has become our primary tool because it allows for continuous monitoring of brain activity during both of these activities.

Evidence is also beginning to appear which suggests that the EEG alpha correlates suggested by Deikman (1971, 1976) can be used to identify people having differing cognitive styles. Davidson and Schwartz (1977) found that musically non-proficient subjects showed significantly greater relative right hemisphere activation while whistling a song vs. reciting the lyrics of a song; whereas, musically proficient subjects did not show EEG asymmetry (using alpha ratios) between these tasks. Based on their results, Davidson and Schwartz concluded that musical training is associated with the adoption of a more sequential and analytical processing mode.

Differences in alpha activity have also been shown between occupational groups assumed to have different processing styles based on the nature of their profession (Doktor and Bloom 1977; Ornstein and Galin 1976). The study of Doktor and Bloom is of particular interest since some fairly clear differences were found between an occupational group assumed to have an analytical processing style (Operations Researchers) and another assumed to use a more holistic mode (Corporate Executives). These investigators gave both occupational groups two problem sets to complete during which bilateral alpha recordings were taken. One problem set contained verbal-analytical problems, the other more holistic problems. The results showed that the analytical processors produced less alpha in the left hemisphere when solving verbal problems than when solving spatial ones. The executives, on the other hand, showed an inconsistent pattern with half producing alpha similar to the analyticals and the other half producing just the opposite pattern.

Because of the questionable choice of holistic thinkers, these results are not as clear as one would like them to be. While many executive positions do require people who focus more on wholes than on parts, many others require or attract persons who have a more analytical style (e.g., college faculty chairpersons). Thus Doktor and Bloom's holistic thinkers probably contained a mixture of both types. Still, the results of their work are promising.

Sex differences in lateral specialization of hemispheric functioning have also been found (e.g., Davidson and Schwartz 1977; Ray, Morell, Frediani, and Tucker 1976). The Ray et al. study showed that when males and females were given right and left hemisphere cognitive tasks, the ratios of EEG power measured from the temporal lobes were statistically significant for males, but not for females. These results suggest that males and females may process the same environmental stimuli with different patterns of brain activity. Since evidence of hemispheric processing differences between the sexes has also been indicated in visual half-field studies using words (Bradshaw, Gates and Nettleton 1977; as well as faces Rizzolatti and Bushtel 1977), it could be argued that sex of subjects should be a major variable of study.

WEAKNESSES OF PAST EEG RESEARCH

Amazingly, little of the research relating individual differences in modal processing to differences in brain activity has actually measured behavioral preformance on the cognitive tasks used to elicit that activity.[2] Differences in brain activity during task processing are interesting, but could be considered of little practical or theoretical value unless that activity is consistently reelated to individual differences in task performance.

Our first attempt to investigate differences in bimodal processing as indexed by physiological brain activity (Hymes, Dunn, Gould and Harris 1977), was a memory study which used measures of recall and clustering performance. It will be instructive at this point to relate this research in detail, since our study was specifically designed to test some of the notions proposed by Deikman (1971, 1976) concerning physiological correlates of modal processing. Deikman suggests that the active (analytical) mode is accompanied by decreased alpha production and increased basal muscle tension, while the opposite holds true for the receptive (holistic) mode. He also argues that shifts in modal processing could occur within an individual, and that individual differences in the balance of these two modes may exist. Therefore, one person may tend to be analytical, while another could possess a more holistic style, although both are capable of some shifting of their modal balance. Deikman's views are similar to those proposed by Levy and Trevarthen (1976), who suggest the integration of hemispheric functions through a metacontrol system. They are also supported by research showing that mode of processing indexed by alpha production is a relatively stable trait (e.g., Doktor and Bloom 1977).

Since Deikman does not speak of differences in alpha asymmetry, but in terms of magnitude of alpha production, our early research reported immediately below did not address differences in hemispheric processing. However, our later research on prose memory, discussed at the end of this chapter, did investigate this issue. Given the new integrated view of bimodal processing, this later research on prose memory is of particular interest.

Subjects in our first study were divided into those more analytical vs. those more holistic on the basis of two-minute, eyes open, integrated recordings of their right-hemisphere alpha activity. They were not dichotomized using both the EEG and the EMG measures suggested by Deikman (1971, 1976), because a Pearson Product Moment correlation between subjects' baseline alpha and EMG data showed a negative but statistically non-significant relationship. Although the correlation was in the predicted direction, a dichotomization based on both physiological measures resulted in too few subjects scoring above the median on one measure and below the median on the other to provide a sufficiently powerful analysis of bimodal memory differences. Therefore, subjects were dichotomized into analytical and holistic processors using only their integrated alpha activity, because alpha was assumed to be a more direct correlate of mental activity than EMG. Holistic subjects were defined as those subjects whose scores fell above the median; analytical subjects were defined as those whose scores were below it.

After screening, subjects returned for a learning task. Half the subjects in the analytical and holistic groups were instructed to relax, and the other half to be alert during learning. This resulted in a 2 (type of processor: analytical/holistic) by 2 (instruction: alert/relax) factorial design for data analysis. The learning task was similar to that used by Bousfield (1953), and consisted of a 40-item word list containing five difficult 8-word categories derived from the McConkie and Dunn (1969) word-sorting norms. The words were presented in quasi-random order, with no two members of the same category being contiguous. The list was shown twice using a slide projector, with each word presented individually for 5 seconds. After presentation, the subjects were allowed 5 minutes to recall the list in any order they wished.

A two-way unweighted means ANOVA performed on the recall data showed only the main effect of type of processor to be statistically significant. Mean recall was greater for analytical than for holistic subjects (20 vs. 16 words, respectively). In order to determine if analytical and holistic subjects encoded differently, the subjects' recall protocols were scored for the amount of obtained vs. expected clustering (categorical organization) using a method reported by Bousfield and Bousfield (1966). Type of clustering score was treated as a repeated measure, and a three-way unweighted means ANOVA was performed on these data. Several main effects and interactions were found to be significant including the important two-way, processor by type of score, and the three-way interaction. These interactions, coupled with appropriate F tests for simple effects, showed two unique patterns: Analytical subjects produced significant clustering, whereas the clustering of holistics was not better than chance. In addition, analytical subjects given alert instructions produced higher mean clustering than the other conditions.

Subjects' recall data were then plotted as a function of the serial position of the words during presentation. The curve generated by the holistics showed the typical serial position effect; however, because of their clustering, the analytical subjects' curve did not. This indicates that the holistic subjects encoded the information more in the order in which it was presented than did the analytical subjects, who tended to organize the material into categories.

The results of this study provide support for bimodal consciousness theory, and show that at least one of the physiological measures suggested by Deikman (1971, 1976), the EEG alpha band, can be used to identify students who are relatively more analytical than others in their processing. Further, it appears that the use of relaxation and alert instruction can differentially shift the modal balance used by subjects.

Some investigators may prefer to view the differences we have ascribed to differences in bimodal processing as due to differences in "arousal" level. However, the old notion that alpha is a correlate of simple arousal and follows the traditional inverted "U" shape function was seriously questioned in a clever set of experiments reported by Orne and Wilson (1977) who showed that, among other things, subjects can produce high alpha even under conditions of high stress. (The interested reader will find many other arguments against the simple arousal notion in the article as well as evidence for systematic individual differences in alpha production.) Further, "arousal" is a very generic and somewhat nebulous term covering a wide range of human functioning including motivational and emotional behavior. It clearly does *not* describe the disparate recall patterns (and inferred differences in cognitive processing) that can be accounted for using our dichotomization. That is, to assume that our high analytic subjects are just highly aroused, not only does not adequately represent their logical and categorical patterns produced at recall, but also implies that "arousal" is somehow a direct causal agent. It is just as easy to assume that measurements of "arousal," such as the alpha band, are merely the correlates of higher-order cognitive processes, rather than the other way around. This latter assumption is, of course, the one taken in this chapter.

These findings are also particularly promising since college students were used as subjects. It could be argued that, if anything, college students are more analytical than most other people because of their academic characteristics and training. For this reason, the holistic processors identified in this study probably were analytical, yet were relatively less analytical when compared to those who were actually termed analytical processors. Whether or not a truly holistic style exists will have to be determined by future research using different populations and stimulus material than was used in the experiments reported in this chapter. Given the differential clustering performance of the two styles as a function of learning and recall instructions (holistics produced their greatest clustering when asked to relax, whereas analyticals produced their greatest clustering when asked to be alert), a weak argument could be made for a unique holistic style. However, some readers may wish to insert the term "low analytic" whenever the word "holistic" appears in the following pages. Regardless, it appears that the type of processing used by subjects (whether high vs. low analytic or perhaps analytic vs. holistic) may be a powerful variable determining which kind of information will be learned, how it will be encoded, and subsequently recalled.

SEMANTIC THEORY, PROSE GRAMMARS, AND RELATED RESEARCH

During the past two decades, the study of memory and retrieval processes has become the primary research interest of most cognitive psychologists. Until quite recently, the major theories in this area have been based on research which has used simple verbal items, such as word lists, as stimulus material (e.g., Mandler 1967, 1970; Tulving 1968). Much of this stimulus material has had little or no inherent semantic structure, and it was assumed that the subject produced a categorically organized cognitive structure on which to base his or her recall. Further, with the exception of Paivio's (1975a) dual-coding theory, most learning psychologists and theorists have regarded information as being processed either through a series of stages (e.g., the stage theory of Atkinson and Shiffrin 1968) or through a more unitary processing system containing a series of levels (Craik and Lockhart 1972). This latter theory, called levels-of-processing theory, currently favored by many learning psychologists, allows for some parallel processing to occur. The long-term memory code for any item is seen as highly semantic, and the retrieval of that item is viewed as a function of the amount of processing, particularly the amount of deep semantic processing, it has received. A similar viewpoint concerning long-term memory is held by stage theorists. It should be noted, however, that both stage theory and levels of processing theory do not directly address bimodal coding or individual differences in that coding.

One of these theories specific to the long-term stage of memory (Mandler 1967, 1968a, 1970) argues that people code information into simple categories during acquisition, and then organize these categories into a hierarchy with the most inclusive category placed on top. This hierarchy of categories is seen as the memorial representation of learned material, and thus serves as the basis for retrieval. In this and similar theoretical systems (Collins and Quillian 1969; Tulving 1968), little attention is given to describing specific relations (like cause and effect) which could exist among the categories contained in the hierarchy.

Because of this lack of description, several researchers have suggested that these simple category schemes may not be adequate for describing the encoding and storage of complex information like sentences and paragraphs (Dunn 1973; Dunn and McConkie 1972). Dunn (1973), for example, found that when subjects were required to categorically organize related main topic sentences from prose passages, they did not use those categories as the basis for their recall. In contrast, studies using word lists (Mandler 1967, 1968b; Mandler and Pearlstone 1966; McConkie and Dunn 1971; Tulving and Pearlstone 1966; Tulving and Psotka 1971) and *unrelated* sentences as stimulus material (Dunn and McConkie 1972) have consistently indicated that subjects do form simple category structures during learning and use them as the basis for their recall.

Moreover, Meyer (1975, 1977a) points out that many of the basic learning principles based on recall of simple word lists, like serial position effects, etc., are rarely found using written text. After reading a prose passage, few people are able to produce verbatim recall, nor are they able to recall all the content information contained in it. Even when several people read the same passage, some concepts are recalled by nearly everyone, while others are recalled by very few. This suggests that subjects form simple memory structures when stimulus information is semantically weak and somewhat unrelated, but form much more elaborate structures or codes when more semantically complex information is encoded. Thus, it appears that the study of encoding and retrieval of complex information requires more sophisticated approaches which account for the complex interrelationships contained among the various concepts stored in memory.

Fortunately, two promising and somewhat contrasting approaches to discourse structure and how it affects comprehension and memory have developed recently: the *schema-based* approach and the *text-based approach* (Frederiksen 1977b). Rather than being founded on radically different theoretical views, these two approaches appear to differ mainly in the relative importance given to past-knowledge structures (schemata) as opposed to the present stimulus properties of text as aids for comprehension and subsequent memory retrieval. An interesting outcome of these slightly different orientations is that the grammars based on a text-based approach are best suited for describing expository text, whereas those developed from the schema view are limited exclusively to describing narrative discourse. Further, like the similar stage and levels-of-processing memory theories, both approaches ignore individual differences in encoding, while construing memory and retrieval as basically functions of semantic processing that uniformly condition human recall.

The grammars which have been developed using the schema view (e.g., Kintsch 1977; Mandler and Johnson 1977; Rumelhart 1975; Thorndyke 1977; van Dijk 1977a) purport to reflect the general knowledge schemata or general cognitive structures used during the process of text-comprehension, rather than just describing the specific semantic structure of the narrative text being read.[3] That is, these grammars are meant to be descriptions of the set of schemata necessary to describe the structure of prototypical stories in a given culture. Thorndyke's (1977) grammar, for example, describes the highest-order schema as consisting of *setting, theme, plot*, and *resolution*. These categories (like the similar ones postulated by Kintsh 1977; and van Dijk 1977a, 1977b) are broken down further into smaller, more detailed subordinate units, which for Thorndyke consist of character, location, setting, time, etc.

Since we all share similar basic experiences on which to form story schemata or superstructures (van Dijk 1977a, 1977b), it is assumed that we use these schemata during encoding and use the least portions of them as the basis for recall of a given text (Kintsch 1977; Mandler and Johnson 1977; Rumelhart and Ortony 1977; Thorndyke 1977; van Dijk 1977a). Thus, one could expect that when a story structure is analyzed by one of these grammars, encoding (inferred from recall data) should reflect this structure. Experimental tests of this hypothesis have been positive and quite impressive (Kintsch 1977; Kintsch and Kozminsky 1977; Kintsch, Mandel and Kosminsky 1977; Mandler and Johnson 1977; Mathews, Yussen, and Evans in press; Stein 1982; Stein and Trabasso 1982; Thorndyke 1977).

In contrast, text-based grammars (e.g., Meyer 1975) focus on describing the semantic organization of the text *per se* and the effects of that text's organization on encoding and recall. Rather than refuting "schema" theory, text-based grammarians merely stress the influence of the text's semantic content on subsequent memory formation (a limited *text-based* schema if you like), which is later used as the basis for retrieval. This is particularly the case when expository text is used and the reader has limited knowledge of the subject matter presented.

Since expository prose can be much more semantically complex than simple narratives and can take many different forms depending on the topic, any grammar used for describing the semantic structure of expository prose must be able to deal with its varied topics and inherent complexity. Because of this, many of the grammars which are capable of dealing with expository text typically have a general set of intra- and inter-sentence semantic relations which can be applied to any particular piece of text, regardless of its difficulty. For this reason, and because the bimodal processing research presented at the end of this chapter exclusively utilized expository text as stimulus material, only selected text-based grammars will be discussed further.

TEXT-BASED GRAMMARS

Development of a reliable system for identifying similarities and differences among passages has marked a major milestone in natural prose research. This is particularly the case for expository text. Past attempts at developing such a system met with little success because they dealt exclusively with the *surface structure of prose* (actual physical arrangement of prose) and not with the meaning of prose and the way content is structured to convey meaning to the reader (Meyer 1975). Three text-based grammars (Frederiksen 1975a; Kintsch 1974; Meyer 1975) are particularly suited for research using expository prose. But since it is difficult to use the Frederiksen and the Kintsch (1974) systems to describe higher-order semantic relations, such as interparagraph relations in text (Bieger and Dunn in press; Meyer 1975), only the Meyer system will be discussed at this point. Further, this system provided the basis for our research which is to be discussed later on.[4]

Meyer's Prose Analysis System and Related Research. The discourse analysis system devised by Meyer (1975) is based on the theoretical notions of the linguist Grimes (1975). This analysis produces for any given passage, a semantic content or logical structure composed of a single hierarchically arranged tree. Nodes in the structure contain actual content (words) from the passage, and the lines connecting the nodes show graphically how the content is semantically organized. Figure 1 contains the analysis of the Kintsch et al. (1975) *sea floor* passage (shown in Table 1) as analyzed by Meyer's procedure.

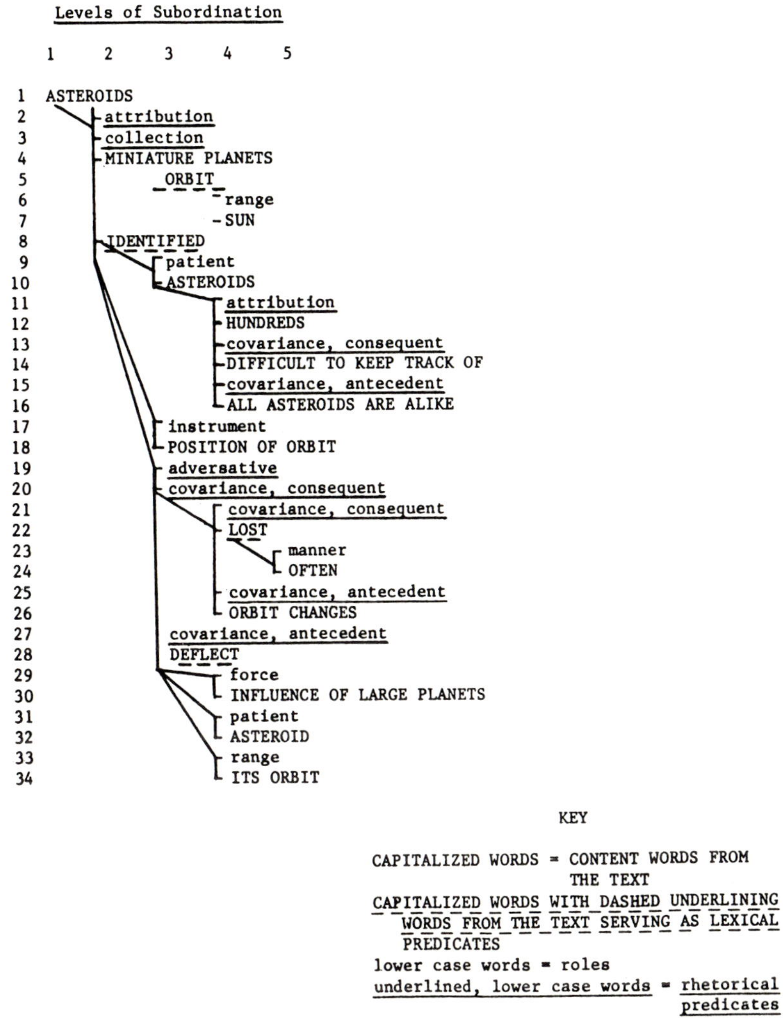

Figure 1

Content-Structure of "Asteroid" Passage as Analyzed using Meyer's (1975) Procedure.

The content structure of a passage shows the superordinate and subordinate pattern of the ideas contained within it. Some ideas from a passage are located at top levels of the content structure, others at the middle, and the remainder at lower levels. The items at the far left of Figure 1 are at the highest level of the passage's content structure, and those at the lower levels are at the far right. The top-level ideas dominate their subordinate ideas, while the lower-level ideas describe or give more information about the ideas above them.

In addition to showing a hierarchial pattern, Meyer's content structure defines the specific relations among the ideas in a passage. The labels describing these relations are of two major types: *role relations* and *rhetorical relations*, and are printed in lower-case letters in Figure 1.

Rhetorical relations or predicates are often found at the top levels of the content structure and show how various subordinate ideas are related together. Unlike role relations, rhetorical predicates are not necessarily dominated by words from text. A *rhetorical proposition* has a rhetorical predicate and often takes entire lexical propositions or other rhetorical propositions as its arguments. In other words, a rhetorical proposition is usually used to relate larger segments of text together rather than just segments of simple sentences. These larger segments may include entire paragraphs or chapters of text. Thus, rhetorical propositions are used primarily to represent the *macrostructure* of text, although they also can be used to relate items occurring at subordinate levels of discourse.

The macrostructure or "gist" of an adaptation of Meyer's (1975) *breeder reactor* passage (see Table 1) used in our research is shown in Figure 2. As can be seen from this figure, a type of *response* rhetorical predicate, consisting of an equally weighted problem(s) and solution, describes the passage's superordinate semantic structure. The *collection* rhetorical predicate indicates that more than one problem was listed in the passage. Other examples of the more frequently occurring rhetorical predicates are: *attribution*, which describes the qualities of a proposition (see lines 2 and 11 of Figure 1), and *covariance*, which is typically used to specify cause (antecedent) and effect (consequent) relations as shown in lines 27 and 20 of Figure 1.

In contrast to rhetorical predicates, role relations are typically (although not exclusively) used to relate information at the lower or micro-levels of text. Role relations are similar to Fillmore's (1968) cases and are always placed directly under certain types of words in the content

- response
- problem
- collection
- NEED TO GENERATE ELECTRICITY
- NEED TO PROTECT ENVIRONMENT
- RATIONAL UTILIZATION OF FINITE RESERVES
- solution
- NUCLEAR BREEDER REACTORS

After Meyer, 1975. Copyright © 1975 by the North Holland Publishing Company. Reprinted by Permission.

Figure 2
Superordinate Structure of *Breeder Reactor* Passage, Using Meyer's Analysis

structure which dominate them (see lines 9 and 17 of Figure 1 for examples). These specialized content words, actually contained in the text, are called *lexical predicates* (see lines 8 and 28). In Meyer's prose analysis, a predicate is something that relates ideas together and does not necessarily mean verb. Role relations classify the manner in which these lexical predicates are related to other content words which are not lexical predicates. The lexical predicate and the words related to it, called arguments, together form a *lexical proposition*. Lines 28 through 34 show an example of a lexical proposition.

The major thrust of Meyer's (1975) research was to test the effects of the height or level of information in the content structure on the recall of that information while controlling for the actual semantic content of the information found at those levels. Actual content was controlled by writing two passages with an identical paragraph, called the *target paragraph*, embedded in each passage. The passages were written so that the target paragraph was *high* in the content structure of one passage and *low* in the content structure of the other. The passages were of equal length, and the target paragraph came at the *same* serial position in both passages.

The results of Meyer's study clearly showed that the position of information in the content structure influences recall of prose. Information high in the content structure of one passage was recalled significantly better than when that same information was placed low in the content structure of another passage. This effect was particularly dramatic in the case of delayed free recall where, one week after reading, information high in the content structure of passages was recalled at least twice as well as that same information when placed low in the content structure. Even when cues were provided, information high in the content structure was recalled better than low information.

Meyer (1975) also found that the recall frequency of an item high in a passage's content structure was determined more by the item's functional relationship to other items than by its topic. This was found to be true for items low in the content or semantic structure. Thus, if two different passages had the same structure of specific relations, but dealt with different topics (e.g., parakeets and schizophrenia), the recall probability of the item was more positively correlated with the height of the item in the content structure than with the topic *per se*.

These results, as well as others (e.g., Frederiksen 1975b, 1975c; Kintsch and Keenan 1973; Kintsch et. al. 1975; Meyer 1971, 1977a, 1977b; Meyer and McConkie 1973), suggest that when subjects encode expository discourse into memory: (1) they produce a logical memory structure somewhat similar to the semantic structure of the discourse; and (2) they use that memory structure as the basis for their recall.

In a recent and important study, Meyer, Brandt, and Bluth (1980) found evidence for individual differences in the ability to encode and retrieve higher-order semantic information from prose. These researchers gave ninth-grade students of high, average, and low reading ability either a signalled or a non-signalled version of two passages to read and recall. Each passage dealt with a different topic, with the signalled or staged version (Grimes 1975) giving special emphasis to the important aspects of the passage's organization by using lexical cues such as: *the most important*, *in contrast*, etc. Of primary interest was the effect of the type of rhetorical predicate used to organize the top-level structure (macrostructure) of the experimental passages on the encoding and retrieval of those passages by the various ability groups. Previous research using homogeneous groups of college students had found that the types of relations (rhetorical predicates) used to produce the macrostructure of a text positively affected the number of idea units recalled (Meyer, Freedle, and Walker 1978).

Several of the more important findings by Meyer et al. indicate that: (1) Most students high in reading ability encode text by forming a memory structure (schema) similar to the organization used by the author of the passage (identified by the content structure) and use it as basis for retrieval, while most students having low comprehension do not. (2) Students employing the strategy of utilizing the higher-order structure of the passage recall much more information than those who do not, particularly in the case of delayed recall. (3) There is some indication that signalling increases the immediate recall of poorer comprehenders, who tend not to use the high-order structure. These effects, however, are not maintained in delayed recall.

While of significant importance, the Meyer et al. study did not specifically investigate the effects of *lower-level* semantic relations, described by rhetorical predicates, on recall. Although this study used a free-recall task, it was concerned solely with the effects of the highest-level semantic relations in a given passage as described by Meyer's (1975) system. However, recent research conducted in our laboratory suggests that when rhetorical predicates are placed at the lower levels of the content or logical structure of text, they can produce individual differences in recall (Dunn, Mathews, and Bieger 1982).[5] In two experiments, fourth- and sixth-grade children were given expository passages to read and recall. Each passage contained a selected rhetorical predicate placed at the lower or more micro-levels of the passage's content structure. Results clearly indicated that good readers recall significantly more of these predicates and their related arguments than do poor comprehenders. Thus, both our results and as those of Meyer et al. show that Meyer's (1975) grammar provides a sensitive metric for identifying individual differences in the recall of semantic information from text.

Although the expository prose research reported above strongly suggests that subjects encode text using hierarchically arranged semantic relations (text-based schemata), it could be argued that this type of memory structure is produced when the analytical mode rather than the holistic mode of conscious processing is used. This statement has some face validity since: 1) most psycholinguistic research uses college students as subjects—most of whose college work, it could be argued, requires the use of analytical thought for successful completion; and 2) most of the experimental tasks given to subjects contain instructions which require their "strained attention" during acquisition and recall. Therefore, it could be assumed that much of the research results (e.g., Kintsch et al. 1975; Meyer 1975) are probably indicative of the type of memory structure produced by the analytical rather than the holistic mode of consciousness.

It is quite possible that people who typically use or are instructed to use the holistic mode of processing form a memorial representation based on some other types of relationships. Because of their hypothesized mode of processing, holistic thinkers may encode prose into either a surface, syntactic deep structure, or some yet unknown paralogical form. Thus, when analytical and holistic processors are given passages containing information in various locations in the semantic structure, they may differ in either the frequency of recall or the type of the items or ideas recalled. As reinforcement, our earlier research (i.e., Hymes, Dunn, Gould, and Harris 1977) found significant differences between analytical and holistic processors in both the number of words recalled and the organizational *patterns* produced at recall.

In the next section, I report an exploratory study by Mike Singer, Jay Gould, and myself (Dunn, Gould, and Singer 1981) and a recent dissertation (Rust 1982) conducted in our laboratory in which written expository and descriptive texts were used as stimulus material. These studies represent attempts to extend bimodal processing theory to the difficult area of memory for complex prose. They will also serve as the focus for integrating the schema and the bimodal views of human information processing previously discussed in this chapter. In order to gain more power, several of the major weaknesses inherent in our previous work (Hymes et al. 1977) were corrected: (1) dichotomization of analytical and holistic processors was based on the average amount of alpha activity produced by both the right and left hemispheres during the baseline period, rather than based solely on the integration of the right hemisphere. Note that the practice of averaging across hemispheres is in harmony with Deikman's views concerning the use of alpha as a correlative of bimodal processing. It is also consonant with the other integrative approaches (presented earlier) which suggest that both hemispheres are involved in analytical as well as holistic processing; (2) the power in the alpha band was determined by a Fourier analysis of the EEG spectrum (1 to 50 Hz) which is far more accurate than most simple integrations using an alpha bandpass filter; and (3) EEG recordings were taken during the experimental tasks and subsequently analyzed using the Fourier procedure in order to determine if the alpha activity of analytical and holistic processors continues to differ while the subject is reading and recalling expository text.

BIMODAL PROCESSING AND ITS EFFECTS ON MEMORY OF EXPOSITORY TEXT

The specific purpose of the Dunn, Gould, and Singer (1981) study was to test whether individual differences in modal processing style affect the *type*, and perhaps even the amount, of semantic information encoded and recalled from expository text. Expository text was used because it is generally more semantically complex than narrative discourse, consequently requiring increased analytical processing. Such text, then, should maximize the differences in processing (as identified by free recall) of those persons identified as having a predominantly analytical, versus a holistic cognitive style.

One of the major advantages of the new semantic grammars is that they can identify the pattern of subordination of semantic information contained in text, regardless of where it physically occurs in the passage. In the case of Meyer's (1975) content-structure grammar, the type of relationships between this information is also described, typically by using rhetorical predicates.

Armed with these tools, it is quite possible to investigate whether the major hypothesized difference between analytical and holistic processors, (i.e., that they have different processing strategies which produce different memory structures) has any validity when complex text information is learned. If the hypothesis is true, it could be expected that analytical processors, because of their categorical and logical style (Deikman 1971, 1976; Hymes et al. 1977), should recall more of the superordinate information of a passage when compared to holistics who supposedly possess a gestalt processing style. Further, based on the results of Hymes et al., learning instructions should differentially shift the modal balance used by these two groups, thereby affecting their recall performance. That is, each group should perform best with instructions appropriate for their mode, with analyticals' greatest performance occurring when instructed to concentrate, and holistics' when asked to relax. In order to test these and other notions, the following experiment was undertaken.

Method

Subjects and Physiological Recording Techniques. Bilateral EEG measurements were taken from 40 upper-division university students during a baseline period and during subsequent reading and recall tasks. Recordings were made using a Grass Model 7 polygraph, and were stored both on paper and on magnetic tape, with the latter being recorded using a Tanberg Series 100 instrumentation FM recorder. Prior to running each subject, the polygraph was internally calibrated. Further, the complete recording system was checked periodically by sending a 10 Hz signal from the electrode leads through the outputs of the tape recorder. The tape-recorded EEG data were later analyzed into conventional frequency bandwidths using a Hewlett-Packard 5441 Fourier analysis computer. Power in the alpha bandwidth was used as the brain activity correlate in this experiment.

The recordings were made from two parietal-temporal sites; i.e., from a point midway between P_3 and T_3 on the left hemisphere, and midway between P_4 and T_4 on the right, in accordance with the 10-20 Electrode System (Jasper 1958). Both sites were referred to C_Z because it allowed for eventual comparison with past research which also used this reference (e.g., Doyle et al. 1974; Ornstein and Galin 1976). Since good electrode contact is essential for maximizing the signal-to-noise ratio, contact impedance was checked just prior to, and immediately after, the experimental tasks were completed.

General Procedures. After electrode placement, the subject was asked to sit quietly for 10 minutes, because previous research has suggested that a rest period facilitates alpha production (e.g., Paskewitz and Orne 1973). The baseline EEG records were made during the last 2 minutes of this period. Immediately after the baseline was taken, half the subjects, randomly chosen, were instructed to be alert and to concentrate as much as possible during the reading and recall tasks which followed. The other half were instructed to remain as relaxed as possible. Each subject was given three passages to read, with a written recall following the presentation of each passage. (Again, physiological recordings were taken during this period). Passages were reproduced on 35mm slides and were rear-projected onto a screen placed directly in front of the subject. The two shorter passages were placed on a single slide each. The longer *breeder reactor* passage was reproduced on three slides, with each paragraph contained on a separate slide.

Subjects initiated the reading/recall sequence for each passage by pressing a button to present each slide. They were instructed to read at their normal rate and, when finished, to press the button again. They were then asked to immediately write down what they could remember about the passage in any order they wished and to push the button again after they finished their recall. Clocks and printing counters were programmed to each button press, allowing reading and recall time data to be recorded. A rest period of 3 minutes was given after each passage reading/recall sequence. After these tasks were completed, the subject was released and informed as to the nature of the experiment.

Specific Nature of the Passages. The two shorter of the three experimental passages were used in previous research by Kintsch and his associates (Kintsch et al. 1975). Both these passages were also analyzed using Meyer's (1975) content-structure analysis, an example of which can be seen in the analysis of the *asteroid* passage shown in Figure 1. According to the results of Kintsch et al. (1975), the *asteroid* passage, which contained fewer different arguments, should be recalled better and take less reading time than the *sea floor* passage, which contained many more different arguments in its text-base.

The third longer passage, concerning nuclear breeder reactors, was derived from one used originally by Meyer (1975). Table 1 contains the three experimental passages.

It should be noted that this passage is not only longer than the others, but also has considerably more internal structure. That is, it is semantically "tighter" in that specific problems and a possible solution are offered. In contrast, the Kintsch passages basically contain a listing of attributes and details. This observation has also been made by Meyer (personal communication).

Because of its length, the content or semantic structure of the Meyer passage is not presented here. The interested reader can easily generate its semantic organization by using the content analysis of the longer passage given on pp. 206–208 of Meyer's (1975) book.

General Design. Dichotomization into analytical or holistic processors was based on subjects' baseline alpha production summed across the two hemispheres, because of past research which has shown that EEG activity is a direct correlate of processing style (e.g., Doktor and Bloom 1977; Hymes et al. 1977). Holistic subjects were defined as those whose summed alpha production exceeded the median, whereas analytical subjects were defined as those whose scores fell below it.

TABLE 1

Passages Used in Dunn, Gould and Singer Study

Asteroids Passage

Asteroids are miniature planets that orbit around the sun. Hundreds of asteroids have been identified, but it is difficult to keep track of them, since all asteroids are alike. An asteroid is identified only by the position of its orbit. Even after an orbit has been determined, it is often lost because the orbit changes due to the influence of the large planets which deflect the asteroid from its orbit.*

Sea Floor Passage

New sea floor and mantle are currently being added to the crust of the earth at spreading centers under deep-sea ridges. The sea floor spreads laterally away from these centers and sinks into the interior of the earth in deep-sea trenches. Volcanoes are created by the consumption process and flank the trenches. Thus, the volcanoes mark the borders between the plates which comprise the shell of the earth.*

Breeder Reactor Passage

The need to generate enormous additional amounts of electric power while at the same time protecting the environment is taking form as one of the major social and technological problems that our society must resolve over the next few decades. The Federal Power Commission has estimated that during the next 30 years the American power industry will have to add some 1,600 million kilowatts of electric generating capacity to the present capacity of 300 million kilowatts. As for the environment, the extent of public concern over improving the quality of air, water, and landscape hardly needs elaboration.

A related problem of equal magnitude is the rational utilization of the nation's finite reserves of coal, oil and gas. In the long term they will be far more precious as sources of organic molecules than as sources of heat. Moreover, any reduction in the consumption of organic fuels brings about a proportional reduction in air pollution from their combustion products.

The breeder type of nuclear reactors holds great promise as the solution to these problems. Breeder reactors produce more nuclear fuel than they consume; they would make it feasible to utilize enormous quantities of low-grade uranium and thorium ores dispersed in the rocks of the earth as a source of low-cost energy for thousands of years. In addition, these reactors would operate without adding noxious combustion products to the air.

*After Kintsch et al., 1975.

As previously mentioned, there is mounting evidence that there are sex differences in hemispheric activity (Ray et al. 1976) and that these differences may be related to performance (Rizzolatti and Buchtel 1977). There are also several prose memory studies which have shown sex differences in prose recall (Dunn and McConkie 1972; Frederiksen 1975b, 1975c). For these reasons, sex was treated as an independent variable in the statistical analysis performed on both the physiological and prose recall data.

In summary, this resulted in a general 2 (sex) by 2 (type of processor: analytical/holistic) by 2 (instructions: concentrate/relax) factoral design. Because dichotomization into holistic and analytical processors was made after all subjects were run and the experiment completed, unequal cell sizes were produced. The unequal cell sizes were, of course, accounted for in the statistical analyses of the data presented below.

Results and Discussion

Recall Scoring Procedures. Subjects' numerically coded recall protocols were scored independently by two of the experimenters. The recall data from the three passages were scored against the Meyer content-structure analysis of that particular passage's semantic content. The recall scoring procedures followed those by Meyer (1975, pp. 99-201) and will not be reported here. Given the complexity of the prose recall data, scoring reliability was acceptably high, averaging 91% across passages and scoring methods.

Because the two brief passages contained approximately the same number of words and propositions, but differed on the number of different arguments each contained (see Kintsch et al. 1975 for details), the recall data of these two passages were treated as a repeated measure in the following statistical analyses. The recall data for the lengthier *breeder reactor* passage, however, were analyzed separately because it had more internal coherence and differed in the number of levels of subordination when compared to the two shorter passages.

Meyer Recall Data. For the primary purpose of determining if analytical and holistic processors differ on the total number of semantic propositions recalled, the total number recalled from the two short passages was analyzed using a four-way mixed analysis of variance. The independent variables were sex, type of processor, instructions, and passage, which was a repeated measure. The only main effect which reached statistical significance was instructions ($p < .03$), with concentration instructions producing greater mean total propositional recall (12.1) than relaxation instruction (9.5). The two-way sex by passage interaction was the only interaction found to be signficant ($p < .02$), indicating that females' mean total recall decreased very slightly with the few-argument *asteroid* passage, compared to the many-different-argument *sea floor* passage (few 10.81 vs. many 10.15); males, on the other hand, showed the opposite pattern (few 10.35 vs. many 11.9).

When the total propositional recall data from the longer, but more semantically structured *breeder reactor* passage were analyzed using a three-way analysis of variance (sex; type of processor; instructions), the main effect of type of processor was the only source of variation to reach even marginal significance ($p < .06$), with analyticals' mean total recall being slightly greater than holistics' (22.7 vs. 18.3). Although weak, this finding is similar to the significant word-list recall results of our earlier study (Hymes et al. 1977).

In spite of these marginal results, the most important prediction for bimodal theory, as presented in this chapter, is that analytical and holistic processors form, and subsequently recall, information using different memory structures. Specifically, this would be indicated if analytical processors were found to recall more of the superordinate information contained at the higher levels of the semantic structure of a passage than were the holistics. In order to test this notion, the number of idea or semantic units (propositions and their related predicates and arguments) recalled by each subject at each level of subordination in the passage's content-structure was converted to the proportion of the total number of units possible at each level of that structure. The content-structure analyses of both short passages produced five levels of subordination each. The semantic analysis of the more organized *breeder reactor* passage produced four levels. Figure 1, for example, shows the Meyer content-structure analysis of the short *asteroid* passage and its five levels of subordination.

The proportional recall data of the two short passages were analyzed first using a five-way mixed analysis of variance. The two repeated measures for this analysis were passage and levels in the content structure, and the three between variables were again: sex, type of processor, and instructions. The main effects of passage and levels were highly significant ($p < .001$) with the few-different-argument *asteroid* passage having greater mean proportional recall (.38) than the many-different-argument *sea floor* passage (.24). The levels main effect showed the typical pattern, with the more superordinate idea units being recalled at a higher proportion on the average than the lower level items (.62; .45; .26; .22; .04; respectively). Both these results are in keeping with the earlier findings of Kintsch et al. (1975), and the latter, with those of Meyer (1975) and Thorndyke (1977).

Two of the two-way interactions were also significant, the sex by levels ($p < .005$), and the passage by levels interaction ($p < .001$). The sex by level interaction indicated that females tend to recall proportionally more items from the superordinate levels than do males. The passage by levels interaction showed that the few-argument passage produced the typical levels effect, whereas the many different-argument passage produced a less consistent pattern (.38; .42; .20; .16; .04). The second level of subordination, for example, had slightly greater mean proportional recall (.42) than the highest level of subordination (.38). This interaction, coupled with the main effect of passage, suggests that of the two, the many-different-argument passage was the more difficult to comprehend, thus replicating the results of Kintsch et al. (1975).

Of greater importance is the signficant three-way, passage by sex by mode interaction ($p < .04$), which is shown in Table 2 as two-way interaction components for ease of interpretation. It appears from these data that male holistics have approximately the same low mean proportional recall from either passage. In contrast, the subjects in the other conditions appear to have greater mean proportional recall of the few-argument passage, relative to the one containing many different arguments, suggesting possible sex differences in modal processing.

As promising as these results are, they are not strong evidence that analytical and holistic processors encode and recall using different organizational patterns or memory schemata. What was needed was some interaction involving the variables of type of processor and levels of the content structure. A possible reason for the lack of interaction may have been the two short passages used, since neither had a great deal of semantic structure. This would tend to make both of them difficult to comprehend. It could be possible that analyticals, because of their hypothesized logical skill, show differential recall of superordinate information when the text is more logically or semantically organized than were either of the two short passages.

This speculation basically was confirmed by proportional recall data from the third, more semantically organized, *breeder reactor* passage.

TABLE 2

Mean Proportional Semantic Recall as a Function of Type of Processor, Sex, and Passage, Scored Using Meyer's Text Analysis Procedure

Type of Processor	*n*	Passage	
		Few Argument	Many Argument
Analyticals			
Females	10	.41	.26
Males	10	.41	.24
Holistics			
Females	10	.44	.21
Males	10	.30	.27

These data were analyzed using a four-way mixed analysis of variance, with levels in the content structure serving as the repeated measure. The levels main effect was again highly significant ($p < .001$), showing the now typical pattern of higher recall of superordinate, relative to subordinate information. Further, although the main effect of type of processor did not reach significance ($p < .07$), the highly important three-way, type of processor by instructions by levels interaction was found to be highly significant, $F\,(3,96) = 5.11$, $p < .003$.

The proportional recall data contributing to this interaction are shown in Table 3, where it appears that analyticals, particularly when asked to concentrate, recall proportionally more of the superordinate items than those at lower levels, whereas holistics, when asked to concentrate, do not recall as much high-level information. Also, when holistics are asked to relax during the reading and recall tasks, they appear to have considerably lower recall of the lower level items, as compared to when they are asked to concentrate. Analyticals on the other hand, tend to produce the same basic, declining pattern, regardless of instructions. These were confirmed by tests of simple interaction effects and related simple main effects (Kirk 1968), thus lending credence to the notions presented at the first part of this section; namely, that analyticals would tend to recall more superordinate information than holistics, and that the recall pat-

TABLE 3

Mean Proportional Semantic Recall of a Function of Type of Processor, Instructions and Levels in the Context-Structure, Scored Using Meyer's Procedure

		Levels in Content-Structure			
Type of Processor	*n*	1	2	3	4
Analyticals					
Concentration Instructions	9	.67	.28	.24	.17
Relaxation Instructions	11	.52	.29	.22	.23
Holistics					
Concentration Instructions	11	.39	.33	.24	.23
Relaxation Instructions	9	.49	.20	.08	.09

terns of the two types of processors would be differentially affected by the learning and recall instructions they were given.

Further, partial confirmation of these results is provided by comparing the mean proportional recall data of the two shorter passages as a function of type of processor, instructions, and levels in the content structure. Although the necessary four-way interaction (type of processor by instructions by passage by levels in the content structure) did not reach statistical significance ($p < .09$), the data are shown for comparison purposes in Table 4.

It will be recalled that of the two shorter passages, the *asteroid* passage was the more semantically structured and, therefore, the most easily comprehended. Thus, if our earlier speculations are correct (i.e., that analyticals, when asked to concentrate, will show greater recall of superordinate information than holistics), it could be expected that the recall pattern of the *asteroid* passage produced by these two groups should be similar to the significant pattern found with the highly structured *breeder reactor* passage, reported above. In contrast, the recall pattern of the extremely loose *sea floor* passage should not show an advantage for analytical processors. As can be seen from the data in Table 4, these recall patterns are basically as predicted.

Before concluding, it is important to note that although increased time spent reading or rehearsing the passages by the analyticals could have caused some of the positive differences in their recall data, the analysis of the reading time data showed that holistics actually spent slightly *more* time reading than did analyticals. (For the sake of brevity these data are not reported). A similar finding also occurred with the recall time data. More importantly, when reading time was statistically controlled using analyses of covariance, the results of the total, as well as the proportional recall data just reported, were virtually unaffected.

In summary, these results, particularly the significant three-way interaction with the *breeder reactor* data, strongly suggest that individual differences in bimodal processing affect the encoding (inferred from

TABLE 4

Mean Proportional Semantic Recall for the Two "Short" Passages as a Function of Type of Processor, Instructions, and Levels in the Semantic Content-Structure Using Meyer's Scoring Procedure

		Levels in Content-Structure [a]				
Type of Processor	*n*	1	2	3	4	5
Few Different Argument Passage						
Analytical						
Concentration Instructions	9	1.00	.58	.34	.31	.00
Relaxation Instructions	11	.82	.47	.25	.30	.00
Holistic						
Concentration Instructions	11	.72	.50	.24	.19	.00
Relaxation Instructions	9	.89	.36	.28	.18	.11
Many Different Argument Passage						
Analytical						
Concentration Instructions	9	.33	.48	.30	.17	.00
Relaxation Instructions	11	.39	.33	.17	.10	.09
Holistic						
Concentration Instructions	11	.41	.48	.26	.20	.04
Relaxation Instructions	9	.37	.44	.09	.15	.00

[a]Passage and levels in content-structure were repeated measures.

recall) as well as the type of semantic information recalled from complex text. They also generally replicate the findings of the Hymes et al. (1977) study, which also obtained recall pattern differences as a function of bimodal processing style and instructions. Thus, they imply that these effects are not limited merely to simple stimulus material.

Reading and Recall Alpha Data. As previously mentioned, bilateral EEG recordings were taken from subjects during the reading and recall tasks they were given. Since the time spent reading and recalling the passages varied across subjects, the total amount of alpha activity recorded from *each* cerebral hemisphere was divided by the total amount of time spent at that task. This of course "normalized" the data, and allowed the reading and recall alpha data to be analyzed across all three passages using a separate analysis of variance for each.

Reading Alpha Data. The bilateral alpha data generated by each subject during reading were analyzed using a five-way mixed analysis of variance having three between independent variables (type of processor, sex, and instructions) and two within or repeated measures (hemisphere and passage).[6] Three main effects, type of processor, passage, and hemisphere, were found to be highly significant (*p*'s © .001). There was less mean alpha (1.26) in the recordings from analyticals than holistics (3.10), and *post hoc* testing confirmed that less mean alpha was found during the reading of the most semantically structured passage (*breeder reactor*) relative to the other two passages (*breeder reactor* = 1.16; *sea floor* = 2.48; and *asteroid* = 2.96). Note that units of measurement are expressed in relative power units.

Surprisingly, more mean alpha was generally recorded from the left hemisphere than the right during the reading tasks (2.43 vs. 1.93). This results, although contrary to some other research (e.g., Doyle et al. 1974; Ornstein and Galin 1976), appears to be primarily a function of the P/T recording sites used in our research and was not due to any equipment malfunction. Confirmation of this finding comes from a recent master's thesis conducted in our laboratory (Hunt 1979) and from an independent study by Ehrlichman and Wiener (1979). Both studies were similar to ours in that the same recording sites were used, and EEG activity was recorded during the performance of complex verbal tasks. In both cases, the left hemisphere was shown to produce more alpha power or amplitude than the right hemisphere.[7] The neurophysiological explanation for this disparate activity is left for future research and is not of crucial importance for arguments made here, because none of our predictions were dependent on any *differential* activity being recorded from the two cerebral hemispheres. Our subjects were labeled as either analytical or holistic processors based on the magnitude of their alpha production from both hemispheres, rather than on either alone, or in some ratio to one another. However, for the interested reader the alpha data produced when reading each experimental passage are shown as a function of type of processor and hemisphere in the top half of Table 5.

TABLE 5

Mean Alpha Power Recorded During Reading and Recall, as a Function of Type of Processor, Hemisphere and Pasage

Type of Processor	Passage: Asteroid	Sea-Floor	Breeder Reactor
Reading Alpha Data			
Analytical			
Left Hemisphere	1.96	1.71	.73
Right Hemisphere	1.59	1.12	.46
Holistic			
Left Hemisphere	4.29	3.90	1.98
Right Hemisphere	3.79	3.18	1.45
Recall Alpha Data			
Analytical			
Left Hemisphere	1.11	.79	.79
Right Hemisphere	.77	.50	.39
Holistic			
Left Hemisphere	1.74	1.47	1.07
Right Hemisphere	1.39	.96	.76

The only interactions to reach a significance were the three-way sex by instruction by passage interaction and the four-way type of processor by sex by instruction by passage interaction ($p < .009$; $p < .006$, respectively). Although rather complex, examination of the four-way interaction suggested that most of the variation was caused by a large increase of alpha activity recorded from male holistics, instructed to relax, when they read the highly structured breeder reactor passage. Over 25% more alpha was recorded from these subjects when reading this passage, as compared to the other two passages. In contrast, less alpha was recorded from subjects in the other conditions when reading this passage, relative to their activity during the reading of the other two passages.

Recall Alpha Data. The alpha data recorded at recall were compared using the same type of analysis of variance as used with the reading alpha data above. In most cases, similar patterns were found (see bottom half of Table 5). The main effects of type of processor, passage, and hemisphere were again found to be highly significant (p's $< .003$), and were in the same direction as the reading alpha data. Less mean alpha was recorded from analyticals than holistics (.72 vs. 1.24); and less mean alpha was recorded during the recall of the *breeder reactor* passage (.76) than during the less structured *sea floor* (.93) or *asteroid* (1.25) passages. Like the reading alpha data, recorded left hemisphere alpha was greater than the right (1.16 vs. .79) during recall.

Only the two-way type of processor by instructions, and the three-way type of processor by sex by instruction interactions reached statistical significance. The two-way interaction showed that when analyticals were asked to relax, less alpha was recorded than when they were asked to concentrate (concentrate = 1.13 vs. relax = .39); in contrast, holistics mean recorded alpha increased when asked to recall in a relaxed state (concentrate = 1.08 vs. relax = 1.39). However, examination of the significant three-way interaction indicated that the holistics' increased alpha under relaxation instructions was produced by the female holistics (concentrate = .99 vs. relax = 1.63), rather than by the male holistics (concentrate = 1.16 vs. relax = .93).

Albeit somewhat messy and in need of further examination, the interactions occurring with both the reading and recall alpha data suggest that possible sex differences in modal processing exist, particularly with relaxation instructions. Regardless of these interactions, the remarkable and consistent differences in alpha activity found between analytical and holistic subjects across tasks is highly important, and in fact crucial, for the arguments made in this chapter; i.e., that total power from the alpha band when measured at baseline can be used to *reliably* identify analytical as opposed to holistic processors. That is, the relative difference in the magnitude of alpha activity recorded at baseline between these two groups appears to be maintained even during the subsequent performance of complex cognitive tasks. This "between subject" consistency in recorded alpha does not appear to be temporary either. Subjects have been shown to maintain their relative positions (using the same P/T and C_Z recording sites) over two sessions containing verbal and spatial tasks, with at least one week separating the sessions (Ehrlichman and Wiener 1979). This suggests that power in the alpha band is a stable correlate of processing style. These results are in keeping with Deikman's (1971, 1976) bimodal theory, as well as our previous findings (Hymes et al. 1977) and are not best described by differences in "arousal" level (see discussion on Page 52).

COMPREHENSIVE STYLE DIFFERENCES: DETERMINED BY TRADITIONAL READING TESTS VERSUS BIMODAL PROCESSING INDEXES

The results of the previously reported study are promising, however, two criticisms can be made. First, although alpha power measurements were taken during reading by Dunn, et al. they were calculated across the entire reading period. Thus it was impossible to determine differential activity of analytic and holistic processors during the encoding of *specific* information from text. If truly qualitative differences in processing style exist, then analytics and holistics not only should show recall differences but should produce divergent patterns of alpha, particularly during the encoding of a given piece of information. Second, previous research on analytical cognitive style has used college students exclusively as subjects. If this dimension is to have any general import for education, it should be able to distinguish individual style differences from a non-college age population.

A recent study, completed in our laboratory by Dorvan Rust for his dissertation (Rust 1982), corrected for most of these problems. Because of this, it is presented in detail below:

Method

Subjects and Recording Procedures. Rust chose two groups of ten male subjects each, all from public schools. The first group consisted of below average readers and the second average to good readers as determined by the Comprehensive Test of Basic Skills, (CTB/McGraw-Hill 1973). Both group's average chronological age was 11 years, 6 months. All recording procedures were similar to those used in the previous study with the exception that linked ears rather than C_Z was used at the reference electrode site. This choice eliminates the problems of using an active reference site like C_Z (see Footnote 7).

Passages. Two forms of the "Loss of Body Water" passage, used by Meyer, Freedle, and Walker (1978) were employed. One of the passages had a relatively "tight" *covariance*, top-level (cause and effect) structure while the other had a less "tight" *attribution* relation (a mere listing of facts) at the highest level of its semantic structure. In addition, two other passages, each dealing with a different topic, i.e, "The Use of Chemical Pesticides" were used in this study. Both were modified from a passage developed by Howell (1979). Each of the passage forms contained approximately the same number of words, and although they differed in basic topics and top-level rhetorical content-structures, they were virtually the same at the more subordinate levels of their semantic structures. Table 6 shows the attribution and covariance version of the chemical pesticides passage.

The passages were reproduced on 35mm slides with a given passage being shown in segments using seven slides. All were rear projected on to a screen directly in front of the subject. The subject initiated the reading sequence for each passage by pushing a button for the presentation of a slide. Timers and printers again were programmed to record the reading time of each slide. Even though four passages were used during the experiment, each subject was given only two of the four passages (one chemical and one body water passage) in order to reduce learning transfer effects. Note, however, each subject received the attribution version from one passage and the covariance version from the other. A written recall followed the presentation of the passage. Again, EEG recordings were made during each slide segment of the passages as well as the written recall period.

Results

A Pearson Product Moment correlation was computed between subjects' CTBS scores and total baseline alpha measured at T_3/P_3. The obtained correlation was not statistically significant ($r(19) = -.25$, $p < .25$), suggesting that traditional measures of reading ability are not related to

TABLE 6

Passages Used in Rust (1982) Study

Covariance Version of the Use of Chemical Pesticides Passage

It is true that the use of chemical pesticides is frequently required by American Commercial growers of corn, potatoes, tomatoes, lettuce and cotton so that their crops will reach certain standards of quality. These standards are much higher than those found in less, developed countries.

As a result, tremendous damage is unintentionally caused by the commercial growers requiring the use of chemical pesticides on their cops. This damage occurs due to the fact that use of chemical pesticides interferes with the balance of complex environmental systems. More specifically, the use of small amounts of chemical pesticides can harm a variety of small creatures like fish and birds. The use of medium amounts can result in harm to bigger animals such as squirrels and gophers. Moreover, large amounts of chemical pesticides can kill deer and bear. The excessive use of many chemical pesticides results in the development of chemical resistant insects, and water pollution; if not controlled, irreversible damage can be the result.

Attribution Version of the Use of Chemical Pesticides Passage

Several aspects of the use of chemical pesticides will be discussed. First, the utilization of chemical pesticides is frequently required by the American commercial growers of corn, potatoes, tomatoes, lettuce and cotton so that their crops will reach certain standards of quality. These standards are much higher than those found in less developed countries.

Second, very large amounts of chemical pesticides are normally used by commercial growers each year.

Third, the use of chemical pesticides can harm the environment. More specifically, the use of small amounts of chemical pesticides can harm a variety of small creatures like fish and birds. The use of medium amounts can result in harm to bigger animals such as squirrels and gophers. Moreover, large amounts of chemical pesticides can kill deer and bear. The excessive use of many chemical pesticides results in chemical resistant insects and water pollution; if not controlled, irreversible damage could result.

alpha measurements of processing style, a point which will be explicated later in this chapter.

In order to determine if total alpha power produced during the reading of specific information could distinguish among individuals' styles, conditional probabilities between reading alpha power scores and proportional recall scores were computed separately as a function of reading ability (as determined by the CTBS) and analytic processing style (as determined by alpha power scores). Specifically, the total alpha produced by a given subject while reading a particular slide was computed. The alpha power produced during the reading of the slides was then averaged. Conditional probabilities were then computed on a slide by slide basis. For example, starting with slide 1, it was determined if the total alpha produced during the reading of that slide was above or below that subject's mean alpha averaged across all seven reading slides. If it was below his median, the proportion of recalled information contained in that slide was recorded. Slide 1, for example, had information at levels, 1, 2, and 3 of the Meyer content-structure analysis of that passage. Thus if the subject recalled .66 of the level 1 information, .50 of level 2 information, and .17 of level 3 information, all three proportions were recorded. The same procedure was used in scoring the remaining slides.

Although with slide 1 it was impossible to determine if the alpha production was related specifically to the encoding of level 1, 2, or 3 information (or some combination of all three) the negative effects of this confounding was lessened to some extent because other slides also contained levels 1, 2, or 3 information. Thus (using the attribution versions as examples) it was possible to obtain three conditional probabilities for a given subject concerning level 1 information, five conditional probabilities for level 2 information, and so on.

Because each of the two passage versions, attribution and covariance, contained differing levels of information per slide, the conditional probability data from each version were analyzed separately. All data were transformed using arc sine transformations and were subjected to a 2 (type of reader: good vs. poor *or* type of processor: analytic vs. holistic depending on analysis) by 2 (level of alpha production: above vs. below) by 5 (levels in the content structure: levels 1–5). All variables were treated as between measures because of the inequality of the number of conditional probabilities that could be computed by level (see above). This is a highly conservative procedure, thus reducing the probability of making an alpha error.

Attribution and Covariance Data as a Function of Type of Reader. When subjects were dichotomized into good and poor readers based on their CTBS reading tests scores, only quantitative differences between reading groups were found. For example, the three-way ANOVA run on the attribution conditional probability data found only the main effects of reader and content structure levels to be significant (p's $< .009$). The mean conditional recall of good readers (.16) was greater than the poor readers' (.08). The levels main effect, like the previously reported study, again showed an erratic pattern (L1 = .23; L2 = .08; L3 = .11; L4 = .05; L5 = .17). The only interaction to reach significance was the type of alpha by content-structure levels interaction ($p < .005$) which indicated that when subjects were producing greater than their mean alpha during reading, their mean conditional probability recall was relatively stable across levels in contrast to when they were producing less than their average alpha. In the latter case, the pattern was more erractic, with greater mean recall occuring at level 1 and less recall at the lower levels.

When the covariance data were analyzed, similar patterns were found, with the exception that the type of alpha by content structure levels interaction did not reach significance. Good readers again had greater mean probability scores than poor readers (.18 vs. .10), and recall as a function of levels again showed an erratic, non-hierarchical pattern (L1 = .35; L2 = .09; L3 = .11; L4 = .16; L5 = .00). No other effects approached significance. Since reader did not interact with any other variable with either the attribution or covariance conditional probability data, it is clear that the CTBS is sensitive to quantitative rather than qualitative differences among reading groups.

Attribution and Covariance Data Split by Type of Processor. In contrast to the CTBS dichotomization reported above, evidence for qualitative differences in processing occurred when subjects were grouped into analytic and holistic processors based on their alpha baseline measurements. It should be noted that five "poor" readers and five "good' readers (based on their CTBS scores) were reclassified as analytic processors with the same distribution being reclassified as holistic processors. Conditional probabilities were then computed as above but with cognitive style rather than reading ability serving as a factor on the ANOVAS performed on these data.

Like the previously reported "sea floor" and "asteroids" passage data, no differences between styles were found when the "non-logically" structured attribution passage conditional probability data were analyzed. The three-way ANOVA computed on the attribution data found the levels main effect to be significant which again followed an erratic, non-hierarchial pattern. The only interaction to reach significance was the type of alpha score by levels in the content-structure interaction which was isomorphic to the significant two-way interaction reported earlier

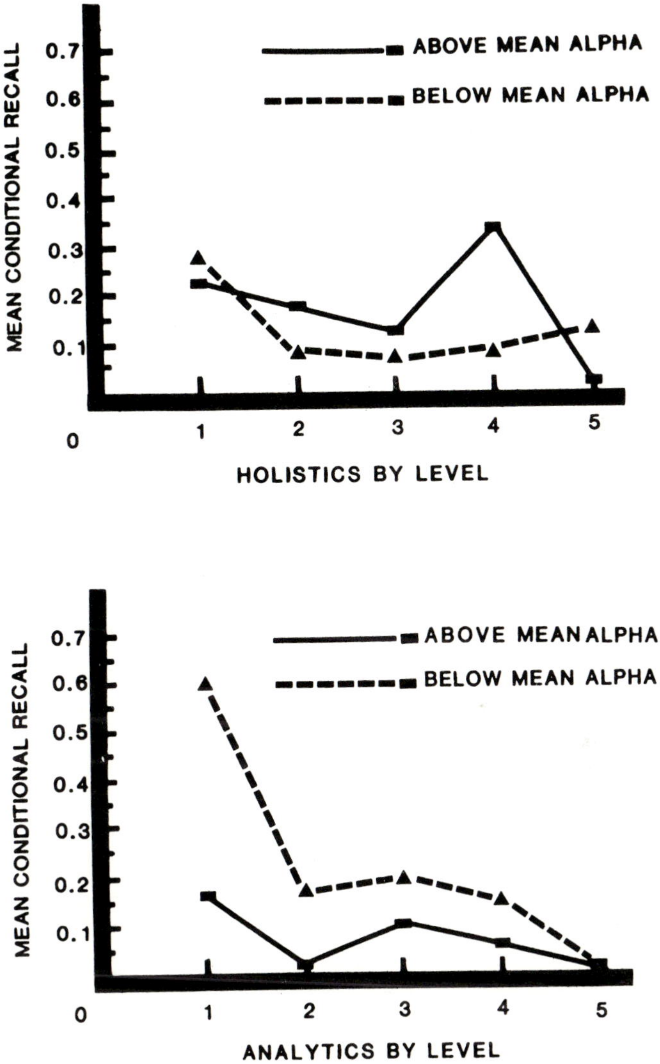

Figure 3.
Conditional Recall by Levels as a Function of Cognitive Style and Type of Alpha Score.

when subjects were dichotomized into good vs. poor readers using the attribution data. However, when the passage increased in logical (covariance) structure, the conditional probability data suggested that analytics and holistics use qualitatively different processes when encoding this type of passage. The ANOVA performed on these data again yielded significance for the main effect of levels in the content structure. More importantly, however, a significant three-way, cognitive style by type of alpha score by levels interaction was found ($p < .04$). For ease of production, the interaction is shown in Figure 3 as two, 2-way (type of alpha by levels) interaction components, for analytic and holistic cognitive style subjects.

The pattern of recall of analytics and holistics appears to differ as a function of their alpha production. Analytics recall more across levels when they are producing less than their mean alpha while reading. In contrast, holistics' best recall (especially at levels 2, 3, and 4) occurs when they are producing *greater* than their mean alpha during reading. This coupled with the differing amount of recall across levels for the two groups suggests that these two cognitive styles may use different encoding strategies. These strategies appear to be more qualitatively different than quantitatively different and occur when subjects read text having a "tight" logical structure. This differential recall by analytics and holistics as a function of semantic structure "tightness" again parallels the previously reported finding of Dunn et al., (1981).

Summary of Results

The data from both reported experiments, when taken together, begin to offer reasonably strong support for the basic tenets of bimodal theory. The recall results of the Dunn et al., study, using Meyer's (1975) content-structure analysis of text, indicate that analytical processors tend to recall slightly more semantic information (propositions); but more importantly, they appear to encode and subsequently recall information using a different and more logical pattern than do holistics. Like past research (e.g., Hymes et al. 1977), instructions again appeared to cause shifts in the mixture of bimodal processing and there was some indication of sex differences in recall.

Also, analyses of subjects' EEGs showed that the recordings of analytical processors contained less bilateral alpha activity than that of holistics during the reading and recall tasks, indicating that power in the alpha band is a reliable physiological correlate of modal processing style. Several interactions occuring with these data suggest possible sex differences in bimodal processing; the explanation for these interactions is, however, far from clear at this stage of research.

Rust's (1982) study is important for several reasons. First, it suggests an improved methodology to be used in individual difference research; namely, through the use of conditional probabilities, neurophysiological data recorded on line can be directly combined with subsequent behavioral measurements. In Rust's case, alpha measurements recorded during encoding of a specific piece of text information were related to the probability of the recall of that information. The probability of that item's recall was determined as a function of the subject's alpha level at the time of encoding, i.e., whether he was producing greater or less than his mean alpha level for the whole passage. This method is similar to that used by Sandman and his associates who use heart rate measurements to predict perceptual and cognitive performance (see Sandman and Walker chapter this volume). Of major import for education are Rust's results showing that when a traditional reading ability measure is used to dichotomize subjects into good and poor readers, only quantitative differences in recall are found as a function of alpha activity. However, when those subjects are divided into analytic and holistic processors using alpha baseline measurements, qualitative differences in recall are obtained when logically structured passages are read.

Since traditional reading measures show primarily quantitative differences in reading comprehension (measured by free recall) then it follows that instruction to improve the reading skills of the poor reader would tend to be quantitative as well. That is, curricula would probably be designed to teach the poor reader more of the same skills exhibited by the good reader, since the test would lead one to conclude that the poor reader merely has less efficient, not different, reading strategies. However, when our analytic and holistic cognitive style dimension is used it is found that some of the good and poor readers are analytic while others are more holistic in their processing. Assuming as we do that the strategies used by analytics are, in part, qualitatively different from holistics, then it would suggest that the teaching of reading should reflect these differences.

Even though our research is promising, considerably more work needs to be done in order to test the overall predictive power of bimodal theory, specifically as it applies to the learning and memory of complex information. For example, the above experiments were limited to the reading and recalling of expository and descriptive text—tasks which, it could be argued, are highly analytical in nature. It would be interesting to determine if these results would hold if narrative text or poetry were utilized as stimulus material. Given the description of holistic processors presented earlier, one might expect better performance from holistics than from analyticals when given these latter types of text. One clear prediction derived directly from bimodal "memory" theory, and demanding investigation, is the notion that holistic processors should show better performance on tasks postulated to require spatial or gestalt-type processing (e.g., perceptual tests like cube comparisons or hidden patterns, etc.) If the holistics do not perform better, then it would provide strong evidence that the cognitive style identified in this chapter was based on an analytical continuum rather than an analytical/holistic dimension.

Admittedly needing a great deal of expansion, our research also has an important implication for memory theories in general, particularly those theories, like schema theory and levels of processing theory, which either play down or ignore individual differences in cognitive style. This chapter will, therefore, conclude with a brief discussion of this issue.

GENERAL IMPLICATIONS AND CONCLUSIONS

Traditionally, the incorporation of individual differences into the major theories of learning and memory has been avoided because of the assumption that these theories should be abstract enough to describe universal cognitive functioning. Therefore, the study of individual differences has been relegated, at best, to a secondary and somewhat unprestigious position in the learning field. This is quite surprising given the wealth of research literature showing that people having differing personality styles, like field-dependence (see Goodenough 1976 for a review) and extraversion (see Eysenck 1976) as well as processing styles (Hunt 1978; Hymes et al. 1977), do *not* behave in the way that various "universal" models of long-term memory would predict.

The irony (in the minority opinion of this author) is that such universal theories will probably continue to be shown to have little applicability to "real" problems, such as reading instruction and remediation, *because* of their stated strength of universality. Many of these theories are, in fact, too over-generalized, and thus too simplified, to have major predictive power in a large portion of individual cases. Admittedly overstating the case, the descriptions of encoding and retrieval processes by the current major theories of memory, like levels of processing theory (Craik and Lockhart 1972), are analogous to a bureaucrat's description of the average American family which owns an 1101.23 sq. ft. house and contains 1.5 children. While there is some limited use for data like these, it is obvious that no family has exactly this hypothetical combination of attributes. Even schema prose theory, which does allow for various cultures to have differing general story schemas (e.g., Kintsch 1977), falls into the same trap by stating little about individual coding differences *within* a given culture.

The question then becomes, how much attention should be paid to individual differences, particularly in theories related to memory of text? It is possible, for example, that too much attention to minute differences may actually create problems of its own by producing theories too detailed and cumbersome to be of much use. Therefore, some compromise between the extreme positions concerning the study of individual differences is needed—the very least of which should include the identification and the incorporation of major classes of individual differences into our future models of memory. Hopefully, the classifications of analytical and holistic processors made in this paper will be of some use for theorists who attempt this difficult task.[8] Regardless, the era of "benign neglect" needs to come to a close.

ENDNOTES

[1]It is interesting to note that because of recent research findings, Paivio (Marschark and Paivio 1977) has suggested a modification to his dual-coding theory by postulating a common, perhaps amodal, representational system in addition to the two modality-specific codes.

[2]A notable exception is a study recently conducted by McLeod and Peacock (1977), who measured their subjects' spatial ability using half the Minnesota Paper Board Test prior to monitoring their EEG during verbal and spatial tasks. No relationship was found between spatial test scores and degree of task-related hemispheric asymmetry, although the degree of asymmetry increased with age. However, only 16 subjects were used, and all were male. Thus there negative results should be viewed with caution.

[3]In general, schemata refer to networks of generic and interacting knowledge structures stored in memory (including representations of separate objects, situations and events, as well as sequences of events and actions), used for all perceptual and cognitive functioning. Thus, schemata are the primary meaning and processing units of the human information processing system (Rumelhart and Norman 1978; Rumelhart and Ortony 1977; Winograd 1977).

Please also note the similarity between this usage of the term "schema" and the descriptions provided by Piaget (1952) and Bartlett (1932). This has been mentioned previously by Rumelhart and Ortony (1977), who also point out that the recent definitions in the literature, particularly the artificial intelligence literature, closely parallel the definition provided by Kant (1787) in his *Critique of pure reason*. Further note that "schema" has recently been given a variety of names including: "frames" (Minsky 1975); "scripts" (Shank and Abelson 1977); "definitions" (Norman, Rumelhart and LNR 1975); "plans" (Schmidt 1975).

[4]In an earlier draft of this chapter, all the recall data in the Dunn, Gould and Singer (1981) study reported later were analyzed using the Kintsch (1974) text analysis system. Like the results of Bieger and Dunn (in press), none of the statistical analysis performed on these data showed any systematic recall differences as a function of cognitive style. Due to the lack of sensitivity and for sake of brevity, neither these data nor the Kintsch (1974) text analysis system of related prose comprehension models (e.g., Kintsch and van Dijk 1978; Kintsch and Vipond 1979; Vipond 1980) will be discussed further.

[5]As stated earlier, the primary purpose of rhetorical predicates is to relate superordinate semantic information. They are, however, occasionally used to relate information at the subordinate or micro-levels of discourse.

[6]Note that at least from the recording sites used, the reading and recall alpha data analyses showed that hemisphere did not significantly interact with any of the other independent variables. It is also of some interest to point out that several of the traditional ratio measures and difference measures (e.g., RH/LH) between the two hemispheres' alpha activity have been calculated. None, however, provided any more information than did our summed power measurements.

[7]The use of an active reference site can cause possible problems in assessing differential hemispheric activity. When an active site like Cz is used, an increase in *recorded* alpha activity does not necessarily reflect an increase in *generated* alpha. That is, an increase in recorded alpha may only reflect an increased difference in alpha generated at the site of interest (in our case the P/T sites) and the reference site. This increased difference could be produced by an increase or decrease at either site, or by changes in the phase relationships between sites, etc.

While still a possible problem for those interested in hemispheric activity, a recent study by Amochaev and Salamy (1979) found only slightly larger task-related EEG asymmetries when a "neutral" reference site (ipsilateral ears) was compared with the active Cz reference.

[8]In his highly important paper, Hunt (1978) argues that there are three main sources of individual differences to deal with complex information: general knowledge, controlled attention-demanding processes, and automatic processes. The latter, which Hunt defines as stable individual processing traits, appears to be similar to the relatively permanent analytical and holistic processing styles identified in this chapter.

REFERENCES

Amochaev, A., and Salamy, A. 1979. Stability of EEG laterality effects. *Psychophysiology* 16:242–246.

Atkinson, R.C., and Shiffrin, R.M. 1968. Human memory: A proposed system and its control processes. In *The psychology of learning and motivation*, Vol. 2, eds. K.W. Spence and J.T. Spence. New York: Academic Press.

Bartlett, F.C. 1932. *Remembering: A study in experimental and social psychology.* New York: Cambridge University Press.

Barton, M.I.; Goodglass, H.; and Shai, A. 1965. Differential recognition of tachistoscopically presented English and Hebrew words in right and left visual fields. *Perceptual and Motor Skills* 21:431–437.

Basso, A.; Bisiach, E.; and Capitoni, E. 1977. Decision in ambiguity: Hemispheric dominance or interaction? *Cortex* 13:96–99.

Ben-Dov, G., and Carmon, A. 1976. On time, space and the cerebral hemispheres: A theoretical note. *International Journal of Neuroscience* 7:29–33.

Bennett, J.E., and Trinder, J. 1977. Hemispheric laterality and cognitive style associated with transcendental meditation. *Psychophysiology* 14:293–296.

Bieger, G.R., and Dunn, B.R. n.d. A comparison of the sensitivity of two prose analysis models to developmental differences in free recall of text. *Discourse Processes.* In Press.

Bogen, J.E. 1969. The other side of the brain: An apposition mind. *Bulletin of Los Angeles Neurological Societies* 34:135–162.

Bogen, J.E., and Gazzaniga, M.S. 1965. Cerebral commissurotomy in man: Minor hemisphere dominance for certain visuo-spatial functions. *Journal of Neurosurgery* 23:394–399.

Bousfield, W.A. 1953. The occurence of clustering in the recall of randomly arranged associates. *Journal of General Psychology* 49:229–240.

Bousfield, A.K., and Bousfield, W.A. 1966. Measurement of clustering and sequential constances in repeated free recall. *Psychological Reports* 19:935–942.

Bradshaw, J.L.; Gates, A.; and Nettleton, N.C. 1977. Bihemispheric involvement in lexical decisions: Handedness and a possible sex difference. *Neuropsychologia* 15:277–286.

Broadbent, D. 1974. Division of function and integration of behavior. In *The neurosciences: Third study program,* eds. F.O. Schmitt and F.G. Worden. Cambridge, MA: MIT Press.

Bryden, M.P. 1963. Ear preference in auditory perception. *Journal of Experimental Psychology* 65:103–105.

________. 1965. Tachistoscopic recognition, handedness, and cerebral dominance. *Neuropsychologia* 3:1–8.

Cohen, G. 1975. Hemisphere differences in the effects of cuing in visual recognition tasks. *Journal of Experimental Psychology: Human Perception and Performance* 1:366–373.

Collins, A.M., and Quillian, M.R. 1969. Retrieval time from semantic memory. *Journal of Verbal Learning and Verbal Behavior* 8:240–247.

Craik, F.I.M., and Lockhart, R.S. 1972. Levels of processing: A framework for memory research. *Journal of Verbal Learning and Verbal Behavior* 11:671–684.

CTB/McGraw-Hill. 1973. *California Achievement Tests-Reading.* Original edition by Earnest W. Tiegs and Willis W. Clark. Monterey, CA: CTB/McGraw-Hill.

Das, J.P. 1973. Structure of cognitive abilities: Evidence for simultaneous and successive processing. *Journal of Educational Psychology* 65:103–108.

Davidson, R.J., and Schwartz, G.E. 1977. The influence of musical training on patterns of EEG asymmetry during musical and non-musical self-generation tasks. *Psychophysiology* 16:58–63.

Davis, R., and Schmit, V. 1973. Visual and verbal coding in the interhemispheric transfer of information. *Acta Psychologica* 37:229-240.

Deikman, A.J. 1971. Bimodal consciousness. *Archives of General Psychiatry* 25:481–489.

________. 1976. Bimodal consciousness and the mystic experience. In *Symposium on consciousness*, eds. P.R. Lee, R.E. Ornstein, D. Galin, A.J. Diekman, and C.T. Tart. New York: The Viking Press.

Dimond, S.J.; Gibson, A.R.; and Gazzaniga, M.S. 1972. Cross field and within field integration of visual information. *Neuropsychologia* 10:379-381.

Doktor, R., and Bloom, D.M. 1977. Selective lateralization of cognitive style related to occupation as determined by EEG alpha asymmetry. *Psychophysiology* 14:385-387.

Doyle, J.C.; Ornstein, R; and Galin, D. 1974. Lateral specialization of cognitive mode 11: EEG frequency analysis. *Psychophysiology* 11:567-578.

Dunn, B.R. 1973. *The effects of subjective organization on the recall of prose.* Paper presented at the meeting of the American Educational Research Association, New Orleans.

Dunn, B.R.; Gould, J.E.; and Singer, M. 1981. *Cognitive style differences in expository prose recall.* (Technical Report 210). The Center for the Study of Reading, University of Illinois.

Dunn, B.R.; Mathews, S.R.; and Bieger, G.R. 1982. Deviation from hierarchical structure in recall: Is there an "optimal" structure? *Journal of Experimental Child Psychology* 34:371-386.

Dunn, B.R., and McConkie, G.W. 1972. An examination of the effects of a self-instructional curriculum technique on retention and understanding. Final Report for U.S. Office of Education Grant #OEG-2-700037 (509), May, 1972. Abstract in *Research in Education* 7:103.

Ehrlichman, H., and Wiener, M.S. 1979. Consistency of task-related EEG asymmetries. *Psychophysiology* 16:247-252.

Eysenck, M. 1976. Extraversion, verbal learning, and memory. *Psychological Bulletin* 83:75-90.

Fillmore, C.J. 1968. The case for case. In *Universals in linguistic theory*, eds. E. Bach and R.T. Harms. New York: Holt, Rinehart and Winston.

Frederiksen, C.H. 1975a. Representing logical and semantic structure of knowledge acquired from discourse. *Cognitive Psychology* 7:371–458.

________. 1975b. Effects of context-induced processing operations on semantic information acquired from discourse. *Cognitive Psychology* 7:139-166.

________. 1975c. Acquisition of semantic information from discourse: Effects of repeated exposures. *Journal of Verbal Learning and Verbal Behavior* 14:158-169.

________. 1977a. Semantic processing units in understanding text. In *Discourse production and comprehension*, ed. R.O. Freedle, Norwood, NJ: Ablex Pub.

________. 1977b. Structure and process in discourse production and comprehension. In *Cognitive processes in comprehension*, eds. M.A. Just and P.A. Carpenter. Hillsdale, NJ: Lawrence Erlbaum Associates.

Freides, D. 1977. Do dichotic listening procedures measure lateralization of information processing or retrieval strategy? *Perception and Psychophysics* 21:259-263.

Galin, D. 1974. Implications for psychiatry of left and right cerebral specialization. *Archives of General Psychiatry* 31:572-583.

Geffin, G.; Bradshaw, J.L.; and Wallace, G. 1971. Interhemispheric effects on reaction time to verbal and nonverbal visual stimuli. *Journal of Experimental Psychology* 85:415–422.

Goldberg, E., and Costa, L.D. 1981. Hemisphere differences in the acquisition and use of descriptive systems. *Brain and Language* 14:144–173.

Goodenough, D.R. 1976. The role of individual differences in field-dependence as a factor in learning and memory. *Psychological Bulletin* 83:675–694.

Grimes, J.E. 1975. *The thread of discourse.* The Hague, Holland: Mouton and Co.

Haaland, K.Y. 1974. The effect of dichotic, monaural and dichotic verbal stimuli on auditory evoked potentials. *Neuropsychologia* 12:339–345.

Hardyck, C.; Tzeng, O.J.L.; and Wang, W. 1978. Cerebral lateralization of functions and bilingual decision processes: Is thinking lateralized? *Brain and Language* 5:56–71.

Heeschen, C., and Jürgens, R. 1977. Pragmatic-semantic and syntactic factors influencing ear differences in dichotic listening. *Cortex* 13:74–84.

Hellige, J.B., and Cox, P.J. 1976. Effects of concurrent verbal memory on recognition of stimuli from the left and right visual fields. *Journal of Experimental Psychology: Human Perception & Performance* 2:210–221.

Hines, D. 1976. Recognition of verbs, abstract nouns and concrete nouns from the left and right visual half-fields. *Neuropsychologia* 14:211–216.

Howell, W.L. 1974. The effects of extra sensory perception, sex, and locus of control on free recall and clustering. Master's thesis, The University of West Florida, Pensacola.

Hunt, D. 1979. Value of a selected battery of psychological tests for predicting EEG activity. Master's thesis, The University of West Florida, Pensacola.

Hunt, E. 1978. Mechanics of verbal ability. *Psychological Review* 85:109–130.

Hymes, D.; Dunn, B.R.; Gould, J.E.; and Harris, W. 1977. *Effects of mode of conscious processing on recall and clustering.* Paper presented at the 1977 meeting of the Southeastern Psychological Association, Hollywood, Florida.

Jasper, H.H. 1958. The ten-twenty electrode system of the international federation. *Electroencephalography and Clinical Neurophysiology* 10:371–375.

Kimura, D. 1964. Left-right differences in the perception of melodies. *Quarterly Journal of Experimental Psychology* 15:166–171.

________. 1966. Dual functional asymmetry of the brain in visual perception. *Neuropsychologia* 4:275–285.

________. 1969. Spatial localization in the left and right visual fields. *Canadian Journal of Psychology* 23:445–458.

Kintsch, W. 1974. *The representation of meaning in memory.* Hillsdale, NJ: Lawrence Erlbaum Associates.

________. 1977. On comprehending stories. In *Cognitive processes in comprehension*, eds. M.A. Just and P.A. Carpenter. Hillsdale, NJ: Lawrence Erlbaum Associates.

Kintsch, W., and Keenan, J. 1973. Reading rate and retention as a function of the number or propositions in the base structure of sentences. *Cognitive Psychology* 5:257–274.

Kintsch, W., and Kozminsky, E. 1977. Summarizing stories after reading and listening. *Journal of Educational Psychology* 5:491–499.

Kintsch, W.; Kozminsky, E.; Streby, W.; McKoon, G.; and Keenan, J. 1975. Comprehension and recall of text as a function of content variables. *Journal of Verbal Learning and Verbal Behavior* 14:196–214.

Kintsch, W.; Mandel, T.W.; and Kozminsky, E. 1977. Summarizing scrambled stories. *Memory and Cognition* 5:547–552.

Kintsch, W., and van Dijk, T.A. 1978. Toward a model of text comprehension and production. *Psychological Review* 85:363–394.

Kintsch, W., and Vipond, D. 1979. Reading comprehension and readability in educational practice and psychological theory. In *Proceedings of the conference on memory*, ed. Lars-Goran Nilsson. Hillsdale, NJ: Lawrence Erlbaum Associates.

Kirk, R.E. 1968. *Experimental design: Procedures for the behavioral sciences.* Belmont, CA: Brooks-Cole.

Levy-Agresti, J., and Sperry, R.W. 1968. Differential perceptual capacities in major and minor hemispheres. *Proceedings of the National Academy of Sciences,* U.S.A., 61:1151.

Levy, J., and Trevarthen, C. 1976. Metracontrol of hemispheric function in human split-brain patients. *Journal of Experimental Psychology: Human Perception and Performance* 2:299–312.

Levy, J.; Trevarthen, C.; and Sperry, R.W. 1972. Perception of bilateral chimeric figures following hemispheric disconnection. *Brain* 95:61–78.

Luria, A.R., and Simernitskaya, E.G. 1977. Interhemispheric relations and the functions of the minor hemisphere. *Neuropsychologia* 15:175–178.

Mandler, G. 1967. Organization and memory. In *The psychology of learning and motivation: Advances in research and theory* (Vol. 1), eds. K.W. Spence and J.T. Spence. New York: Academic Press.

________. 1968a. Association and organization: Facts, fancies and theories. In *Verbal behavior and general behavior theory,* eds. T.R. Dixon and D.L. Horton. Englewood Cliffs, NJ: Prentice-Hall.

________. 1968b. Organized recall: Individual functions. *Psychonomic Science* 13:235–236.

________. 1970. Words, lists, and categories: An experimental view of organized memory. In *Studies in thought and language*, ed. J.L. Cowan. Tucson: University of Arizona Press.

Mandler, G., and Pearlstone, Z. 1966. Free and constrained concept learning and subsequent recall. *Journal of Verbal Learning and Verbal Behavior* 5:126–131.

Mandler, J.M., and Johnson, N.S. 1977. Remembrance of things parsed: Story structure and recall. *Cognitive Psychology* 9:111–151.

Marschark, M., and Paivio, A. 1977. Integrative processing of concrete and abstract sentences. *Journal of Verbal Learning and Verbal Behavior* 16:217–231.

Mathews, S.; Yussen, S.; and Evans, R. n.d. Remember that story? An investigation of the robustness and temporal course of the story schema's influence. *Journal of Experimental Psychology: Human Learning and Memory.* In press.

McConkie, G.W., and Dunn, B.R. 1969. *Word sorting norms for 180 common words.* Cornell University, in mimeo.

________. 1971. Word sorting and free-recall. *Psychonomic Science* 24:75–76.

McKeever, W.F., and Huling, M. 1970. Left cerebral hemisphere superiority in tachistoscopic word recognition performance. *Perceptual & Motor Skills* 30:763–766.

McLeod, S.S., and Peacock, L.J. 1977. Task-related EEG asymmetry: Effects of age and ability. *Psychophysiology* 14:308–311.

Meyer, B.J.F. 1971. Idea units recalled from prose in relation to their position in the logical structure, importance, stability and order in the passage. Master's thesis, Cornell Universal.

________. 1975. *The organization of prose and its effects on memory.* Amsterdam: North-Holland Publishing Co.

________. 1977a. The structure of prose: Effects of learning and memory and implications for educational practice. In *Schooling and the acquisition of knowledge,* eds. R.C. Anderson, R.J. Spiro, and W.E. Montague. Hillsdale, NJ: Lawrence Erlbaum Associates.

________. 1977b. What is remembered from prose: A function of passage structure. In *Discourse production and comprehension*, ed. R.O. Freedle. Norwood, NJ: Ablex Pub.

Meyer, B.J.F.; Brandt, D.M.; and Bluth, G.J. 1980. Use of top-level structure in text. Key for reading comprehension of ninth-grade students. *Reading Research Quarterly* 16:72–103.

Meyer, B.J.F., and McConkie, G.W. 1973. What is recalled after hearing a passage? *Journal of Educational Psychology* 65:109–117.

Meyer, B.J.F.; Freedle, R.O.; and Walker, C.H. 1978. *Effects of discourse type on the recall of young and old adults.* Unpublished manuscript, Arizona State University.

Minsky, M.A. 1975. A framework for representing knowledge. In *The psychology of computer vision*, ed. P. Winston. New York: McGraw-Hill.

Nebes, R.D. 1971. Superiority of the minor hemisphere in commissurotomised man for the perception of part-whole relationships. *Cortex* 7:333–349.

Norman, D.A.; Rumelhart, D.E.; and the LNR Research Group. 1975. *Explorations in cognition.* San Francisco: W.H. Freeman & Co.

Orne, M., and Wilson, S. 1977. Alpha, biofeedback and arousal/activation. In *Biofeedback and behavior,* eds. J. Beatty and H. Legewie. New York: Plenum Press.

Ornstein, R.G., ed. 1973. *The nature of human consciousness: A book of readings.* San Francisco, CA: W.H. Freeman & Co.

Ornstein, R.E. 1977. *The psychology of consciousness* (2nd ed.). San Francisco, CA: W.H. Freeman & Co.

Ornstein, R.E., and Galin, D. 1976. Physiological studies of consciousness. In *Symposium on consciousness*, eds. P. Lee, R. Ornstein, D. Galin, A. Deikman and C. Tart. New York: The Viking Press.

Osborne, K., and Gale, A. 1976. Bilateral EEG differentiation of stimuli. *Biological Psychology* 4:185–196.

Paivio, A. 1971. *Imagery and verbal processes.* New York: Holt, Rinehart and Winston.

________. 1975a. Imagery and synchronic thinking. *Canadian Psychological Review.* 16:147–163.

________. 1975b. Perceptual comparisons through the mind's eye. *Memory and Cognition* 3:635–647.

Paskewitz, D., and Orne, M. 1973. Visual effects on alpha feedback training. *Science* 181:360–363.

Patterson, K., and Bradshaw, J.L. 1975. Differential hemispheric mediation of nonverbal stimuli. *Journal of Experimental Psychology: Human Perception and Performance* 1:246–252.

Piaget, J. 1952. *The origins of intelligence in children.* New York: Norton.

Pirozzolo, F.J., and Rayner, K. 1977. Hemispheric specialization in reading and word recognition. *Brain and Language* 4:248-261.

Ray, W.J.; Morell, M.; Frediani, A.W.; and Tucker, D. 1976. Sex differences and lateralization of hemispheric functioning. *Neuropsychologia* 14:391-394.

Repp, B.H. 1975. Dichotic forward and backward "masking" between CV syllables. *Journal of Acoustical Society of America* 57:483-496.

———. 1976. Effects of fundamental frequency contrast on discrimination and identification of dichotic CV syllables at various temporal delays. *Memory and Cognition* 4:75-90.

Rizzolatti, G., and Bushtel, H.A. 1977. Hemispheric superiority in reaction time to faces: A sex difference. *Cortex* 13:300-305.

Rizzolatti, G.; Umilta, C.; and Berlucchi, G. 1971. Opposite superiorities of the right and left cerebral hemispheres in discrimination reaction time to physiognomical and alphabetical material. *Brain* 94:431-442.

Rumelhart, D.E. 1975. Notes on a scheme for stories. In *Representation and understanding: Studies in cognitive science,* eds. D. Bobrow and A. Collins. New York: Academic Press.

Rumelhart, D.E., and Norman, D.A. 1978. Accretion, tuning, and restructuring: Three modes of learning. In *Semantic factors in cognition*, eds. J. Cotton and R. Klatsky. Hillsdale, NJ: Lawrence Erlbaum Associates.

Rumelhart, D.E., and Ortony, A. 1977. The representation of knowledge in memory. In *Schooling and the acquisition of knowledge*, eds. R.C. Anderson, R.J. Spiro, and W.E. Montague. Hillsdale, NJ: Lawrence Erlbaum Associates.

Rust, D.T. 1982. EEG Alpha responses related to semantic recall in two groups of children. Doctoral diss., Walden University.

Schank, R.C., and Abelson, R.P. 1977. *Scripts, plans, goals and understanding: An inquiry into human knowledge and structures.* Hillsdale, NJ: Lawrence Erlbaum Associates.

Schmidt, C. 1975. Understanding human action. In *Theoretical issues in natural language processing: Proceedings of an interdisciplinary workshop,* eds. B.L. Nash-Webber and R.C. Schank. Cambridge, Massachusetts.

Searleman, A. 1977. A review of right hemisphere linguistic capabilities. *Psychological Bulletin* 84:503-528.

Sergent, J. 1982a. About face: Left-Hemisphere involvement in processing physiognomies. *Journal of Experimental Psychology: Human Perception and Performance* 8:1-14.

———. 1982b. The cerebral balance of power: Confrontation or cooperation? *Journal of Experimental Psychology: Human Perception and Performance* 8:253-272.

Sergent, J., and Bindra, D. 1981. Differential hemisphere processing of faces: Methodological considerations and reinterpretations *Psychological Bulletin* 89:541-554.

Sperry, R.W.; Gazzaniga, M.S.; and Bogan, J.E. 1969. Interhemispheric relationships: The neocortical commissures; syndromes of hemispheric disconnection. In *Handbook of clinical neurology* (Vol. 4), eds. P.J. Vinken and G.W. Bruyn. Amsterdam: North-Holland Publishing Company.

Stein, N.O. 1982. The definition of a story. *Pragmatics* 6.

Stein, N.L., and Trabasso, T. 1982. Children's understanding of stories: A basis for moral judgment and dilemma resolution. In *Verbal processes in children: Progress in cognitive development research,* eds. C.J. Brainerd and M. Pressley. New York: Springer-Verlag.

Thorndyke, P.W. 1977. Cognitive structures in the comprehension and memory of narrative prose. *Cognitive Psychology* 9:77–110.

Trevarthen, C. 1978. Modes of perceiving and modes of acting. In *Modes of perceiving information,* eds. H.L. Pick, Jr. and E. Saltzman. Hillsdale, NJ: Lawrence Erlbaum Associates.

Tulving, E. 1968. Theoretical issues in free recall. In *Verbal behavior and general behavior theory,* eds. T. Dixon and D. Horton. Englewood Cliffs, NJ: Prentice-Hall, Inc.

Tulving, E., and Pearlstone, Z. 1966. Availability versus accessibility of information in memory for words. *Journal of Verbal Learning and Verbal Behavior* 5:381–391.

Tulving, E., and Psotka, J. 1971. Retroactive inhibition in free recall: Inaccessibility of information available in the memory store. *Journal of Experimental Psychology* 87:1–8.

van Dijk, T.A. 1977a. Semantic macrostructures and knowledge frames in discourse comprehension. In *Cognitive processes in comprehension,* eds. M.A. Just and P.A. Carpenter. Hillsdale, NJ: Lawrence Erlbaum Associates.

———. 1977b. *Text and content: Explorations in the semantics and pragmatics of discourse.* London: Longman.

van Dijk, T.A., and Kintsch, W. 1977. Cognitive psychology and discourse. In *Trends in text linguistics,* ed. W.V. Dressler. Berlin and New York: De Gruyter.

Vipond, D. 1980. Micro-Macroprocesses in text comprehension. *Journal of Verbal Learning and Verbal Behavior* 19:276–296.

White, M.J., and White, K.G. 1975. Parallel serial processing and hemispheric function, *Neuropsychologia* 13:377–381.

Winograd, T. 1977. A framework for understanding discourse. In *Cognitive processes in comprehension*, eds. M.A. Just and P.A. Carpenter. Hillsdale, NJ: Lawrence Erlbaum Associates.

Zaidel, E. 1977. Unilateral auditory language comprehension on the token test following cerebral commissurotomy and hemispherectomy. *Neuropsychologia* 15:1–18.

Chapter 3

Cardiovascular Relationships to Attention and Thinking

by Curt A. Sandman and Barbara B. Walker

INTRODUCTION

The study of the physiological basis of cognitive processes has developed rapidly within the field of psychology. For the most part psychologists have attempted to understand the relationship between physiology and behavior by lesioning areas of the brain and then assessing the residual behavioral deficits. The early, elegant work of Lashly and the contemporary advocates of this approach have provided convincing evidence that particular structures of the brain subserve unique behaviors. For instance, it is reasonably well accepted that the left and right hemispheres of the brain process information differently (Sperry 1974). Sufficient data support the notion that the left cerebral hemisphere (in right-handed persons) is most proficient with verbal, logical and sequential analysis whereas the right cerebral hemisphere is specialized for spatial and analogical processing. Further, it is believed that topographic areas of the cortex (frontal, temporal, parietal and occipital lobes), the thalamic nuclei related to these areas and the networks of subcortical structures are the reservoirs of distinctive behaviors. Some (Jackson 1958) have argued that the brain is structured hierarchically such that the cortex elaborates the processes of deeper subcortical structures, and that the complexity of behavior may be a function of increasing cortical mass. Others (Bard 1934) have suggested that the cortex has a censoring or suppressive influence on the more primitive subcortical structures. While resolution of this issue is not the province of this chapter it is important to acknowledge that sufficient evidence indicates there are reliable neuroanatomical relationships with behavior. In fact, by the 1930's evidence of anatomical relationships with behavior had gained such scientific credibility that persons with deviant behaviors or thought processes were subjected to alteration of brain structures. Even though there is very little support for the therapeutic benefits of lobotomies or destruction of various brain structures, the practice continues (Mark and Ervin 1970).

An obvious assumption of this popular theoretical orientation and approach is that the brain serves as the undisputed and supreme controller of behavior and thought. All other processes are subservient to the demands and commands of this unilateral decision maker. This view received its strongest support from Cannon (1929), whose early analysis of the relationship between the mind and body or physiology and behavior is represented in Figure 1. Cannon maintained that the flight or fight response critical for survival was associated with a unidimensional nervous system response. The peripheral systems were passive executors of the commands received from the brain. As such, qualitative distinctions among psychological states (e.g., fear and anger) were not assumed to be reflected or affected by the peripheral systems. Since such states were assumed to differ quantitatively and that the response systems were coupled and controlled by the central nervous system, any single peripheral response was as adequate as any other for determining the organism's state of arousal. These tenuous assumptions resulted in a simplistic methodological strategy yielding spurious conclusions, and separated even further the brain and body.

A radically different viewpoint had been expressed with the metascientific approach of William James. James (1892) suggested that emotional experience was a product of visceral and autonomic input to the brain. He proposed that perception gained meaning as a result of the context in which it was experienced and that the peripheral systems provided this context. This view is characterized in Figure 2. It is apparent that the viscera, the muscles, the heart and the endocrine system provide information to the brain and thereby participate in the determination of the behavior and thoughts of the organism. The notion that "we are afraid because we run" represents this view. The intuitive appeal of this approach is evident in our everyday activity. Imagine driving your car down a residential street when all of a sudden a small child darts in front of

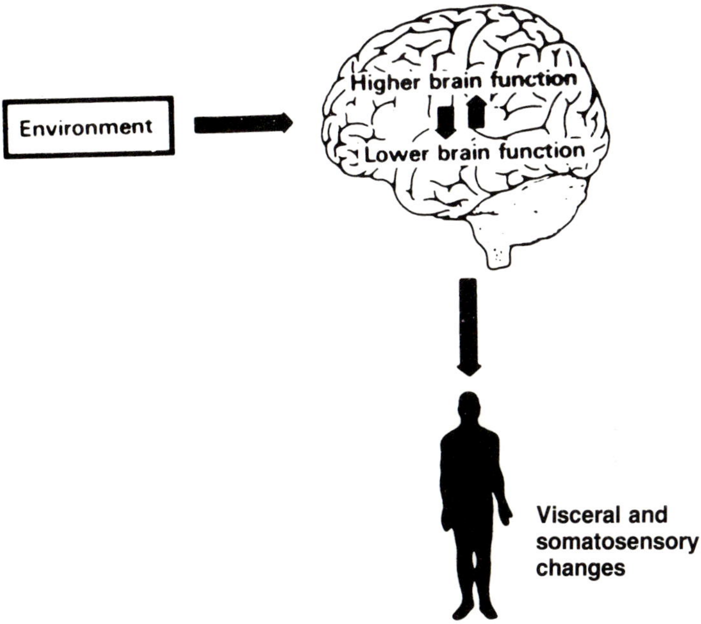

Figure 1.
Illustrates the brain-body formulation of Cannon. The brain receives information from the environment and simultaneously directs information upward (to the cortex) and downward (to the body). Except for homeostatic functioning there is no provision for afferent input from the body to the brain.

your car. It is likely that you immediately step on the brakes and, assuming you have missed the child, you sit there and ponder your close call. All of a sudden you begin to shake, your heart is beating, your palms are moist, and your emotional state climaxes. This scenario illustrates that we first act, then as the consequences of physiological and psychological action become "conscious" we experience an emotion.

The converse view, representative of the centralist position, is that "we run because we are afraid." Thus, while we drive our car, and the child darts out in front of us, we scream, experience the emotion and step on the brakes, hopefully in time. Refinements of the centralist position suggested that subcortical areas processed environmental information and simultaneoulsy relayed information upward to the cortex resulting in elaboration of emotion and downward to the peripheral system resulting in action.

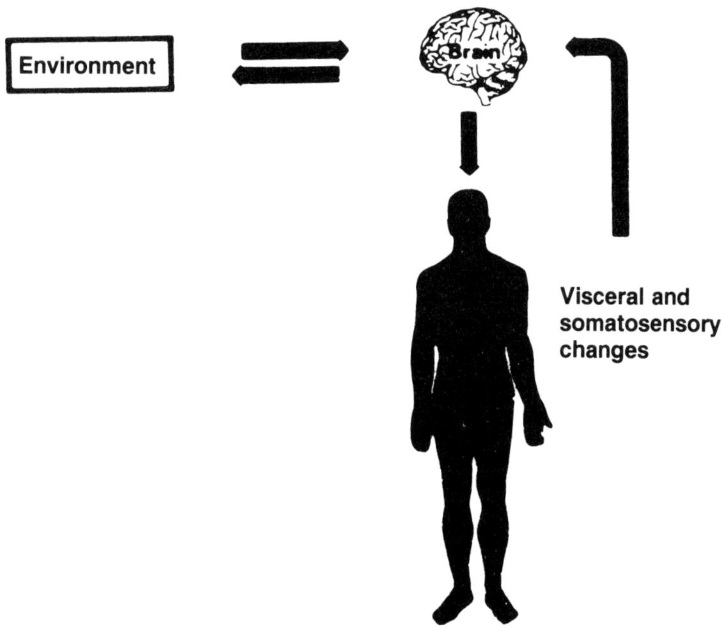

Figure 2.
Represents the brain-body views of James. The brain not only directs changes in but also receives information from the body. This afferent information provides a context for evaluating the environment.

Evidence secured in our laboratory (Sandman 1971, 1975) suggested that both theoretical views may be accurate. Some people (field-independent) appear to use visceral or bodily information more readily than others. These individuals are able to make accurate perceptual judgments about the environment even though they are presented with distracting information. However, field dependent subjects tend to base their perceptual judgments primarily upon the distracting information. Field-independent individuals tend to show qualitative differences in physiological responding during various emotional experiences. Further they are able to provide more accurate information about their physiological state and display concordance between how they say they feel, and how they respond physiologically. Field-dependent persons utilize environmental rather than internal information to assess their state. Consistent with Cannon's formulations they tend to show less "emotional complexity" and respond to stimuli with differing degrees of arousal. Interestingly, subjects become more field independent after learning to control a physiological response, a theme we shall pursue later in this chapter.

By the 1950's a new field was emerging as a dominant force in the study of physiology-behavior relationships. The field, psychophysiology, gave prominence to the study of relationships among the autonomic nervous system, central nervous system and behavior in *intact* organisms. Although the majority of the early studies supported the concept of arousal, studies from the laboratories of Davis (1957) and the Laceys (1963, 1967, 1970) began to indicate that neo-Jamesian principles provided a more complex description of the mind-body relationships than the centralist's position. Prominent among the findings was that patterns of autonomic responses differentiated stimulus content. That is, different stimuli or situations, even though they may be stressful, resulted in distinctive physiological patterns. These findings suggested that responses of the nervous system were not necessarily related. Thus, it became apparent that the physiological (and the psychological) state of the organism could not be determined solely by measurement of a single response. The outstanding example of this phenomenon is the relationship of the cardiovascular system to the brain and behavior.

NEUROPHYSIOLOGICAL RELATIONS BETWEEN THE CARDIOVASCULAR SYSTEM AND THE CENTRAL NERVOUS SYSTEM

Pressure sensitive cells in the wall of the carotid sinus and aortic arch which detect changes in blood pressure are called baroreceptors. The baroceptors increase their firing when blood pressure increases and decrease their rate of firing when blood pressure decreases. The homeostatic significance of these structures is evident by the fact that nerves from the carotid sinus and aortic arch join the vagus and glossopharyngeal nerve and terminate in the lower brain stem to assist in controlling blood pressure and ensuring the survival of the organism. However, these structures may serve functions in addition to ones classified as homeostatic.

Bonvallet, Dell and Hiebel (1954) mechanically distended the carotid sinus of cats in order to produce an experimental analog of increased pressure. They discovered that increased pressure shifted electrocortical activity from low-voltage fast activity, to high-voltage slow activity. Thus when the baroreceptors in the wall of the carotid sinus detects increases in pressures, the electrocortical activity is inhibited. Decreases in blood pressure should release the cortex from this inhibitory influence. Indeed, Bonvallet et al. (1954) discovered that by severing the vagus and glossopharyngeal nerves the inhibitory influence dissipated.

While the significance of the cortical inhibitory influences of the baroreceptors may not be as readily apparent as the homeostatic control of blood pressure, this inhibition may have survival value for the organism. For instance, the heart is responsive to environmental stimulation and these cardiovascular changes are detected in structures of the bulbar area of the brain (see Figure 3). Further, there is evidence that the baroreceptors may be responsive to environmental stimulation (Obrist et al 1979). Cells firing with a cardiac rhythm have been recorded in this area (Humphrey 1967; Smith and Pearce 1961) and coagulation in the bulbar region tends to prolong effects of a stimulus. Thus Lacey (1967) has suggested that the function of this area may be to "control the duration of an episode of stimulus-produced process in the brain."

Unfortunately the functions of the baroreceptors are not as simple and straightforward as the foregoing might suggest. For instance the carotid sinus has its own properties, such as stiffness of the vascular wall, which may determine its responsiveness. Further, not every change in blood pressure or heart rate will influence cortical activity since the central nervous system can modify the impact of changes of the cardiovascular system. Therefore some manipulations such as exercise may have profound cardiovascular effects without directly influencing the negative feedback system of the carotid sinus and the brain. (In fact, it is conceivable that the most dramatic effects on behavior occur when heart-rate changes are observed relatively independently of systemic physiological responses.) To multiply the complexities, there are baroreceptors all over the body about which virtually nothing is known. Thus no simple formulae can be presented to account for the relationship among the heart, the brain and behavior.

The complexity of cardiovascular events and the proposed relationship with behavior is simplified in Figure 3. Each ventricular contraction of the heart (the R wave) propogates a bolus of blood through the vascular system which is detected as a resonating pulse. As is evident in Figure 3 the peak of the carotid pulse wave begins to ascend at about the R wave and reachs a peak value (systolic pressure) several milliseconds later. The firing rate of the baroreceptors is related to both peak of the carotid pulse

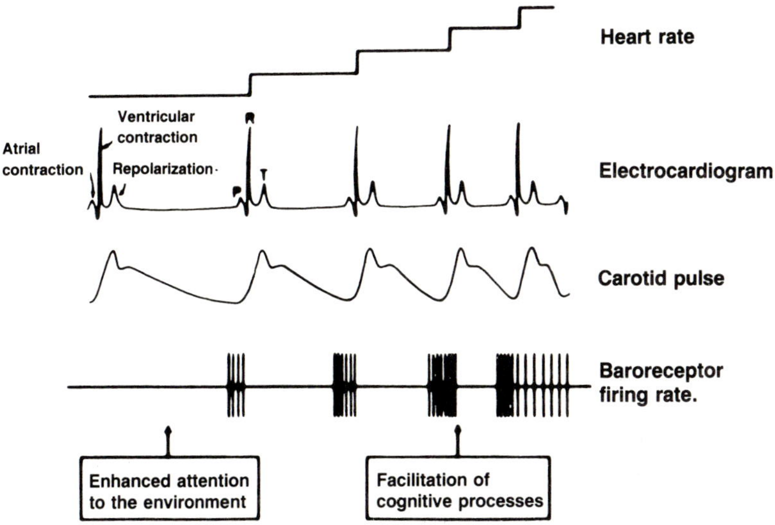

Figure 3.
The relationships among heart rate, the electrocardiogram, the carotid pulse, baroreceptor activity and psychological processes.

and to the level of heart rate. Thus, as heart rate increases, the firing rate of the baroreceptors increases during each pulse. The Laceys were the first to recognize the significance of these neurophysiological relationships for the study of behavior. In a series of elegant studies they have demonstrated clearly that the heart influences the mind.

CARDIOVASCULAR RELATIONS TO BEHAVIOR

In a series of tasks ranging from those requiring attention to the external environment (i.e., detection of flashes) to those in which attention to the environment may interfere with performance of the task (i.e., mental arithmetic) it was discovered that heart rate and blood pressure were the physiological responses which best differentiated the cognitive-perceptual processes (Lacey 1967; Lacey et al. 1964). Heart rate decreased during tasks requiring environmental attention, whereas tasks demanding "mental concentration" or "rejection of the environment" were related with heart-rate acceleration. These findings were related cogently to the neurophysiological evidence reviewed above which indicated that decelerating heart rate would release the cortex from inhibitory control of the baroreceptors. Thus, during decelerating heart rate, fast frequency electroencephalographic activity would result and this activity has been related consistently with vigilant behavior (Lindsley 1969). Conversely, increased heart rate may stimulate baroreceptors and thereby inhibit cortical activity. Slow wave formations would develop, which has been related to problem solving behavior.

The influence of cardiac activity on attention received substantial support from studies of reaction time. In a typical reaction time experiment subjects are presented with two stimuli. The first stimulus is a warning signal informing the subject that the second stimulus (imperative stimulus) will be forthcoming. The subject is instructed to depress a telegraphic key as soon as the imperative stimulus appears. The warning period may vary but usually it is within 2–8 seconds and in most experiments it is fixed. That is, all warning periods will be of the same duration. It was observed that heart rate characteristically decelerated several beats before the imperative stimulus, with the slowest beats occurring just prior to the stimulus. Since decreased reaction time (i.e., faster response) has been used as a classical measure of attention, heart-rate decleration should correlate with faster reaction time. Indeed data collected from several laboratories have confirmed this expectation (Duncan-Johnson and Coles 1974; Lacey and Lacey 1970, 1974; Obrist, Webb and Sutterer 1969).

Studies from our laboratory (Sandman 1971, 1975; Walker and Sandman 1977) and others (Hare et al. 1970; Libby, Lacey and Lacey 1973) indicated that subjects responded with decelerated heart rate while viewing unpleasant stimuli. This response was surprising since heart-rate acceleration commonly is believed to be an aspect of the overall sympathetic nervous system response to stressful stimuli. The findings were interpreted as indicating that stressful stimuli can involve a strong attentional component and that viewing these stimuli also involves "morbid fascination." In a refined analysis of this issue Cacioppo and Sandman (1978) presented subjects with stressful visual stimuli (pictures of accident victims) and stimuli which were equated with the pictures of accident victims on the dimension of unpleasantness but required "cognitive effort." These latter stimuli included arithmetic problems, anagrams and strings of digits to be memorized. Thus two sets of stressful stimuli were generated, one set depicting gruesome material and involving emotional reactions and another set reflecting cognitive stress. Consistent with previous studies, heart rate decelerated during viewing of the accident victims but increased for the equally unpleasant stimuli which required "mental effort." Thus it appears that heart rate reflects the type of processing required by the task but does not reflect its affective components. Specifically, heart rate decelerates during processing which requires only "attention to the environment," whereas tasks requiring "cognitive elaboration" or "rejection of the environment" results in heart-rate acceleration.

INFLUENCE OF THE HEART ON ATTENTION

In a recent set of experiments we (Sandman et al. 1977) attempted to examine the influence of heart rate and cardiac phase on detection of stimuli. During daily activities and while sitting passively in the laboratory subjects evidence a broad range of heart rate. The range of heart rate may vary from 2 to 40 beats per minute (bpm). The average variation tends to be approximately 14 bpm. Thus at any one time our heart rate may be 63 bpm and during the next beat it may be 77 bpm. Obviously the range is greater for some individuals than for others. As illustrated in Fig. 4, the students' fluctuating heart rates were detected by a computer and when a fast beat (upper decile of subjects' resting heart rate), a low beat (lowest decile of subjects' resting heart rate) or a midrange beat (average of fast and low) was emitted, a digit of extremely brief exposure (6, 10, or 20 ms) was flashed on a screen in front of them. The subjects were required to report the digit (single digits from 0–9 were presented) they perceived. If attention to the external environment is related to low heart rate, better performance would be expected during low than during high heart rate.

The results of this experiment provided dramatic support for the bradycardia (decelerating heart rate) of attention. When heart rate was low, subjects perceived the stimuli which were presented for the briefest exposure significantly better than when heart rate was fast. This profound influence of the heart on behavior is illustrated in Figure 5. In addition to the behavioral changes seen in this study, cerebral perfusion (blood flow to the brain), a measure of brain activity (Ingvar 1972), indicated that increased blood flow to the brain was associated with decelerating heart rate.

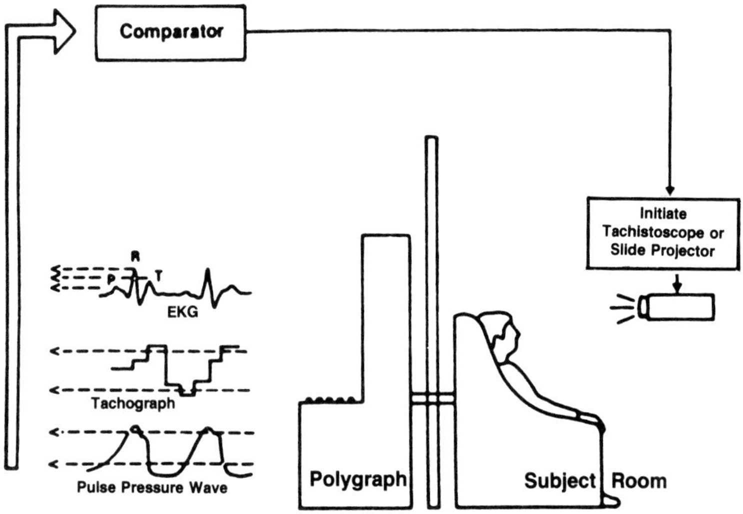

Figure 4.
The paradigm employed permitting the electrocardiogram, heart rate or pulse pressure waves to trigger stimulus. Subjects' physiological signals are recorded by a polygraph and compared by a computer with a pre-set criterion. If the criterion is met or exceeded a stimulus is automatically activated.

Similar influences on the baroreceptors may be expected during low heart rate and during the P wave of the cardiac cycle and during fast heart rate and the R-T interval of cardiac cycle (see Figure 3). Thus in a second experiment we examined the behavioral significance of the discrete waves during each cardiac cycle. Previous investigations yielded equivocal results; some studies reported greater attention to the environment during the early components of the cycle (Birren, Cardon and Phillips 1963; Callaway and Layne 1964) while other studies found no significant influence of the cardiac cycle on behavior (Delfini and Campos 1972; Elliott and Graf 1972; Thompson and Botwinick 1970). Just as in the previous study, and illustrated in Fig. 4, digits were presented for brief periods of time but were synchronized with the waves of the cardiac cycle. The stimuli were presented approximately during the P wave (atrial contraction), R wave (ventricular contraction) and the T wave (repolarization) of the EKG (see Figure 3). We discovered that stimuli presented during the P wave were perceived more accurately than stimuli presented during the T wave, just a half of a second later. Although cardiovascular influences on the brain and behavior are expected from the neurophysiological evidence, it is remarkable that awareness of environmental events can be modified by such subtle changes in physiological activity. Hence, it is clear from these experiments that a single heart beat can exert a significant influence on attention.

We reasoned further that if heart rate has an important or adaptive influence on attention or perception, the cardiovascular system should reflect a person's intention to receive information.

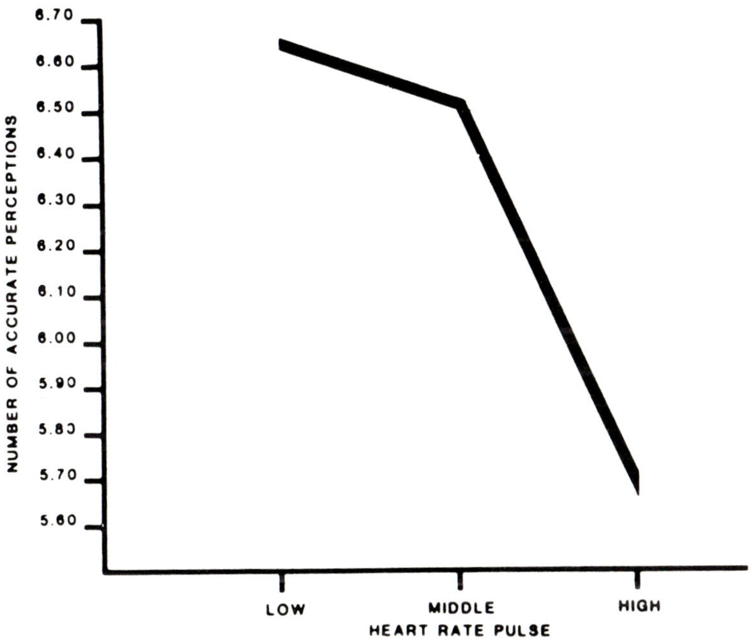

Figure 5.

Accuracy of perception as a function of heart rate. During low heart rate, subjects perceived tachistoscopic stimuli more accurately than during high heart rate (from Sandman et al. 1977).

A study was designed in which subjects were instructed to depress a telegraphic key whenever they "felt ready to perceive a stimulus." The stimuli, as before, were digits presented for just an instant. As Figure 6 indicates, the depression of the key, indicating the subjects' intention to perceive, was associated with heart-rate deceleration and further, accurate perception was related to greater deceleration than inaccurate perception. These data suggested that changes in the cardiovascular system were coupled with intention to receive information. Remarkably, the extent of the deceleratory response was related to accuracy of the subjects' perception. These findings provide additional support for the influence of extremely subtle changes in the body on behavior.

INFLUENCE OF THE HEART ON COGNITIVE ACTIVITY

As already suggested, the Laceys have related increases in heart rate to "rejection of the environment" or to tasks requiring cognitive processing. They and others (Tursky, Schwartz and Crider 1970) have found that tasks requiring mental concentration or cognitive elaboration were consistently related to increases in heart rate. For instance Kaiser and Sandman (1975) found that solution of anagrams was related to heart rate increase such that the most difficult problems (reflecting more processing) produced the greatest acceleration and easiest problem produced the least acceleration. Further the rate of problem solution was positively correlated with heart rate.

In a recent study (Baker, Sandman and Pepinsky 1975) subjects were required to prepare "mentally" a two-minute speech. One "speech" was to be about a visible object (to which they could attend and then describe) or about "someone they disliked very much." Heart rate (and other responses) was measured during the preparation interval, during the speech and then several minutes after the speech. Increases in heart rate were recorded only during the rehearsal period for the nonvisible object (requiring imagery and fantasizing). Further, a significant relationship between heart rate increases and verbal output was observed. These findings have been replicated (Baker and Sandman, unpublished) and indicated that as heart rate increased more words (and hence more thought) were produced. While no causal link can be developed from these studies, a clear relationship between the magnitude of heart rate increases and an

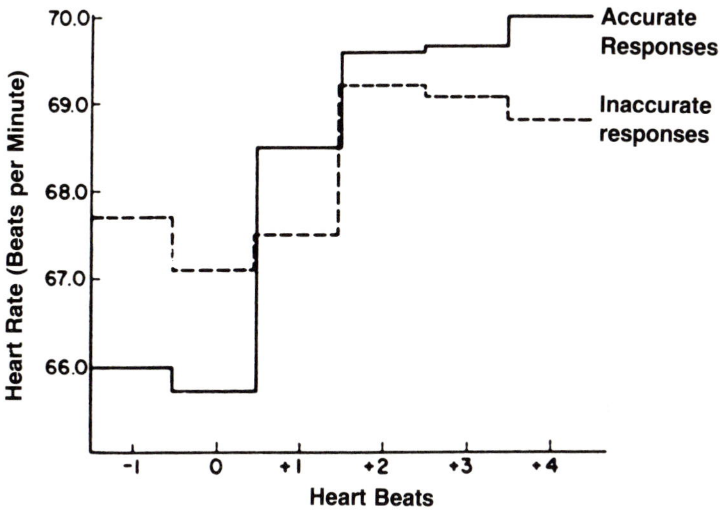

Figure 6.
Heart rate decelerated during key depression (heart beat 0). Greater deceleration was related to accurate perception of tachistoscopic stimulation.

objective measure of underlying thought was developed.

Simple reaction time (when the subject does not have to make a decision but only responds during the presentation of a stimulus) is related to decelerating heart rate and facilitation of attention. However, Duncan-Johnson and Coles (1974) have illustrated that the heart rate deceleration can be attenuated if the subject is required to make a decision before responding. Utilizing the same design employed for assessing the impact of the heart on perception (Figure 4) we attempted to elaborate the relationship between heart rate and cognitive processing. Stimuli were presented to subjects during either fast, slow or midrange heart rate (as described earlier). The subjects were shown either a circle or a square; when a circle was presented they were to depress a telegraphic key as rapidly as they could. During the second stimulus, a square, they withheld their response. The time required to respond to the circle is a measure of decision making. In this study we expected that increases of

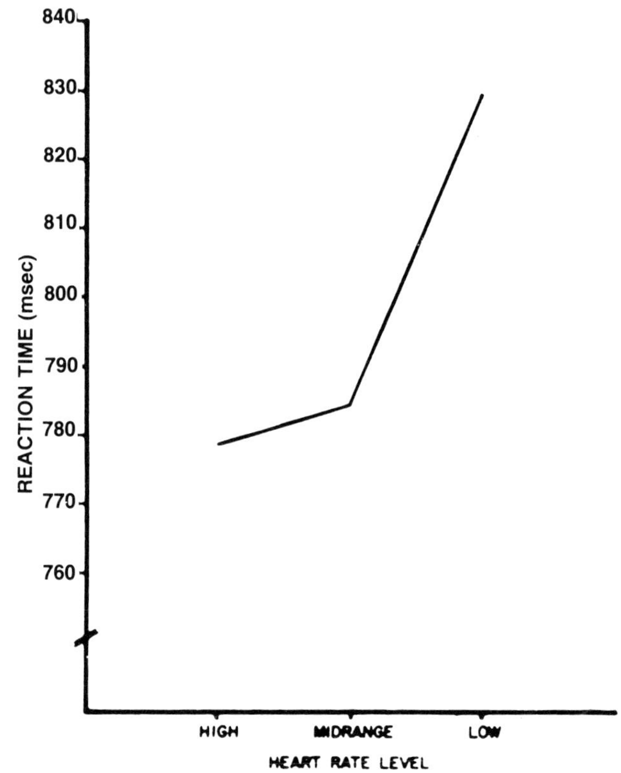

Figure 7.
Faster choice reaction time (requiring cognitive processing) is related to increased heart rate.

heart rate would relate to faster reaction time since we assumed that cognitive processing induced by elevated heart rate would be facilitated.

Indeed, the findings provided support for our expectations. The clear influence of heart rate on a reaction time task which reflected cognitive processing or decision making is illustrated in Figure 7. During elevated heart rate, reaction time decreased (thus decision-making was facilitated), and conversely, during lower heart rate, reaction time slowed.

In a second part of this experiment the influence of cardiac phase on this task was examined. Unlike the results for heart rate and perception, no effect of cardiac phase upon reaction time was observed. These results suggested that heart rate and cardiac phase do not influence behavior identically. Perhaps the physiological mechanisms underlying these behaviors are not as similar as was once thought.

THE EFFECTS OF "BIOFEEDBACK" ON BEHAVIOR

The process of biofeedback, illustrated in Figure 8, involves providing information to a subject about his/her body. While most of us are aware of our heart beat, few of us are conscious of our heart rate, the status of our blood vessels, or the frequency of the electrical waves of the brain. However, with biofeedback techniques, we can be acquainted with our body. While many responses can be controlled (see McCanne and Sandman 1975; Miller 1969 for reviews) the focus of our discussion will be on cardiac activity. Since the heart can influence profoundly the psychological or cognitive state of the organism, we have taught subjects to control their heart rate in order to measure the impact of such control on attention and thinking.

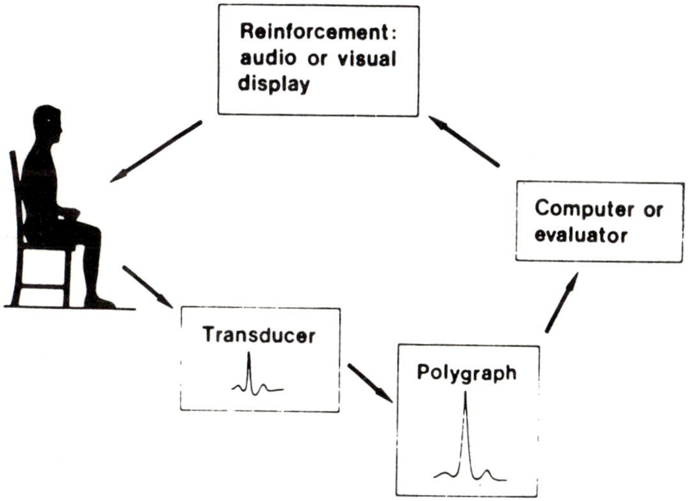

Figure 8.
The process of biofeedback. Very small electrical potentials are recorded with transducers (electrodes) and amplified (polygraph). The information is evaluated by a computer and presented to the subject as audio or visual feedback.

In our initial experiment (McCanne and Sandman 1974) we attempted to link control of heart rate to changes in attention or perception of environmental stimuli. Using an operant conditioning procedure (see McCanne and Sandman 1975) subjects were "shaped" to produce increases and decreases in their heart rate on cue. The cue was a light; when it was blue the subjects were required to increase their heart rate and when it was yellow they were to decrease their rate. A clock was automatically activated informing the subject of the amount of time his/her heart was above or below the criterion. Subjects were trained with this procedure for 6 consecutive days before they were tested for effects on attention. The tests of attention involved presenting digits at very brief exposures while subjects were reinforced for heart rate deceleration or acceleration. Consistent with earlier findings subjects perceived digits more accurately during reinforced heart rate deceleration. These data were among the first experimental demonstrations that self control of specific bodily processes could exert a discrete effect on the mind.

In a related experiment we (McCanne and Sandman 1976b) found that learned control of heart rate was related to increased accuracy of Rod-and Frame performance. Improvement of performance in this task requires the ability of subjects to ignore distracting information in order to align a rod to a vertical position. Accuracy (which is labeled field independence) has been related to the selectivity of attention. As such our findings lend further support to the relationship postulated between the cardiovascular system and attention.

However, these findings have other implications as well. As discussed earlier, field-independent and field-dependent subjects differ not only in perceptual style but also in terms of accessibility to information about their body. Field-independent subjects appear to have greater access to bodily states than field-dependent subjects and indeed some (e.g., Cohen 1967) have argued that performance of the Rod-and Frame is a function of this accessibility. Thus, in addition to indicating that control of the cardiovascular system may influence attention, it is also possible that such control will sensitize subjects to the state of their bodies. Thus in view of our earlier discussion these physiological changes, if they are persistent, may have clinical utility. Augmented sensitivity to bodily states may result in a richer perceptual and emotional life. Further research, aimed especially at examining the duration of these changes, is needed to establish the reliability of these findings.

Another paradigm was employed to examine the influence of learned

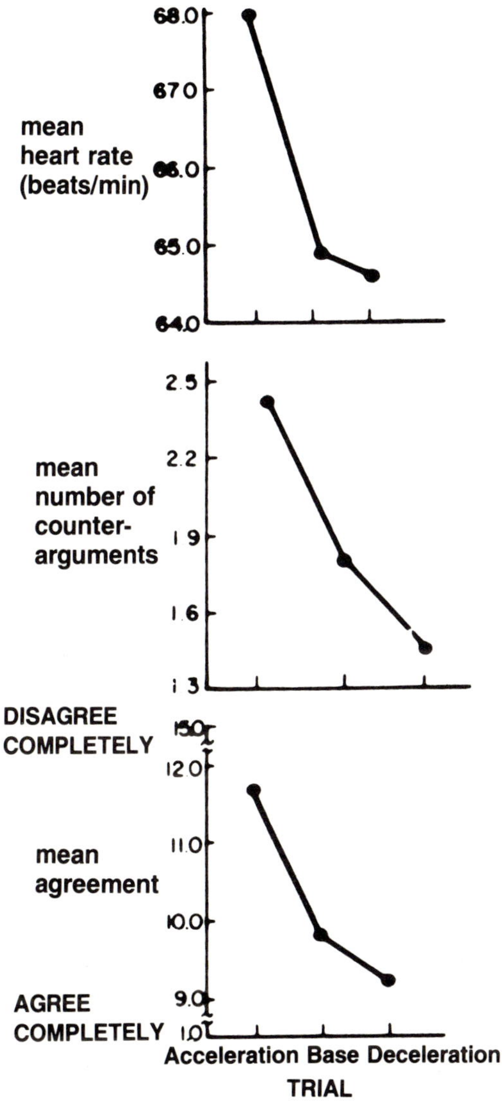

Figure 9.
The relationship among controlled heart rate, number of counterarguments and attitudes (From Cacioppo et al. 1978).

heart rate control on cognitive activity (Cacioppo, Sandman and Walker 1978). Resistance to persuasion is, in part, a function of the number of counterarguments subjects can generate to rebut an issue. The greater the number of reasons (counter-arguments) subjects develop to reject a message, the less likely they will be persuaded by the message. We hypothesized that controlled increases in heart rate would enhance cognitive activity. During elevated heart rate subjects should generate more counterarguments and be less susceptible to persuasion. Conversely, subjects should become more susceptible to persuasion during low heart rate since their "thinking" ability is comprised. Thus we believed by controlling heart rate we could influence attitudes. As in the previous experiment, subjects were trained to control their heart rate for several days with operant procedures prior to behavioral testing.

Figure 9 indicates that during reinforced accelerated heart rate the subjects generated more counterarguments (assessed after presentation of the message) and were less willing to endorse the persuasive message. However, during reinforced decelerated heart rate the subjects provided fewer counterarguments and were much more susceptible to persuasion. We believe this occurred because during high heart rate cognitive elaboration tends to be facilitated and self-convincing arguments can be generated against a persuasive message. However, during lowered heart rate our cognitive functioning gives way to environmental attention and we may tend to become a slave to the demands of the environment. Thus, with diminished cognitive activity we can be more accepting of the information we receive.

We have demonstrated that psychological activity is related to physiological activity. Further, we have indicated that access to the mind can be gained by controlling the body. We believe that these data are difficult to reconcile with views which ascribe all intellectual abilities solely to the brain. However, very little information is available regarding the impact of the body on the brain. The following studies are among the first to describe the influences of the heart on the brain.

INFLUENCES OF THE HEART ON THE BRAIN

We have assumed that the changes in behavior we observed were the result of influences of the heart on the brain. Although it is difficult to assess cause and effect relationships of this sort, we nevertheless con-

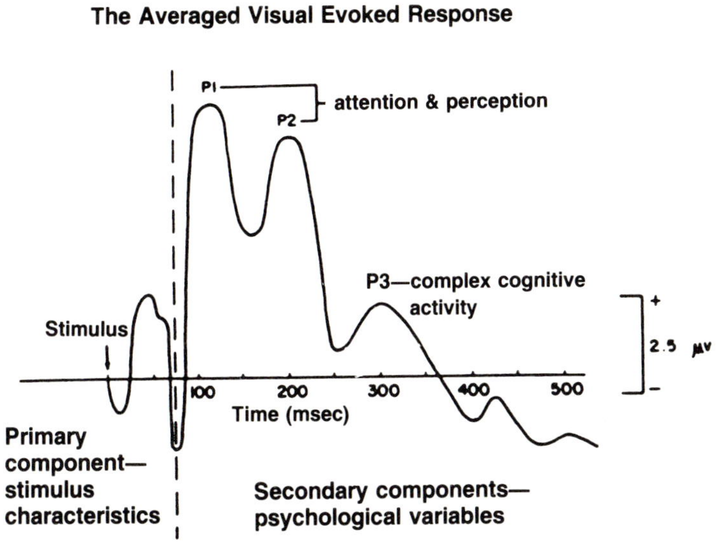

Figure 10.
The averaged visual evoked potential recorded in our laboratory from the occipital cortex.

ducted a series of studies which were identical in design to the behavioral ones, and were intended to determine the impact of the cardiovascular system on the electrical activity of the brain. In order to probe the influence of the heart on the brain we chose to study cortical averaged evoked potentials (AEP) (Walker and Sandman 1979). The AEP is electrical activity recorded from the brain which is time-locked to a specific stimulus. In order to obtain a visual evoked response, flashes of light are presented to a subject while the electroencephalogram (EEG) is measured. The electrocortical responses to each flash of light are summed by a computer and the activity which is not related to the light is randomly dispersed and equals approximately zero. The components of the wave which are evoked by the stimulus are then clearly identifiable against this background. The form of the AEP recorded in our laboratory is presented in Figure 10. As shown in the figure, different components have been associated with discrete behaviors.

The early aspect of the wave, the "primary response," is related to sensation and is usually unchanged by psychological or physiological interventions. The secondary components, P1 and P2 (occurring approximately 100 and 200 msec after the stimulus), are sensitive to changes in attention and perception. Large P1 and P2 waves are usually related to improved attentional or perceptual processing. The P3 wave (occurring approximately 300 msec after the stimulus) is related to more complex cognitive activity such as decision-making.

In our experiment brief flashes of light were presented to the subject during fast, slow and midrange heart rates (as in earlier experiments, Figure 4), while AEP's were recorded from the right and left hemispheres of the brain. The paradigm of the present study relates most directly to changes in P1 or P2, since the subjects were not required to think or make any behavioral response.

The results (illustrated in Figure 11) indicated that the heart exerted dramatic influences on the AEP's of the right but not the left hemisphere. Furthermore, the amplitudes of P1 and P2 were larger when flashes of

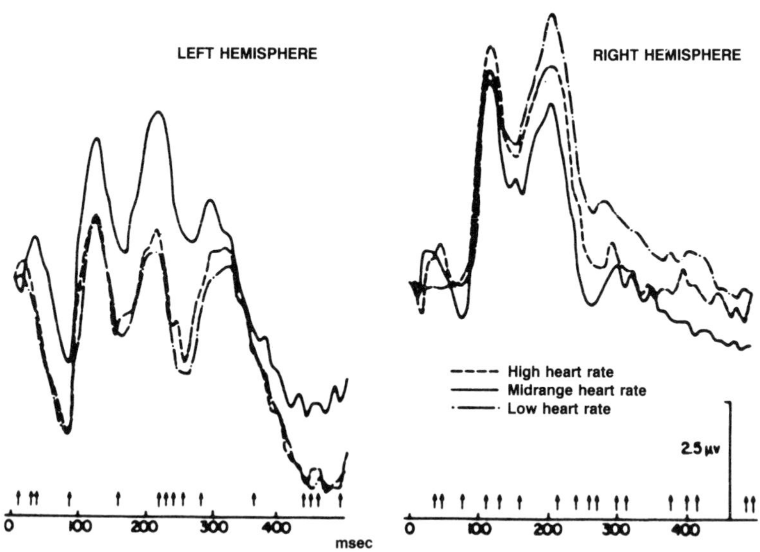

Figure 11.
The differential influence low, midrange and high heart rate on visual evoked potentials recorded from the left and right hemispheres.

light were presented during low heart rate than during high heart rate. Although it may be peculiar to the paradigm we used, it is apparent that the influence of the heart on the brain is lateralized. These findings are conceptually consistent with the growing body of literature which suggests that tasks requiring attention to the environment are associated with AEP's recorded from the right hemisphere (Dustman, Schenkenberg and Beck 1976) and with low heart rate (Lacey and Lacey 1974; Sandman et al. 1977). Thus the heart may influence attention processing by specifically affecting the right hemisphere. Further tests of the lateralized influences of the cardiovascular system have confirmed our initial report.

As illustrated in Figure 3, each ventricular pulse of the heart sends a bolus of blood rushing through the arteries. This bolus of blood is received as a transient shift in pressure and is reflected as a pulse pressure wave. At the peak of the wave (systolic pressure), pressure is the greatest and the baroreceptors increase their firing rate. During the lowest point of the wave (diastolic pressure) the baroreceptors are relatively quiescent. Since pulse pressure is intricately tied to the pumping action of the heart, systolic and diastolic pressure coincide with electrical components of the electrocardiogram (ECG). From Figure 4 it is apparent that diastolic pressure coincides with the early components of the ECG (P wave) and systolic pressure coincides with the T wave. Therefore, as with the earlier studies which examined the relation of heart rate, cardiac phase and perception, we chose to study the influence of transient changes in pulse pressure on the AEP (Walker and Sandman 1982). The paradigm was identical to the study of heart rate and AEP's (Walker and Sandman 1979) except pulse "peaks" (systolic pressure) and "valleys" (diastolic pressure) were used to trigger the stimuli. Since similar (but not identical) pressure changes are detected by the baroreceptor during low heart rate and diastolic pressure, and during high heart rate and systolic pressure we expected to observe similar influences on the brain in this study as with the study of heart rate. We reasoned further that the effects of pulse pressure on the brain were "time-locked," and displacement of stimulation in time may alter the impact of the heart on the brain. Therefore, we also synchronized the flashes of light with changes in pulses to the brain (occurring approximately 30 msec after carotid pulse changes) and to the finger (occurring approximately 180 msec after carotid pressure changes).

It is apparent from Figure 12 that changes in AEP coincide with changes in the carotid artery and the brain. When pulse pressure is low the amplitude of P1 is augmented only in the right hemisphere. This find-

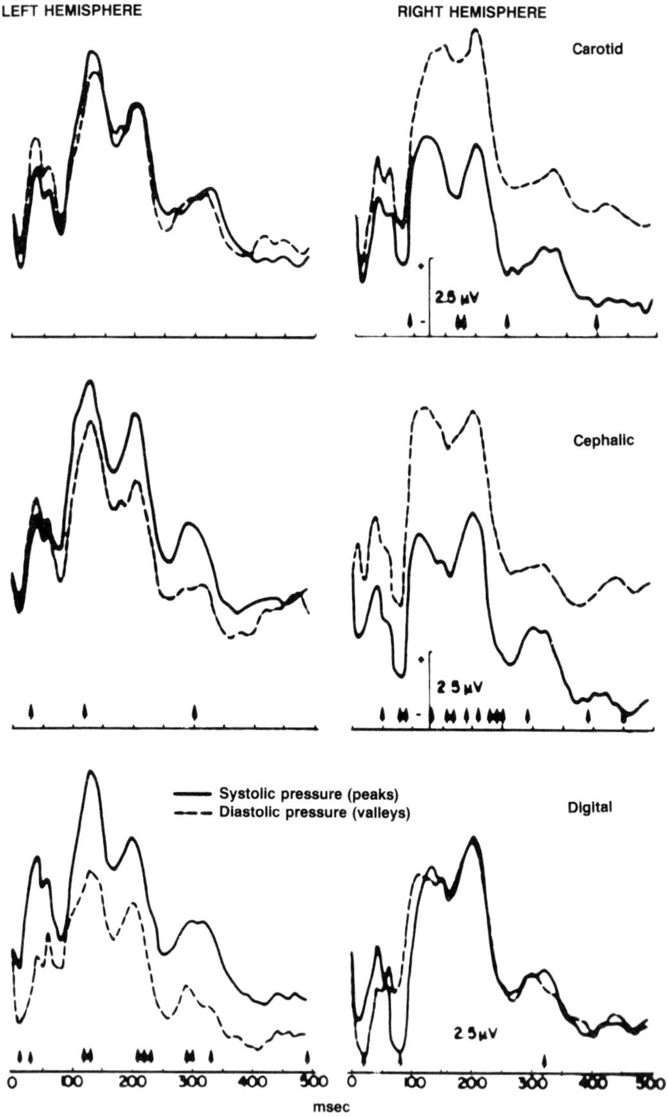

Figure 12.
Visual evoked potential recorded from the left and right hemisphere when stimulated during systolic and diastolic pressure recorded from the area of the carotid artery, the brain and peripherally.

ing is in accord with the data reported for heart rate. However, several differences in the AEP-associated change in heart rate and carotid pulse pressure were detected. Specifically, the primary component was diminished during low heart rate but enhanced during diastolic pressure, and P2 was enhanced during low heart rate but suppressed during diastolic pressure. These findings are consistent with the neurophysiological evidence suggesting that while similarities exist between change of rate and pulse pressure, each mechanism may operate independently. When stimulation was delayed approximately 180 msec, the changes in the right hemisphere associated carotid and cephalic pressure disappear. The impact of pulse pressure changes in the finger shifts to the left hemisphere. Further, as seen in Fig. 12, stimulation during diastolic pressure relates to augmented AEP's, while stimulation during diastolic pressure coincides with a diminished AEP. This pattern is opposite to that observed in the right hemisphere with stimulation during carotid and cephalic pulse pressure.

There are several implications of this series of experiments. First, it appears that the heart is "wired" to the brain in very specific ways (see Sandman, O'Halloran and Isenhart, 1984). Distinctive components of the AEP were related to the cardiovascular events (either changes in heart rate or pulse pressure) which controlled the stimuli. Thus the influence of the heart on the brain (and behavior) is not diffuse but highly specific and may exert a significant influence on consciousness. Fascinating support for the notion that the heart may "pulse" consciousness derives from a report by Oswald (1959). In an examination of after-images, Oswald discovered that after about 5 seconds some subjects reported that the images pulsated. With an ingenious procedure it was determined that the pulsating image was perfectly syncrhonized with heart rate. The shift of cardiovascular influence from the right to left hemisphere as a function of stimulation either during pulse changes in the carotid artery of following a delay suggests a finely tuned and possibly highly adaptive mechanism. Although purely speculative, these data suggest that the heart may "pulse" each hemisphere of the brain during each cardiac cycle.

It is tempting to conjecture that the heart's impact on consciousness or awareness is dynamic and fluctuates between liberating and suppressing the left and right side of the brain. It appears that not only may this control pertain to heart rate but also fluctuates during each beat of the heart. Thus cardiovascular influences on consciousness of the right and left hemisphere may vary from second-to-second and the ability of the organism to detect and react to the environment may be intimately tied to these mechanisms.

TABLE 1

The Putative Relationship Between Various Physiological Responses and Psychological Activity

PHYSIOLOGICAL ACTIVITY	PSYCHOLOGICAL ACTIVITY
Heart rate increases	Cognitive processing and problem solving
Heart rate decreases	Attention to environment
Muscle tension	Covert vocalization and thinking
EEG beta 	Vigilance
alpha 	Passive acceptance and relaxation
theta 	Problem solving and ecstasy
Increased blood in brain	Response to novel stimuli
Decreased blood in periphery	Response to stressful stimuli
Skin response (GSP) tonic 	Cognitive activity
phasic 	Emotional activity

OTHER RESPONSE SYSTEMS

Although the focus of this chapter has been the cardiovascular system, it is apparent from Table 1 that several physiological response systems have been related to psychological activity. Even though this list is far from exhaustive, the complexity of considering several physiological responses simultaneously is obvious. Nevertheless, organisms tend to respond in complex ways, and a more complete understanding of behavior will require the development of technologies for determining the influence of patterns of physiological response on behavior.

CONCLUSION

As mentioned in the first part of the chapter we have two brains, a left brain which is primarily verbal and logical and right brain which is primarily spatial and analogical. While obviously the two brains are connected, it appears that one side of the brain tends to dominate. The educational process in our culture appeals to, and possibly even develops, an overdependence on left-hemispheric domination of our mode of thinking. Curricula are designed to develop our verbal and logical skills, with minimal concern for alternative styles of thinking. This volume attests to the concern of educators about the noticeable intellectual limp associated with overemphasis on training one side of the brain. But how is our atrophied "other half" stimulated and developed?

The work done with physiological feedback may have implications for a holistic educational paradigm. The data from our experiments suggest that the mind, as ephemeral and undefinable as it is, develops from the interaction between the brain and the body. As reviewed earlier, the brain receives a contiunual flow of information from the body. This information is an important mediator between the environment and the organism, and is a critical factor in a developing definition of the mind or intelligence. It appears unwise to dismiss the interaction between central and autonomic nervous system activity as purely homeostatic and as extraneous to the process of education. Although we have only unveiled a small portion of the picture, our data suggest that the body (heart) exerts a "time-locked" and lateralized impact on the brain. Further, we indicated that under certain circumstances the heart may provide access to the right hemisphere.

The technology for controlling physiological responses is well developed. Although there are undoubtedly several procedures for discretely stimulating cerebral hemispheric activity, it is clear that one possible approach may be related to developing refined control of the body. As such, physiological techniques and procedures for self control may have important implications for the development of holistic concepts of education and learning.

REFERENCES

Baker, W.M.; Sandman, C.A.; and Pepinsky, H.P. 1975. Affectivity of task rehearsal time and physiological response. *Journal of Abnormal Psychology* 84:539.

Bard, P. 1934. On emotional expression after decortication with some remarks on certain theoretical views. Parts I and II., *Psychological Review* 41:309, 424.

Birren, J.; Cardon, P.; and Phillips, S. 1963. Reaction time as a function of the cardiac cycle in young adults. *Science* 140: 195.

Bonvallet, M.; Dell, P.; and Hiebel, B. 1954. Tonus sympathetique et activite electrique corticale. *Electroencephalography and Clinical Neurophysiology* 6:119.

Cacioppo, J.T., and Sandman, C.A. 1978. Physiological differentiation of sensory and cognitive tasks as a function of warning, processing demands and reported unpleasantness. *Biological Psychology* 6:181.

Cacioppo, J.T.; Sandman, C.A.; and Walker, B.B. 1978. The effects of operant heart rate conditioning on cognitive elaboration and attitude change. *Psychophysiology* 15:330.

Calloway, E., and Layne, R. 1964. Interaction between the visual evoked response and two spontaneous biological rhythms: The EEG alpha cycle and the cardiac arousal cycle. *Annals of the New York Academy of Sciences* 112:424.

Cannon, W.B. 1929. *Bodily changes in pain, hunger, fear and rage: An account of recent researches into the function of emotional excitement.* New York: Appleton.

Davis, R.C. 1957. Response patterns. *Transactions of the New York Academy of Sciences.* 19:731.

Delfini, L., and Campos, J. 1972. Signal detection and the "cardiac arousal cycle." *Psychophysiology* 9:484.

Duncan-Johnson, C., and Coles, M. 1974. Heart rate and disjunctive reaction time: The effects of discrimination requirements. *Journal of Experimental Psychology* 103:1160.

Dustman, R.E.; Schenkenberg, T.; and Beck, E.C. 1976. The development of the evoked response as a diagnostic and evaluative procedure. In *Developmental psychophysiology of mental retardation*, ed. R. Karrer. Springfield: C.C. Thomas.

Elliott, R., and Graf, V. 1972. Visual sensitivity as a function of phase of cardiac cycle. *Psychophysiology* 9:357.

Hare, R.; Wood, K.; Britain, S.; and Shadman, J. 1970. Autonomic responses to affective visual stimulation. *Psychophysiology* 7:408.

Humphrey, D.R. 1967. Neuronal activity in the medulla oblongata of cat evoked by stimulation of the carotid sinus nerve. In *Baroreceptors and hypertension*, ed. P. Kedzi. New York: Pergamon Press.

Ingvar, D.H. 1972. Patterns of thought recorded in the brain. *Totus Homo* 4:98.

Jackson, J.H. 1958. Evolution and dissolution of the nervous system. In *Selected writing of John Hughlings Jackson,* ed. J. Taylor. New York: Basic Books.

James, W. 1892. *Psychology.* New York: Henry Holt.

Kaiser, D.N., and Sandman, C.A. 1975. Physiological patterns accompanying complex problem solving during warning and non-warning conditions. *Journal of Comparative and Physiological Psychology* 89:357.

Lacey, B.C., and Lacey, J.I. 1974. Studies of heart rate and other bodily processes in sensorimotor behavior. In *Cardiovascular psychophysiology*, eds. P.A. Obrist, A.H. Black, J. Brener, and L.V. DiCara. Chicago: Aldine.

Lacey, J.I. 1967. Somatic response patterning and stress: Some revision of activation theory. In *Psychological stress: Issues in research*, eds. M.H. Appley and R. Trumbull. New York: Appleton.

Lacey, J.I., and Lacey, B.C. 1970. Some autonomic-central nervous system interrelationships. In *Physiological correlates of emotion*, ed. P. Black. New York: Academic Press.

Lacey, J.I.; Kagan, J.; Lacey, B.C.; and Moss, H. 1963. The visceral level: Situational determinants and behavioral correlates of autonomic response patterns. In *Expression of the emotions in man*, ed. P.H. Knapp. New York: International Universities Press.

Libby, W.L.; Lacey, B.C.; and Lacey, J.I. 1973. Pupillary and cardiac activity during visual attention. *Psychophysiology* 10:270.

Lindsley, D. 1969. Average evoked potentials—achievements, failures and prospects. In *Average evoked potentials: Methods, results and evaluation,* eds. E. Donchin and D. Lindsley. Washington, DC: NASA.

Mark, V.H., and Ervin, F.R. 1970. *Violence and the brain.* New York: Harper & Row.

McCanne, T.R., and Sandman, C.A. 1974. Instrumental heart rate responses and visual perception: A preliminary study. *Psychophysiology* 11:283.

________. 1975. Determinants of human operant heart-rate conditioning: A systematic investigation of several methodological issues. *Journal of Comparative and Physiological Psychology* 88:609.

________. 1976a. Human operant heart rate conditioning: The importance of individual differences. *Psychological Bulletin* 83:587.

________. 1976b. Operant autonomic conditioning and rod-and-frame test performance. *Journal of Personality and Social Psychology* 34:821.

Miller, N.E. 1969. Learning of visceral and glandular responses. *Science* 163:434.

Obrist, P.A.; Webb, R.A.; and Sutterer, J.R. 1969. Heart rate and somatic changes during aversive conditioning and a simple reaction time task. *Psychophysiology* 5:696.

Obrist, P.A.; Light, K.C.; McCubbin, J.A.; Hunchenson, J.S.; and Hoffer, J.L. 1979. Pulse transit time: Relationship to blood pressure and myocardial performance. *Psychophysiology* 16:292.

Oswald, I. 1959. A case of fluctuation of awareness with the pulse. *Quarterly Journal of Experimental Psychology* 11:45.

Sandman, C.A. 1971. Psychophysiological parameters of emotion. Ph.D. diss., Louisiana State University.

________. 1975. Physiological responses during escape and non-escape from stress in field indpendence and field dependent subjects. *Biological Psychology* 2:205.

Sandman, C.A.; O'Halloran, J.P.; and Isenhart, R. 1984. Is there an evoked vascular response? *Science.*

Sandman, C.A.; McCanne, T.R.; Kaiser, D.N.; and Diamond, B. 1977. Heart rate and cardiac phase influences on visual perception. *Journal of Comparative and Physiological Psychology* 91:189.

Smith, R.E., and Pearce, J.W. 1961. Microelectrode recordings from the region of the nucleus solitarius in the cat. *Canadian Journal of Biochemical Physiology* 39:933.

Sperry, R.W. 1974. Lateral specialization of cerebral function in the surgically separated hemispheres. In *The Psychophysiology of thinking*, eds. F.J. McGuigan and R.A. Schoonover. New York: Academic Press.

Thompson, L.W. and Botwinick, J. 1970. Stimulation in different phases of the cardiac cycle and reaction time. *Psychophysiology* 7:57.

Tursky, B.; Schwartz, G.E.; and Crider, A. 1970. Differential patterns of heart rate and skin resistance during a digital transformation task. *Journal of Experimental Psychology* 83:451.

Walker, B.B., and Sandman, C.A. 1977. Physiological response patterns in ulcer patients: Phasic and tonic components of the electrogastrogram. *Psychophysiology* 14:393.

———. 1979. Relationship of heart rate on the visual evoked potential. *Journal of Comparative and Physiological Psychology* 93:717.

———. 1982. Visual evoked potentials change as heart rate and carotid pressure change. *Psychophysiology* 19:520.

Chapter 4

The Utility of Psychophysiological Measures for Reading Research

by Victor M. Rentel, Christine Pappas, and Barbara Pettegrew

INTRODUCTION

Increasingly, psychophysiological measures of reading activity have been employed by researchers in their efforts to understand this commonplace but complex skill. A literature of sufficient quality and size has emerged from this research to permit a tentative, initial appraisal of the utility of such measures for reading research. Roughly, these measures may be categorized as follows: (a) electroencephlographic (EEG) measures such as percentage or amplitude of brain waves in specified frequency bands, averaged evoked potentials (AEP), event related potentials (ERPs) and contingent negative variation (CNV); (b) cardiovascular measures such as heart rate (HR) and blood pressure (BP); (c) blood flow measures such as regional cerebral blood flow (rCBF), isotopic measures of brain parameters such as brain tomography (BT) and electrical stimulation mapping (ESM). Other psychophysiological measures frequently employed in reading research such as oculograms and eye-movement photography as well as electrodermal measures such as galvanic skin response have been reviewed extensively elsewhere and thus will not be included in this appraisal (Just and Carpenter 1980; Levy-Schoen and O'Regan 1979; McConkie et al. 1979). Our review of the utility of these psychophysiological measures in reading research will extend to their use in research on such factors as attention, memory, lateralization, and other constructs typically thought to be necessary aspects of reading. Our appraisal, too, will venture away from the standard research literature on reading to draw upon the experimental literature in psychology, psychobiology, and learning disabilities. Before doing so, however, we will state briefly several basic assumptions about the measurement of reading.

Any system of measurement requires clear and consistent definitions of the things being counted. Reading is, of course, the result of many complex cognitive activities, some of which are well established as theoretically defensible constructs in cognitive theory while others lack such reassuring backing. Reading, presumably, also is an extension of more basic linguistic capabilities, distinct not just visually, but adapted nicely to the unique conventions of written discourse. Linguistic science has made remarkable advances in the last two decades, but like cognitive theory, linguistic theory has few universally accepted constructs, and many that are the subject of intense, lively, scientific debate. In short, both evidence and backing for many hypothesized cognitive and linguistic attributes of reading remain at issue; a state of affairs not likely to yield clear and consistent definitions. It follows, then, that attempts to measure attributes of reading ability will be crude, sometimes questionable, and nearly always subject to intense controversy and criticism.

The development of technologically sophisticated new techniques for studying both physiological and brain functions with the capability to relate them to behavior has given researchers opportunities to observe heretofore opague activities of the intact body and brain under conditions where the relationship between brain changes, physiological changes, specific events and the behavioral responses to them are discernable. For example, technology has made it possible to study the metabolic activity of neurons in the brain through isotopic blood flow. Other procedures are within reach for measuring metabolic changes such as glucose utilization at specific brain sites during specific tasks. Each technique requires explicit, well-designed behavioral tasks to isolate corresponding alterations in brain function and locations within the brain. Each technique, of course, has limitations that must be considered when interpreting these measures and the data yielded by them. To realize the full potential of these psychophysiological measures in reading research, their dazzling technological sophistication must not numb our critical awareness of these limitations. We have written the chapter in this spirit. We have organized the chapter as follows. In each section we will define a hypothetical construct and its relationship to reading. Then we will consider how a variety of psychophysiological measures relate to each construct, summarizing rebuttals and alternative accounts of what these measures imply about each construct. In a final section, we will state our conclusions about the utility of these measures for reading research.

HEART RATE

The notion that attention may be related to cardiovascular activity was first advanced by Lacey (1959). He noted that across a wide variety of tasks and stimuli, heart rate decelerated when subjects attended to events in their immediate environment. Conversely, cognitive activity requiring the rejection of external stimuli produced accelerated heart rates. Lacey observed that other physiological measures taken concurrently over the same tasks and stimuli correlated positively, negatively, or not at all with heart rate. To characterize this configuration of assorted somatic response parameters, Lacey coined the phrase "directional fractionation," implying that different components of a somatic response pattern have their own unique specificity rather than a correlated directionality. These findings run counter to traditional expectations that stimulation should produce correlated physiological effects, and paradoxically, cardiac deceleration, a parasympathetic effect, rather than acceleration, the expected sympathetic effect (Obrist 1976).

The Laceys (1974) explained these effects as a function of baroreceptor feedback. The cardiovascular system contains detectors—baroreceptors—that inform the central nervous system about blood pressure. The Laceys argued that blood pressure affects the central nervous system through the baroreceptors, whose afferents fire at rates reflective of blood pressure and heart rate. These afferents activate systems in the brain stem, which in turn act on the cortex, the motor, and the autonomic systems, affecting their levels of activity, responsiveness, and duration (Lacey 1967; Lacey et al. 1963; Lacey and Lacey 1974; Lacey and Lacey 1978). According to the Laceys, " . . . attention and response intention can be explained as the consequence of the neurophysiological fact that the increases in blood pressure and heart rate determine the frequency of impulses along the visceral afferent feedback pathways from the baroreceptors of the carotid sinus, aortic arch, and other structures (Lacey and Lacey 1974, 539)." This feedback stimulates central processes that increase vagal tone, which then slows the heart and thus reduces blood pressure. As blood pressure is reduced, the excitatory influence of the baroreceptors on central processes is reduced, vagal tone is inhibited, and the organism theoretically is better prepared to respond.

Neither the Laceys' attention construct nor their physiological explanation of heart-rate deceleration immediately preceding reaction-time tasks has escaped criticism. Hahn (1973), for example, argued that a more convincing test of the "attention" hypothesis would require a demonstration that heart rate instrumentally affects information intake or "attention" to the external environment. McCanne and Sandman (1974) attempted such a test and found that subjects trained to raise and lower their heart rates could recognize tachistoscopically presented stimuli more often during deceleration than during heart-rate acceleration. Another criticism of the Laceys' explanation comes from Obrist (1968) and Obrist et al. (1974) who argued that heart-rate variability merely indicates metabolic demand—that the heart beats faster to supply blood to tissues that need it. To Obrist's way of thinking, heart-rate deceleration only reflects quiescent muscle tissue demand, while acceleration reflects muscle tension that typically accompanies solving a mental problem, and thus higher somatic demand. However, regardless of how heart rate may be coupled to somatic demand, somatic coupling does not rule out the possibility that heart rate may reflect other factors as well, a conclusion reached by Obrist (1981) recently.

Despite substantial evidence indicating a strong relationship between heart rate and somatomotor activity, still there are inconsistencies that somatic coupling cannot explain. For example, there are data (Lawler, Obrist and Lawler 1976) indicating that while phasic increases in heart rate were affected by incentives and response certainty, somatomotor activity was not. Other data (Coles and Duncan-Johnson 1975) indicated that heart-rate changes were better indicators of decision making and information processing than were measures of somatomotor activity. Other works suggests a dissociation of tonic heart rate levels from somatomotor activity (Engle, Gottlieb and Hayhurst 1976; Elliot 1974, 1975; Obrist et al. 1975). Finally, there are data suggesting phasic decreases in heart rate facilitated a range of somatomotor activities: finger tapping (Obrist, Webb, and Sutterer 1969) eyeblink (Bohlin and Graham 1977) and monosynaptic leg reflexes (Brunia 1979). Quite obviously, a somatic account of these heart-rate findings would be untenable.

Not just the "heart-rate" aspects of the Laceys' attention hypothesis have been criticized. Central to their theory is the activity of the baroreceptors. Green (1980), in an extensive review of literature on the relationships between blood pressure, baroreceptor activity, and central nervous system activity, argued that the Laceys' physiological hypothesis implies that increases and decreases in blood pressure and related baroreceptor activity should respectively inhibit and excite central nervous system processes. From his review, Green concluded that animal studies indicate blood pressure and baroreceptor activity do influence central nervous system activity, but he questions the applicability of this evidence to humans. Drawing on a small corpus of studies where baroreceptor afferent activity in humans has been investigated, Green concluded that the evidence does not support the Laceys' physiological hypothesis. Green relied heavily on work by Brooks et al. (1978), and on clinical studies of hypertensive patients who, through a surgical implant, are able to regulate baroreceptor afferent activity (Bilgutay and Lillehei 1965; Brest, Weiner and Bachrach 1972; Epstein et al. 1969; Tuckman, Reich and Lyon 1968). Both sets of studies seemed to pose problems for the Laceys' attention hypothesis. Data from Brooks et al. (1978) indicated that during mental arithmetic problems, a task requiring rejection of the environment, baroreflex sensitivity decreased, which, according to the Laceys' hypothesis, is contrary to expectations. Likewise, the clinical data reviewed by Green suggested that direct stimulation of baroreceptors of the carotid sinus produced no changes in alertness associated with stimulation. Green concluded that the studies he reviewed offered little support for the Laceys' physiological hypothesis.

Previous reviews (Carroll and Anastasiades 1978; Elliot 1972; Obrist, 1976) of the Laceys' attention hypothesis were equally pessimistic. Elliot (1972) argued that relatively direct tests of the relationship between heart rate and attention provided only equivocal support for the hypothesis. In addition, basic terms in the hypothesis such as attention, environmental intake and environmental rejection lack sufficiently clear and independent definition to permit adequate prediction. These assessments were echoed by Carroll and Anastasiades (1978), who not only concluded that interpretation of heart rate data often has rested on internal, unobservable constructs, but that existing data generally do not support the hypothesis.

According to Hassett (1978), even the Laceys would accept the view that heart rate is primarily an indication of metabolic demand. The question is, what else does heart rate measure? Obrist (1976) also makes situational distinctions relating to heart rate. During passive coping situations, where a person has no control of the environment, cardiovascular increases and decreases covary with somatic responses via cardiac-somatic coupling. However, in an active coping situation, where a person has some control or influence over the environment, heart rate increases occur that do not directly reflect somatic activity. Critical tests explaining mechanisms underlying the relationships between heart rate, baroreceptor feedback, central nervous system activity, and behavior thus far have not been devised. Despite rather interesting new evidence that average evoked potentials in the right and left hemispheres are related differentially to normal heart-rate fluctuations (Walker and Sandman 1979) as well as to diastolic and systolic blood pressure (Walker and Sandman 1982), these data still do not explain the relationships between behavior, cardiovascular activity, and central nervous system processes. They simply are consistent with the Laceys' baroreceptor feedback hypothesis and suggest that hemispheric specialization must be incorporated into explanations of baroreceptor influences on central processes. The Laceys' hypothesis remains just that, a provocative hypothetical construct that existing data support equivocally at best.

Given the important position that the construct of attention occupies in several current reading theories (LaBerge and Samuels 1977; Schneider and Shiffrin 1977), and in the learning disability literature (Kinsbourne and Caplan 1979; Knights and Bakker 1976), it is surprising how little use has been made of heart rate to assess attentional deficits in reading disabled children. In one study that did use heart rate and heart-rate variability as indices of attention in readers, Levine (1976) compared normals with two groups of deficient readers, one defined as having primary reading deficiencies and the other as having secondary reading deficiencies (Rabinovitch et al. 1954).

Primary reading deficiency hypothetically stems from an underlying neurological or genetic source while secondary deficiency is predicated on nonorganic educational, psychological, or environmental origins. Leaving aside the definitional ambiguity and circularity of this classification (Rutter 1978), Levine found that when subjects were presented with auditory and visual stimulus pairs for both intra- and inter-sensory conditions requiring paired and serial verbal recall, heart-rate deceleration occurred only for the "normal" reading group during stimulus presentation. Heart-rate variability, a different heart-rate measure employed by Levine, and, like heart rate, thought to be related to attention (Porges

1972), remained essentially stable during stimulus onset for the normal group, but increased significantly during recall. For the secondary deficiency group, heart-rate deceleration, as noted above, did not occur during stimulus presentation. But, the secondary group's heart-rate variability, unlike the normal group's which remained essentially stable during onset, decreased during stimulus presentation, though, like that of normal readers, increased significantly during recall. For the primary deficiency group, neither heart-rate deceleration nor changes in heart-rate variability were observed during stimulus presentation and recall.

It is important to note at this point that Levine employed one additional measure of cognitive activity, galvanic skin response. These findings, along with those for heart rate and heart rate variability, together comprised the data from which Levine drew her conclusions. Levine interpreted the absence of heart-rate deceleration in deficient readers as an indication of flawed attentional capabilities. Changes in heart-rate variability across tasks were common for the normal reading group, but were not observed for the primary reading group. For the secondary reading group, heart-rate variability did not change significantly across tasks. Levine attributed the secondary group's decrease in heart-rate variability at stimulus onset to emotional stress which, she reasoned, led to excessive attention at the time of onset, thus preventing early efficient cognitive processing during recall as seen in this group's pattern of heart-rate variability. The primary group, on the other hand, simply failed to attend at any significant level at stimulus onset, preventing later cognitive processing altogether for them. Galvanic skin response data indicated that all three groups of readers were engaged in processing at the time of recall, but that only normal readers seemed able to adjust cognitive activity to the character of the tasks themselves.

Levine went on to theorize that cardiovascular changes not explained fully by somatic demand associated with physical work were related to levels of oxygen required for cognitive "work" (Pribram and McGuinness 1975) supplied to cortical centers by large biosystems switching to anaerobic modes during intensive mental activity. She hypothesized that these biosystems may be implicated in the reading difficulties of poor readers.

Since Levine's explanation rests heavily on the Pribram and McGuinness (1975) account of attentional mechanisms, a brief summary of their notions is appropriate before assessing Levine's conclusions. Pribram and McGuinness attempted to reconcile contradictions and to accomodate both Obrist's cardiac-somatic coupling hypothesis and the Laceys' attention hypothesis in a model of attention incorporating three separate but interacting component systems: "arousal," a phasic physiological response to stimulation; "activation," a tonic physiological readiness to respond; and "effort," a system that coordinates arousal and activation. Reviewing both neurophysiological and psychological evidence for the construct of "attention," Pribram and McGuinness explained the relationships between behavior, central nervous system processes, and heart-rate changes as follows. They argued that activation and arousal may operate separately or successively depending on task demands. During categorizing tasks, for example, arousal precedes activation but during reasoning tasks, activation precedes arousal. Where neither reasoning nor categorizing are required by a task, arousal and activation are coupled. When the coordination of activation and arousal are necessary, such as during a reasoning or a categorizing task, heart-rate acceleration reflects the effort involved in centrally representing the requirements of the task. In these circumstances, stimulus intake must alternate with concentration. During stimulus intake, heart rate is under sympathetic control, resulting in an initial phasic heart-rate acceleration varying in magnitude with stimulus intensity. This initial change is followed by heart-rate deceleration stemming from vagal control whose function is to stabilize the system. These rate changes prepare the somatic system to initiate an action. During a categorizing task, this vigilance or "readiness" phase is extended. Extraneous movements are eliminated, resulting in further deceleration. When a response—such as a choice in a categorizing task—is initiated, heart rate comes under control of the somatomotor system, the motor response determining tonic heart-rate acceleration.

If the task is constructed as a reasoning problem, a different course of events occurs. Activation precedes arousal and the emphasis is on which response to produce, thus reversing the somatomotor and cardiovascular relationship. Highly refined changes in response and constant shifts between relevant stimuli are characteristic of reasoning. These changes are accompanied by both isotonic and isometric muscle activation (Berdina et al. 1972) and are responsible for increases in blood flow and heart rate. Thus, the locus of demand for effort in reasoning tasks differs from that in categorizing tasks, with the course of the physiological response depending on how the task is constructed.

Very distinct patterns of response emerge from two decades of research on heart rate—those associated with control conditions and those connected with various response dimensions (Somsen, Van der Molen and Orlebeke 1983). Clearly, a very complicated relationship exists between task parameters and heart-rate components. It is doubtful that heart rate deceleration or acceleration reflect a simple linear relationship between attention or cognition and cardiovascular processes. Until it becomes clear just what underlying processes elicit various components of heart rate and blood pressure, conclusions about the cardiovascular relationship to attention must be viewed with some caution. Without a clear connection between factors that influence or are influenced by heart rate, it follows that, at the present time, cardiovascular measures will add little to our understanding of reading disability.

ELECTROENCEPHALOGRAPHIC MEASURES

Various facets of attention have been probed using components of electroencephalographic (EEG) waves as measures. "Alpha blocking" or alpha attenuation is one of the more traditional EEG measures. This procedure involves an analysis of amplitude decreases among spontaneous alpha waves (8–13 Hz) during stimulus presentation and/or task performance. Berger (1929) first described and constrasted spontaneous brain rhythms: *alpha* waves (around 10 Hz) were associated with a state of relaxed wakefulness; *beta* waves (higher frequency) appeared to accompany states of relative alertness. Through the years, many investigators have observed that a simple, inverted, U-shaped function describes the relationship between attention and alpha activity (1). As "attending" increases, alpha activity attenuates; as "attending" decreases, alpha activity heightens. As observed above, learning disabled children often are described as disractible and inattentive. Not surprisingly, EEG measures have been employed to examine attention disorders arising from subtle anomalies in brain function. Generally speaking, psychological and most neurological measures are not sufficiently sensitive to tease out these subtleties. But many diagnostically useful features of the EEG can now be discerned through computer methods that permit reliable quantification of brain functions associated with cognitive processes, learning, and memory. Quantitative neurometric data from carefully defined populations now permit rather sophisticated, objective, operational classification of many disorders that previous schemes handled inadequately at best (John et. al. 1977).

Just how complex these classification issues are can be illustrated in a study that attempted to compare learning disabled children with normal children where it was assumed that alpha attenuation would reveal attention differences between the two groups (Fuller 1977). Fuller's findings indicated that overall EEG alpha activity for the normal group attenuated more than that of the learning disabled group. Such a finding suggests the possibility of attention deficits in the learning disabled population. However, three levels of task were incorporated in the experiment, and in only one task were there significant differences in alpha attenuation between the learning disabled and normal groups. On the other two tasks, considerable overlap in the scores of the two groups occurred, producing a finding of no significant differences. Thus, it is not clear whether tasks, attention disorders, or the assumed relationship between alpha attenuation and attention are at issue.

Individual differences in alpha density are commonplace (Orne and Wilson 1977). Consider the two studies that follow. Paskewitz and Orne (1973) predicted that anticipation of electric shock should induce concern, fear, and apprehension in subjects that would lead to attenuation of alpha. Alpha attenuation, however, did not occur and the data failed to support a relationship between arousal and alpha density. Instead, some subjects increased alpha, others decreased alpha, and some evidenced no response to the stimulus. Reevaluation of this shock experiment demonstrated that group means masked these individual differences, differences that remained consistent within individual subjects (Orne and Wilson 1977).

Data from a second experiment (Paskewitz and Orne 1973) produced similar findings regarding individual differences. Subjects counted backwards, followed by a task that required them to subtract in a descending order. Differences were not attributable to success or speed in these tasks. Subjects who blocked alpha while counting backwards also did so in the more difficult descending subtraction task; subjects who enhanced alpha on the counting task also increased alpha on the subtraction task. As Orne and Wilson (1977) observed, many assumptions about the relationship between activation and arousal as reflected in alph density are questionable. Moreover, systematic individual differences must be considered in any experiment employing alpha as a dependent measure.

Another common procedure employing EEG components involves measuring relative differences in EEG activity between the hemispheres while subjects perform verbal-analytical and visuospatial categorizing tasks. Using this procedure, Galin and Ornstein (1972) devised an index of laterized function by calculating a power ratio for the hemispheres across a wide range of frequency bands (1-35 hz.). Recording from parietal and temporal sites in normal, right-handed adults, they found asymmetrical electrical activity for verbal and spatial tasks. As hypothesized, the ratio of right to left hemisphere power was greater during verbal-analytic tasks than during visuo-spatial tasks. In this and later works (Doyle, Ornstein and Galin 1974; Galin 1979; Galin and Ellis 1975; Ornstein and Galin 1976), most task-specific activity has been associated with the alpha band (8–13 Hz.), providing support for the use of alpha in EEG studies of hemispheric asymmetry.

Studies focusing on alpha rhythm distribution in the hemispheres assume that relative suppression of alpha indicates increased information processing in that hemisphere. Within this framework, several studies report more alpha activity in the right hemisphere during verbal-analytic tasks (Morgan, Macdonald and Hilgard 1974; Morgan, McDonald and Macdonald 1971; Robins and McAdams 1974), but investigations of children, or of individuals engaged in more complex language-cognitive tasks like reading, indicate more complicated patterns of activity. For example, a study by Cole and Cummings (1977) investigated alpha differences among 4 to 6 year-old children, reporting increases in left-hemipshere alpha as children watched a silent cartoon film over that recorded when they listened to a story read aloud to them. Presumably, alpha inversely indexes information processing: increased alpha should predict reduced information processing and vice versa. On this basis, listening to a story requires greater left-hemisphere activity than viewing a story, thus modality and task appear to interact. Similarly, a study by Kraft (1976) recorded bilateral alpha rhythm in 6 to 8 year-old children during several cognitive tasks including silent reading. By comparing alpha power ratios over right and left hemispheres between the initial period when subjects were silently reading a passage and a subsequent period when subjects were thinking about comprehension questions concerning the passage, Kraft detecting a shift pattern from right-hemisphere activity during the silent reading phase to left-hemisphere activity during the "reflection" phase. These findings suggest that different aspects of performance during reading involve bilateral activity, with both hemispheres contributing to the overall performance.

It would be misleading to suggest that general agreement exists regarding what cognitive processes and functions alpha indexes (Gevins et al. 1979). Differences have been observed between sensory modalities, scalp sites, tasks, conditions, and subjects. Nor can it be said that brain mechanisms underlying bilateral changes in alpha are particularly well understood (Galin, Johnstone and Herron 1977). Brainstem and thalamic processes may be involved in lateralized alpha-level fluctuations as well as inhibition from the brainstem or the corpus callosum (Galin et al. 1977). In short, it is not yet possible to distinguish among various classes of bilateral alpha change, nor to specify mechanisms underlying such change. (For more extensive critiques of bilateral functions and processes, see Chapter 2).

Contingent negative variation (CNV) is another EEG correlate that has attracted interest as a potential indicator of sources of reading disability. Contingent negative variation refers to slow changes in brain electrical potential shifting from positive to negative. It is thought to reflect readiness of the brain for processing (Hillyard 1973; Pribram and McGuinness 1975). In situations where responses must be serially organized, such as in a reaction time task, the first input alerts the subject to get ready to respond to the second signal. During the interval between signals, slow changes in brain electrical activity have been observed (Walter et al. 1964). At the end of negativity, a sharp positive spike or deflection is observed. The slow negative potential thus is thought to indicate expectancy or readiness for processing. As is typical of other EEG components, CNV also is difficult to interpret unambiguously.

The difficulty is illustrated by the following reaction-time experiment (Grunewald-Zuberier et al. 1978) in which matched samples of normal 11 and 12 year-olds with varying ability to concentrate were compared on the basis of CNV, evoked potentials, wave forms elicited by precisely defined stimuli, and alpha attenuation. This study attempted to determine the extent to which these three measures discriminated differences between attention and concenration. There were no direct and dependent relationships observed during the interstimulus interval between alpha attenuation and CNV, and it appeared that each was functionally related to tasks. In addition, each measure varied significantly as a function of attention differences among the three groups of subjects.

Tecce (1972) contends that three types of negative potentials interact depending on the characteristics of an experiment. The first reflects variation attributable to expectancy or attention; the second indicates motor readiness signaling; and the third suggests spontaneous shifts which as yet have not been linked to task dimensions but may reflect individual differences. Or, the sites at which CNVs or transcortical negative variations are produced may reflect local configurations of brain strata maintaining a readiness for processing (Hillyard 1973). Thus, as indicated earlier, CNV should not be considered a unitary phenomenon indicative of a given psychological state or reflecting only one attribute of performance (Weinberg, Michalewski and Koopman 1976).

The 40-Hz frequency range has been another EEG correlate of interest to researchers probing the nature of reading disability. Sheer (1976) has observed a consistent relationship between 40-Hz rhythms and the acquisition period in learning. He argues that the 40-Hz rhythm indicates attention to input stimuli. His account of this mechanism asserts that the 40-Hz signal is related to successive repeated stimulation of a limited number of cells for a brief time at a constant frequency. This repeated stimulation creates negative feedback or inhibitory excitation that serves to focus arousal and provide autonomic control over excitation during problem solving (Spydell and Sheer 1982). Negative feedback depresses synapses that are weakly excited and sharpens the focus of attention. Behaviorally, the result is a sharpening of attention to relevant stimuli and a reduction of responses to extraneous stimuli. Sheer contends that deficits in focused arousal, that is, the absence of selective facilitation of attention, may account for learning difficulties in children who cannot attend to tasks. Sheer noted significant increases in the 40-Hz signal in the left and right parietal leads for a normal group of subjects, but not for two learning-disabled groups. Sheer concluded that the absence of 40-Hz rhythms in the learning disabled groups indicated their inability to focus arousal, which, in turn, affected their ability to maintain information stored in short-term memory. This instability of short-term storage, he argued, prevents consolidation and coding for long-term storage.

EEG wave forms, while obviously informative and provocative, still remain problematic for reading research. Galin (1979) nicely summarized these problems in a study of 90 subjects who responded to continuous text. EEGs were recorded while subjects sang, spoke, wrote, read and listened to text. Findings indicated that no single verbal task's hemispheric patterns mirrored those of other tasks or were representative of a general language pattern. Galin concluded, "Any single test used to assess 'language lateralization,' such as tachistoscopic presentation of words to be read in each hemifield, or dichotic listening, is likely to mislead by oversimplifying (p. 137)." Until procedures are developed that sort out the nature of interactions between two recording areas; that disentangle individual differences from asymmetric dimensions of brian function; and that stem from adequate assumptions regarding hemispheric interactions; EEG waveforms, amplitudes, and frequencies cannot adequately explain normal and deficient reading. But developments in EEG technology as well as refinements in experimental procedures should eventually lead to the sort of evidence needed to frame adequate explanations of both.

EVENT RELATED AND EVOKED POTENTIALS

Another potentially useful approach to understanding the neurophysiological mechanisms underlying reading utilizes evoked potentials (EP) recorded from the scalp. The technique typically involves measuring wave potentials elicited by a well-defined stimulus presented to normal and disabled readers (Connors 1971; Ross, Childers and Perry 1973; Shipley and Jones 1969; Sobotka and May 1977). Connors (1971), for example, employed averaged evoked potentials (AEP), a technique that averages subtle wave potentials evoked by repeated light flashes, to detect functional hemispheric asymmetries in a comparison of normal and reading disabled subjects. Left-parietal (P3) anomalies in the late components of the evoked potentials were recorded for the reading disabled subjects as well as waveform changes and amplitude attenuation over the left hemisphere. Connors concluded that these results suggest different information processing strategies among disabled readers.

Other studies have attempted to measure potentials related to events (ERP) either as elicited by words presented to subjects (Preston 1979; Preston, Guthrie and Childs 1974; Preston et al. 1977), or by repeated presentations of simple sentences word by word (Friedman et al. 1975; Goto et al. 1979). One approach to ERP analysis entails evaluating gross changes in the entire waveform as a function of hypothesized states of a subject. A more complex approach involves analyzing the waveform conceptualized as a mixture of components. The latter procedure requires that regions of variance—amplitude, latency, etc., be isolated in terms of specific aspects of tasks performed by subjects. Each source of variance is treated as a component, linking stimulus characteristics and componential variation of the waveform. For example, one of the better understood waveform components is labeled P300. Following the presentation of two categories of tasks or stimuli in a series wherein each category has complementary probabilities of occurence, subjects are instructed to respond by counting or predicting either or both categories of stimuli. The waveform is analyzed to determine its direction (positive or negative), latency (number of milliseconds from stimulus onset to wave peak), and scalp distribution. P300 would indicate a positive direction and a minimum latency of 300 milliseconds over specific scalp regions.

In a sophisticated application of these techniques, Kutas and Hillyard (1980) recorded ERPs from three midline and two lateral sties while subjects silently read 160 seven-word sentences presented one word at a time. The typeface of the last word in 25 percent of these sentences was emboldened. Each sentence, though a meaningful and grammatically acceptable whole, bore no relationship to any other sentence presented. Subjects were told to read each sentence silently in order to answer questions about them at the end of the experiment. The first two components produced by words 1–6 (N144 and P204) were present fronto-centrally in all subjects. But, at roughly 250 msec. considerable inter-subject waveform variability was observed with half of the subjects generating P3 "expectancy" components to word presentations. The same subjects produced identical responses to a repeated control word. All words in each sentence, except the first one, produced ERPs with late positivity significantly higher in the left hemisphere than the right over the temporoparietal region. The change in typeface for the last word produced a complex ERP with three late positive components more distinct and larger than those produced by standard typeface words occupying final sentence positions. These three components were explained as a response to a simple physical deviation from a constant ground; Apparently, given time and opportunity, the P3 system (expectancy) can be triggered by both irrelevant and relevant stimuli.

Of some interest is the fact that each word in a sentence did not generate a large P3 component or "expectancy." Instead, the sustained asymmetry over words in a sentence context raises a number of tantalizing possibilities. First, does the left-higher-than-right asymmetry indicate the functioning of language ensembles in the left hemisphere? Or, is the asymmetry a reflection of some interpretive process, given the symmetric ERPs for repeated, highly predictable control words from which it is unlikely that new semantic information might by gleaned? Or, is it possible that the asymmetry represents increasing transitional probabilities typically identified with words in later sentence positions? These and other possible explanations must await resolution of what various components of event related potentials signify.

In a later study using similar procedures but substituting semantically anomalous words for the typeface variations in the previous experiments,

Kutas and Hillyard (1982) recorded ERPs from adults reading the same 160 sentences. Semantically anomalous words appeared to elicit a negative component (N400) in the late positive shift of the ERPs to the seventh word. The late positive shift for the congruent seventh word was significantly larger over the right than the left hemisphere for each lateral electrode pair. The difference wave between congruous and anomalous seventh words for N400 was slightly larger and more prolonged over the right hemipshere but neither difference was statistically significant. As in the previous study, a left-greater-than-right asymmetry in the low positive wave (400–700 msec.) for the first six words was recorded. The results for anomalous and congruent seventh words suggest the possibility of right hemisphere involvement in language comprehension, an interpretation supported by other recent evidence (Cicone, Wapner and Gardner 1980; Wapner, Hamby and Gardener 1981; Winner and Gardner 1977).

The significance of waveshape, amplitude, direction, and distribution of wave components is not really well understood. What stimulus properties and response dimensions they reflect is at best hypothetical. Nor is it clear why different subjects produce such widely divergent ERP waveforms while individual subjects produce very consistent waveforms. But, event related potentials constitute a promising set of variables from which answers to these and a host of other questions may emerge. Still in their infancy as measures, ERPs eliminate many objections associated with other psychophysiological measures, particularly those regarding the logic of generalizing from psychological constructs assumed to be required for skilled reading to reading itself, and of generalizing from letters and words to natural reading. To their credit, ERPs are sufficiently complex to permit very fine-grained analyses of language in many contexts of use, reading among them.

Several cautions are in order however (Donchin and McCarthy 1979) since, as just noted, experimenters frequently define stimuli solely according to values presumed operative in their instructions and presentations. But they also argue that intrinsic processes under the control of subjects account for variations in wave components. Such processes presumably are related temporally to eliciting tasks and stimuli, yet, what is reflected in ERP components is under subject rather than experimenter control.

Variations in information processing over trials, in other words, will affect signal variation in ERP components. Signal averaging over wave components, therefore, may obscure or confound persistent individual differences observed in nearly all ERP studies. ERPs must be analyzed appropriately, and signal averaging, when it is done, should be guided by fairly strict ground rules. Donchin and McCarthy (1979) recommend the following procedures. First, signal averaging should be accompanied by thorough analysis of all available performance data on subjects. Second, measurements of wave components should be taken for single trials of each category of trials to capture possible fine gradations in performance. If signal averaging is still necessary, it may then be employed after trial-by-trial variability is established. Third, wave-component latencies may vary considerably as a function of internal processing differences in subjects. Signal averaging may make it difficult if not impossible to sort out amplitude fluctuations from latency variability. Since averaging will assume a common stimulus onset, the amplitude of a given averaged signal may be reduced by individual latency variability (Brazier 1964). Signal averages therefore must be analyzed with considerable care.

ELECTRICAL STIMULATION MAPPING

Techniques for mapping electrically stimulated brain sites have been employed for about thirty years (Penfield and Jasper 1954; Penfield and Perot 1963; Penfield and Roberts 1959). These techniques are applied to patients undergoing neurosurgery under a local anesthetic; therefore, findings cannot be generalized readily to normal reading and neurologically intact populations. But electrical stimulation of brain sites does have the advantage of identifying discrete localization of brain and behavior relationships better than any other known technique (Ojemann 1983). Electrical stimulation of the brain introduces substantial but reproducible disruption in behavior. Thus, designs have evolved that permit mapping cortical and thalamic sites where stimulation has been shown to affect specific behaviors such as naming simple objects, reading brief phrases, identifying speech sounds, mimicing facial movements, and recalling names of visually depicted objects. A site is selected randomly, stimulated throughout one of these tasks, and the effects of stimulation on performance are measured. Performance is then compared with that elicited on interspersed control trials where no stimulation is applied during performance of these tasks. The location of a cortical site is pinpointed by comparing venous phase arteriography done before surgery with photographs of cortical veins taken during surgery.

From stimulation mapping have come a number of important observations about the organization of language and language related functions in the brian's dominant hemisphere. First, it appears that different language functions are localized to specific cortical sites, but there also appear to be cortical areas that subserve several language functions (Ojemann 1983). One such location, an area of peri-Sylvian cortex, is common to both language production and comprehension. This finding indicates a brain substrate that would lend support to a motor theory of speech perception and comprehension (Liberman et al. 1967).

Second, particular language functions are disrupted by stimulation within a very closely circumscribed area of cortex with abrupt transition to areas of cortex where the response is unaffected by stimulation. But within the affected area, some sites produce disruption on every trial, others only sporadically, and still others not at all. The purpose of stimulation mapping is to identify areas of function that will be affected by surgery so that, if possible, the surgeon may avoid intruding on these areas. When, however, a patient's condition requires that the surgeon encroach on an area where stimulation always disrupts a language function, language impairment often follows surgery (Whitaker and Ojemann 1977). But when surgery has intruded on sites where only occasional disruption of function has been caused by electrical stimulation, no language disturbance follows surgery (Ojemann 1979a). Ojemann (1983) suggests that sites where stimulation always produces disruption are primary to language while sites where stimulation produces occasional disruption are secondary areas that may be involved in recovery of language function when primary areas have been damaged.

Ojemann (1983) reports that reading has been disrupted at 17 cortical sites, both reading and naming at nine sites, reading and memory at seven sites, and reading along with orofacial movements and phoneme discrimination at half the sites where reading was disrupted by stimulation. Reading alterations that occurred without any other language disruption produced a very distinctive error pattern. Errors were confined to verb endings, prepositions, pronouns, and conjunctions. These findings suggest a possible syntactic origin or a potential textual explanation, and perhaps even both. Stimulation of the final motor pathway also disrupted language functions, with an interesting association between phoneme identification and orofacial mimicry. Phoneme identification was disrupted at half of all final motor pathway sites dispite the fact that current was not applied at the time of phoneme production, thus it would appear that final motor pathways are involved in phoneme identification. In addition, final motor pathway sites that produce disruption in sequential orofacial movements represents 85 percent of the motor pathway sites where phoneme identification is disrupted. These sites appear crucial to the production of speech and the discrimination of phonemes. They may account both for some aspects of language production and some aspects of speech perception.

Stimulation mapping also has been a useful technique in identifying a thalamic alerting system that appears sensitive to verbal stimuli, and responsible for simultaneously preventing retrieval of already stored material from short- and long-term memory (Ojemann 1975; Ojemann, Blick and Ward 1971). The procedures are essentially the same as those employed in cortical stimulation except that a more restricted range of tasks has been investigated: naming and short-term visual memory have been measured. Stimulation of left-thalamic areas disrupts performance of naming tasks, overlapping with left-lateral thalamic areas where stimulation also produces short-term memory disruption. The nature of these memory errors suggests how this alerting mechanism works (Ojemann 1982). Left thalamic stimulation during retreival from short-term memory doubles error rates over those obtained in nonstimulated control trials. Stimulation of the same sites at input, however, halves error rates over those obtained in control trials, while stimulation during storage produces error rates equivalent to control trials. At input, short-term memory appears to be activated by these thalamic sites, but they appear to block retrieval while permitting material already available in memory to be stored. Furthermore, left-lateral thalamic stimulation appears to affect verbal but not spatial tasks, while the reverse is true of right-lateral thalamic stimulation.

The value of these stimulation mapping techniques is that they have provided rich new evidence for language localization in the brain and have supported a theory of speech perception wherein the brain is thought to produce a "motor" model of speech as part of the speech decoding process (Liberman et al. 1967). Furthermore, stimulation mapping provides unusually discrete results and seems a particularly useful technique for locating anatomic substrates related to language (Ojemann, 1976). Identification of these substrates cannot help but clarify how specific brain mechanisms affect and explain aspects of both normal reading and reading disability. At the very least, so long as the technique's limitations are borne in mind, stimulation mapping will continue to produce discrete effects that, in combination with corroborative data from complementary techniques, can lend much greater precision to concepts of brain organization for language and reading.

Finally, stimulation mapping, like other psychophysiological techniques, underscores the pervasiveness of individual differences. Findings indicating that certain language functions are localized within the dominant hemisphere also demonstrated that exact locations for these sites varied considerably among individuals (Ojemann 1979b). This variability may simply reflect the unique population studied (Ojemann 1983). Subjects were patients suffering from intractible epilepsy, from chronic pain, or from dyskinesias. These conditions may effect how language is organized in the brain. But these differences may reflect the more general tendency for individuals to vary in all respects. Indeed, localization may be as highly individualized as fingerprints or voice qualities.

REGIONAL CEREBRAL BLOOD FLOW

Localized measures of the distribution of blood in hemispheric gray matter, regional cerebral blood flow (rCBF), have been used to explore changes in the resting blood flow pattern within and between hemispheres as a function of mental activity (Ingvar and Risberg 1967; Maximilian et al. 1978; Risberg et al. 1975; Risberg and Ingvar 1973). Blood-flow increases are taken to indicate gray-matter metabolic activity, thus reflecting neuronal information processing in the cortex. Using an inter-carotid injection technique that allows only unilateral measurements, Risberg and Ingvar explored intrahemispheric blood flow changes in the dominant hemisphere during verbal and spatial reasoning tasks. While increased blood flow was found in brain areas typically associated with auditory and visual tasks, increased flow also was observed in the pre-orlandic and anterior frontal cortex, areas postulated to be involved in conscious intellectual and logical operations (Luria 1977; Penfield and Roberts 1959). More recently, bilateral measurements of rCBF have been attempted using a radioactive gas inhalation technique. Interhemispheric results with this technique were similar to those obtained with inter-carotid injection techniques, but Risberg et al. (1975) made one important further observation:

> The results also showed that rCBF increases during 'unilateral' activity take place in both hemispheres indicating the importance of integration of brain activity mediated by the cerebral commissures, especially the corpus callosum. The

bilateral increases also indicate that the tests used activate complex and mixed mental processes. It is, for example, possible that part of the solving of the spatial test is of linguistic character, the subject silently discussing with himself the possible solutions (p. 521).

Regional cerebral blood flow studies have not been conducted extensively with children, no doubt due to the invasive and traumatic nature of these techniques. In a rare applicaiton to normal children (Jacquy et al. 1977), modification of cerebral circulation was studied during silent reading. Children ranged from ages 6 to 11. Results suggested that patterns of rCBF in children differ from adult patterns. The "hyperfrontality" at rest (higher than mean hemisphere values in the frontal cortex accompanied by lower than mean hemispheric values in parietal and temporal areas) exhibited by adults was not observed in children. At rest, children showed higher than mean values in the temporal area. Reading induced increased rCBF values in both children and adults. For adults, this increase was more marked in the dominant hemisphere, while for children, the blood-flow increase was symmetrical in both hemispheres. This suggests that regional and hemispheric specialization for language is much more flexible in children than in adults.

COMPUTERIZED BRAIN TOMOGRAPHY

A strikingly different approach to investigating the structural asymmetry of the human cerebral hemispheres involves using a noninvasive radiologic technique to measure cytoarchitectural variation in regions of the brain assuming that greater size may provide a more favorable substrate for the functions subserved by particular regions. *Post mortem* investigations have shown that the posterior region of the left hemisphere, a region long thought to be critical for language functioning, is larger than the right in most brains (Geschwind 1974; Witelson and Pallie 1973). A recent investigation of a group of dyslexic but otherwise neurologically normal subjects using non-invasive brain tomography revealed an intriguing reversal of the typical size relationships between the hemispheres in subjects ranging in age from 14 to 44 (Hier et al. 1978). Of the 24 dyslexics studied, ten had brains that were wider in the right parietooccipital region, six had brains that appeared symmetrical, while only eight had brains that were wider on the expected left side. In addition, the ten in whom the typical structural asymmetry was reversed had significantly lower mean verbal intelligence quotients than the other dyslexic subjects, but did not differ significantly from the others in their performance intelligence quotients.

While no other cytoarchitectural differences between the hemispheres have been observed, vascularization differences between them have been reported (Selnes and Whitaker 1977). Hier et al. (1978) speculated that reversal of asymmetry may result in lateralization to a hemisphere "less suited to support language functions and act as a risk factor for the development of reading disability (p. 90)." While acknowledging that only a minority of those with a reversed pattern of structural asymmetry will show evidence of dyslexia, Hier et al. estimated that these persons are five times more likely to be dyslexic than individuals with the more usual pattern. Thus, computerized tomography may be useful in diagnosing "at risk" populations, which may lead to careful consideration of environmental factors affecting or triggering this predisposition. Also, the technique may be useful for identifying subgroups within the broad diagnostic category of dyslexia leading, hopefully, to greater precision and reliability in classifying types of reading disability.

PSYCHOPHYSIOLOGICAL MEASUREMENT IN READING RESEARCH: ISSUES AND PROBLEMS

Enormous leaps in the ability of the biological sciences to probe the body, peer through its profound complexities, and solve age-old puzzles has been one of the splendid accomplishments of this quarter century. Nowhere has this been more true than in the brain sciences. The foundation for these achievements has been the powerful impetus provided them by the invention and technological improvement of enormously ingenious measurement techniques. The computer has been instrumental to these developments. Its continued evolution will spur even further progress in the biological sciences, thus what we have noted in this chapter will soon be dated and of historical rather than current scientific interest. But the problems of applying findings in the basic sciences to practical pursuits; instruction and clinical appraisal of reading disability here; will not yield as easily to technology and invention, for the issues are ones that require linkage to discoveries in linguistic, psychological, and social theory, fields now undergoing rapid intellectual and theoretical development. We shall consider two broad issues of linkage and their attendant problems. One is the issue of oversimplification.

Far too many of the experimental paradigms and tasks employed to identify psychophysiological correlates of various language activities presumed to underlie reading were oversimplified in the studies we reviewed. As a result, findings and conclusions from one study after another were in conflict or were so restricted as to have almost no practical significance, or that permitted justification for almost any practice. To overcome these problems, we suggest two basic solutions. One is to further define global concepts such as *attention, localization*, and *memory*. The other is to set aside poorly defined global constructs in favor of precisely defined relationships between specified behavioral conditions and the interactive physiological response systems presumed to underlie them.

To illustrate, consider how the concept of "attention" has evolved over the past decade and a half. Initially, the dichotomy between outward versus inward attention had great appeal (Lacey et al. 1963), but after a decade of controversy it was discarded in favor of a more complex construct. In its place, for example, Pribram and McGuinness (1975) posited three separate but interacting subsystems to account for attention: arousal, activation, and effort. In our view, the precision and clarity of these distinctions have provided a much better explanation of the cardiovascular component of attention and how it might function in normal or disabled reading.

Attention is a construct that attempts to account for the capacity of living organisms to notice and apply themselves to things that impinge on their sensibilities. Since readers presumably must attend to written language, it is not surprising that failure to learn to read sometimes is attributed to hypothesized attention deficits (Levine 1976). But, attention is a construct quite apart from reading. Theoretical bridges between measures of physiological activity and attention are still under construction. Using these measures to establish relationships between attention and reading assumes that both reading and attention are well understood. We are not arguing that attention plays no role in reading or that it is not an important factor in reading. Indeed, linguistic performance may vary as a function of arousal or attention systems. We simply argue that precision and clarity are necessary conditions for building these bridges.

We also noted with concern that experimental tasks employed to identify pyschophysiological correlates of reading often are presumed to be related directly to given psychophysiological response parameters. However, our assumption is that events in the environment are part of a dynamic and active set of processes that determine responses. In our view, the organism continuously interprets and constructs a representation of the environment. Therefore, how a task is interpreted or constructed by subjects affects physiological responses. Pribram and McGuinness (1975) argue, for example, that heart rate depends upon how a task is constructed—whether it is viewed as a categorizing task or a reasoning task. When a subject is required to maintain attention over a period of time in a categorizing task, extraneous movement is reduced and heart rate adjusts to the reduced demands of the somatomotor system. But in a reasoning task, a task naturally requiring trial and error responses, the cardiovascular-somatomotor relationship is the opposite: heart rate increases. Also, a subject's control or lack of control of the environment in a situation may be a determining factor in heart rate increases or decreases (Obrist 1976). The point is that the study of physiological correlates must isolate variance that corresponds both to specific aspects of tasks and to how tasks are viewed by subjects. In the specific instance cited above, normal reading involves both categorizing and reasoning (Rumelhart and Ortony 1977), as well as control of the environment. It may well be that certain components of reading responses are controlled by the physical characteristics of the stimulus, but other components may reflect processing required by the text, the task, or by the context in which the text is read (Donchin and McCarthy 1979). These subject, text, task and context variables must be enumerated in the variance observed for any psychophysiological measure employed in studying reading or factors presumed to underlie reading (For a detailed discussion of these issues, see Dunn, this volume.).

Similarly, there is a need for caution in conceptualizing both lateralization and language processes too simplistically. A simple dichotomy between language versus nonlanguage, with language lateralized in the left hemisphere for most individuals, may be counterproductive of further understanding of the cognitive aspects of linguistic behavior. Language is often equated with speech production, ignoring the important distinction between language as a formal system and language in use as a medium of expression. A great deal is known about the formation of an idea to be expressed and the planning of an utterance (MacNeilage and Ladefoged 1976). In a comprehensive review of right-hemispheric linguistic abilities, Searlman (1977) emphasized the necessity of separating production from comprehension when investigating hemispheric specialization for language. To do otherwise only obscures aspects of linguistic performance that appear to be lateralized. The notion of hemispheric specialization can be a valuable starting place from which structural and functional asymmetries in language and reading may be pursued if care is taken to avoid overly simple dichotomies between left and right or linguistic and nonlinguistic.

Over and over again we noted in the studies that came under our review that individual differences interacted with experimental tasks and classifications. This was particularly true of experiments that contrasted supposedly deficient or abnormal populations with normal ones. Performance of both experimental and control groups overlapped considerably. The issues and problems associated with sample classification are complex and highly intricate. This is one instance however where we believe that definition alone will not solve these problems. Poorly defined parameters such as normal and abnormal should be set aside in favor of highly discriminated population categories. The conceptual and measurement issues involved are subtle and subject to error arising from how little is known about reading itself. Measures of reading ability lack rigorous construct validity (Anderson 1972; Bormuth 1970; Johnston 1983). Classification of subjects based on typical standardized reading achievement measures inevitably must result in misclassification, because the measures themselves are insensitive to critical subject differences and substantive aspects of reading itself.

What we suggest is a classification system based on rate or frequency of responses by subjects to single trials in a series of trials designed to establish trial-by-trial variability of tasks and measures of interest. Responses may be classified using discriminant function analysis to determine whether or not a given response is rare or frequent in given subjects for specific tasks and trials. In this way, the classification system should identify stimuli generating identical responses, blocks of subjects who respond differentially to identical stimuli, and patterns in the measure of interest. The important thing is to specify the conditions under which subjects perform, the variability in subjects' performances, the variability associated with trials, and the associated dimensions of a psychophysiological parameter of interest. These techniques have been employed to test sets of labeled observations (Donchin and Herning 1975) and waveforms from the P300 region (Squires and Donchin 1976; Squires, Donchin, Herning and McCarthy 1977). To us, they seem very hopeful procedures for eliminating the measurement clouds that obscure the etiology of dyslexia and reading in all of its variety.

We are confident that these sophisticated new techniques for probing the psychophysiological manifestations of reading and language processing have made and will continue to make substantive contributions to our understanding of the psychobiology of language. These measures and the techniques for obtaining them are undergoing rapid development and refinement. From them we can expect new criteria for determining the efficacy of traditional diagnostic procedures in cases of severe reading disability, new standards for judging the appropriateness of instructional and therapeutic interventions, and new directions for theory construction. Not many of the psychophysiological measurement techniques we reviewed are fully understood or have achieved a status where they can be accepted uncritically. As individual measures become better understood and more refined, we think certainly that reading research stands to profit from their capacity to illuminate the physiology and biology on which ultimately all behavior rests.

ENDNOTES

[1]As might be expected, a substantial literature exists on electroencephalographic measures, a literature too rich and complex to review in the present chapter. Two excellent volumes dealing with such measures present a comprehensive analysis of EEG measures and the constructs they are presumed to index. A volume edited by Burch and Altshuler, *Behavior and Brain Electrical Activity*, 1974, Plenum Press, delves into what have now become standard approaches to measuring brain activity. In several interesting chapters this book provides substantive early accounts of the relationships between EEG measures and behavior. A more recent book edited by E. Roy John and Robert Thatcher, *Neurometrics*, 1979, Lawrence Erlbaum, presents a variety of EEG techniques capable of probing many aspects of brain function through sophisticated computer methods. These two volumes will supply the interested reader with considerable background on electroencephalography as well as detailed information on transient electrical oscillations, evoked potentials, and other EEG components elicited by sensory stimuli.

[2]For an interesting and comprehensive examination of the use of evoked potentials in the study of reading disability, we refer you to a volume edited by H. Beglieter, *Evoked Poetentials and Behavior* published by Plenum Press in 1979. In particular, the chapter by M. Preston deals with the many difficult issues involved in defining reading disability and with a full discussion of techniques, procedures and problems associated with the measurement of evoked potentials.

REFERENCES

Anderson, R. 1972. How to construct achievement tests to assess comprehension. *American Educational Research Journal* 42:145–170.

Begleiter, H., ed. 1979. *Evoked potentials in psychiatry*. New York: Academic Press.

Berdina, N.; Kolenko, O.; Kotz, I.; Kuzetzov, A.; Rodinov, I.; Savtchencko, A.; and

Thorevsky, V. 1972. Increase in skeletal muscle performance during emotional stress in man. *Circulation Research* 6:642–650.

Berger, H. 1929. Uber das elektrenkephalogram des menschen. *Archiv fur Psychiatric und Nervenkrankheiten* 87:527–570.

Bilgutay, A., and Lillehei, C. 1965. Treatment of hypertension with implantable electronic device. *Journal of the American Medical Association* 191:649–653.

Bohlin, G., and Graham, F. 1977. Cardiac deceleration and reflex blink facilitation. *Psychophysiology* 14:423–430.

Bormuth, J. 1970. *On the theory of achievement test items.* Chicago: The University of Chicago Press.

Brazier, M. 1964. Evoked response recorded from the depths of the human brain. *Annals* of the New York Academy of Science 112:35–59.

Brest, A.; Wiener, L.; and Bachrach, B. 1972. Bilateral carotid sinus nerve stimulation in the treatment of hypertension. *American Journal of Cardiology* 29:821–825.

Brooks, D.; Fox, P.; Lopez, R.; and Sleight, P. 1978. The effect of mental arithmetic on blood pressure variability and baroreflex sensitivity in man. *Journal of Physiology* 280:75P.

Brunia, C. 1979. Some questions about the motor inhibition hypothesis. In *The orienting reflex in humans*, eds. H.D. Kimmel, E.H. van Olst, and J.F. Orlebeke. Hillsdale, New Jersey: Lawrence Erlbaum Associates.

Burch, N., and Altshuler, H. 1974. *Behavior and brain electrical activity.* New York: Plenum Press.

Carroll, D., and Anastasiades, P. 1978. The behavioral significance of heart rate: The Laceys' hypothesis. *Biological Psychology* 7:249–275.

Cicone, M.; Wapner, W.; and Gardner, H. 1980. Sensitivity to emotional expressions and situations in organic patients. *Cortex* 16:145–158.

Cole, R., and Cummings, N. 1977. Bilateral alpha rhythm in children during listening and looking. In *Language development and neurological theory*, eds. S. Segalowitz and F. Gruber. New York: Academic Press.

Coles, M., and Duncan-Johnson, C. 1975. Cardiac activity and information processing: The effects of stimulus significance, and detection and response requirements. *Journal of Experimental Psychology: Human Perception and Performance* 1:418–428.

Connors, C. 1970. Cortical visual evoked response in children with learning disorders. *Psychophysiology* 7:418–428.

Donchin, E., and Herning, R. 1975. A stimulation study of the efficacy of stepwise discriminant analysis in the detection and comparison of event related potentials. *Electroencephalography and Clinical Neurophysiology* 38:51–68.

Donchin, E., and McCarthy, G. 1979. Event-related potentials in the study of cognitive processes. In *The neurological bases of language disorders in children: Methods and directions for research,* eds. C. Ludlow and M. Doran-Quine, 109–128. NINCDS Monograph No. 22. (NIH Publication No. 79–440)

Doyle, J.; Ornstein, R.; and Galin, D. 1974. Lateralization of cognitive mode: II. EEG frequency and analysis. *Psychophysiology* 11:567–578.

Elliot, R. 1972. The significance of heart rate for behavior: A critique of Laceys' hypothesis. *Journal of Personality and Social Psychology* 22:398–409.

________. 1974. The motivational significance of heart rate. In *Cardiovascular psycho-*

physiology: Current issues in response mechanisms, biofeedback and methodology, eds. P. Obrist, A. Black, J. Brener, L. DiCara. New York: Aldine.

________. 1975. Heart rate, activity and activation in rats. *Psychophysiology* 12:298–305.

Engel, B.; Gottlieb, S.; and Hayhurst, V. 1976. Tonic and phasic relationship between heart rate and somato-motor activity in monkeys. *Psychophysiology* 13:288–295.

Epstein, S.; Beiser, G.; Goldstin, R.; Stampfer, M.; Wechsler, A.; Glick, D.; and Braunwald, E. 1969. Circulatory effects of electrical stimulation of the carotid sinus nerves in man. *Circulation Research* 40:269–276.

Friedman, D.; Simson, R.; Ritter, W.; and Rapin, I. 1975. The late positive component (P300) and information processing in sentences. *Electroencephalography and Clinical Neuropsychology* 38:255–262.

Fuller, P. 1977. Computer estimated alpha attenuation during problem solving in children with learning disabilities. *Electroencephalography and Clinical Neuropsychology* 42:149–156.

Galin, D. 1979. EEG studies of lateralization of verbal process. In *The neurological bases of language disorders in children. Methods and directions for research*, eds. C. Ludlow and M. Doran-Quine, 129–141. NINCDS Monograph No 22. (NIH Publication No. 79–440)

Galin, D., and Ellis, R. 1975. Asymmetry in evoked potentials as an index of laterized cognitive processes: Relation to EEG alpha asymmetry. *Neuropsychologia* 13:45–50.

Galin, D.; Johnstone, J.; and Herron, J. 1977. Effects of task difficulty on EEG measures of cerebral engagement. *Neuropsychologia* 16:461–472.

Galin, D.; and Ornstein, R. 1972. Lateral specialization of cognitive mode: An EEG study. *Psychophysiology* 9:412–419.

Geschwind, N. 1974. *Selected papers on language and the brain.* Dordrecht, Holland: D. Reidel Publishing Company.

Gevins, A.; Zeitlin, G.; Doyle, J.; Schaffer, R.; Yingling, C.; Callaway, E.; and Yeager, C. 1979. Electroencephalogram correlates of higher cortical functions. *Science* 203:665–667.

Goto, H.; Adachi, T.; Utsunomiya, T.; and Chen, I. 1979. Late positive component (LPC) and CNV during processing of linguistic information. In *Human evoked potentials applications and problems,* eds. D. Lehman and E. Calloway. New York: Plenum Press.

Green, J. 1980. A review of Lacey's physiological hypothesis of heart-rate change. *Biological Psychology* 1:63–80.

Grunewald-Zuberbier, E.; Grunewald, G.; Rasche, A.; and Netz, J. 1978. Contingent negative variation and alpha attenuation response in children with different abilities to concentrate. *Electroencephalography and Clinical Neurophysiology* 44:37–47.

Hahn, W. 1973. Attention and heart rate: A critical appraisal of the hypothesis of Lacey and Lacey. *Psychological Bulletin* 79:59–70.

Hassett, J. 1978. *A primer of psychophysiology*. San Francisco: W.H. Freeman and Co.

Hier, D.; LeMay, M.; Rosenberger, P.; and Perlo, V. 1978. Developmental dyslexia. *Archives of Neurology* 35:90–92.

Hillyard, S. 1973. The CNV and human behavior: A review. In *Event related slow potentials of the brain: Their reaction to behavior,* eds. W. McCallum and J. Knott. Amsterdam: Elsevier.

Ingvar, D.; and Risberg, J. 1967. Increase of regional cerebral blood flow during mental effort in normals and in patients with focal brain disorders. *Experimental Brain Research* 3:195–211.

Jacquy, J.; Noel, P.; Segers, A.; Huvelle, R.; Piraux, A.; and Noel, G. 1977. Regional cerebral blood flow in children: A rheoencephalographic study of the modifications induced by reading. *Electroencephalography and Clinical Neurophysiology* 42:691–696.

John, E.R., and Thatcher, R. 1979. *Neurometrics.* Hillsdale, New Jersey: Lawrence Erlbaum Associates.

John, E.R.; Karmel, B.; Corning, W.; Easton, P; Brown, D.; Ahn, H.; John, M.; Harmonym, T.; Prichep, L.; Toro, A.; Gerson, I.; Bartlett, F.; Thatcher, R.; Kaye, H.; Valdes, P.; and Schwartz, E. 1977. Neurometrics. *Science* 196:1393–1410.

Johnston, P. 1983. *Reading comprehension assessment.* Newark, Delaware: International Reading Association.

Just, M., and Carpenter, P. 1980. A theory of reading: From eye fixations to comprehension. *Psychological Review* 87:329–354.

Kinsbourne, M., and Caplan, P. 1979. *Children's learning and attention problems.* Boston: Little, Brown.

Knights, R., and Bakker, D., eds. 1976. *The neuropsychology of learning disorders.* Baltimore: University Park Press.

Kraft, R. 1976. An EEG study: Hemispheric brain functioning of six to eight year old children during Piagetian and curriculum tasks with variation in presentation mode. Doctoral diss., The Ohio State University, Columbus.

Kutas, M.; and Hillyard, S. 1980. Reading between the lines: Event-related brain potentials during natural sentence processing. *Brain and Language* 11:354–373.

________. 1982. The lateral distribution of event-related potentials during sentence processing. *Neuropsychologia* 20:579–590.

LaBerge, D., and Samuels, S.J., eds. 1977. *Basic processes in reading: Perception and comprehension.* Hillsdale, New Jersey: Lawrence Erlbaum Associates.

Lacey, B., and Lacey, J. 1974. Studies of heart rate and other bodily processes in sensorimotor behavior. In *Cardiovascular psychophysiology: Current issues in response mechanisms, biofeedback and methodology,* eds. P. Obrist, A. Black, J. Brener, and L. DiCara. Chicago: Aldine.

________. 1978. Two-way communication between the heart and the brain: Significance of time within the cardiac cycle. *American Psychologist* 33:99–113.

Lacey, J. 1967. Somatic response patterning and stress: Some revisions of activation theory. In *Psychological stress: Issues in research,* eds. M. Appley and R. Trumbull. New York: Appleton-Century-Crofts.

________. 1959. Psychophysiological approaches to the evaluation of psychotheraputic process and outcome. In *Research in psychotherapy,* eds. E. Rubenstein and M. Parloff. Washington, D.C.: American Psychological Association.

Lacey, J.; Kagan, B.; Lacey, B.; and Moss, M. 1963. The visceral level: Situational determinants and behavioral correlates of autonomic response patterns. In *Expression of the emotions in man,* ed. P. Knapp. New York: International Universities Press.

Lawler, K.; Obrist, P.; and Lawler, J. 1976. Cardiac and somatic response patterns during a reaction time task in children and adults. *Psychophysiology* 13:448–455.

Levine, M. 1976. Physiological responses in intrasensory and intersensory integration of auditory and visual signals by normal and deficit readers. In *The neuropsychology of learning disorders,* eds. R. Knights and D. Bakker. Baltimore: University Park Press.

Levy-Schoen, A., and O'Regan, K. 1979. The control of eye movements in reading. In *Processing of visible language*, eds. P. Kolers, M. Wiebstad, and H. Bouma. New York: Plenum Press.

Liberman, A.; Cooper, F.; Shankweiler, D.; and Studdert-Kennedy, M. 1967. Perception of the speech code. *Psychological Review* 74:431–461.

Luria, A. 1977. Cerebral organization of conscious acts: A frontal lobe function. In *Brain function and reading disabilities,* eds. L. Tarnopol and M. Tarnopol. Baltimore: University Park Press.

MacNeilage, P., and Ladefoged, P. 1976. The production of speech and language. In *Handbook of perception VII. Language and speech,* eds. E. Carterette and M. Friedman. New York: Academic Press.

Maximilian, V.; Prohovnik, I.: Risberg, J.; and Hakansson, K. 1978. Regional blood flow changes in the left cerebral hemisphere during word pair learning and recall. *Brain and Language* 6:22–31.

McCanne, T., and Sandman, C. 1974. Instrumental heart rate responses and visual perception: A preliminary study. *Psychophysiology* 11:283–287.

McConkie, G.; Hogaboam, T.; Wolverton, G.; Zola, D.; and Lucas, P. 1979. Toward the use of eye movements in the study of language processing (Technical Report No. 134). Center for the Study of Reading, Urbana, Illinois: University of Illinois.

Morgan, A.; MacDonald, H.; and Hilgard, E. 1974. EEG alpha: Lateral asymmetry related to task and hypnotizability. *Psychophysiology* 11:275–282.

Morgan, A.; McDonald, J.; and MacDonald, H. 1971. Differences in bilateral alpha activity as a function of experimental task, with a note on lateral eye movements and hypnotizability. *Neuropsychologia* 9:459–469.

Obrist, P. 1976. The cardiovascular-behavioral interaction—As it appears today. *Psychophysiology* 13:95–107.

________. 1968. Heart rate and somatic-motor coupiing during classic aversive conditioning in humans. *Journal of Experimental Psychology* 77:180–195.

________. 1981. *Cardiovascular psychophysiology: A perspective*. New York: Plenum Press.

Obrist, P.; Galosy, R.; Lawler, J.; Gaebelein, C.; Howard, J.; and Shanks, E. 1975. Operant conditioning of heart rate: Somatic correlates. *Psychophysiology* 12:445–455.

Obrist, P.; Howard, J.; Lawler, J.; Galosy, R.; Meyers, K.; and Gaebelein, C. 1974. The cardiac somatic interaction. In *Cardiovascular psychophysiology: Current issues in response mechanisms, biofeedback and methodology,* eds. P. Obrist, A. Black, J. Brener, and L. DiCara. Chicago: Aldine.

Obrist, P.; Webb, R.; and Sutterer, J. 1969. Heart rate and somatic changes during aversive conditioning and a simple reaction time task. *Psychophysiology* 5:696–723.

Ojemann, G. 1975. Language and the thalamus: Object naming and recall during and after thalamic stimulation. *Brain and Language* 2:101–120.

________. 1976. Subcortical language mechanisms. *Studies in Neurolinguistics* 1:103–138.

________. 1979a. Altering memory with human ventrolateral thalamic stimulation. In *Modern concepts in psychiatric surgery*, eds. E. Hitchcock, H. Ballantine and B. Meyerson. Amsterdam: Elsevier.

________. 1979b. Individual variability in cortical localization of language. *Journal of Neurosurgery* 50:164–169.

________. 1982. Interrelationships in the localization of language, memory and motor mechanisms in human cortex and thalamus. In *Modern perspectives on cerebral localization*, eds. R. Thompson and J. Green. New York: Raven.

________. 1983. Interrelationships in the brain organization of language-related behaviors: Evidence from electrical stimulation mapping. In *Neuropsychology of language, reading, and spelling*, ed. U. Kirk. New York: Academic Press.

Ojemann, G.; Blick, K.; and Ward, A., Jr. 1971. Improvement and disturbance of short-term verbal memory with human ventrolateral thalamic stimulation. *Brain* 94:225–240.

Orne, M., and Wilson, S. 1977. Alpha, biofeedback and arousal/activation. In *Biofeedback and behavior*, eds. J. Beatty and H. Legewie. New York: Plenum Press.

Ornstein, R., and Galin, D. 1976. *Physiological studies of consciousness*. New York: Viking Press.

Paskewitz, D., and Orne, M. 1973. Visual effects on alpha feedback training. *Science* 181:361–363.

Penfield, W., and Jasper, H. 1954. *Epilepsy and the functional anatomy of the human brain*. Boston: Little, Brown.

Penfield, W., and Perot, P. 1963. The brain's record of auditory and visual experience—A final summary and discussion. *Brain* 86:595–696.

Penfield, W.; and Roberts, L. 1959. *Speech and brain mechanisms*. Princeton: Princeton University Press.

Porges, S. 1972. Heart-rate variability and deceleration as indices of reaction time. *Journal of Experimental Psychology* 92:103–110.

Preston, M. 1979. The use of evoked response procedures in studies of reading disability. In *Evoked brain potentials and behavior*, ed. H. Begleiter.

Preston, M.; Guthrie, J.; and Childs, B. 1974. Visual evoked responses (VERs) in normal and disabled readers. *Psychophysiology* 11:452–457.

Preston, M.; Guthrie, J.; Kirsch, I.; Gertmen, D.; and Childs, B. 1977. VERs in normal and disabled adult readers. *Psychophysiology* 14:8–14.

Pribram, K., and McGuinness, D. 1975. Arousal, activation, and effort in the control of attention. *Psychological Review* 82:116–149.

Rabinovitch, R.; Drew, A.; De Jong, R.; Ingram, W., and Withey, A. 1954. A research appraoch to reading retardation. *Association for Research in Nervous and Mental Disease* 34:363–396.

Risberg, J.; Halsey.; Wills, E.; and Wilson, E. 1975. Hemispheric specialization in normal man studied by bilateral measurements of the regional cerebral blood flow: A study with the 133-Xe inhalation technique. *Brain* 98:511–524.

Risberg, J., and Ingvar, D. 1973. Patterns of activation in the grey matter of the dominant cerebral hemisphere during memorizing and reasoning: A study of the regional cerebral blood flow changes during psychological testing in a group of neurologically normal patients. *Brain* 96:737–756.

Robins, K., and McAdams, D. 1974. Interhemispheric alpha asymmetry and imagery mode. *Brain and Language* 1:189-193.

Ross, J.; Childers, D.; and Perry, N. 1973. The natural history and pyschophysiological characteristics of familial language dysfunction. In *The disabled learner: Early detection and intervention,* eds. P. Satz and J. Ross. Rotterdam: University of Rotterdam Press.

Rumelhart, D., and Ortony, A. 1977. The representation of knowledge in memory. In *Schooling and the acquisition of knowledge*, eds. R. Anderson, R. Spiri, and W. Montague. Hillsdale, New Jersey: Lawrence Erlbaum Associates.

Rutter, M. 1978. Prevalence and types of dyslexia. In *Dyslexia: An appraisal of current knowledge*, eds. A. Benton and D. Pearl. London: Oxford University Press.

Schneider, W., and Shiffrin, R. 1977. Automatic and controlled information processing in vision. In *Basic processes in reading: Perception and comprehension*, eds. D. LaBerge and S.J. Samuels. Hillsdale, New Jersey: Lawrence Erlbaum Associates.

Searleman, A. 1977. A review of right hemisphere linguistic capabilities. *Psychological Bulletin* 84:503-528.

Selnes, O., and Whitaker, H. 1977. Neurological substrates of language and speech production. In *Sentence production: Developments in research and theory*, ed. S. Rosenberg. Hillsdale, New Jersey: Lawrence Erlbaum Associates.

Sheer, D. 1976. Focused arousal and 40Hz EEG. In *The neuropsychology of learning disorders*, eds. R. Knights and D. Bakker. Baltimore: University Park Press.

Shipley, T., and Jones. R. 1969. Initial observations on sensory interaction and the theory of dyslexia. *Journal of Communcation Disorders* 2:295-311.

Sobotka, K., and May, J. 1977. Visual evoked potentials and reaction time in normal and dyslexic children. *Psychophysiology* 14:18-24.

Somsen, R.; Van der Molen, M.; and Orlebeke, J. 1983. Phasic heart rate changes in reaction time, shock avoidance, and unavoidance shock tasks: Are hypothetical generalizations about S1-S2 tasks justified? *Psychophysiology* 20:88-94.

Spydell, J., and Sheer, D. 1982. Effect of problem solving on right and left hemisphere 40 hertz EEG activity. *Psychophysiology* 19:420-425.

Squires, K., and Donchin, E. 1976. Beyond averaging: The use of discriminant functions to recognize event-related potentials elicited by single auditory stimuli. *Electroencephalogy and Clinical Neurophysiology* 41:440-459.

Squires, K.; Donchin, E.; Herning, R.; and McCarthy, G. 1977. On the influence of task relevance and stimulus probability on event-related potential components. *Electroencephalography and Clinical Neurophysiology* 42:1-14.

Tecce, J. 1972. Contingent negative variation (CNV) and psychological process in man. *Psychological Bulletin* 77:73-108.

Tuckman, J.; Reich, T.; and Lyon, A. 1968. Electrical stimulation of the sciatic nerves in hypertensive patients. *Hypertension* 16:23-28.

Walker, B., and Sandman, C. 1982. Visual evoked potentials change as heart rate and carotid pressure change. *Psychophysiology* 19:520-527.

________. 1979. Influences of heart rate on the human visual evoked response. *Journal of Comparative and Physiological Psychology* 93:717-729.

Walter, W.; Cooper, R.; Aldridge, V.; McCallum, W.; and Winter, A. 1964. Contingent negative variation: An electrical sign of sensorimotor association and expectancy in the human brain. *Nature* 23:380-384.

Wapner, W.; Hanby, S.; and Gardner, H. 1981. The role of the right hemisphere in the apprehension of complex linguistic materials. *Brain and Language* 14:15–33.

Weinberg, H.; Michalewski, H.; and Koopman, R. 1966. The influence of discriminations on the form of the contingent negative variation. *Neuropsychologia* 14:87–95.

Whitaker, H., and Ojemann, G. 1977. Graded localization of naming from electrical stimulation mapping of left cerebral cortex. *Nature* 270 (5632):50–51.

Winner, E., and Gardner, H. 1977. Comprehension of metaphor in brain-damaged patients. *Brain* 100:719–727.

Witelson, S., and Pallie, W. 1973. Left hemisphere specialization for language in the newborn: Neuroanatomical evidence for asymmetry. *Brain* 96:641–646.

Chapter 5

Emotional Stress: Pyschophysiologic Effects on Learning and Health[1]

by Samuel A. Corson and Elizabeth O'Leary Corson

I. WHAT IS STRESS?

In summarizing the discussion at the closing session of the First International Interdisciplinary Symposium on Society, Stress and Disease, Selye (1971) expressed doubt that any single indicator could give us an overview of all the detrimental and defensive consequences of stress. He pointed out the need to develop a *stress index based on a battery of measurements* (heart rate, GSR, urinary catecholamines and corticosteroids, psychologic tests, etc.) in order to lay the basis for a truly scientific analysis of stress in man. In this presentation we propose to describe one such attempt at recording *patterns of psychophysiologic reactions to repeated exposure to psychologically stressful situations.*

We are proposing the term "biopsychogenic stress" in order to emphasize the idea that *all stress reactions involve integrated physiologic and psychologic factors*, even in cases where the stressors are physical or chemical.

Selye's definition of stress as a "nonspecific response of the body to any demand made upon it" is a logical outgrowth of Cannon's concept of homeostasis. It may be more appropriate to use the term "homeokinesis," since in living systems we are dealing with a kinetic or flux equilibrium, and not with a static equilibrium. In this sense, stress represents a reaction of an organism to any stimuli which would tend to disturb the homeokinetic state or which could meet the particular drives (needs) of the organism at a particular time.

Mason (1975), in a thoughtful review of the stress field, questioned the adequacy of Selye's global stress syndrome concept and the idea of a nonspecific response produced by diverse noxious agents.

Mason argued correctly that "it has become increasingly evident that *conventional* laboratory situations designed for the study of physical stressors . . . very often also elicit an appreciable degree of emotional disturbance." Mason cites his experiments demonstrating that "in fasting . . . little or no corticosteroid change occurs in monkeys, if fruit-flavored non-nutritive cellulose fiber, i.e., placebo food, is given in place of similarly flavored and shaped regular food pellets."

Mason further states that "in heat studies with both humans and monkey subjects, it appears that heat *per se* either does not change or actually *suppresses* adrenal cortical hormone levels when measures are taken to avoid such factors as novelty or extremely sudden or severe temperatures." Mason concludes that "such experimental results, if generally confirmed, cast serious doubt upon the validity of the nonspecificity concept as originally formulated. From our experimental standpoint, *the question raised is basically one of recognition and control of independent variables*, namely the inadvertent psychological stimuli contaminating many stress experiments on physical stressors."

This apparent "impasse" between the views of Mason and those of Selye is in reality a question of semantics. Psychologic stimuli can no more be considered as contaminants of physical stress experiments than the seed could be considered a "contaminant" of a fruit. While Selye did not specifically speak about psychological components of the stress syndrome, he certainly did not specifically deny their participation. Mason is correct in stating that "the unrecognized first mediator in many of Selye's experiments simply may have been the psychological apparatus involved in emotional arousal."

Mason's experiment of filling the fasting monkey's stomach with placebo pellets probably eliminated the neural (and possibly also endocrine) messages to the lateral hypothalamus and thus eliminated the stimuli that would lead to corticosteroid changes. Similarly, in heat stress studies, if measures are taken to avoid such factors as novelty or abrupt or severe temperature changes, one is simply permitting the animals to develop physiologic and psychologic adaptation.

The point is that in an unanesthetized living organism with an intact nervous system, all stress responses involve an intricate pattern of physiologic as well as psychologic factors.

Our stress studies on several breeds of dogs are in agreement with Mason's findings that, in addition to Selye's nonspecific stress responses, there are *specific patterns* of physiologic and psychologic reactions which involve genetic and experiential factors. Selye refers to these as "conditioning factors."

II. CONSTITUTIONAL DIFFERENCES IN BIOPSYCHOGENIC STRESS REACTIONS AND LEARNING: ARE ALL CHILDREN CREATED EQUAL?

Ye sages, be heedful with your words,
lest ye incur the penalty of exile
and be exiled to a place of evil waters,
and your disciples who come after you
drink thereof and die,
and the heavenly name be profaned.

Ethics of the Fathers, Ch. 1, 11

It would have served our educational system well had the framers of the U.S. Constitution paid heed to the admonition of the sages to "be heedful with your words." The phrase "all men are created equal" was a poor choice with which to express the noble idea of the need to offer all people equal opportunities and equality before the law. In fact, an educational system that neglects to take into account constitutional differences in general and specific abilities and in rates of maturation represents a perversion of democratic principles because it does not offer to each student appropriate opportunities to develop his or her specific potentialities.

Teachers and parents, medical and veterinary clinicians, animal breeders, and observant farmers have long been aware of marked individual differences in the susceptibility of living organisms to disease, responsivity to injury and drugs, and behavioral and learning patterns. Yet, scientific investigations of individual differences in the biological and behavioral sciences have lagged far behind the massive efforts expended on studies of average reactions.

As early as 1865, Claude Bernard cautioned biologists against the misuse of statistical methods in describing averages that have no relationship to biologic reality. He quoted as an example of such a pursuit of a mythical average the case of "a physiologist who took urine from a railroad station urinal where people of all nations passed, and who believed he could thus present an analysis of average European urine!"

Just as Bernard foreshadowed the development of the concept of biochemical and physiologic homeostasis and cybernetics, so he was also able to discern the principles of biologic individuality. Thus, Bernard stated: "By destroying the biological character of the phenomena, the use of averages in physiology and medicine usually gives only apparent accuracy to the results . . . Averages . . . confuse while aiming to unify and distort while aiming to simplify."

Reductionist physiologists succeeded in obliterating biologic individuality not only by the misapplication of statistical methods but also by limiting their experiments to anesthetized (and often macerated) animals and isolated organs and tissues. In this manner they managed to obliterate not only constitutional differences but also variations associated with biological rhythms and environmental changes.

This is not to disparage reductionism *per se* or the fractional-analytic approach in biomedical and psychobiologic research. Such analytic studies have made, and will continue to make, essential contributions to biological and behavioral sciences. The argument is not for abolishing reductionist-analytic studies. Rather, it is to assert that: a) the functioning of biologic organisms cannot be understood by merely studying the individual components of the living machinery and b) the mechanisms of sexual reproduction run counter to the concept of an "average standard machinery" in living organisms.

Hirsch (1967) epitomized the glaring neglect of individual differences in the behavioral and psychobiological sciences by the following rather pithy statement: "The 50-year fiasco that was behaviorism, what the Brelands (1961) correctly called 'a clear and utter failure of conditioning theory,' resulted from a blind fixation on the impossible task of trying to generalize about 'laws' of environmental influence." Hirsch and Tryon (1956) pointed out that "it is patent . . . that environmental influence must be an influence on something and therefore the laws of such influence must differ as the object influenced differs."

It was I.P. Pavlov who must be credited with initiating one of the first systematic longitudinal investigations of individual behavioral and psychophysiologic differences in dogs. As early as 1907–08, three of Pavlov's students published dissertations on individual differences exhibited by dogs in the course of elaboration of conditioned reflexes

(Pimenov, 1907; Perel'tsveig, 1907; Zavadskii, 1908). These early observations were related chiefly to differences in general motor behavior on the Pavlovian stand during salivary conditioning experiments and in the dog kennels.

There has been a great deal of confusion regarding Pavlovian typology in the Western and even the Russian literature. This confusion can be ascribed to three factors: 1) Pavlov gradually evolved different conceptual constructs for typology; 2) temporary perversion of the Pavlovian typology concepts generated by the Lysenkoist brand of behaviorism; and 3) the word "typology" has been used by some American behavior-geneticists in a different sense from that used by the Pavlovian school. We therefore propose to review briefly the development of Pavlovian typology concepts and to relate these concepts to current studies on individual differences.

The first systematic attempt in Pavlov's laboratory to classify dogs according to their individual differences in patterns of behavior was made by Nikiforovskii (1910). He classified the dogs into three types: a) extremely exictable, nervous, sensitive dogs; b) extremely inhibitory, unexcitable dogs; and c) a central intermediate type in which he placed the majority of dogs he studied. This classification was based entirely on relatively superficial indices of the balance between excitation and inhibition in general patterns of behavior in dogs during conditioning experiments.

In 1925 in a paper entitled "Normal and Pathological States of the Cerebral Hemipsheres" (see Pavlov, 1954), Pavlov proposed his first typology scheme based on observations of *general patterns of behavior* and also on *basic properties of the central nervous system* as derived from studies on the development of conditional reflexes. Two properties of the central nervous system were considered: the strength of cortical cells ("the supply of excitatory substance in the cortical cells") and the balance between excitation and inhibition. He proposed four types: 1) an extreme excitatory type—strong (sanguinic); 2) an extreme inhibitory—weak (melancholic); and two intermediate types—choleric (approximating the sanguinic) and phlegmatic (approximating the melancholic).

In 1927 in a paper entitled, "Physiological investigations on the Types of Nervous System, i.e., of Temperaments" (see Pavlov, 1954), Pavlov switched the positions of the sanguinic and choleric types. These confusing changing classifications were due to the fact that Pavlov initially used, as criteria for his typology, indices derived from investigations on the basic properties of the central nervous system, as well as from observations of the general behavior of the dogs. For example, one of the indices for classifying a dog as belonging to the "weak" type was "cowardice" (timidity) or the presence of a "passive defense reflex."

However, Vyrzhikhovskii and Maiorov (1933) and Zeval'd (1938) demonstrated that timidity does not necessarily indicate that the dog belongs to a "weak" type in terms of basic properties of the central nervous system as derived from salivary conditioning experiments. Vyrzhikhovskii and Maiorov took eight puppies from two litters and raised half of them in isolation cages for a period of two years and the other half in the usual laboratory conditions with a comparatively enriched environment. All the dogs raised in the isolation cages turned out to be timid, but none of them belonged to the "inhibitory" or "weak" type when tested in salivary conditioning experiments. It thus appeared that while early isolation may modify the general behavior of dogs, it did not seem to change significantly the basic properties of the nervous system.

For this reason, during the years 1933–36 Pavlov eliminated the consideration of general patterns of behavior from the typologic classification. From this period on, the Pavlovian typology was based entirely on the following criteria derived solely from salivary conditioning experiments: strength of the nervous system, balance between excitation and inhibition, and mobility or lability of the nervous system. This definitive classification scheme was as follows:

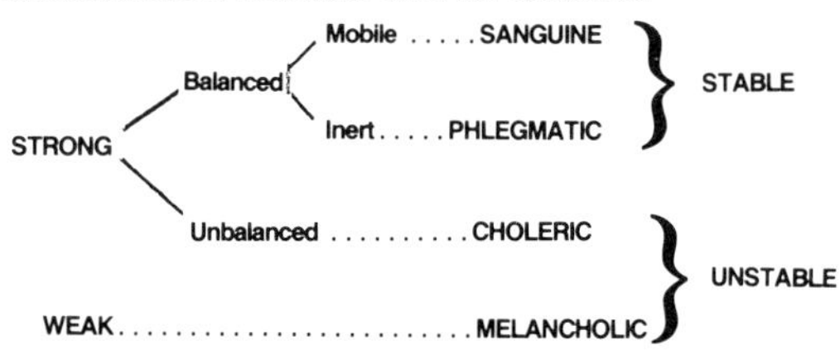

It is not feasible within the limits of this short survey to describe the details of the methods of determining Pavlovian typology. Briefly, the strength of the nervous processes is estimated by determining the threshold of the appearance of the so-called "supramaximal inhibition" (also translated as "supramarginal" or "transmarginal") in response to the application of progressively stronger or more prolonged stimuli or stimuli presented at higher frequencies. The Russian phrase Pavlov used was "zapredel'noe tormozhenie," which literally means "inhibition beyond the limit." In physiological terms this phrase could best be rendered as "supraoptimal inhibition." It implies that for an individual animal there is an optimal intensity, frequency, or duration of stimuli that will evoke inhibition. "Strong" types will exhibit a higher threshold before supraoptimal inhibition will appear.

The balance of nervous processes is determined by the relative ease of elaboration of positive and negative conditional reflexes, i.e., by the number of reinforcements required to produce a positive CR and the number of presentations of unreinforced differentiating stimuli required to develop differentiation or a negative CR.

Mobility or lability is estimated by the ease of conversion of a positive conditional reflex into a negative conditional reflex and vice versa; e.g., in so-called "switching" experiments, when a negative conditional stimulus is reinforced while the previously positive conditional stimulus is not reinforced.

Numerous other experimental procedures have been used for the estimation of the three basic properties of the nervous system and the final determination of the typology. They are all based on longitudinal conditioning experiments. The original battery of tests devised in Pavlov's laboratories during the years 1934–41 is known as the "large standard" and requires experiments lasting one and one-half to two years. Kolesnikov and Troshikhin (1951) introduced the so-called "small standard" requiring only about six months.

The significant conclusions that emanate from reviewing Pavlovian typology studies may be summarized as follows:

1. Pavlov recognized the importance of conducting longitudinal studies (what he referred to as "chronic experiments") in discerning consitutional differences.
2. In his final formulation, after some 30 years of experimentation, Pavlov spoke about "type of nervous system," which he equated to the *"genotype"* and also to the animal's *"temperament."* The pattern of general behavior of the dogs resulting from genetic and environmental interactions, Pavlov referred to as the *"phenotype"* or *"character."* In other words, Pavlov concluded that, whereas the general behavior of the animals may be significantly modified by environmental events, the basic types of the central nervous system remain relatively stable.

What Pavlov tried to emphasize was that the three basic CNS properties as tested in the laboratory could not be significantly changed by modifying the environment, including early postnatal experience. Pavlov realized the inadequacy of their rather limited attempts to modify the early postnatal experience of the dog and also the inadequacey of their tests to determine typology. Because of the widespread confusion on this score in the Russian and English literature, it is worth quoting Pavlov (1935, "General Types of Higher Nervous Activity in Animals and Man"; see Pavlov, 1954, p. 144):

> We must emphasize one very essential and thus far almost insurmountable difficulty in the determination of the types of nervous activity. The pattern of human and animal behavior is determined not only by congenital properties of the nervous system, but also by those influences which have impinged and continue to impinge on the organism during its individual existence, i.e., on the continuous education and training in the broad sense of these words. This is so because, side by side with the above-mentioned properties of the nervous system [Corsons' note: Pavlov is referring to strength, balance, mobility], another most important characteristic continually manifests itself—marked plasticity. Consequently, since we are talking about the innate type of nervous system, we must take into account all those influences to which a given organism has been exposed from the day of its birth until now. With regard to our experimental material (dogs), thus far in the overwhelming majority of cases, this requirement remains only a fervent wish. We shall be able to achieve this *only when all our dogs will be born and reared before our eyes under our unremitting observation* [emphasis Corsons']. For the elimination of the above difficulty, thus far there is only one remedy—*to increase and diversify the forms of our diagnostic tests*, with the idea that in this or that case the specific changes in the innate type of nervous system occasioned by definite influences on the individual existence will become manifest [emphasis Corsons'].

In his latest writings, Pavlov used the terms "congenital" or "innate" rather than "inherited" types because Kupalov (cited by Teplov, 1961, p. 384) demonstrated that the "innate" properties of the nervous system may be influenced by intrauterine development and by very early postnatal environmental conditions.

In the West, as well as the USSR, there has been some misinterpretation of Pavlov's tentative classification by transforming it into a rigid catechism of four types, no more and no less. Pavlov actually estimated at least 24 possible types (Teplov, 1961, p. 465). Krasuskii (1964), in his analysis of data on 116 dogs at the Pavlov Institute of Physiology at Koltushi, came up with 48 types.

Teplov (1961) pointed out that the typology of a given dog may vary depending on: a) the type of reinforcement used, b) the kind of conditional responses used as indices, and c) the modality of the conditional stimuli used. For example, Vatsuro (1949) reported that in dogs the auditory analyzer exhibits greater mobility than the visual analyzer. In the anthropoids, the kinesthetic analyzer exhibits greater mobility than the visual analyzer. Vatsuro referred to these observations as the "principle of leading afferentation."

The confusion regarding the principles of Pavlovian typology was compounded by the fact that in the English literature on behavior genetics the word "typology" has been used in a different sense from that used by Pavlov and his students. Whereas Pavlov in his latest formulation considered the types of nervous system in dogs as genotypes, Mayr (1958, 1959) and Hirsch (1962, 1967) used the word "typology" to describe behavioral-science research which "was pre-Mendelian, in fact pre-Darwinian" (Hirsch, 1967). Mayr (1958) described his typology concept thus: "The philosophical basis in much of early science was typological, going back to the *eidos* of Plato. This implies that the 'typical' aspects of the phenomenon can be described, and that all variation is due to imperfect replicas of the type . . . The typological concept has been completely displaced in evolutionary biology by the population concept. The basis of this concept is that in sexually reproducing species no two individuals are genetically alike . . . The time has come to stress the existence of genetic differences in behavior." Hirsch (1967) stated: "There is no place for individual differences in the typological frame (uniformity is axiomatic)."

It is unfortunate that the word "typology" came to be used in such a manner as to denote precisely opposite concepts. This again suggests the usefulness of a careful study of the classics in biology. Since Pavlov used "types of nervous system" to describe individual inborn differences in CNS functioning, it obviously would have been desirable not to use the same word to describe the behaviorist denial of individual differences. Because Pavlovian "typology" is based on the recognition of individual genetic differences in higher nervous activity, it does not represent "typological" thinking as defined by behavior geneticists.

Some of the most extensive studies on individual differences were conducted by Petrova (1955) on dogs and by Fedorov (1952) on dogs, mice, and human subjects. Krushinskii (1960) initiated behavioral studies on pure breeds of dogs raised in a relatively enriched environment (private homes) and in restricted laboratory kennels. He reported that in both environments a greater proportion of German shepherds developed timidity than Airedale terriers. When German shepherds and Doberman pinschers were raised in isolation cages, 49 percent of the German shepherds developed excessive timidity, whereas only 12 percent of the Doberman pinschers developed timidity, and only of a minimal kind.

Kavetskii et al. (1961), at the Bogomolets Institute of Physiology in Kiev, studied a number of visceral-autonomic reactions of dogs with respect to Pavlovian typology. However, these workers limited their observations to the recording of one or two parameters without any attempts to investigate patterns of adaptive reactions. Firsov (1961) reported individual differences in some visceral reactions of chimpanzees. Monaenkov (1963) summarized rather extensive experiments on individual differences in the development of immunity in rats, rabbits, and horses.

Probably some of the most sophisticated and best-controlled studies in the USSR on individual differences in human subjects have been conducted by Teplov (1961) and Nebylitsyn (1966) at the Institute of Psychology in Moscow. Teplov was one of the first Soviet psychologists to present a critique of the perversion of the concepts of Pavlovian typology and the canonization of a rigid scheme of four types. Some publications from Teplov's laboratories were translated by Gray (1964).

As pointed out earlier, systematic neglect of individual differences fairly well characterized Western biologic and psychologic research until recent times. Roger Williams (1956) pioneered in investigating biochemical individual differences.

Some of the early studies on genetics and behavior were conducted by Tolman (1924), Tryon (1929, 1940), and Heron (1935), who investigated the inheritance of maze-learning in rats. Searle (1949), a student of Tryon, pointed out that fear of the mechanical maze was partly responsible for the slow learning of the "dull" rats. Hall (1941), Broadhurst and Levine (1963), and Broadhurst and Eysenck (1965) reported on genetic differences in emotional responses of rats (defecation). Broadhurst (1960) summarized his extensive experiments in biometrical psychogenetics involving the diallele cross method on six strains of rats in which ambulation and defecation scores were recorded. Ginsburg (1967) studied genetics of audiogenic seizure susceptibility in mice. Bovet et al. (1969) summarized their extensive studies on genetic aspects of learning and memory in mice.

Comparatively few studies have been conducted in the West on individual differences in dogs. Stockard et al. (1941) attempted to investigate variations in the size of different endocrine glands in relation to behavior in several breeds of dogs. Unfortunately, Stockard died before these studies were completed.

Fuller and Thompson (1960) summarized the investigations in this area in their monograph, *Behavior Genetics*. Scott and Fuller (1965) presented a thorough and critical review of their work in *Genetics and the Social Behavior of the Dog*.

Parnell (1958) and Oganesyan (1961) summarized investigations relating somatotypes and behavior in human subjects. Anastasi (1954, 1958), Benjamin (1962), Kallmann (1954, 1962), and Vandenberg (1965) summarized the literature on genetic factors in psychiatric disturbances.

Eysenck (1960, 1963) attempted to relate Pavlov's concepts on the interaction of excitation and inhibition to extroversion and introversion in human subjects. Eysenck postulates that extroverts are characterized by a high and relatively persistent cortical inhibition, whereas introverts are characterized by a low level of cortical inhibition. When Eysenck speaks of a high degree of cortical inhibition he does not use this term in the same sense in which it is commonly used, i.e., inhibition exerted by the cortex on subcortical structures. Rather, Eysenck uses this expression to signify that the inhibited cortex has a low excitability and therefore *does not inhibit the subcortical structures* and thus leads to uninhibited behavior. He further reasons that because of the low cortical inhibition (i.e., high cortical excitation) "introverts should condition better than extroverts." Using eyeblink conditioning tests, Eysenck reports that this is indeed so. He then goes on to say that since "phobias, anxieties, obsessional and compulsive behavior patterns, etc. are nothing more than conditioned autonomic and skeletal responses . . . such conditioned responses are more likely to occur in individuals predisposed to the development of conditioned responses by the possession of a central nervous system which conditions easily. Thus we would expect . . . that neurotics of this type would be introverts . . . and would also condition extremely well. There is much impressive evidence to support both these deductions."

Few systematic studies have been conducted with regard to physiologic, endocrine, and biochemical mechanisms underlying individual differences in responses to psychologic stressors. Levine and Treiman (1964) reported significant differences in the temporal patterns of plasma corticosterone responses to noxious stimuli or novel situations in four inbred strains of mice. Hamburg (1967), in an erudite review on "Genetics of Adrenocortical Hormone Metabolism in Relation to Psychological Stress," reported evidence on "genetically determined enzymatic differences in the synthesis or disposal of adrenocortical hormones." He also reported unpublished observations by Mason and Hamburg on "individual differences (in human subjects) in 17-hydroxycorticosteroid excretion, consistent over several months and through several stressful experiences." Mason (1968), in a thought-provoking review of his extensive concurrent measurements of endocrine responses in 72-hour avoidance sessions in monkeys, called attention to significant individual differences. He concluded that "the individual difference phenomenon is emerging as a central problem in psychoendocrine research and the need for long-term systematic investigations in this area . . . seems increasingly evident."

Apart from the confusion regarding Pavlovian typology, Pavlovian psychobiology is often being confounded in the West with mechanistic reductionist behaviorism. It is curious that in reviewing extensively the background for the development of organismic biology, Bertalanffy (1969) failed to mention Sechenov or Botkin and referred to Pavlov's contributions as furnishing support for the mechanistic approach in biology. This is precisely where the Sechenov-Botkin-Pavlov school does not belong.

Pavlov's significant contributions to integrative psychobiology may be summarized as follows:

1. The recognition that living organisms are goal-directed self-regulating systems. Pavlov referred to this as the "reflex of purpose or goal reflex" (Pavlov, 1903, 1916).
2. The development of techniques for psychophysiologic studies of intact unanesthetized animals.
3. The recognition of psychophysiologic constitutional differences (Pavlovian typology).
4. The emphasis on the need for longitudinal chronic studies in psychophysiologic investigations.
5. *The recognition of specific human psychophysiologic characteristics and the delineation of the importance of the second signal system (language).*

Pavlov's recognition of the importance of symbolic and cultural factors in human behavior can be seen from his remarks in his paper on the Reflex of Purpose (Pavlov, 1916, 1941): "The Reflex of Purpose (goal reflex) has great vital significance; it represents the basic form of vital energy in everyone of us . . . all of life, all its improvements, all its culture is achieved through the reflex of purpose, is achieved only by those individuals who strive to reach this or that life goal which they placed before themselves . . . In contrast, life ceases to be attractive as soon as the purpose disappears. Do we not often read in the notes left by suicide victims that they ended their life because it was purposeless."

It is impossible within the confines of this introductory article to encompass the broad sweep of Pavlovian psychobiology. In closing, one should mention the achievements of one of Pavlov's most brilliant and imaginative students, Peter Kuz'mich Anokhin. Having studied with Vladimir Bekhterev (at the Brain Research Institute) before coming to Pavlov's laboratory, Anokhin attempted to achieve a synthesis of Pavlov's basic conditioning studies with Bekhterev's keen clinical psychiatric and neurologic observations and his pioneering studies on behavior modification and group psychotherapy methods.

Anokhin (1935, 1974) was one of the first in the USSR to initiate systematic utilization of electrophysiologic techniques in the investigation of conditional reflexes and their role in biological adaptation. Anokhin also had the unique distinction of initiating a systematic dialogue and synthesis between the Pavlovian school and Western neurophysiology, experimental psychology, and cybernetics. As early as 1935, Anokhin published a paper in which he developed the concept of the functional system as the basic unit of neurophysiologic integration incorporating into this concept the notion of "return afferentation," thus foreshadowing the development of the concepts of feedback, and a systems approach in psychobiology long before the publication of Wiener's *Cybernetics* in 1948. Anokhin's extensive studies and original concepts are elegantly summarized in an expanded English translation of his latest book (Anokhin, 1974).

III. A SYSTEMS APPROACH IN THE DEVELOPMENT OF ANIMAL MODELS OF BIOPSYCHOGENIC STRESS REACTION PATTERNS

A. Rationale

As mentioned earlier, we are using the term "biopsychogenic stress" in order to emphasize the proposition that all stress reactions involve *integrated physiologic and psychologic factors.*

We embarked on the development of an animal model of psychophysiologic stress reactions because of the important role played by biopsychogenic stress in the development of psychosomatic and behavioral disorders. In modern industrial societies, and even in many developing countries, the types of stressful situations to which people are exposed are not primarily related to physical stressors. People are not generally involved in working excessively long hours or at tasks requiring excessive or prolonged expenditures of physical energy. Similarly, people in industrialized societies are not generally exposed to severe or prolonged deprivation of food or water, although malnutrition is still a problem contributed by nutritional ignorance and poverty. In industrial societies, as well as in developing countries, chemical pollutants have largely taken the place of physical stressors.

The major ubiquitous source of stress, however, is related to psychosocial factors engendered by large dehumanized and dehumanizing industrial and socioeconomic bureaucratic organizations; high population density and mobility; and progressive disintegration of the psychosocial support which stable neighborhoods, stable family structures, and stable social and religious institutions offer. Psychosocial stress-inducing factors are further augmented by the increased reliance on huge mechanized military arsenals in international relations and the development and accumulation of megaquantities of atomic weapons and atomic waste products, representing a threat to the existence of life on this planet. The overriding psychological component operating here is the feeling of helplessness and loss of control over these psychosocial, economic, and political forces. All these factors have created a complex of psychosocial stressors of enormous magnitude, challenging the psychobiological limitations of human adaptability.

That psychosocial stressors represent a serious threat to mental and emotional health is suggested by the 1978 Report of the President's Commisison on Mental Health (Levi, 1979) which summarizes evidence that about 25 percent of the USA population may suffer from mild to moderate depression, anxiety, and other emotional disorders and about nine million Americans are involved with alcohol abuse problems, representing an estimated annual cost of about $40 billion.

Levi (1979) reports similar findings in surveys conducted in Sweden. According to a study performed for the years 1968–1974, on a random sample of the Swedish population aged 15–75, "one Swede out of three reported experiencing impaired mental well-being."

It thus appears that the very survival of mankind and of our social institutions makes it imperative that we institute systematic studies on the nature of psychosocial stress reactions, methods of preventing and ameliorating psychophysiologic and behavioral disorders, and methods of developing psychosocial, economic, and political institutions compatible with human psychobiologic capabilities and conducive to the achievement of optimal physical, mental, and emotional health.

In attempting to develop an animal model for psychogenic stress studies, we were guided by the following considerations:

1. The need to investigate constitutional differences in psychogenic stress reactions. We define constitutional differences as differences resulting from the interaction between genetic, experiential, and environmental factors.

2. The importance of a longitudinal study design, i.e., the need to study psychogenic stress responses to repeated or chronic exposure to stressful situations in order to gain some knowledge about psychophysiologic and behavioral reactions to what Lazarus (1978) refers to as "chronic daily hassles."

3. The importance of investigating *patterns* of psychophysiologic and behavioral stress reactions and not merely isolated single parameters. The aim should be to delineate the significance of the variables observed in *terms of the total integrative adaptive activities of the organism* in the process of maintaining or restoring psychophysiologic homeostasis.

TABLE I

RESEARCH DESIGNS

I. NOMOTHETIC (ASSUMPTION: UNIFORM POPULATION)	II. IDIOGRAPHIC (ASSUMPTION: CONSTITUTIONAL DIFFERENCES)
* STUDY COHORTS, GROUPS	* STUDY INDIVIDUAL
* STATISTICAL REPRESENTATION OF ENTIRE CLASS	* REPEATED MEASURES — IPSATIVE METHOD
* SINGLE MEASUREMENT	* TIME SERIES
* SURVEY ORIENTED	* STUDY INTERVENING VARIABLES

In essence, as outlined in Table 1, our research design is process-oriented and incorporates idiographic-ipsative (i.e., intraindividual), as well as nomothetic-normative (i.e., interindividual), observations. This ipsative-normative method has been discussed in detail by Broverman (1962), Marceil (1977), and Lazarus (1978).

Our initial studies were conducted on mongrel dogs. Later we shifted to the investigation of several distinct breeds, including dogs obtained from the Jackson laboratory. Thus far we have investigated about 70 dogs.

The rationale for choosing dogs as our experimental animals is based on the fact that a great variety of standard breeds is available. As pointed out by Scott and Fuller (1965), "We chose the dog because it shows one of the basic hereditary characteristics of human behavior: a high degree of individual variability . . . The dog is a veritable genetic gold mine. Besides the enormous differences between breeds, all sorts of individual differences appear at the shake of a genetic pickaxe, in this case the technique of mating two closely related animals. Anyone who wishes to understand a human behavior trait or hereditary disease can usually find the corresponding condition in dogs."

Another reason for using dogs is the fact that these animsls exhibit a variety and intensity of emotional reactions approximating those shown by human beings. These animals are large enough to permit biochemical and endocrine studies of body fluids. They are generally cooperative and relatively easily trained and they will tolerate reasonably well surgical implants and experimental paraphernalia without having to resort to such extreme unphysiological and stressful restraints as a primate restraining chair. Moreover, a wealth of data on higher nervous functions of dogs has been accumulated by the Pavlovian school and by Gantt (1944, 1953, 1962, 1974) and his students. Stockard (1941) and his collaborators presented a good amount of material on genetics in relation to endocrine morphology and some behavioral parameters. And finally, we have the elegant studies of Scott and Fuller (1965) on genetics and the social behavior of dogs.

B. Experimental Design

Longitudinal psychophysiologic experiments were performed on 70 dogs. Since we wanted to study the psychophysiologic and behavioral characteristics of our dogs during their entire life span, and we wanted to investigate the psychobiologic reactions of these animals in their kennels, as well as in different psychologic settings, we placed our kennels adjacent to our laboratories and conditioning rooms.

Our dogs were kept in indoor runs (3 x 1 meters) maintained at 21–23 °C. This was similar to the temperature range maintained in our Pavlovian and operant conditioning rooms (20–22 °C). Each run contained a wooden bed or dog house where the animals could rest or sleep. This permitted the maintenance of our dogs under hygienic and pleasant conditions. In addition, the dogs were taken outdoors routinely for walks. Caging of dogs (particularly those used for longitudinal studies) is physiologically and psychologically stressful, especially for certain breeds of dogs. Keeping dogs in cages without opportunities for exercise is not only physiologically and psychologically unsound, but is also not in keeping with humanistic goals of scientific research.

Our dogs were maintained on a controlled regimen of food intake designed for optimal weight and health maintenance. We found that controlling nutritional and psychoenvironmental variables enabled us to secure reproducible and reliable psychophysiologic and behavioral data.

Our experimental design involved studying the same dogs repeatedly in four distinct psychologic environments:

1. A neutral control room where baseline control data were recorded.
2. A psychologically aversive room where Pavlovian motor defense responses were elaborated by reinforcing neutral tones with electric stimuli to a leg.
3. An operant conditioning room where, although similar tones were reinforced with electrocutaneous stimuli, the dogs were permitted to develop escape, and eventually, discriminated avoidance responses.
4. A room with positive emotional connotations where Pavlovian conditional salivary responses were recorded, using food reinforcement procedures and techniques for determining Pavlovian typology.

In order to obtain reproducible data, we found it essential that a *different experimenter* conduct the experiments in each of the four rooms. Moreover, we found it necessary to bring the dogs to each of the experimental rooms *via a different route.* Failure to observe these precautions led to variable and confusing results.

The Pavlovian term "conditional motor defense reflex" is rather misleading. The fact is that in a Pavlovian paradigm the conditional leg lift response does not have any defense function, inasmuch as lifting the leg does not prevent the application of the electric stimulus. Therefore, the animal is not in a position to develop a consummatory adaptive response. This is in contrast to Pavlovian experiments with alimentary reinforcement where conditional salivation does represent an adaptive reaction.

Pavlovian conditioning with electrocutaneous reinforcement is essentially equivalent to a "no solution" problem situation and may therefore be conducive to the development of frustration, anxiety, and neurotic manifestations. This is in contrast to electrocutaneous reinforcement in an operant paradigm where the animals are permitted to develop avoidance responses.

Our early experiments were conducted on mongrel dogs. Because we observed striking individual differences in psychovisceral reactions of these animals, we decided to concentrate on the investigation of several pure breeds of dogs in order to enable us to study the interaction of genetic and psychoenvironmental factors.

Detailed descriptions of our Pavlovian conditioning techniques have been published (Corson, 1966 a and b; Corson, 1971a; Corson and O'Leary Corson, 1969, 1971; Corson et al., 1970). Therefore, only a brief outline of the methods will be presented here. After a standard period of food and water withdrawal, the dogs were given a water load (25 ml/kg) via stomach tube or gastic fistula at the beginning of each experiment. The purpose of the standard water load was to enable us to measure, among other variables, the influence of psychologic stress on the time course of a water diuresis and on the osmolality and chemical composition of the urine. The introduction of a large water load is equivalent to a temporary diabetes insipidus. This enabled us to study the effects of emotional stress on the dynamics of vasopressin release.

Several weeks before the experiments were initiated, some of the dogs had bilateral cystostomy tubes implanted into a small portion of each urinary hemibladder. In our later experiments we found it more convenient to use dogs with implanted urinary bladder cannulae with tightly fitting obturators which were removed during the experiments. Between experiments the cannulae were closed, so that the dogs could utilize the normal urinary tract. Each of these techniques eliminated the complications of urinary bladder reflexes.

All experiments were started punctually at the same time of day. Food and water were withdrawn 12 hours before each experiment. Before the Pavlovian conditioning experiments were initiated, each dog was studied daily for a period of several weeks on a Pavlovian stand in a sound-attenuated control room where behavioral, physiologic, and endocrine data were recorded for a period of two hours. The following parameters were recorded: ECG, heart rate, respiratory rate and depth, rectal and skin temperature, oxygen consumption and CO_2 production, and electromyogram. Urine collections were made (outside the room) every 20 minutes. The experiments in the control room were continued until reproducible baseline values were obtained. The number of days required for these control experiments varied with different dogs.

The Pavlovian conditioning experiments (with electrocutaneous reinforcement) were conducted by a different experimenter in a conditioning room that was distinctly different externally and internally from the neutral control room. As in the control room, the experiments were of two hours duration and were composed of six 20-minute data collection periods (Figure 1).

Before conditioning experiments were started, control sessions were again instituted in the Pavlovian conditioning room until reproducible data were obtained for the various parameters. In essence, these are tonic orienting responses to the conditioning room complex. The number of sessions required for the stabilization of the tonic OR varies for different dogs. Thereafter, phasic orienting sessions were initiated during which 20 orienting tones were presented, *always during the fourth 20-minute data collection period.* The first three 20-minute periods were intended to serve as pre-stimulus control periods. Periods 5 and 6 were to serve as post-stimulus control periods, as depicted in Figure 1. All physiologic and behavioral data were recorded continuously in a remote control monitoring room equipped with closed circuit television instrumentation, so that the dog was isolated from adventitious stimuli.

The tones presented were of conversational intensity (70 db). Two kinds of tones were presented:
1. "A" tones of 400 cps which eventually were to be reinforced with electrocutaneous stimuli to a leg, leading to the elaboration of conditional motor defense responses (leg lift);
2. "B" tones of 1000 cps. These tones were eventually used as differentiating (inhibitory) signals and were never reinforced with electrocutaneous stimuli.

After extinction of the phasic OR to both tones (i.e., after habituation), Pavlovian aversive conditioning experiments were initiated, in which the A tones were reinforced with electrocutaneous stimuli to a leg by means of a constant current generator. This eventually led to the development of a motor defense response (leg lift).

In some experiments, all the A tones were reinforced with electric stimuli. In other experiments ten reinforced A tones were presented and ten inhibitory B tones were randomly interspersed. On some days only inhibitory B tones (20) were presented, while in other sessions 20 *unreinforced A tones* were given (extinction sessions). In some experiments the dog was placed in the Pavlovian room but no tones at all were presented, in order to determine the influence of the conditioning room complex per se on visceral and behaviorarl parameters.

Energy metabolism during conditioning experiments was determined

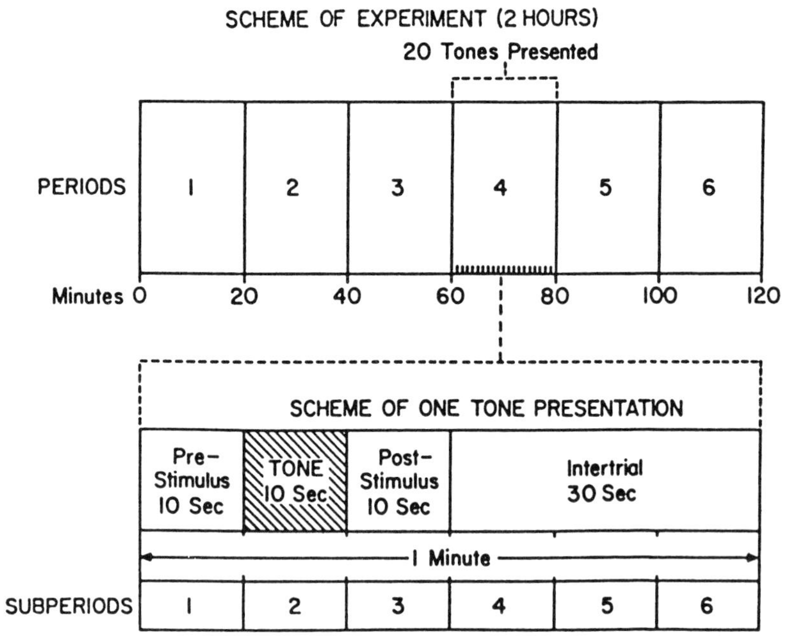

Figure 1:

The upper part of the diagram depicts the scheme of the experiments which were the basis of all phases of our work. Each experimental session lasted two hours and was subdivided into six 20-minute periods corresponding to standard renal clearance procedures. Throughout the 2-hour experiment, behavioral and physiological data were recorded continuously in a remote control monitoring room equipped with closed circuit television instrumentation so that the animal was isolated from adventitious stimuli.

The lower part of the diagram depicts the scheme of the tone presentation period (period 4), in which 20 tones (each of 10 sec duration) were presented, once each minute for 20 minutes. A further subdivision of each one-minute period into six subperiods, each of 10 seconds duration, allows for detailed analysis of psychophysiologic responses occuring in anticipation of the tone, during the tone, and during recovery from the tone.

by a modification of a Beckman Biomonitor, which permits continuous recording of oxygen consumption, CO_2 production, and respiratory quotients without resorting to the use of masks and valves.

Discriminated avoidance conditioning studies were conducted in the same dogs in a distinctly different conditioning room by a different experimenter. The tones used were of the same modality as those presented in the Pavlovian aversive conditioning room. The tone frequencies were sufficiently different to permit discrimination between them and those used in the Pavlovian room. The excitatory (E) tones were reinforced with the same type of electric stimuli used in the Pavlovian conditioning room.

The dog was able to develop an escape and eventually an avoidance response by lifting his head and causing two parallel strips of copper-wire cloth to come in contact. This closed the circuit and either terminated or prevented the administration of the electric stimulus to the dog's leg. The dog could avoid the shock by lifting his head within a period of five seconds after the onset of the presentation of the E tones.

IV. EMOTIONAL STRESS AND SOMATOVISCERAL DICHOTOMY: PERSISTENT GENETICALLY PROGRAMMED DIFFERENCES IN PSYCHOPHYSIOLOGIC REACTIONS OF DOGS TO AN AVERSIVE PAVLOVIAN CONDITIONING ROOM; RELEVANCE TO TYPE A AND TYPE B BEHAVIORAL PATTERNS IN HUMANS

Results of the preliminary analysis of the longitudinal experiments conducted in the Pavlovian aversive conditioning room were published elsewhere. (Corson, 1971a; Corson and Corson, 1971, 1976). We described two major types of psychophysiologic (genetically influenced) reactions to repeated exposure to the psychologically stressful environment represented by the Pavlovian aversive conditioning room (see Table 2). Some dogs (e.g., beagles, most hounds, and some mongrels) exhibited rapid psychophysiologic adaptation (*high adaptation dogs* = *HA*). Other dogs (e.g., wirehair fox terriers, cocker spaniels, some border collies, German shepherds, and some mongrels) exhibited a persistent, almost inextinguishable integrated octet of psychophysiologic reactions to the *entire conditioning room complex*: tachycardia; polypnea; profuse salivation; increases in energy metabolism, rectal temperature, and electromyographic reactions; vasopressin release; and increased urinary catecholamines (*low adaptation dogs* = *LA*).

TABLE 2

CORSON TYPOLOGY

BASED ON REACTIONS TO REPEATED EXPOSURE TO A PSYCHOLOGICALLY STRESSFUL ENVIRONMENT

LOW ADAPTATION DOGS	*HIGH ADAPTATION DOGS*
Tachycardia	Normal heart rate
Polypnea	Normal respiratory rate
Copious psychogenic thermoregulatory salivation	No psychogenic salivation
Marked increase in:	*Little or no increase in:*
Rectal temperature	Rectal temperature
O_2 consumption	O_2 consumption
Antidiuretic hormone (vasopressin release)	Vasopressin release
Urinary catecholamines (norepinephrine, epinephrine)	Urinary catecholamines
Electromyogram intensity	Electromyogram intensity

These psychophysiologic reactions in the LA dogs were invariably *triggered by the entrance of the dogs into the Pavlovian aversive conditioning room, even in extinction sessions or in the absence of any conditional or unconditional signals* (see Fig. 2). Some of the dogs were studied by us for as long as 10 years during which period the Pavlovian *conditioning room continued to trigger these psychophysiologic stress reactions*. These observations confirm Gantt's postulate on autokinesis. In constrast to the conditional motor defense reflexes (leg lift) which were stimulus-bound, well differentiated, and easily extinguished, the *psychophysiologic visceral reactions in LA dogs were highly generalized*. This phenomenon of *somatovisceral dichotomy* is comparable to the principles of *schizokinesis* reported by Gantt (1953). Thus our *studies suggest that schizokinesis is characteristic primarily for LA dogs*. These observations have some relevance to the problem of the target organ in psychosomatic medicine and to differences in susceptibility to psychosomatic disorders in human subjects who may be exposed to similar stressful situations.

The phenomenon of somatovisceral dichotomy calls into question the universality of the currently popular cognitive paradigm in the behavioral sciences. It appears that in some individuals there may be marked dissonance between overt behavior (which is under cognitive control) and visceral-autonomic reactions (which may not always be under cognitive control). This dissociation may be particularly marked in individuals with certain genetic programs.

This dissociation may become especially evident in the course of extinction sessions (wherein conditional signals are presented but not reinforced). In some LA dogs, during extinction sessions the conditional visceral responses may not only fail to extinguish but may actually become accentuated; in contrast, the motor defense responses become rapidly extinguished. This phenomenon has also been observed in humans and referred to as *incubation* (Champion and Jones, 1962; Furedy et al., 1983).

The acquisition and treatment of phobias in humans may be related to the phenomenon of somatovisceral dichotomy. As pointed out by Marks (1969) and Furedy et al (1983), phobias (like conditional visceral responses) in some individuals are easily acquired, are very difficult to extinguish, and resist cognitive therapeutic interventions.

The phenomenon of somatovisceral dichotomy has also been reported in human subjects by Eliot and Buell (1983) and Eliot et al. (1982) in connection with their studies on the relationship between type A behavior and cardiovascular disorders. These authors stated: "We have found that some individuals are cool reactors, i.e., they have a normal cardiovascular response to stress. Others are hot reactors, with an abnormal cardiovascular response. It is impossible, however, to determine who is a hot or cool reactor simply by observing the behavioral facade. Some people are concordant in that their surface behavior reflects their internal physiologic state. Others are discordant, and their surface behavior does not reflect their internal state."

We suggest that the "hot" reactors would be comparable to our LA dogs, whereas the "cold" reactors would be comparable to our HA dogs. In our studies we found a strong genetic factor involved in these types of psychophysiologic reactions to stressful situations.

All these studies suggest that in future research on the role of behavioral patterns in health and disease it would be fruitful to pay attention to the interaction between genetic and experiential factors and to the problem of cognitive-psychophysiologic dissociation in certain individuals.

Physiologically, the LA dogs respond to the psychologically aversive environment as though they were engaged in intensive muscular effort associated with Walter B. Cannon's "fight or flight" reactions, although these animals generally do not struggle in the conditioning room. These physiologic reactions of the LA dogs would represent appropriate adaptive responses under conditions where the animals were able to engage in "fight or flight" activities. However, in a Pavlovian paradigm with aversive reinforcement, these dogs are not able to achieve an adaptive consummatory response. Therefore, this incessant triggering of visceral arousal in the absence of actual aversive stimuli represents the transformation of an adaptive reaction complex into a maladaptive pattern of psychovisceral pathology. This interpretation of the psychophysiologic reactions of the LA dogs to the Pavlovian room is comparable to the concept developed by Glass for type A behavior in humans "as a style of coping with uncontrollable stressful events" (Glass, 1977, 1978).

It is important to note that in spite of persistent panting (in a room maintained at 21–23 °C) the LA dogs still exhibit increased rectal temperatures. This psychogenic hyperthermia (associated with increased muscle tension) may be related to the observation reported by Friedman (1950) in his review on "Hyperthermia as a Manifestation of Stress." Friedman reported that some 30 percent of his patients with cardiovascular diseases exhibited hyperthermia during their waking hours.

The psychogenic nonadaptive muscle tension observed in the LA dogs and in type A individuals (Friedman and Rosenman, 1959; Rosenman and Friedman, 1977) may serve as an explanation for the reported beneficial effects of what would appear to be two mutually exclusive therapeutic procedures, namely, moderate exercise and progressive deep muscle relaxation (Benson et al, 1974; Jacobson, 1929; McGuigan, 1981; Rosenman and Friedman, 1977). Moderate exercise could be considered as a physiologic outlet for an aborted "fight or flight" reaction. Muscle relaxation would represent a method of preventing or ameliorating a vicious cycle of nonadaptive psychophysiologic reactions.

Our postulate that the psychophysiologic responses of our low adaptation dogs to the Pavlovian room were comparable to a "fight or flight" reaction was supported by highly sophisticated circulation studies of Brod (1960, 1965), Brod et al, (1959 a and b, 1962), and Fencl et al, (1959) in experiments on human subjects. Difficult arithmetical problems were presented at such a rate that the subjects were unable to carry them out. These tasks were "resented by most of the subjects as very unpleasant, exhausting, and producing in some of them a feeling of anger or frustration." *Brod described the circulatory changes in these subjects as being comparable to those observed during strenuous muscular activity*. It is interesting that similar circulatory patterns were reported by Brod et al. (1962) as being characteristic for patients with essential hypertension and for patients with chronic cardiac failure.

The pathophysiologic significance and clinical implications of these psychoenvironmental visceral reactions are suggested by instructive experiments reported by Lown et al. (1973). These authors recorded in dogs the threshold for repetitive ventricular response. When the dogs were placed in a Pavlovian stand where they had previously been shocked, these authors observed a significant decrease in the threshold for a repetitive ventricular response, in comparison with the responses of the same dogs in their home cage. Lown et al. interpreted this decrease in threshold as suggesting a predisposition to ventricular fibrillation, induced by a psychologically aversive environment.

It is tempting to suggest (as a topic for future research) that the reactions of our LA dogs to the psychologically aversive Pavlovian conditioning room may be related to the type A behavior in humans described by Friedman and Rosenman (1959). In other words, these reactions may represent the *psychophysiologic substrates of type A behavior*. Friedman and Rosenman described two types of overt behavioral patterns in human subjects: type A and type B. Type A behavior was characterized by time urgency, chronic impatience, intense striving for achievement, overcommitment to work, excessive agressive drive, competitiveness, and abruptness of gesture and speech. Type B individuals are more relaxed, patient, easygoing, and lack aggression, competitiveness, and time urgency. The authors postulated that individuals exhibiting type A behavior patterns are more likely to develop coronary heart disease than individuals with type B behavior. On the basis of prospective investigations by the Western Collaborative Study Group, Rosenman et al. (1976) reported confirmation of the suggestion that type A behavior patterns do represent an important risk factor for coronary heart disease, independent of other risk factors. Kornitzer et al. (1981) confirmed a relationship between type A behavior and the prevalance of coronary heart disease in the Belgian Heart Disease Prevention Project.

Classification of human subjects into types A or B is based on a structured interview (SI) developed by Rosenman and Friedman (1977), the Jenkins Activity Survey Questionnaire (JAS) (Jenkins et al., 1967; Jenkins, 1978), a Short Rating Scale developed by Bortner (1969), and the Framingham Type A Scale as described by Haynes et al. (1980). In all cases, the classification is based on the judgment of trained interviewers and observers of overt behavior, or self-evaluation responses.

The Review Panel on Coronary-Prone Behavior and Coronary Heart Disease (1981) convened by the National Heart, Lung, and Blood Institute, suggested "the need for improved techniques for assessing type A behavior and systematic investigation of mechanisms by which type A behavior affects disease status." Other recommendations included the need for the elucidation of intervening physiologic mechanisms and the role of genetic factors. The animal models described in this communication may help to find answers to some of these questions.

V. PSYCHOPHYSIOLOGIC REACTIONS TO UNAVOIDABLE AND AVOIDABLE STRESSORS; DEVELOPING CONTROL OVER AVERSIVE SITUATIONS.

We postulated that the persistence of the "fight or flight" psychophysiologic reaction in the low adaptation dogs in the Pavlovian conditioning room is associated with anticipatory triggering of the cardiovascular, respiratory, renal, and thermoregulatory control centers in the face of inability to achieve a consummatory adaptive response.

Exposure of an animal to new stimuli leads to an information deficit (Simonov, 1965) and the triggering of an orienting-investigative reflex. If the stimuli have a biological significance (positive or negative), the central nervous system initiates appropriate adaptive approach or avoidance responses. Anokhin (1958, 1966, 1974) postulated the operation in the central nervous system of control mechanisms for evaluating whether the response has actually achieved biological adaptation. Anokhin referred to such a coordinating evaluating center as an *action acceptor.*

The appropriate adaptive response of our experimental dogs in a Pavlovian paradigm with electrocutaneous reinforcement would be to fight or run. Since this is not permitted by the experimental set-up, the action acceptor will continue to signal that an adaptive response has not been achieved. This then would lead to the perpetuation of a chronic information deficit and a continuous internal (visceral) turmoil evidenced in our dogs by tachycardia, hyperpnea, salivation, antidiuresis, and increased energy metabolism.

We reasoned that if this is true, then exposure of the low adaptation dogs to similar conditional and unconditional stimuli under conditions

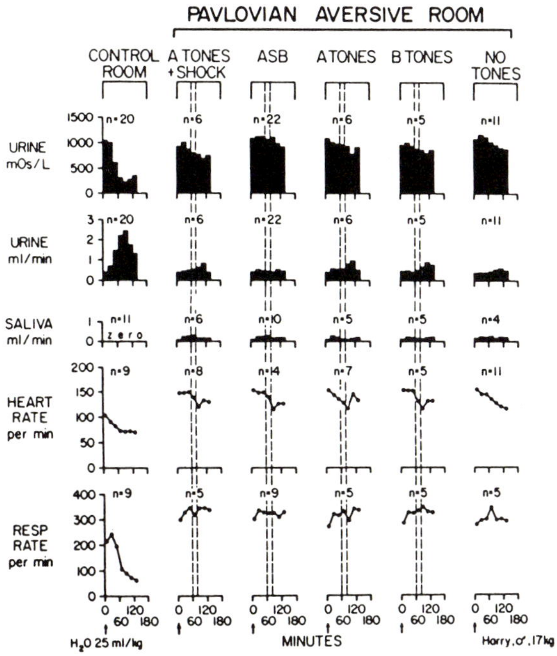

Figure 2:

Conditional respiratory, salivary, cardiac, and antidiuretic responses to psychologic stress in low adaptation dog Harry (male, 17 kg). On the ordinates are plotted (from top to bottom) urine osmolality, rate of urine flow, rate of salivary secretion, heart rate, and respiratory rate. From left to right are plotted mean values (n = number of experiments in a given design) for experiments conducted in the control room (where the animal was never exposed to reinforced or unreinforced signals) and five groups of experiments conducted in a Pavlovian conditioning room (an aversive environment). Broken vertical lines indicate the 20-minute period during which reinforced, unreinforced, or inhibitory tones were presented. "A tone + shock" indicates that 20 reinforced tones were presented at one-minute intervals. "ASB" indicates that 10 reinforced tones wree interspersed at random with 10 inhibitory B tones. "A tones" signifies *extinction sessions during which 20 unreinforced A tones were presented at one-minute intervals.* "B tones" signifies the presentation of 20 inhibitory tones. "No tones" signifies that the animal was placed in the conditioning chamber but no conditional or unconditional stimuli were administered. Note that the conditioning chamber complex acted as a conditional stimulus, the dog exhibiting conditional antidiuretic, cardiac, respiratory, and salivary responses regardless of the experimental design, as long as the animal was in the conditioning chamber.

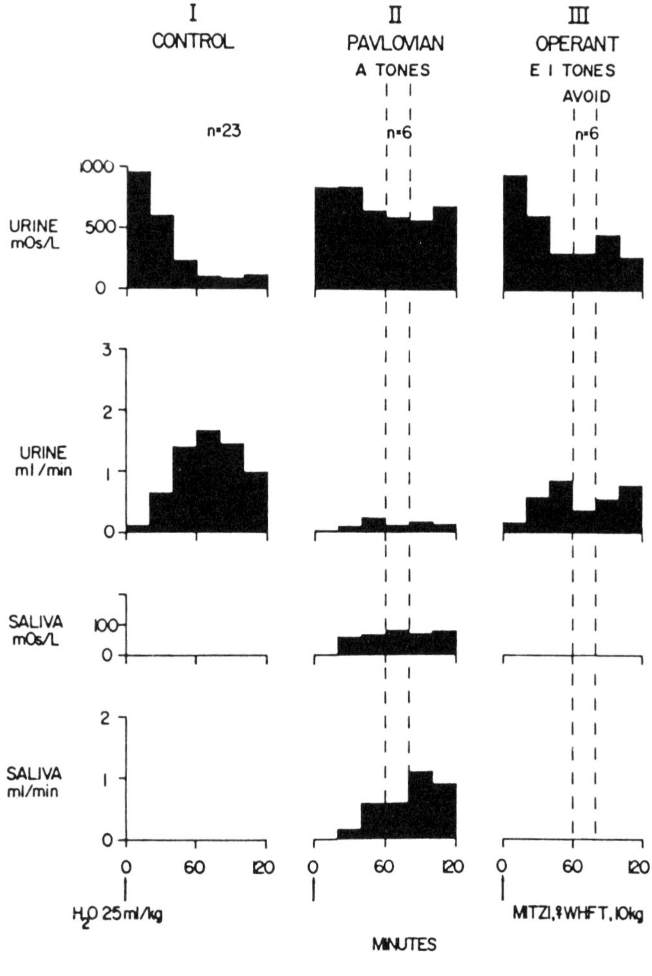

Figure 3:
Comparative renal and salivary responses in low adaptation dog Mitzi in a neutral control room and in Pavlovian and operant conditioning rooms. In column II are depicted the mean values of renal and salivary responses in six extinction sessions conducted in the Pavlovian room (where the dog was exposed to unavoidable shock). In column III are depicted the mean values of six experiments in the operant room after the dog reached 90–100% level of avoidance. Note the amelioration of the antidiuresis and the decrease in urine osmolality in the room where avoidance experiments were conducted. Note also that in the avoidance experiments the psychogenic thermoregulatory salivary responses disappeared.

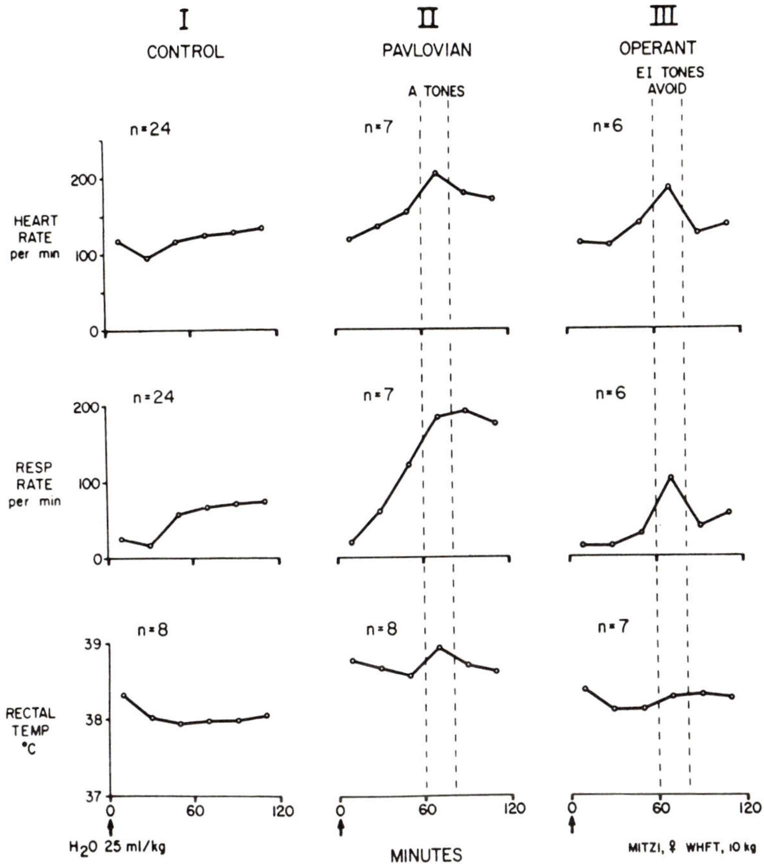

Figure 4:
Comparative values for heart rate, respiratory rate, and rectal temperature observed in a low adaptation dog, Mitzi, in a neutral control room and in Pavlovian and operant conditioning rooms. The experiments are the same as those depicted in figure 3. Note the amelioration of the cardiac, respiratory, and thermal responses in the operant room as compared to the values observed in the Pavlovian room.

where they could develop an avoidance response should tend to ameliorate the psychogenic visceral disquietude.

Figures 3 and 4 illustrate comparative visceral reactions in low adaptation dog Mitzi in the control room (I), the Pavlovian conditioning room

(II), and the operant avoidance room (III). In column II are plotted data derived from extinction sessions when A tones were presented *without electrocutaneous reinforcement*. In column III are plotted data from experiments after the dog reached 90–100 percent level of avoidance. This means that whereas the dog received no shocks at all in the Pavlovian extinction sessions, the dog did receive some shocks in the operant room.

As can be seen in Figure 3 there was a significant decrease in the antidiuresis and in the urine osmolality in the operant room, as compared to the Pavlovian room, in spite of the fact that in the operant room the dog did receive occasional shocks. Note that the psychogenic thermoregulatory salivation also disappeared in the operant room.

Figure 4 depicts similar data in the same dog for heart rate, respiratory rate, and rectal temperature. All these parameters were attenuated in the operant room, so that the values began to approach the baseline magnitudes observed in the control room.

Thus, it appears that it is not the noxious stimuli per se that provoke inappropriate visceral-autonomic hyperactivity but the inability to achieve an adaptive consummatory response. The ability to gain control over stressful situations thus leads to the amelioration of pyschophysiologic distress reactions.

VI. AUTONOMIC ORIENTING REACTIONS AS GUIDES IN PSYCHOPHYSIOLOGIC PERSONALITY ASSESSMENT AND AS POSSIBLE AIDS IN VOCATIONAL GUIDANCE PROCEDURES

In designing classical conditioning experiments, it is customary first to record behavioral and physiologic reactions of the experimental subjects to the neutral signals which will eventually become reinforced with unconditional stimuli and thus develop into conditional signals. The responses to the neutral signals have been referred to by Pavlov (1928, 1954) as orienting reflexes (OR).

If the orienting stimuli are truly neutral, i.e., have no positive or negative biological significance for the organism, then repeated presentation of these signals will eventually lead to extinction or habituation.

Since the dynamics of the development and extinction of OR have significant implications for problems of learning, discrimination, and biological adaptation, investigations in this area have been extensive (Kimmel et al., 1979; Leibrecht, 1974; Sokolov, 1959, 1963; Sokolov and

Vinogradova, 1975). However, some of the reports in the literature have been contradictory and confusing. Some of the reasons for this confusion may be due to differences in OR exhibited by different physiologic and behavioral systems, species differences, and constitutional differences in the same species. This section will describe such stable constitutional differences in the dynamics of OR development and habituation in the HA and LA dogs we investigated and the implications of such OR differences for psychophysiological adaptation.

As indicated earlier, we observed stable constitutional differences in reactions of dogs to a room where these animals were previously exposed to Pavlovian conditioning with unavoidable aversive reinforcement. These psychophysiologic characteristics persisted throughout the entire period during which we studied these dogs (in some cases for as long as 10 years).

A retrospective analysis of our data revealed that *the dynamics of the development and extinction of cardiac and respiratory orienting responses could be used as predictors of high or low adaptation to the psychologically aversive environment.*

Figures 5 and 6 depict the orienting responses of the two types of dogs. As can be seen in the upper graphs of Figure 5:

a. The two HA dogs show little or no tonic cardiac OR (i.e., adaptation to the conditioning room), the heart rates remaining relatively low.

b. The phasic OR (i.e., responses to neutral tones) are of low magnitude and extinguish rapidly.

c. Fluctuations in heart rate within and between experiments are relatively small, i.e., there appears to be good central modulation.

In contrast, in the LA dogs, as can be seen in the lower graph in Figure 5, and in Figure 6:

a. the heart rate remains high throughout the entire series of experiments.

b. The tonic OR (to the conditioning room) failed to extinguish for a total of 50 sessions.

c. The phasic OR to tones persist for another 8 sessions.

d. There is evidence of poor central modulation of heart rate, i.e., there are high fluctuations in heart rate in repeated measures.

Similar constitutional differences were observed in the dynamics and development of respiratory orienting responses. In general, the patterns of respiratory OR dynamics were similar to those of the cardiac OR. However, in some LA dogs, we observed some discordance in the dynamics of the development and habituation of the cardiac and respiratory orienting responses.

Figure 5

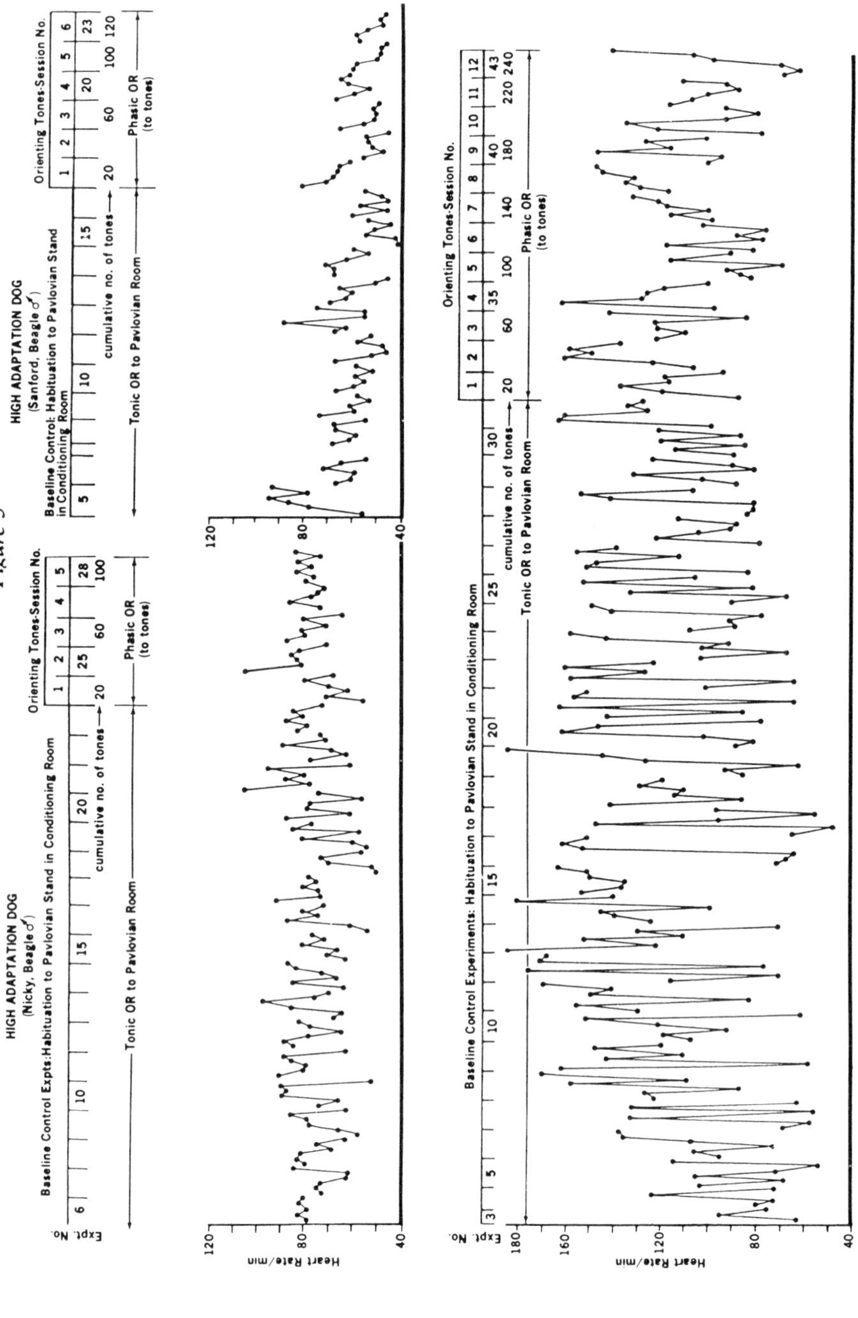
HIGH ADAPTATION DOG
(Nicky, Beagle ♂)
Baseline Control Expts: Habituation to Pavlovian Stand in Conditioning Room
Orienting Tones-Session No.
cumulative no. of tones
Tonic OR to Pavlovian Room
Phasic OR
(to tones)
Expt. No.
Heart Rate/min
HIGH ADAPTATION DOG
(Sanford, Beagle ♂)
Baseline Control: Habituation to Pavlovian Stand in Conditioning Room
Baseline Control Experiments: Habituation to Pavlovian Stand in Conditioning Room
LOW ADAPTATION DOG

Figure 5

The upper two graphs represent orienting case histories of two high adaption dogs, Nicky and Sanford (beagles, male), depicting mean heart rates during habituation to a Pavlovian stand in a conditioning room and during presentation of orienting tones. All experiments were conducted in a sound-shielded Pavlovian room maintained at 21–23 °C. The experiments were of two hours duration and were composed of six 20-min data collection periods. Each data point represents the mean of one of these 20-min periods. Recording of heart rates began with experimental sessions 5 or 6, when electrodes were first placed on the dog (the earlier sessions were training sessions without electrodes).

After baseline control sessions (*tonic* orienting to the Pavlovian conditioning room), *phasic* orienting sessions were initiated during which 20 orienting tones (at 70 dB) were presented, each of 10 seconds duration, one minute apart, one hour after the beginning of each experiment.

Note that in these high adaptation dogs:

1. The heart rates are generally low throughout the entire series of orienting sessions.
2. These dogs show little or no *tonic* orienting responses (to the conditioning room).
3. *Phasic* orienting responses (to the tones) are of low magnitude and extinguish rapidly.
4. Fluctuations in heart rates within and between experiments are relatively small, as contrasted with low adaptation dogs.

The lower graph represents the orienting case history of low adaptation dog, Brigand, (wirehair fox terrier, male) depicting mean heart rates during habituation to a Pavlovian stand in a conditioning room and during presentation of orienting tones. Designations and experimental design are the same as those in the upper graph.

Note that in this low adaptation dog:

1. The heart rates are high throughout the entire series of orienting sessions.
2. This dog shows marked tonic and phasic orienting responses.
3. These orienting responses show poor extinction (poor habituation), as contrasted with those of the high adaptation dogs. The tonic OR (to the room) failed to extinguish in 31 sessions in the Pavlovian stand. The phasic OR (to the tones) failed to extinguish in 12 additional sessions and 240 cumulative tone presentations.
4. There are large fluctuations in heart rates throughout the entire series (poor modulation).

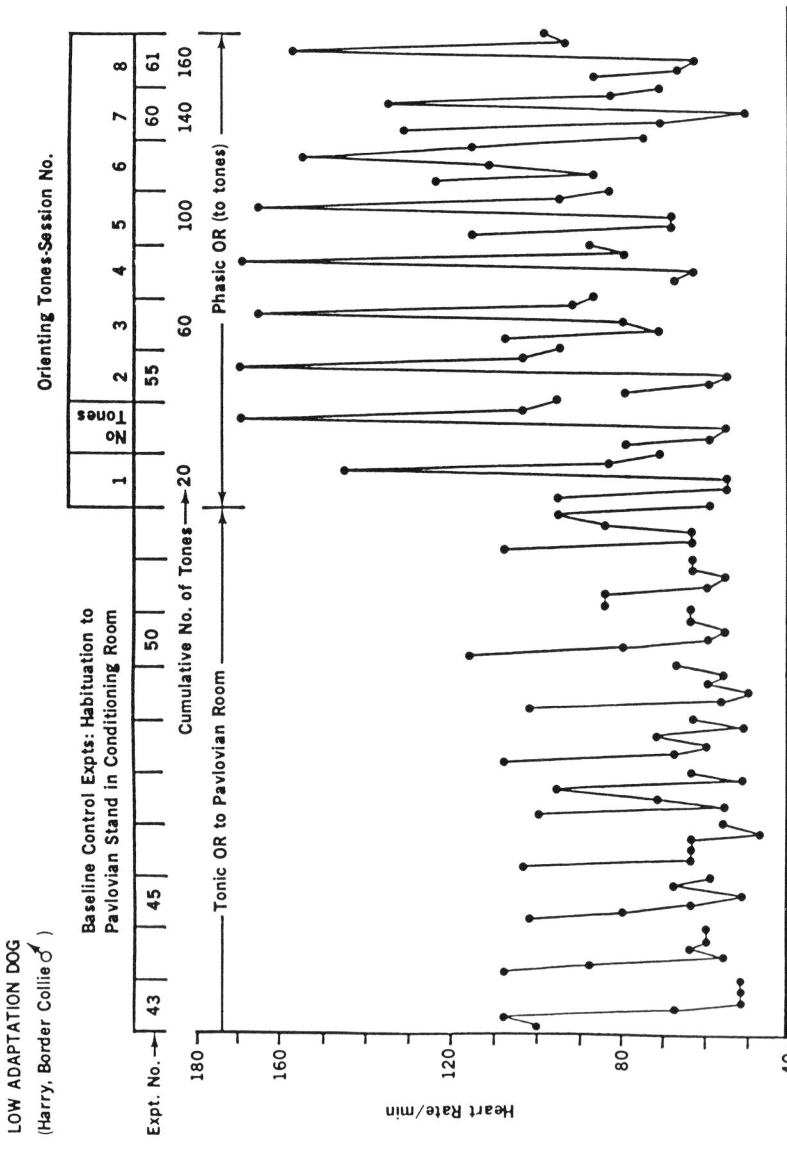
LOW ADAPTATION DOG
(Harry, Border Collie ♂)
Expt. No.
43
45
50
55
60
61
Baseline Control Expts: Habituation to Pavlovian Stand in Conditioning Room
No Tones
1
2
3
4
5
6
7
8
Orienting Tones-Session No.
Cumulative No. of Tones
20
60
100
140
160
Tonic OR to Pavlovian Room
Phasic OR (to tones)
Heart Rate/min
180
160
120
80
40

Figure 6

Figure 6

Orienting case history of low adaptation dog, Harry (border collie, male). Note that this dog continued to exhibit a cardiac OR to the conditioning room during the first 20-minute data collection period up to the 50th experimental session. To conserve space, the first 42 experiments were omitted from this plot. During the tone presentation period (period 4) this dog continued to show phasic OR to the tones for another eight sessions (a total of 160 tone presentations). Also note that in experiment 54 the cardiac OR appears during period 4, even though no tones were presented at this session. Note also the large fluctuations in heart rate.

TABLE 3

t-tests of magnitude of fluctuations of heart rates in 12 high and 18 low adaptation dogs during two phases of their case histories, expressed as the difference between the highest and the lowest mean heart rate in each experimental session.

	1 Tonic OR (to Room)		2 Phasic OR (to Tones)
n_1 (HA) =	125	n_1 (HA) =	51
$\bar{x}$ =	31.16	$\bar{x}$ =	30.29
sd =	± 16.22	sd =	± 16.00
n_2 (LA) =	172	n_2 (LA) =	60
$\bar{x}$ =	48.80	$\bar{x}$ =	50
sd =	±28.09	sd =	± 28.18
t = 6.81	$p < .001$	t = 4.57	$p < .001$

n_1 (HA) = number of values of the dependent variable for the high adaptation group
n_2 (LA) = number of values of the dependent variable for the low adaptation group
$\bar{x}$ = mean
sd = standard deviation
p = probability that the two groups do not differ

A prominent characteristic of the LA dogs is the exhibition of high fluctuations in repeated measures of cardiac and respiratory rates, suggesting poor damping mechanisms. Table 3 depicts t-tests of magnitudes of fluctuations of heart rates in 12 HA and 18 LA dogs, expressed as the differences between the highest and the lowest mean heart rates recorded in each experimental session during adaptation to the conditioning room (tonic OR) and during presentation of orienting tones. The differences between the LA and the HA dogs are significant at the 0.001 level.

TABLE 4

t-tests of magnitude of fluctuations of respiratory rates in 12 high and 18 low adaptation dogs during three phases of their case histories, expressed as the difference between the highest and the lowest mean respiratory rate in each experimental session.

1 Tonic OR (to Room)		2 Phasic OR (to Tones)		3 Experiments with Reinforced Tones (First 10 Sessions)	
n_1 (HA) =	115	n_1 (HA) =	42	n_1 (HA) =	53
$\overline{x}$ =	33.15	$\overline{x}$ =	12.71	$\overline{x}$ =	23.24
sd =	± 41.82	sd =	± 22.51	sd =	± 21.50
n_2 (LA) =	174	n_2 (LA) =	30	n_2 (LA) =	45
$\overline{x}$ =	123.6	$\overline{x}$ =	86.50	$\overline{x}$ =	111.86
sd =	±102.12	sd =	±83.62	sd =	± 69.87
t = 10.41	$p < .001$	t = 4.63	$p < .001$	t = 8.10	$p < .001$

n_1 (HA) = number of values of the dependent variable for the high adaptation group
n_2 (LA) = number of values of the dependent variable for the low adaptation group
$\overline{x}$ = mean
sd = standard deviation
p = probability that the two groups do not differ

Table 4 presents similar data for magnitudes of fluctuations in tonic and phasic respiratory orienting responses, as well as for the first ten experimental sessions involving presentations of tones reinforced with electrocutaneous stimuli. Again the differences in fluctuations are significant at the 0.001 level.

VII. EDUCATIONAL, PSYCHOPHYSIOLOGIC AND CLINICAL IMPLICATIONS OF THE DYNAMICS OF THE DEVELOPMENT AND HABITUATION OF CARDIAC AND RESPIRATORY ORIENTING RESPONSES

One of the objectives of this presentation is to suggest as a topic for further investigation that the basic common denominator underlying the psychophysiologic patterns of the LA dogs and of type A behavior in humans may be a genetically influenced psychophysiologic "fight or flight" reaction complex under conditions where a satisfying consummatory response is not possible. Type A behavior may thus be considered as a dissonance between "fight or flight" psychophysiologic and neuroendocrine reactions and behavioral opportunities for adaptive responses.

Since we demonstrated that cardiac and respiratory orienting responses in dogs made it possible to predict the type of psychophysiologic reactions the animals would exhibit to pyschologically stressful environments, it would appear reasonable that *it may be possible to enhance the predictive power of type A and B classification in humans by adding to the testing repertoire the recording of cardiac, respiratory, and other visceral orienting reactions.* The feasibility of such studies is indicated by the fact that OR recording is noninvasive and innocuous, and requires relatively simple instrumentation.

It may be appropriate to summarize at this point those major characteristics of visceral orienting responses of the LA dogs which may serve as indices of discovering individuals at risk for psychovisceral pathology.

1. Intensity of Visceral Orienting Reactions

The cardiac and respiratory OR in the LA dogs were of a higher intensity than in the HA dogs, often being of magnitudes comparable to reactions to unconditional or conditional aversive stimuli. Sokolov (1959) summarized several reports from Soviet laboratories describing "defensive" patterns of OR in some types of animals and in some humans, particularly in some cases of oligophrenia, infectious psychoses, and some neurotics and schizophrenics. These "defensive" types of OR are interpreted as reflecting a decrease in cerebrocortical inhibitory control, thus leading to exaggerated subcortical defense type reactions, often in response to very weak neutral stimuli.

2. Extinction Rate of Orienting Responses

There is a marked delay in the habituation of orienting responses in the LA dogs, suggesting decreased central inhibitory modulation. Pavlov and many of his collaborators reported that, whereas orienting reflexes are present in decorticated dogs, extinction could not be observed in these animals, suggesting that cortical inhibitory modulation is essential for the extinction of responses to repeated presentation of innocuous stimuli which have no positive or negative biological significance (Pavlov, 1928, 1935, 1954).

In terms of Pavlovian typology classification, the LA dogs would be considered as having a "weak" type nervous system. Several reports from Soviet laboratories indicate that such dogs exhibit poor OR extinction (Sokolov, 1959; Vinogradov, 1938). In fact, poor OR extinction was eventually used as one index of classification of types in dogs and in monkeys (Varukha, 1953; Voronin and Shirkova, 1949). Sokolov (1959) also reviewed several studies indicating poor OR habituation in some aged humans, in senile dementia, oligophrenia, and in some neurotics. Sokolov interpreted these findings as indicating the importance of cortical inhibition in OR habituation. Sokolov also reported that decreased habituation is associated with poor development of discriminative conditional reflexes.

Lader (1971) reported decreased OR habituation in patients with anxiety states and interpreted his findings as indicating that "high arousal is associated with slow habituation." It should be pointed out that the term "arousal," as used by Lader and by Eysenck (1981), implies "arousal" of the autonomic (or of the skeleto-muscular) nervous system, i.e., poor central inhibitory modulation, or "low arousal" of the higher cortical structures. *It would be less confusing to use the terms high or low central modulation, rather than the vague term "arousal."*

3. High Lability of Orienting Reflexes

One of the most dramatic characteristics of the LA dogs is the high fluctuation in cardiac and respiratory parameters, particularly in responses to orienting stimuli, again suggesting poor central damping or the occurrence of large errors in the central regulatory homeostatic mechanisms. It is instructive that Lader (1971) reported that in human subjects "slow habituation is related to many fluctuations (high arousal), much overt anxiety, and high self-assessment of anxiety." Mundy-Castle and McKiever (1953) reported that in recording GSR orienting responses in humans, the labile subjects were also the slowest to habituate. It is instructive that Dembroski et al (1977, 1978) observed greater lability and magnitude of blood pressure in type A individuals than in type B persons. Brod (1971), in reviewing the role of psychosocial stressors in essential hypertension, presented evidence suggesting that labile hypertension (i.e., poor modulation) may be considered as a precursor of essential hypertension. In testing psychophysiologic reactions of subjects with coronary-prone behavior, Horvath and Frantik (1981) reported that labile subjects exhibited higher cardiovascular responses to psychologic stressors.

Wolf (1971, 1972) summarized clinical data suggesting that "disease states are often associated with lability of the involved system." A seven-year study of 65 patients with documented myocardial infarction and 65 matched healthy controls demonstrated that in the MI patients, the variance in a number of physiologic and biochemical parameters was consistently and significantly greater than in the control group. Evidence for poor damping in the MI group was recorded for: systolic and diastolic blood pressure, coronary blood flow, serum cholesterol and uric acid concentrations, plasma fibrinogen, platelet count, and clotting time. According to Wolf (1972), "variance distinguished very sharply between patients and controls and, among patients, predicted recurrent myocardial infarction and sudden death with remarkable accuracy."

Lability in blood pressure as a prognostic sign of the development of persistent hypertension was reported in instructive studies by Sudakov (1976, 1981, 1983) and his collaborators. In these experiments, immobilized rats were exposed to prolonged stimulation of "negative emotiogenic" centers of the hypothalamus (ventromedial and paraventricular nuclei). Marked differences were found in the development of persistent hypertension in different lines of rats. Thus, Wistar rats were highly resistant to the development of hypertension, whereas August line rats were most susceptible. Significant differences in susceptibility were also observed in different rats within the same genetic line. Sudakov reported that a reliable diagnostic sign for the eventual development of persistent hypertension was the lability of blood pressure in the early stages of these experiments. *High initial blood pressure lability was a reliable predictor that these rats would develop persistent high blood pressure.*

All these observations on the significance of lability as a possible index of psychosomatic vulnerability, *suggest the usefulness of repeated measures of physiologic functions as a tool for elucidating the degree of central homeostatic control evidenced in a given organism.* Our own data indicate that, at least in dogs, the dynamics of the development and habituation of cardiac and respiratory orienting responses and their degree of variance appear to serve as predictors of the type of psychophysiologic responses these animals would exhibit to psychologically stressful situations.

If these findings should prove to be applicable to humans, the OR method may turn out to be a useful component for a psychophysiologic personality assessment, and as a method for discovering individuals at risk for psychophysiologic pathology.

The question would naturally arise as to the usefulness of discovering people at risk. On the basis of prospective studies on some 70 dogs, we were able to demonstrate that it is possible to ameliorate the psychogenic visceral turmoil in many LA dogs by appropriate behavioral modification techniques (see Figures 3 and 4), as well as by the judicious use of anxiolytic drugs and some CNS stimulants (Corson and Corson, 1976, 1981). Thus, recording visceral orienting responses in humans may contribute significant links to the development of preventive health care measures. Since OR recording methods are noninvasive and relatively easy to perform, they might also be useful adjuncts to vocational guidance procedures.

VIII. PSYCHOSOCIAL DISTRESS FACTORS IN EDUCATIONAL INSTITUTIONS

A. Statement of the Problem

An old adage has it that charity should begin at home. For several decades (particularly since the pioneering work of Hans Selye) scientists have been studying stress in laboratory settings in animals and humans as well as in field studies, and in human subjects in various occupations (Levi, 1971, 1973). However, very little attention has been paid to the investigation of stressful components of working life in educational institutions. Considering that there are about a half million people involved in teaching and research in academic institutions in the USA, plus many others working in ancillary positions, such an oversight is rather surprising. Since over eight million college students are likely to be influenced (in a positive or negative way) by these academic tutors and researchers, and since many of these students, in turn, are likely to play important roles in the management and directions of our educational, social, economic, and political institutions, the need for data on the psychosocial environment of academic institutions would appear to be imperative. This section (dealing primarily with academic institutions in the USA) is written with the hope that it may stimulate systematic research in this area. Such research may eventually lead to the provision of optimal conditions for creative teaching, research, and public service in academic institutions in all countries.

B. Definitions of terms; stress, distress, anxiety

A major source of psychophysiological distress, which academic institutions share with many industrial and commercial establishments, is the lack of viable feedback and sensitive response channels. The growing self-perpetuating bureaucracies often become self-serving instead of serving the needs of the institutions and their individual constituents. In a previous publication (Corson, 1971) we pointed out that this lack of effective feedback and response channels makes it difficult to correct errors and to maintain social homeostasis and stability. The individuals within these enterprises feel helpless, become alienated, and may develop psychopathologic disturbances characteristic for individuals who feel trapped and unable to develop control of their situation. We postulate that psychopathology is likely to result not from mere exposure to hard work or being faced with difficult problems. Rather, *it is the exposure to no-solution problems* (or the development of a conviction or feeling that the problems are insoluble), i.e., *the inability to achieve an adaptive consummatory response, that leads to psychophysiologic and/or behavior disturbances.* Such behavioral psychopathology was referred to by Seligman (1975) as "learned helplessness."

In Section IV we reported marked and persistent psychophysiologic visceral disturbances in certain types of dogs exposed to Pavlovian conditioning with aversive reinforcement. The psychophysiologic disorders disappeared or became markedly ameliorated when the same dogs were permitted in a different environment to develop discriminated conditional avoidance responses, in spite of the fact that the same aversive stimuli were used for reinforcement (Corson, 1971a; Corson et al., 1970; Corson and E. O'Leary Corson, 1976; see Figures 3 and 4).

A great deal of confusion has arisen in the literature because the concepts of stress and of anxiety have been given different meanings by different authors. In particular, stress and anxiety have been used to denote both biologically positive as well as biologically negative phenomena.

It would be helpful if the term "stress" were to be restricted to the definition proposed by Selye (1971, 1978), the originator of the concept of stress, namely: "the nonspecific responses of the organism to any demand made upon it." The set of reactions of an individual exposed to unavoidable nociceptive stimuli or situations wherein the individual cannot develop adaptive coping mechanisms should be referred to as *distress.* Lennart Levi (1971) and Hans Selye (1971, 1978) have attempted to make such a distinction.

The term "anxiety" has caused even more confusion because it has been used to denote both psychopathology as well as positive motivation for achievement of biologically useful goals. Mowrer (1939) for example stated: "Anxiety is a learned response, occurring to signals [conditioned stimuli] that are premonitory . . . [to] situations of injury or pain . . . anxiety is thus basically anticipatory in nature and has thus great biological utility in that it adaptively motivates living organisms to deal with traumatic events in advance of their actual occurrence . . . . Anxiety, i.e., mere anticipation of actual organic need or injury, may effectively motivate human beings."

It appears to us that it serves no useful purpose to confuse anxiety with biological drive or motivation. The studies of Cattell (1964) and Cattell and Scheier (1961), using factor analysis techniques, demonstrated that there is only one type of anxiety and that it never serves as a motivational drive, but on the contrary always causes an impairment of performance.

Our data suggest that it is exposure to *unavoidable stressors* or *insoluble problems* that may lead to the development of a state of anxiety in *organisms with certain constitutional makeup.*

In cybernetic terms, anxiety may be considered a chronic information deficit. Exposure to new stimuli leads to a temporary information deficit which can be detected in the central nervous system as electrical desynchronization, particularly in the hippocampus. Anokhin (1974) postulated the operation in the central nervous system of a series of feedback loops which eventually include an "action acceptor" involving the hippocampus and frontal areas of the cerebral cortex. The operation of this action acceptor leads to the development of integrated somatic-behavioral and visceral-endocrine adaptive responses, at which point the hippocampal electrical desynchronization disappears. The information deficit is thus eliminated and the animal develops what Pavlov (1903, 1928, 1954) referred to as a "dynamic stereotype." When an organism is repeatedly exposed to unavoidable psychologic stressors under conditions where an adaptive consummatory response cannot be achieved, then Anokhin's action acceptor would continue to signal and a chronic information deficit would develop, thus leading to a persistent "emotional dominant" as described by Simonov (1965). This animal would then simulate some aspects of the psychopathologic conditions of anxiety and frustration.

The fact that the psychovisceral reactions of some of our dogs exposed to Pavlovian reinforcement with nociceptive stimuli were markedly ameliorated when the animals were permitted to develop discriminated avoidance responses supported the proposition that *it is the inability to cope with stressors that provokes anxiety and psychopathology*.This is in accordance with the views expressed so elegantly by Lazarus (1966, 1967). Mowrer and Viek (1948) reported that rats subjected to unavoidable shock (uncontrollable shock) exhibited a greater degree of conditioned suppression than rats shocked but permitted to escape.

Our experimental data on the therapeutic function of developing control over stressful situations appear to be at variance with the reports of Brady (1958) and Brady et al. (1958) regarding the development of gastrointestinal ulcers in the so-called "executive" monkeys who allegedly had control over the aversive stimuli. However, the design of the experiments by Brady et al. is such that the so-called "executive" monkeys were *actually not in control of the situation. Their situation was more like that of galley slaves being driven by a merciless whip*. The Brady experimental design was such that in order to avoid unsignalled electrical shocks the "executive" monkey had to press a lever *every 20 seconds for 6 hours on and 6 hours off every 24 hours for a period of 6–7 weeks.* Such a schedule represents a rather severe form of exposure to exhausting physical and psychological stressors and may be comparable to an extreme form of speedup on a factory assembly line or a chain gang. By contrast, in our experimental design, the reinforcement schedule in the operant room was of the type which permitted relatively easy mastery. The intervals between signaled electrocutaneous reinforcement were one minute. Moreover, the total period of presentation of stimuli in both the Pavlovian aversive room and in the operant room was only 20 minutes during a two-hour experiment.

It should also be mentioned that the so-called "executive" monkeys were selected on the basis of being high avoidance responders. Such a biased selection may have resulted in the assignment of "executive" roles to monkeys with high emotionality and a constitutional predisposition to psychovisceral disorders, such as ulcerations (see Seligman, 1975, pp. 41–42). Since the "executive" monkeys were highly efficient compulsive avoidance bar pressers, the yoked monkeys rarely received any shocks at all and, therefore, should not have been expected to develop psychopathological disorders.

Weiss (1971a, b, c) repeated the Brady experiment on rats using a triadic design ("executive," helpless, and no shock conditions). The "executive" rats showed far fewer and less severe ulcerations than the yoked animals which had no control over the occurrence of shocks. The importance of developing control over situations was pointed out in elegant studies by Masserman (1943, 1971) in his studies on experimental neurosis in monkeys.

The importance of unavoidable psychologic stress and of frustration in the development of psychosomatic disturbances was pointed out in the admirable studies of Stewart Wolf et al. (1948) on human subjects. These authors reported the case of a patient who actually left the interview office to beat up the person he resented. His resting diastolic pressure during the interview was 110 mm. After his return from this rather uninhibited physical aggression, his diastolic pressure decreased to 85 mm.

Stewart Wolf et al. (1955) in an elegant study concluded that the hypertensive patients were generally "fundamentally driving and often hostile, but not able fully to commit or assert themselves." These authors also had the impression that "freer or more fearless self-assertion, brought about by a variety of devices, has been associated among our subjects with a short or long-lasting lowering of arterial pressure."

Hambling (1959) reported cases of hypertensive patients who exhibited marked elevation of diastolic blood pressure whenever they were faced with a frustrating situation that was beyond their control. The same patients remained normotensive in stressful situations which permitted them appropriate response outlets.

Lundberg and Frankenhaeuser (1978) and Frankenhaeuser and Lundberg (1977) reported a series of well controlled experiments on two groups of university students exposed to white noise while performing mental arithemetic. One group had the option of deciding the level of noise intensity they wished to accept (Condition Control group, C). The yoked partners had to accept the same noise level as the C students (NC group). The authors concluded that "subjective and physiological arousal was lower when the subjects were permitted to exert control over noise intensity than when they lacked control." The authors also reported that there were considerable interindividual differences.

On the basis of many elegant laboratory and field studies, Frankenhaeuser (1977) concluded that "a moderately varied flow of stimuli and events, opportunities to engage in psychologically meaningful activities and to exercise personal control over external conditions, may be considered key components in the quality-of-life concept."

The lack of effective feedback and sensitive response channels and the resultant alienation and pyschopathology become more prominent the larger the institution. Because during the past several decades industrial and business institutions have tended to conglomerate (especially in the U.S.A.), the problems of maintaining viable communication in our working places have become progressively more complex. Even secondary and higher educational institutions have become victims of the drive to become bigger, on the questionable assumption that "bigger means better." This unlimited growth in size has been true particularly for many of our state universities, which seem to have developed all the deficiencies of a regimented socialist economy without its benefits.

The need to limit the size of educational institutions was recognized by the Robins report (see Gallant and Prothero, 1972) which recommended the founding of new universities and expanding of regional colleges so as to keep the enrollment of all institutions below 10,000.

It appears that in order to minimize psychopathology and social disorganization in large working institutions it would be necessary to decentralize the institutions into smaller semiautonomous subunits and to broaden decision making processes, so as to involve as many of the workers as possible.

That such broadening of responsibility and authority is possible and desirable, not only in educational institutions but also in factories, has been demonstrated in the U.S.A. by at least two industries, the American Brake Shoe Company, and more recently by the Harman International Industries.

William B. Given, Jr. (1949), President of the American Brake Company, published the results of such decentralized management in a book appropriately entitled "Bottom Up Management." In essence, the philosophy of this type of management can be summarized by the following statement by Given:

> Lately businessmen have come to realize that the success and progress of an enterprise is the sum-total of the success and progress of its people. The management that fails to stimulate their whole-hearted interest and loyalty, and fully utilize their ideas and initiative . . . is shortchanging itself, its stockholders, and

the public it serves . . . . Gradually a philosophy of maximum freedom in management began to evolve, and we found ourselves moving farther and farther away from the conventional top-down techniques of management.

It would be of great interest to compare the incidence of various forms of psychopathology in such a "Bottom Up Management" enterprise with that in the traditional centralized autocratic institutions.

The program on management democratization at the Harman International Industries (HII) was initiated in 1943 by its president, Sidney Harman[1] (1976). In a personal communication, Dr. Harman wrote that he was convinced "that if a program of human development was to grow within the factories, such a program would have to begin at the highest levels of management . . . or face the likelihood, if not the certainty, that it will be destroyed there."

The Harman International Industries employ about 4,000 people in 13 manufacturing plants located principally in the U.S.A., but also in England, Scotland, and Germany. The program in shared management began in 1973 in the Automotive Division Plant at Bolivar, Tennessee, eventually leading to the establishment of an ad hoc "working committee" consisting of five members each from the management and the United Automobile Workers. The "working committee" identified the following four operating principles for the shared management experiment. These principles state that the worker must:

1. Feel secure about his job and be free from fear and anxiety concerning his health, safety, income, and future;
2. Must feel fairness in his treatment;
3. Must feel that his needs are respected and that he can develop his individual capabilities to the fullest;
4. Must have a say in the decisions that affect him, starting with the job itself.

During the life of the program, a fifth and crucial principle evolved; that is, that in any social enterprise the parties must respect each other's differing roles. In short, there must be a sense of mutual respect and trust.

According to Dr. Harman's testimony at the Senate Hearings (1976), this program has had a dramatic favorable effect on the attitudes of the workers toward their jobs and the factory. The program had also resulted in a significant increase in productivity, the submission by workers of many useful innovative suggestions, and the development of a cost-saving-sharing program in which both the management and the union are involved.

C. Are there distress-inducing factors in educational institutions?

But man, proud man
Drest in a little brief authority,
Most ignorant of what he's most assured,
His glassy essence, like an angry ape,
Plays such fantastic tricks before high heaven
As make the angels weep.

William Shakespeare, Measure for Measure, II, 2

There is a dearth of information on the psychosocial environment in academic institutions. Caplan et al. (1975) included scientists and professors in their extensive studies on job demands and worker health. According to these authors, "scientists were chosen to represent a group which was low in stress and low in risk of coronary heart disease." This report also states that "the most satisfied occupations are professors, family physicians, white collar supervisors, police, and air traffic controllers at small sites. Scientists had the lowest blood pressure of the eight occupations measured."

We were unable to find in this publication what kind of scientists or professors were studied and what institutional connections they had. The statement about family physicians is in contrast to the studies reported by C. Thomas (1976, 1977) and others discussed in section E, indicating high morbidity and mortality in physicians.

Sorri et al. (1976) reported on stress in the academic world in Finland. They list several factors involved in the production of stress, among which are:

a. The availability of a very limited number of tenured positions. Thus, the bulk of academic personnel are exposed to economic insecurity, adversary relationships with their colleagues and superiors, and the development of a low self-esteem and depression in the face of nonreappointment or failure to secure a tenured position. This latter fact is particularly stressful since "when a person takes to research, this means selecting a career which will narrow down his possibilities of choosing his place in society, since returning from research work to more practical fields is often difficult."

b. Forced age-related retirement, even if accompanied by an adequate pension. These authors point out that "work plays such an important part in the individual's personal life that his retirement on a pension is liable to lead to a serious identity crisis and even to dejection."

It is generally agreed that the function of a university is transmission and development of knowledge, culture, esthetics, and humanistic values by providing "an atmosphere within which the critical spirit can flourish . . . Its essential bias is in favor of unencumbered criticism" (Shoben, 1970, pp. 695–697).

Free inquiry and free interplay of ideas are essential to a stable, viable social organization. This is the essence of academic freedom, the preservation of which requires that decision-making processes in a university ought to be decentralized to include faculty, as well as students, and all the strata of the public whom the university is supposed to serve.

The exact opposite has been taking place in many American academic institutions, especially state universities. These universities are governed by a board of trustees usually appointed by the governors, who in many cases may have little idea of the nature and functions of an academic institution. Similarly, his appointees generally have little appreciation or understanding of what it is that makes a university tick.

These trustees appoint a president, generally without real faculty input, although there is usually a pretense of such input by the appointment of a search committee, whose function is to search but not to find, and certainly not to appoint.

The president appoints the deans who in turn appoint chairpersons for the departments, all this generally without any real faculty or student input before, or during, the tenure of these administrators. It is essentially an autocratic set-up in violation of all principles of a democratic system or of a well-managed business.

The members of the board of trustees are usually well-to-do business people who have neither the training, experience, time, nor inclination to manage a university. The president, thus, remains essentially the *de facto* "tsar" of the institution, as long as he does not jeopardize the business interests or the particular preferences of the trustees.

According to Epstein (1970) state university board members are "mainly business and professional men with substantial incomes, and they are not young . . . Although overwhelmingly college or university graduates, often with law, medical or other advanced degrees, they are seldom professional educators . . . . Neither are they faculty members from other institutions . . . . In this respect, state university boards differ from those private college boards that have included, notably in recent years, members belonging to the educational community itself, often alumni who have become administrators or professors at other institutions. A similar membership for public university boards would not be impossible.''

The deans and chairpersons in a public university generally serve ''at the pleasure'' of the president, and thus represent the wishes and whims of the president, rather than representing the needs of the faculty or the students or the university as a whole, or, for that matter, the needs of the people whose taxes support the institution. In essence, at many universities there are few viable grievance procedures, few or no means of correcting or preventing errors, and no legitimate means whereby faculty or students can participate in a recall of a university adminsitration or of the board of trustees.

No truly democratic government could long survive with such a ''no feedback'' type of administration, nor could any business enterprise with this type of autocratic management long endure. In a free enterprise economy corrective measures would come from stockholders and/or the marketplace.

In the case of a state university, such corrective measures are lacking. Thus, a state university is perhaps the only institution in a free enterprise economy that seems to have many of the disadvantages of a dictatorial socialist economy without any of its benefits.

It has been said that the human mind is remarkable for being able to resist new ideas and for holding tenaciously to stereotypes. It is remarkable that for all these years, in the U.S.A. in a society where federal, state, and local governments are elected periodically by the people and are subject to public scrutiny and recall, that in the same country, academic institutions (and particularly state universities) should have remained as bastions of undemocratic, unresponsive management.

Stephen R. Graubard (1970) in a preface to the *Daedalus* issue on ''Rights and Responsibilities: The Universities' Dilemma,'' written during the period of student unrest, stated: ''The students (and the universities dare not disclaim or repudiate them) challenge some of the most deeply held beliefs of the society; they remind the society of promises once made; they raise questions about rights and responsibilities, and insist that *authority can be made legitimate again only if it accedes to the founding principles of the nation.*''

In the same issue of *Daedalus*, Robert S. Morison (1970), a distinguished neurophysiologist and university administrator, recognizes that ''the pursuit of academic freedom requires that decision-making in a university be decentralized." Nevertheless, Morison advocates that overall academic policy remain largely with the administration and trustees. The reasons given by Morison for such a recommendation are:

a. possible conflict of interests if faculty members vote on budgetary matters;

b. faculty members lack qualities required by legislators: "tolerance of ambiguity, the ability to compromise, a desire to get on with the job, and a nice sense of the possible";

c. "the administration, and especially the president, is in a way uniquely concerned with the welfare of the university as a whole."

Our argument is not to abolish the office of the university president or the institution of the board of trustees, but to make the administration and the trustees accountable to those whose activities are essential for the functioning of a university (i.e., the faculty and students) and to develop effective feedback and sensitive response channels, so as to permit optimal functioning and social stability in the university community. If a private enterprise involving, on the one hand, profit-oriented owners and stockholders and, on the other hand, workers who are in an adversary position of trying to secure a greater share of the profits—if such a privately owned business (such as Harman International Industries) can devise effective mechanisms for sharing decision-making processes—why should not a non-profit public university be able to broaden its decision-making base so as to *develop cooperative, rather than adversary, relationships with the entire university community*, including faculty, nonacademic personnel, and students?

One of the factors contributing to the inefficient and stress-inducing management in public universities is the progressive (perhaps we should say "regressive") increase in the size of these institutions during the past several decades. Some of these universities have 50,000 or more students. This tends to create a huge, often self-serving, faceless and inefficient bureaucracy, mountains of paperwork, and tremendous waste of taxpayers' funds. Under these conditions, even the most competent and highly motivated administrators tend to become cynical and/or frustrated, thus creating a vicious dehumanizing and demoralizing cycle and creating an atmosphere inimical to intellectual and esthetic growth and to creative teaching or research.

One can cite numerous examples of economic waste and senseless activities which do not promote the interests of the universities or the public as a result of a bulky administration lacking in effective feedback channels. In the face of decreasing budgets for research and teaching, one observes expensive periodic replacement of intact doors, floors, ceilings, and furniture. Without consultation with faculty, laboratories are being dismantled, often against the expressed wishes of faculty. In one large public university, the administration sent in a "demolishing crew" that wrecked, in a few days, a highly sophisticated biobehavioral laboratory that took about a decade of hard work and many multidisciplinary talents and large sums of public money to design and build. Reasoned supplications by the scientists who developed the laboratory and by many clinical colleagues were not only of no avail, but did not even merit a courteous response, to say nothing of a reasonable explanation or an attempt at indicating a willingness at least to listen.

The same administration continued for years to badger a scientist to remove a colony of dogs (used for longitudinal biobehavioral psychosocial stress studies) from kennels adjoining the conditioning and physiologic laboratories to a central animal holding facility in another building. As would be obvious to any elementary student of behavioral sciences, such a move would undercut any possibilities for behavioral control of the dog colony. It would expose experimental animals to a variety of unpredictable and uncontrollable psychosocial and physical stimuli, including extreme weather conditions in transit to the laboratory building, and would invalidate the entire research program. Needless to say, the administration eventually succeeded in removing these animals and in abolishing the interdisciplinary psychobiologic and psychophysiologic studies. The administraton also succeeding in making it impossible to secure psychophysiologic, behavioral, neuroendocrine, and genetic data associated with aging changes in these animals. Many of these dogs had been studied for about a decade before the colony was disbanded.

In a carefully researched paper, Gallant and Prothero (1972) attempt to present an analogy between cell growth and institutional growth, pointing out the principle of size optimization. Although "cells exist in a variety of sizes, each size representing an optimization to one or another set of constraints, yet there are upper bounds. There are no cells the size of basketballs because essential metabolic functions are limited by the surface-to-volume ratio. In the case of the university, no grand theory of education is needed in order to identify dysfunctions of growth that affect essential activities (for example, the diffusion of individuals through, in, and out of the university) or that affect all activities (for example, overall morale). Balanced against these dysfunctions are such advantages of growth as economy, the achievement of a critical mass, and flexibility in staffing."

However, the analysis by these authors of "data from the California system indicates that unit costs of education decline very little above a size of 10,000 or 15,000 students . . . at the same time, the dysfunctions attendant on growth become steadily more severe."

In the case of universities "already well into the dysfunctional size range" these authors suggest either the establishment of a new university or the decentralization of the existing university into two or more campuses. Gallant and Prothero conclude: "Returning to the natural world, we note that cells do not grow indefinitely. Instead they divide."

We suggest another even simpler way of achieving the benefits of decentralization and that is to broaden decision-making processes by permitting more autonomy to different departments within educational institutions and increasing faculty-student participation in decision-making. Many functions could easily be decentralized and performed more efficiently and with less cost. For example, with every appointment of ancillary personnel, one gets involved with the tremendous red tape of a college personnel office, then a central all-university personnel office with all the attendant paper-pollution maneuvers and costly delays. If the funds come from a research grant, the appointment is also channeled through a research foundation. Such appointments could more easily be processed locally by every college. Records of such appointments could, of course, be maintained in a central office, but there would be a saving of time and paperwork.

Similarly, why is it necessary for every order of equipment and supplies to go through the numerous delaying stages of a centralized purchasing department, when it would be more efficient and less costly for every department or even every laboratory to order these items directly from the supplier?

Under such a decentralized system, not only would university functions be performed more efficiently, but it would also save financial resources by making it unnecessary to organize huge bureaucratic superstructures and thus cut down the expense of maintaining a paper-polluting machinery. These funds thus saved could be used for research, education, and service.

The important point is that social organizations, like living systems, function best under conditions wherein effective feedback and sensitive response channels are incorporated into the system. In essence, biological systems represent living proof for the advantages of a truly democratic system which incorporates effective networks of social support and mutually advantageous cooperative arrangements. Such a symbiotic system would tend to stimulate optimal efficiency in learning, teaching, and administration in educational institutions. It also would contribute to optimal health maintenance and would create suitable conditions for life, liberty and the pursuit of happiness.

[1]Dr. Harman was the Undersecretary of Commerce in the Carter administration.

The research work of the authors was supported in part by grants from The Commonwealth Fund, USPHS grants NB 04769, HL 20861, NBLM 05006, LM 00635, MH 12089, MH 18098, the Foundations' Fund for Research in Psychiatry, The Rockefeller Brothers Fund, The Central Ohio Heart Association, the Ohio State University Graduate School Biomedical Research Support Grant, the Grant Foundation, and the Psychiatric Research Foundation of Columbus, Ohio.

REFERENCES

Anastasi, A. 1954. The inherited and acquired components of behavior. In *Genetics and the inheritance of integrated neurological and psychiatric patterns*, eds. D. Hooker and C.C. Hare. Baltimore, MD: Williams and Wilkins Co.

________. 1958. Heredity, environment, and the question, "How?". *Psychol. Rev.* 65:197–208.

Anokhin, P.K. 1935. Problema tsentra i periferii v sovremennoi fiziologii nervoi deyatel' nosti (The problem of center and periphery in modern physiology of nervous activity). In *Problema tsentra i periferri v fiziologii nervoi deyatal'nosti* (The problem of center and periphery in the physiology of nervous activity), ed. P.K. Anokhin. Gorki: Gosizdat.

________. 1958. *Vnutrenee tormozhenie kak problem fiziologii* (Internal inhibition as a problem of physiology). Moscow: Medgiz.

________. 1966. Kibernetika i integrativnaia deiatel'nost' mozga (Cybernetics and the integrative function of the brain). *Vopr. Psikhol.* (Problems of Psychology) 12(3):10–32.

________. 1974. Biology and neurophysiology of the conditioned reflex and its role in adaptive behavior. In *International series of monographs on cerebrovisceral and behavioral physiology and conditioned reflexes*, Vol. 3, scientific and translation editor, S.A. Corson. Oxford, England: Pergamon Press.

Benjamin, J.D. 1962. Some comments on twin research in psychiatry. In *Research approaches to psychiatric problems*, eds. T.T. Tourlentes, S.L. Pollack, and H.E. Himwich. New York: Grune and Stratton.

Benson, H.; Marzetta, B.R.; and Rosner, B.A. 1974. Decreased blood pressure associated with the regular elicitation of relaxation response: A study of hypertensive subjects. In *Stress and the heart*, ed. Eliot. New York: Futura.

Bernard, C. 1865. *Introduction a l'etude de la medecine experimentale.* (English edition:

An introduction to the study of experimental medicine.) 1957. New York: Dover Publications.

Bertalanffy, L.V. 1969. *General system theory. Foundations, development, applications.* New York: George Braziller, Inc.

Bortner, R.W. 1969. A short rating scale as a potential measure of pattern A behavior. *J. Chron. Dis.* 22:87-91.

Bovet, D.; Bovet-Nitti, F.; and Oliverio, A. 1969. Genetic aspects of learning and memory in mice. *Science* 163:139-149.

Brady, J.V. 1958. Ulcers in "executive" monkeys. *Scientific American* 199:95-100.

Brady, J.V.; Porter, R.W.; Conrad, D.G.; and Mason, J.W. 1958. Avoidance behavior and the development of gastroduodenal ulcers. *Journal of the Experimental Analysis of Behavior* 1:69-72.

Breland, K., and Breland, M. 1961. The misbehavior of organisms. *Amer. Psychol.* 16:681-684.

Broadhurst, P.L. 1960. Applications of biometrical genetics to the inheritance of behaviour. In *Experiments in personality*, ed. H.J. Eysenck. New York: Humanities Press.

Broadhurst, P.L., and Levine, S. 1963. Behavioral consistency in strains of rats selectively bred for emotional elimination. *Brit. J. Psychol.* 54:121-125.

Broadhurst, P.L., and Eysenck, H.J. 1965. Emotionality in the rat: A problem of response specificity. In *Stephanos: Studies in psychology presented to Cyril Burt*, eds. C. Banks and P.L. Broadhurst.

Brod, J. 1960. Haemodynamic response to stress and its bearing on the haemodynamic basis of essential hypertension. *WHO symposium on the pathogenesis of essential hypertension,* Prague.

________. 1965. Coordination of circulation during emotion. *XXIII International Congress of Physiological Sciences, Excerpta Medica International Congress* Series No. 87:157-164.

________. 1971. The influences of higher nervous processes induced by psychosocial environment on the development of essential hypertension. In *Society, stress and disease*, ed. Levi, Vol 1, *The psychosocial environment and psychosomatic diseases.* London: Oxford University Press.

Brod, J.; Fencl, V.; Hejl, Z.; and Jirka, J. 1959a. Circulatory changes underlying blood pressure elevation during acute emotional stress (mental arithmetic) in normotensive and hypertensive subjects. *Clin. Sci.* 18(2): 269-279.

________. 1959. Haemodynamics in essential hypertension. *Nature* 184:1643-1644.

Brod, J.; Fencl, V.; Jirka, J.; Hejl, Z.; and Ulrych, M. 1962. General and regional haemodynamic pattern underlying essential hypertension. *Clin. Sci.* 23:339-349.

Broverman, D.M. 1962. Normative and ipsative measurement in psychology. *Psychol. Rev.* 4:259-305.

Caplan, R.D.; Cobb, S.; French, J.R.P., Jr.; Van Harrison, R.; and Pinneau, S.R., Jr. 1975. Job demands and worker health. Washington, D.C.: U.S. Government Printing Office.

Cattell, R.B. 1964. Psychological definition and measurement of anxiety. *J. Neuropsychiat.* 5:396-402.

Cattell, R.B., and Scheier, I.H. 1961. *The meaning and measurement of neuroticism and anxiety.* New York: The Ronald Press Co.

Champion, R.A., and Jones, J.E. 1962. Drive level and extinction in classical aversive conditioning. *J. Gen. Psychol.* 67:61–87.

Corson, S.A. 1966a. Conditioning of water and electrolyte excretion. In *Endocrines and the central nervous system*. Baltimore, MD: Williams and Wilkins Co.

________. 1966b. Neuroendocrine and behavioral response patterns to psychologic stress and the problem of the target tissue in cerebrovisceral pathology. Proc. Conference on Psychophysiological Aspects of Cancer. *Ann. N.Y. Acad. Sci.* 125(3): 890–918.

________. 1971a. Pavlovian and operant conditioning techniques in the study of psychosocial and biological relationships. In *Society, stress and disease,* ed. L. Levi, Vol 1, *The psychosocial environment and psychosomatic diseases.* London, England: Oxford University Press.

________. 1971b. The lack of feedback in today's societies—a psychosocial stressor. In *Society, stress and disease,* ed. L. Levi, Vol. 1, *The psychosocial environment and psychosomatic diseases.* London, England: Oxford University Press.

Corson, S.A., and O'Leary Corson, E. 1969. Neuroendocrine and behavioral correlates of constitutional differences. *Conditional Reflex* 4(4): 265–266.

________. 1971. Psychosocial influences on renal function—implications for human pathophysiology. In *Society, stress and disease*, ed. L. Levi, Vol. 1, *The psychosocial environment and psychosomatic diseases.* London, England: Oxford University Press.

________. 1976. Constitutional differences in physiologic adaptation to stress and distress. In *Psychopathology of human adaptation,* ed. G. Serban. New York: Plenum Press.

________. 1981. Working situations and psychophysiologic pathology—a systems approach. In *Society, stress and disease*, ed. L. Levi, Vol. 4, *The psychosocial environment and psychosomatic diseases.* London, England: Oxford University Press.

Corson, S.A.; O'Leary Corson, E.; and Kirilcuk, V. 1970. Individual differences in respiratory responses of dogs to psychologic stress and Anokhin's formulation of the functional system as a unit of biological adaptation. *Int. J. Psychobiol.* 1(1): 1–12.

Dembroski, T.M.; MacDougall, J.M.; and Shields, J.L. 1971. Physiologic reactions to social challenge in persons evidencing the type A coronary prone behavior pattern. *J. Hum. Stress* 3:2–9.

Dembroski, T.M.; Weiss, S.M.; Shields, J.L.; Haynes, S.G.; and Feinleib, M., eds. 1978. *Coronary-prone behavior.* New York: Springer-Verlag.

Eliot, R.S., and Buell, J.C. 1983. The role of the CNS in cardiovascular disorders. *Hospital Practice* :189–199.

Eliot, R.S.; Buell, J.C.; and Dembroski, T.M. 1982. Bio-behavioral perspectives on coronary heart disease, hypertension and sudden cardiac death. *Acta Med. Scand.* 660 (suppl):203.

Epstein, L.D. 1970. State authority and state universities. *Daedalus* 99(3): 700–712.

Eysenck, H.J., ed. 1960. *Experiments in personality*, Vol. 1, *Psychogenetics and psychopharmacology*. New York: Humanities Press, Inc.

________. 1963. Biological basis of personality. *Nature* 199(4898):1031–1034.

________. 1981. Personality and psychosomatic diseases. *Activ. Nerv. Sup.* (Praha) 23(2):112–129.

Fedorov, V.K. 1952. Znachenie dlya psikhiatrii i psikhologii ucheniya I.P. Pavlova o tipakh vysshei nervoi deyatel'nosti (Significance of I.P. Pavlov's teaching on types of higher nervous activity for psychiatry and psychology). *Zh. Nevropatol. i Psikhiat.* 52(6): 13–19.

Fencl, V.; Hejl, J.; Jirka, J.; Madlafousek, J.; and Brod, J. 1959. Changes of blood flow in forearm muscle and skin during an acute emotional stress (mental arithmetic). *Clin. Sci.* 18(3): 491–498.

Firsov, L.A. 1961. Sravnitel'naya kharakteristika povedeniya i nekotorykh vegetativnykh funktstii u shimpanze (Comparative characteristics of behavior and of some vegetative functions in the chimpanzee). *Dokl. Akad. nauk SSR* 141(6): 1522–1254.

Frankenhaeuser, M. 1977. Quality of life: Criteria for behavioral adjustment. *International Journal of Psychology* 12(2): 99–110.

Frankenhaeuser, M., and Lundberg, U. 1977. The influence of cognitive set on performance and arousal under different noise levels. *Motivation and Emotion* 1(2):139–149.

Friedman, M. 1950. Hyperthermia as a manifestation of stress. In *Life stress and bodily disease.* New York: Hafner Publishing Co.

Friedman, M., and Rosenman, R.H. 1959. Association of specific overt behavior pattern with blood and cardiovascular findings. *J. Am. Med. Ass.* 169:1286–1295.

Fuller, J.L., and Thompson, W.R. 1960. *Behavior genetics.* New York: John Wiley and Sons.

Furedy, J.J.; Riley, D.M.; and Fredrikson, M. 1983. Pavlovian extinction, phobias, and the limits of the cognitive paradigm. *Pavlovian J. of Biol. Sci.* 18(3): 126–135.

Gallant, J.A., and Prothero, J.W. 1972. Weight-watching at the university: The consequences of growth. *Science* 175(4020): 381–388.

Gantt, W.H. 1944. *Experimental basis for neurotic behavior.* New York: Harper & Brothers.

________. 1953. Principles of nervous breakdown—schizokinesis and autokinesis. *Ann. N.Y. Acad. Sci.* 56(2):143.

________. 1962. Factors involved in the development of pathological behavior: Schizokinesis and autokinesis. *Perspectives Biol. Med.* 5(4): 473–482.

________. 1974. Autokinesis, schizokinesis, organ-system responsibility: Concepts and definitions. *Pav. J. Biol. Sci.* 9(4): 187–191.

Ginsburg, B.E. 1967. Genetic parameters in behavioral research. In *Behavior-genetic analysis*, ed. J. Hirsch. New York: McGraw-Hill.

Given, W.B., Jr. 1949. *Bottom-Up management. People working together.* New York: Harper and Brothers.

Glass, D.C. 1977. *Behavior patterns, stress, and coronary disease.* Hillsdale, NJ: Lawrence Erlbaum Associates.

________. 1978. Pattern A behavior and uncontrollable stress. In *Coronary-prone behavior,* eds. T.M. Dembroski, S.M. Weiss, J.L. Shields, S.G. Haynes, and M. Feinleib. New York: Springer-Verlag.

Graubard, S.R., ed. 1970. Preface to the issue Rights and responsibilities: The university's dilemma. *Daedalus* 99(3): 5–14.

Gray, J.A., ed. 1964. *Pavlov's typology.* Oxford, England: Pergamon Press.

Hall, C.S. 1941. Temperament: A survey of animal studies. *Psychol. Bull.* 38:909–943.

Hambling, J. 1959. Essential hypertension. In *The nature of stress disorder*. Springfield, IL: Charles C. Thomas.

Hamburg, D.A. 1967. Genetics of adrenocortical hormone metabolism in relation to psychological stress. In *Behavior-genetic analysis*, ed. J. Hirsch. New York: McGraw-Hill.

Harman, S. 1976. Statement of Sidney Harman, Ph.D., board chairman and chief executive officer of Harman International Industries, Lake Success, Long Island, NY. In *Changing patterns of work in America, 1976: Hearings on examination of alternative working hours and arrangements*, 94th Cong., 2nd sess., 7 and 8 April 1976. Washington, D.C.: U.S. Government Printing Office.

Haynes, S.G.; Feinleib, M.; and Kannel, W.B. 1980. The relationship of psychosocial factors to coronary heart disease in the Framingham study. *Am. J. Epidemiol.* 111:37.

Heron, W.T. 1935. The inheritance of maze-learning ability in rats. *J. Comp. Psychol.* 19:77–89.

Hirsch, J. 1962. Individual differences in behavior and their genetic basis. In *Roots of behavior*, ed. E.L. Bliss. New York: Harper and Brothers.

________. 1967. Behavior-genetic analysis. In *Behavior-genetic analysis*, ed. J. Hirsch. New York: McGraw-Hill.

Hirsch, J.; and Tryon, R.C. 1956. Mass screening and reliable individual measurements in the experimental behavior genetics of lower organisms. *Psychol. Bull.* 53:402–410.

Horvath, M., and Frantik, E. 1981. Testing of psychophysiological reactivity of subjects with coronary-prone behaviour in multifactorial preventive study. *Abstracts of colloquium on psychosomatic risk factors of cardiovascular diseases*. Czechoslovakia: Karlovy Vary.

Jacobson, E. 1929. *Progressive relaxation*. Chicago: University of Chicago Press.

Jenkins, C.D. 1978. A comparative review of the interview and questionnaire methods in the assessment of the coronary-prone behavior pattern. In *Coronary-prone behavior*, eds. T.M. Dembroski, S.M. Weiss, J.L. Shields, S.G. Haynes, and M. Feinleib. New York: Springer-Verlag.

Jenkins, C.D.; Rosenman, R.H.; and Friedman, M. 1967. Development of an objective psychological test for the determination of the coronary-prone behavior pattern in employed men. *J. Chron. Dis.* 20:371–379.

Kallmann, F.J. 1954. The genetics of psychotic behavior patterns. In *Genetics and the inheritance of integrated neurological and psychiatric patterns*, eds. D. Hooker and C.C. Hare. Baltimore, MD: Williams and Wilkins Co.

________. 1962. New genetic approaches to psychiatric disorders. In *Research approaches to psychiatric problems*, eds. T.T. Tourlentes, L. Pollack, and H.E. Himwich. New York: Grune and Stratton.

Kavetskii, R.E.; Solodyuk, N.F.; Vovk, S.I.; Krasnovskaya, M.S.; and Dzgoeva, T.A. 1961. *Reaktivnost' organizma i tip nernvoi sistemy* (Reactivity of the organism and type of nervous system). Kiev: Akademiya Nauk USSR, Institut Fiziologii im. A.A. Bogomol'tsa.

Kimmel, H.D.; Van Olst, E.H.; and Orlebeke, J.F., eds. 1979. *The orienting reflex in humans*. Hillsdale, NJ: Lawrence Erlbaum Associates.

Kolesnikov, M.S., and Troshikhin, V.A. 1951. Malyi standart ispytanii dlya opredeleniya tipa vysshei nervnoi deyatel'nosti sobaki (The small standard of tests for the determination of the type of higher nervous activity in dogs). *Zh. vyssh. nerv. deyat. I.P. Pavlova* 1(5): 739–743.

Kornitzer, M.; Kittel, F.; DeBacker, G.; and Dramaiz, M. 1981. The Belgian heart disease prevention project: Type "A" behavior pattern and the prevalance of coronary heart disease. *Psychosom. Med.* 43(2):133–145.

Krasuskii, V.K. 1964. Metodika ostenki svoistv nervnykh protsessov u sobak, prinyataya laboratoriei fiziologii i genetiki tipov vysshei nervnoi deyatel'nosti. (The method of evaluation of the properties of nervous processes in dogs adopted by the laboratory of the physiology and genetics of types of higher nervous activity). In *Metodiki izucheniya tipologicheskikh osobennostei vysshei nervnoi deyatel'nosti zhivotnykh* (Methods of studying the typologic characteristics of higher nervous activity in animals), ed. V.N. Chernigovskii. Moscow-Leningrad: AN SSSR.

Krushinskii, L.V. 1960. *Formirovanie povedeniya zhivotnykh v norme i patologii* (The formation of animal behavior under normal and pathologic conditions). Moscow: Moscow University.

Lader, M.H. 1971. The responses of normal subjects and psychiatric patients to repetitive stimulation. In *Society, stress and disease*, ed. L. Levi, Vol. 1, *The psychosocial environment and psychosomatic diseases*. London, England: Oxford University Press.

Lazarus, R. 1966. *Psychological stress and the coping process*. New York: McGraw-Hill.

________. 1967. Cognitive and personality factors underlying threat and coping. In *Psychological stress*, eds. M.H. Appley and R. Trumbull. New York: Appleton-Century-Croft.

________. 1978. A strategy for research on psychological and social factors in hypertension. *J. Human Stress* 4(3):35–40.

Leibrecht, B.C. 1974. Habituation: Supplemental bibliography. *Physiol. Psychol.* 2(3B): 1–19.

Levi, L. 1971. The human factor—and the inhuman. In *Society, stress, and disease*, ed. L. Levi, Vol. 1, *The psychosocial environment and psychosomatic diseases*. London, England: Oxford University Press.

________. 1973. Stress, distress and psychosocial stimuli. *Occup. Mental Health* 3(3): 2–10. (Also in *Occupational stress*, ed. A. McLean. Springfield, IL: Charles C. Thomas).

________. 1979. Psychosocial factors in preventive medicine. In *Healthy people: The surgeon general's report on health promotion and disease prevention—background papers*. DHEW (PHS) Publication No. 79-55071A, Washington, D.C.

Levine, S., and Treiman, D.M. 1964. Differential plasma corticosterone response to stress in four inbred strains of mice. *Endocrinology* 75:142–144.

Lown, B.; Verrier, R.; and Corbalan, R. 1973. Psychologic stress and threshold for repetitive ventricular response. *Science* 182(4114): 834–836.

Lundberg, U., and Frankenhaeuser, M. 1978. Psychophysiological reactions to noise as modified by personal control over noise intensity. *Biological Psychology* 6(1978):51–59.

Marceil, J.C. 1977. Implicit dimensions of idiography and nomothesis: A reformulation. *Am. Psychol.* 32:1046–1055.

Marks, I.M. 1969. *Fears and phobias*. London, England: Heineman.

Mason, J.W. 1968. Organization of the multiple endocrine responses to avoidance in the monkey. *Psychosom. Med.* 30(5) Part 2:774–790.

________. 1975. A historical view of the stress field. *J. Human Stress* 1(1): 6–12 and 1(2):22–36.

Masserman, J.H. 1943. *Behavior and neurosis.* Chicago: University of Chicago Press.

________. 1971. The principle of uncertainty in neurotigenesis. In *Experimental psychopathology,* ed. H.D. Kimmel. New York: Academic Press.

Mayr, E. 1958. Behavior and systematics. In *Behavior and evolution,* eds. A. Roe and G.G. Simpson. New Haven, CT: Yale University Press.

________. 1959. Darwin and the evolutionary theory in biology. In *Evolution and anthropology: A centennial appraisal,* ed. B.J. Megges. Washington, D.C.: The Anthropology Society of Washington.

McGuigan, F.J. 1981. *Calm down. A guide for stress and tension control.* Englewood Cliffs, NJ: Prentice-Hall.

Monaenkov, A.M. 1963. *Faktor individual'nosti v protsessakh immuniteta* (The factor of individuality in immune processes). Moscow: Institut normal'noi i patologicheskoi fiziologii, Akademiya Meditsinskikh Nauk SSSR.

Morison, R.S. 1970. Some aspects of policy-making in the American university. *Daedalus* 99(3):609–644.

Mowrer, O.H. 1939. A stimulus-response analysis of anxiety and its role as a reinforcing agent. *Psychol. Rev.* 46:553–565.

Mowrer, O.H., and Viek, P. 1948. An experimental analogue of fear from a sense of helplessness. *J. Abnorm. Soc. Psychol.* 43:193–200.

Mundy-Castle, A.C., and McKiever, B.L. 1953. The psychophysiologic significance of the galvanic skin response. *J. Exp. Psychol.* 46:15–24.

Nebylitsyn, V.D. 1966. *Osnovnye svoistva nervnoi sistemy cheloveka* (Fundamental properties of the human nervous system). Moscow: Prosveshchenie.

Nikiforovskii, P.M. 1910. Farmakologiya uslovnykh refleksov, kak metod dlya ikh izucheniya (Pharmacology of conditioned reflexes as a method for their investigation). Diss., St. Petersburg.

Organesyan, L.A. 1961. *O vzaimootnosheniyakh mezhdu psikhicheskoi i somaticheskoi sferami v klinike vnutrennikh boleznei* (Interrelations between the psychic and somatic spheres in the clinical course of internal diseases). Erevan: Institut Kardiologii, Akademiya Nauk Armyanskoi SSR.

Parnell, R.W. 1958. *Behaviour and physique. An introduction to practical and applied somatometry.* London, England: Edward Arnold Ltd.

Pavlov, I.P. 1903. Eksperimental'naya psikhologiya i psikhopatologiya na zhivotnykh (Experimental psychology and psychopathology on animals). *Izv. Voenno-med. Akad.* (Bulletin of the Military Medical Academy) 7(2): 109–121. (Also in *Dvadtsatiletnii opyt ob''ektivnogo izucheniya vysshei nervnoi deyatel'nosti (povedeniya) zhivotnykh. Uslovnye refleksy* (Twenty years of experience in the objective study of the higher nervous activity (behavior) of animals. Conditioned reflexes), ed. I.P. Pavlov. Moscow: Medgiz. Chapter 1, 1951).

________. 1916. *Refleks tseli* (The reflex of purpose). (Also in Ibid., 1951, Chapter 27).

________. 1928. *Lectures on conditioned reflexes,* trans. and ed. W.H. Gantt. New York: International Publishers Co., Inc.

________. 1935. Obshchie tipy vysshei nervnoi deyatel'nosti zhivotnykh i cheloveka

(General types of higher nervous activity in animals and man). In *Poslednie soobshcheniya po fiziologii i patologii vysshei nervnoi deyatel'nosti* (Latest reports on the physiology and pathology of higher nervous activity), No. 3 Moscow: Akademiya Nauk SSSR. (Also in *O tipakh vysshei nervnoi deyatel'nosti i eksperimental'nykh nevrozakh* (Types of higher nervous activity and experimental neuroses), ed. P.S. Kupalov. Moscow: Medgiz, 1954.)

________. 1935. The conditioned reflex. *Fiziol. zh. S.S.S.R.* (Journal of Physiology of the U.S.S.R.) 19(1):299–313.

________. 1941. *Lectures on conditioned reflexes*, trans. and ed. W.H. Gantt, Vol. 2, *Conditioned reflexes and psychiatry*. New York: International Publishers Co., Inc.

________. 1954. *O tipakh vysshei nervnoi deyatel'nosti i eksperimental'nykh nevrozakh* (Types of higher nervous activity and experimental neuroses), ed. P.S. Kupalov. Moscow: Medgiz (in Russian).

Perel'tsveig (Perelzveig), I.Y. 1907. Materialy k ucheniyu ob uslovnykh refleksakh (Materials on the theory of conditioned reflexes). Diss., St. Petersburg.

Petrova, M.K. 1955. *O roli funktsional'no oslablennoi kory golovnogo mozga v vozniknovenii razlichnykh patologicheskikh protsessov v organizme* (The role of a functionally weakened cerebral cortex in the onset of various pathologic processes in the organism). Moscow: Medgiz.

Pimenov, P.P. 1907. Osobaya gruppa uslovnykh refleksov (A particular group of conditional reflexes). Diss., St. Petersburg.

Rosenman, R.H., and Friedman, M. 1977. Modifying type A behavior pattern. *J. of Psychosom. Res.* 21:323–331.

Rosenman, R.H.; Brand, R.J.; Sholtz, R.I.; and Friedman, M. 1976. Multivariate prediction of coronary heart disease during 8.5 year follow-up in the western collaborative group study. *Am. J. Cardiol.* 37:903.

Scott, J.P., and Fuller, J.L. 1965. *Genetics and the social behavior of the dog.* Chicago: University of Chicago Press.

Searle, L.V. 1949. The organization of hereditary maze-brightness and maze-dullness. *Genet. Psychol. Monograph* 39:279–325.

Seligman, M.E.P. 1975. *Helplessness: On depression, development and death.* San Fransisco, CA: W.H. Freeman and Co.

Selye, H. 1971. The evolution of the stress concept—stress and cardiovascular disease. In *Society, stress and disease*, ed. L. Levi, Vol. 1, *Environment and psychosomatic diseases.* London, England: Oxford University Press.

________. 1978. On the real benefits of eustress. Interview by L. Cherry. *Psychology Today* Mar:60–70.

Shoben, E.J., Jr. 1970. Cultural criticism and the American college, ed. S.R. Graubard. *Daedalus* 99(3):676–699.

Simonov, P.V. 1965. O roli emotsii v prisposobitel'nom povedenii zhivykh sistem (The role of emotions in adaptive behavior of living systems). *Vop. Psikhol.* (Problems of Psychology) 11(4):75–84 (in Russian).

Sokolov, E.N., ed. 1959. *Orientirovochnyi refleks i voprosy vysshei nervnoi deiatel'nosti v norme i patologii* (The orienting reflex and problems of higher nervous activity under normal and pathologic conditions). Moscow: Akademiia Pedagogicheskikh Nauk RSFSR, Institut Defektologii (Institute of Defectology, RSFSR Academy of Pedagogical Sciences Publishing House).

Sokolov, E.N. 1963. *Perception and the conditioned reflex.* Oxford, England: Pergamon Press.

Sokolov, E.N., and Vinogradova, O.S. 1975. *Neuronal mechanisms of the orienting reflex.* Hillsdale, NJ: Lawrence Erlbaum Associates.

Sorri, P.; Achte, K.; and Varilo, E. 1976. Work and stress in the academic world. *Psychiat. Fennica*:195–200.

Stockard, C.R. 1941. The genetic and endocrine basis for differences in form and behavior. In *American anatomical memoirs*, No. 19. Philadelphia, PA: Wistar Inst. of Anatomy and Biology.

Stockard, C.R.; Anderson, O.D.; and James, W.T. 1941. The genetic and endocrinic basis for differences in form and behavior. In *American anatomical memoirs*, No. 19. Philadelphia, PA: Wistar Inst. of Anatomy and Biology.

Sudakov, K.V. 1976. *Emotsional'nyi stress i arterial'naia gipertenziia-Obzor eksper-mental'nykh dannykh* (Emotional stress and arterial hypertension-Review of experimental data). Moscow: VNIIMI (in Russian).

________. 1981. *Sistemnye mekhanizmy emotsional'nogo stressa* (Systems mechanisms in emotional stress). Moscow: Meditsina Publishers (in Russian).

________. 1983. *Emotional stress and arterial hypertension—Review of experimental data*, scien. and trans. eds. S.A. Corson and E. O'Leary Corson. New Delhi: Amerind Publishing Co., Oxonian Press; distributed by the U.S. Dept. of Commerce, National Technical Information Service, Springfield, VA.

Teplov, B.M. 1961. *Problemy individual'nykh razlichii* (Problems of individual differences). Moscow: Akademiya Pedagogicheskikh Nauk RSFSR.

The Review Panel on Coronary-Prone Behavior and Coronary Heart Disease. 1981. Coronary-prone behavior and coronary heart disease: A critical review. *Circulation* 63(6):1199–1215.

Thomas, C.B. 1976. What becomes of medical students: The dark side. *The Johns Hopkins Medical Journal* 138:185–195.

________. 1977. Habits of nervous tension: Clues to the human condition. *The Precursors Study.* Baltimore, MD: The Johns Hopkins University School of Medicine.

Tolman, E.C. 1924. The inheritance of maze-learning ability in rats. *J. Comp. Psychol.* 4:1–18.

Tryon, R.C. 1929. The genetics of learning ability in rats. *Univ. Calif. Publ. Psychol.* 4:71–89.

________. 1940. Genetic differences in maze-learning ability in rats. In *Yearbook National Soc. Stud. Educ.* 39(1):111–119.

Vandenberg, S.G., ed. 1965. *Methods and goals in human behavior genetics.* New York: Academic Press.

Varukha, E.A. 1953. Sravnitel'naia otsenka tipa vysshei nervnoi deitael'nosti sobak po orientirovochnym refleksam (Comparative evaluation of the type of higher nervous activity of dogs on the basis of orienting reflexes). *16^{oe} Sovessch. po problemam vyssh. nerv. deiat. Tezisy i referaty 1953*(16th Conference on problems of higher nervous activity).

Vatsuro, E.G. 1949. Printsip vedushchei afferentatsii v uchenii vysshei nervnoi deyatel'nosti (The principle of leading afferentation in the study of higher nervous activity). *Fiziol. zh. SSSR* 35(5).

Vinogradov, N.V. 1938. Slabyi tormoznyi tip nervnoi systemy (Weak inhibitory type of nervous system), Vol. 5, *Trudy fiziol. lab. im. I.P. Pavlova* (Publications of the I.P. Pavlov Laboratory).

Voronin, L.G., and Shirkova, E.N. 1949. Ugasheniie orientirovochno-issledovatel'skogo refleksa u obez'ian kak odin iz testov opredeleniaa ikh tipov nervnoi sistemy (Extinction of the orienting-investigatory reflex in monkeys as one of the tests for determining their type of nervous system). *Biull. eskp. biol. i med.* 28(9).

Vyrzhikhovskii, S.N., and Maiorov, F.P. 1933. K voprosu o vliyanii vospitaniya na sklad vysshei nervnoi deyatel'nosti u sobak (The influence of rearing on the constitution of higher nervous activity in dogs). *Tr. fiziol. lab. I.P. Pavlova* (Publications of the I.P. Pavlov Laboratory) 5:169–191.

Weiss, J.M. 1971a. Effects of coping behavior in different warning signal conditions on stress pathology in rats. *J. Comp. Physiol. Psychol.* 77:1.

________. 1971b. Effects of punishing the coping the response (conflict) on stress pathology in rats. *J. Comp. Physiol. Psychol.* 77:14.

________. 1971c. Effects of coping behavior with and without a feedback signal on stress pathology in rats. *J. Comp. Physiol. Psychol.* 77:22.

Wiener, N. 1948. *Cybernetics.* New York: John Wiley and Sons.

Williams, R.J. 1956. *Biochemical individuality.* New York: John Wiley and Sons.

Wolf, S. 1971. Psychosocial forces in myocardial infarction and sudden death. In *Society, stress and disease*, ed. L. Levi, Vol. 1, *The psychosocial environment and psychosomatic diseases.* London, England: Oxford University Press.

________. 1972. Sudden cardiac death. In *The artery and the process of arteriosclerosis measurement and modification*, ed. S. Wolf. New York: Plenum Press.

Wolf, S.; Pfeiffer, J.B.; Ripley, H.S.; Winter, O.S.; and Wolff, H.G. 1948. Hypertension as a reaction pattern to stress: Summary of experimental data on variations in blood pressure and renal flow. *Ann. Internal Med.* 29:1056–1076.

Wolf, S.; Cardon, P.V., Jr.; Shepard, E.M.; and Wolff, H.G. 1955. *Life stress and essential hypertension.* Baltimore, MD: Williams and Wilkins Co.

Zavadskii, I.V. 1908. Materialy k voprosu o tormozhenii i rastormazhivanii uslovnykh refleksov (Inhibition and disinhibition of conditional reflexes). Diss., St. Petersburg.

Zeval'd, L.O. 1938. K voprosu o vliyanii uslovii vospitaniya na sklad vysshei nervnoi deyatel'nosti u sobak (The influence of the conditions of rearing on the constitution of higher nervous activity in dogs), Vol. 8, *Tr. fiziol. lab. I.P. Pavlova.*

Chapter 6

Asymmetric Brain Specialization: Proposed Relationship Between Its Development and Cognitive Development

by R. Harter Kraft

NATURE OF HUMAN BRAIN ASYMMETRY

We have known for years that asymmetric deficits may develop following lesions, surgery, or damage to the left or right cerebral hemisphere (Benton 1972; Broca 1863; Corkin 1965; Dax 1836; Kinsbourne and Smith 1974; Milner 1975; Mountcastle 1962), and recent research has demonstrated that the two hemispheres in the intact human brain are specialized in function (Dimond 1972; Dimond and Beaumont 1974; Dimond and Blizard 1977; Harnad et al. 1977; Kinsbourne 1977a; 1984; Segalwitz and Gruber 1977b; Springer and Deutch 1981; Teuber 1975), yet the specific nature of the asymmetry and the underlying mechanisms of the specialization remain under investigation and debate. There is debate, for instance, about the specific role in the specialized asymmetric function of the limbic system and subcortical structures such as the thalamus and midbrain structures (Brown 1975; Goldman 1977; Ojemann 1977; Pribram 1976, 1977; Riklan and Cooper 1977; Robinson 1976) and about hypothesis that the left cerebral hemisphere possesses certain detectors for specific features of natural speech, such as phonological and syntactical information (Cole 1977; Liberman 1975; Pribram 1976; Segalowitz and Gruber 1977a).

Although most researchers and theorists characterize the hemispherical specialization in dichotomous terms, the differences (whether qualitative or quantitative) are probably relative rather than exclusive. Nevertheless, the terminology used most commonly to define this specialization is verbal (for the left) and visual-spatial or non-verbal (for the right). There is evidence, however, that language *per se* is not the common denominator of left-hemispheric specialization. The left hemisphere has been found to be superior to the right also in perceiving temporal patterns and performing fine temporal-order judgments (Carmon and Nachson 1971; Halperin, Nachson and Carmon 1973; Papcun et al., 1974) and sequential motor programming (Kimura and Vanderwolf 1970; see Krashen 1976a, 1977 for a review of this literature) independent of linguistic processing.

In addition the right cerebral hemisphere has been found to possess some language skills. For example, global asphasic patients have often been reported to have a residum of semantic knowledge although they retain no syntactic or grammatical abilities (Rudel 1978). Moreover, when input is restricted to the right hemisphere in "split-brain" patients, they have been found to have an auditory single-word recognition vocabularies of ages eight to sixteen (mean at eleven years, seven months); their major deficits seem to stem from poor short-term verbal/sequential memory (Zaidel 1976, 1977a, b) and a lack of syntactic abilities (Gazzaniga and Hillyard 1971; Zaidel 1977a). In addition, Yamadori (1975) and Sasanuma and Fujimara (1971) report that left hemispheric damage destroyed Japanese patients' ability to read and write Kana (a phonographic system) while leaving intact their ability to read and write Kanji (an ideographic system). From reviewing the literature on the right hemisphere's linguistic ability, Searleman (1977) concludes that the left hemisphere appears to have control of expressive language but the right hemisphere also has receptive language abilities. Clearly then, the right hemisphere does possess some language skills. What is not known is whether right-hemispheric linguistic processing is qualitatively or quantitatively different from that of the left. Rudel (1978) suggests that the left and right hemispheres have different linguistic functions, complementing each other, but she does not specifically define the nature of the differences.

Of the researchers positing broader differences between hemispheric function systems than linguistic-nonlinguistic, Semmes (1968) puts forward perhaps the most succint hypothesis. Presenting research on brain-injured veterans who demonstrated focal representation (of sensory and motor capabilities of the hands) in the left hemisphere and diffuse representation of the same abilities in the right, she suggests that "hemispheric specialization in language stems from a basic difference in sensorimotor organization" (p. 21). This contrast then is one of focal representation (in the left hemisphere) versus diffuse representation (in the right hemisphere). The complex coordination of the elementary functions that characterize the higher centers is brought about by convergence of lower-level (neutral) units. She argues that when functionally similar lower-level units are concentrated heavily in a small area (focally represented), their integration and convergence into the next level "would bring about a more precise coding of the input and would thus make possible a more finely modulated control of the output. This finer control could be based not only on concentration of similar input elements, but also on an analogous concentration of similar output elements. The development of such precise control of the articulatory apparatus may provide an optimal substrate for speech representation in the left hemisphere" (pp. 21-22). Conversely, Semmes suggests that right-hemispheric processing is based upon a diffuse organization that confers an advantage for spatial abilities by frequent convergence of unlike units, bringing about "heteromodal integration to an extent surpassing that possible in a focally-organized hemisphere. In contrast to functions which may depend on a high degree of convergence of like elements, spatial function might depend instead on convergence of unlike elements—visual, kinesthetic, vestibular, and perhaps others—combining in such a way as to create through experience a single supermodal space" (p. 24). In accord with the foregoing, Kimura (1976) cites research suggesting relationships between manual skill and speech lateralization in the brain of normal, deaf, and lesioned subjects. She suggests that underlying the functional specialization of the left hemisphere is a superiority for programming complex sequential motor movements, which includes speech production.

However, despite the elegant simplicity of Semmes' hypothesis, some evidence suggests subcortical "attentional" differences between the left and right brain systems, including perception of verbal versus nonverbal stimuli as well as speech motor-control mechanisms. At the basis of evidence that the ventrolateral and pulvinar thalamic nuclei of right-handed subjects are involved asymmetrically specific alerting response model with a verbal-nonverbal material, Ojemann (1977) suggests an asymmetric specific alerting response model with a verbal-nonverbal dichotomy. Stimulation of the left thalamus increased recognition and recall memory during the presentation of verbal stimuli and objects easy-to-label-verbally but decreased recognition and recall of objects difficult to code verbally. In addition, the left thalamus was found to be involved in the mechanical processes underlying speech, such as the respiratory oral-facial muscle control. In contrast, stimulation of the right thalamus facilitated recognition and recall of nonverbal stimuli. Since the thalamus is thought to be involved in motor memory and evidences a similar, though probably not asymmetric, alerting response in animals, and since the ventral-lateral thalamic nucleus is considered part of the motor system, Ojemann suggests that the human brain, through evolution, has incorporated this motor memory system into a mechanism for verbal and nonverbal memory via ipsilateral channels. The human left lateral thalamus is "an interface between motor, automatic and alerting processes and language functions (that) represent an interface between evolutionary more complex processes such as language" (p. 393). Conversely, the right thalamus evidences a similar interface with visual-spatial material that is difficult to code verbally. Thus, according to this model, the human brain is asymmetric at the subcortical level as well, with the left thalamus functioning as an alerting mechanism to the left cerebral hemisphere for memory, perception, processing, and production of linguistic information. Although Ojemann's model involves a verbal-nonverbal dichotomy, the functional specialization posited also includes an asymmetric control of the musculature related to speech production.

Further support for the asymmetric motor-control hypothesis comes from evidence that the left hemisphere may be specialized for motor control of the tongue. Sussman (1971) and Sussman and MacNeilage (1975) and subjects perform a pursuit auditory tracking task. The stimulus tone was played in one ear while subjects were to match it to a second stimulus which was placed in the other ear. In addition, they had subjects control the matching tone either with their left or right hand or with their tongue. They found that subjects could match the tone significantly better in the right-ear (left-hemisphere)- tongue condition than the left-ear (right-hemisphere)-tongue condition, and no difference was found for either of the hand-control conditions. On the basis of the Sussman data, Segalowitz and Gruber (1977a) suggest that the left hemisphere may be specialized for control of speech mechanisms independent of language *per se*. They further argue that this specialization may explain the localization of Broca's area (the motor-speech area) in close physical proximity to the motor control area for the tongue in the left hemisphere. Thus, the nature of the functional specialization of the left hemisphere may be a built-in sensorimotor superiority for rapid sequencing; for analyzing rapid sequential stimuli (such as linguistic inputs) and for programming rapid sequential motor movements (such as speech). This left hemisphere superiority appears to include subcortical attentional or alerting system(s) for perceiving and programming this sequential processing and, as Semmes suggests, a cortical organizationn that facilitates and supports it.

Evidence for the cortical units suggested by Semmes and of their differential organization within the two hemispheres is circumstantial, however, as is much recent research and subsequent hypotheses on the nature of cerebral functional asymmetry which appears to support Semmes' hypothesis. Therefore a consensus of opinion has not been reached among researchers (e.g., Kinsbourne 1775a, b, 1977a, b; Kinsbourne and Hiscock 1977). The supprting hypothesis included analytic versus synthetic-gestalt perception (Levy-Agresti and Sperry 1968), temporal-analytic versus spatial- synthetic operations (Levy, Trevarthen and Sperry 1972), analytic versus holistic processing (Bever, 1975) sequential versus parallel processing (Cohen 1973), linear versus nonlinear processing, rational versus intuitive (Ornstein 1972a, b) and propositional versus appositional thinking (Bogen 1969).

The human brain thus appears to have two asymmetrically functioning systems that include both subcortical and cortical components. For most adults the left-hemisphere system is thought to be specialized for verbal, linear, and analytic processing and learning by the sequential building of constructs; it is primarily involved in analyzing parts of a whole, propositional thinking, and temporal structuring of the world. It appears also to possess an asymmetric motor control of the speech musculature as well as being superior at programming rapid sequential motor movements. The right-hemisphere system is thought to be primarily involved in gestalt, synthetic, imaginal, and simultaneous processing input; it mediates learning by holistic synthesizing of constructs, and is the site of the mechanism involved in filling in missing pieces to understand the whole picture and the spatial structuring of the world.

This description, however, may apply only to adults and perhaps only to right hand-eye preference adult males with no left handed ancestors (Hardyck 1977; Kraft 1981b, 1983). The existence of predictable invidivual and group differences in brain organization is yet another area of current investigation and debate.

SEX DIFFERENCES IN BRAIN DEVELOPMENT AND ORGANIZATION

Sex differences in the functional maturation of the cerebral cortex that may depend in part on differences in cerebral organization (Bryden 1979; Harris 1977b; McGlone 1978) and/or early hormonal differences (Reinisch 1974) have been suggested. A series of studies by Goldman and associates (Goldman 1976b; Goldman et al. 1974) involving bilateral orbital prefrontal lesions in infant and juvenile rhesus monkeys demonstrated that, by two and one-half months, the operated males showed impaired performance on object-discrimination reversal tasks or spatial delayed-response deficits but that females did not evidence the same deficit until 15 to 18 months of age. The same deficit was immediately observable postoperatively in male and female juvenile and adult monkeys. Those results suggested that this area became functionally involved in these tasks earlier in the males than the females. When, however, females were injected with testosterone propionate before ablation (postnatally), the evidenced deficits at about the same age as the males (two and one-half months) (Goldman 1975, 1976a; see also Rudel 1978, and Young 1977, for discussions). Similar differential maturation may underlie the observed early differences in language acquisition favoring females and the increasing superior spatial abilities in males (Garai and Scheinfeld 1968; Harris 1977a, b; Kamptner, Kraft and Harper 1984; Maccoby and Jacklin 1974).

Several models of sex differences in hemispheric development have been suggested. Buffery and Gray (1972) proposed sex differences favoring girls in terms of left-hemispheric functions, reflected in their earlier development of linguistic skills. They further posited that bilateral functioning of spatial information is common in boys and is the basis for their superiority on spatial tasks. Witelson (1976b, 1977c) reviewed the developmental literature on lateralization and concluded that although there is little evidence of sex differences in left-hemispheric linguistic processing, there is reason to conclude that males have an earlier development of specialized functioning in the right hemisphere. From an extensive review of the sex-differences literature, Harris (1977b) concludes that although both the Buffrey and Gray and Witelson hypotheses have some supporting childhood data they do not account for the available adult data. He thus proposes a model of greater lateralized functioning in adult males than adult females. He suggests that early on females use a verbal intellectual style and males a nonverbal spatial style, with males eventually "catching up" with the females as their left hemispheres become the main linguistic processing center and their right hemispheres are left free to process most of the nonverbal and spatial information. According to this model, adult females tend to process linguistic information with both hemispheres and this impairs their spatial abilities.

Kraft (1982a) found evidence of the intellectual style or strategy differences between the sexes in 7 to 12 year old children. In recalling dichotically presented nonverbal stimuli (environmental sounds), boys showed a left-ear (right hemisphere) advantage and outperformed the girls, who showed a right-ear (left hemisphere) advantage. This finding suggests that males tended to use a spatial right-hemispheric strategy when remembering and identifying dichotically presented environmental sounds and females a less efficient verbal left-hemispheric strategy. Furthermore, this sex difference in ear advantage increased with task difficulty revealing that whether appropriate or not, as the task became harder females increased their tendency to utilize verbal strategies and males a spatial strategy (see Bryden 1978 for an excellent discussion of strategy effects in hemispheric assessment).

THE INFLUENCE OF ENVIRONMENT ON LATERALIZATION

There is reason to suspect that environmental stimulation is necessary for the development of certain neuronal functioning (see Witelson 1977c and Rudel 1978 for discussions). For instance, environmental deprivation during a critical period of brain development will result in permanent visual deficits (Hirsch and Spinilli 1970; Wiesel and Hubel 1965; reviewed in Berry 1976).

Evidence also suggests that linguistic experience may be necessary for the development of left-hemispheric language lateralization. Studies show that congenitially deaf subjects do not develop clearly lateralized language functioning. McKeever et al. (1976) report that college-educated, congenitally deaf adults have marginal visual field asymmetries on linguistic tasks and Neville (1977) reports that only deaf children who have acquired a sign language system evidence even minimal brain-wave asymmetries for linguistic stimuli. Illiterate subjects also have been reported to have less lateralized functioning. For instance, two studies show that both left- and right-hemispheric lesions will equally produce aphasia in illiterate adults (Cameron, Currier and Haerer 1971; Wechsler

1976), and a third investigation indicates that illiterate preadolescent children tend to show less right-ear superiority on verbal tasks than do matched literate controls (Khadem 1977). Children from lower socioeconomic settings are reported to have less language experiences (Hess 1970; Hunt 1964) and may not be as lateralized for language functioning as their middle-class peers (Geffner and Hochberg 1971; Kimura 1967, versus Dorman and Geffner 1974; Geffner and Dorman 1976). Finally, severe sensory and linguistic deprivation, as in the case of Genie[1], may totally disrupt left-hemispheric language development (Curtis, et al. 1976; Fromkin, et al. 1974).

THE INFLUENCE OF HEREDITY ON LATERALIZATION

Evidence is accumulating suggesting that in addition to possible sex differences there are other heritable aspects of brain organization. For example, having left-handed ancestors is associated with decreased lateral specialization. This greater bilateral processing particularly for verbal information, has been reported for both left-handed and right-handed individuals (Hecaen and Sauguet 1971; Hecaen, DeAgostini and Monzon-Montes 1981, Luria 1970) including right-handed children 6 to 12 years of age (Kraft 1981a) and preschoolers as young as 2½ years (Kraft 1982b, 1984).

Bilateral verbal processing has been found to be associated with high Wechsler verbal intelligence scores and high WRAT spelling and reading scores in right hand/eye familial sinistral children 6–15 years of age. In contrast, their right-eyed, right-handed classmates from right-handed lineages who evidenced a strong degree of hemispheric specialization had higher Wechsler verbal intelligence scores, higher Wechsler objects assembly scores, and higher WRAT achievement scores (Reading, Spelling and Math) than the familial dextral children who were not well lateralized (Kraft 1981a, 1983, forthcoming).

Familial sinistrality, however, may be related to delays in language acquistion (Kraft 1982b), particularly for boys (Kraft and Kamptner, forthcoming). Many other studies report that boys lag behind girls in brain maturation (reviewed in McGlone 1978). The findings from this laboratory indicate that familial sinistrality and sex interact in some way (e.g., hormonal influences on inherited brain organization patterns) effecting the maturation (functional plasticity) of the cortex (Kraft 1982b; Kraft and Kamptner forthcoming; Kraft 1984; Worley 1982).

EARLY FUNCTIONAL PLASTICITY OF THE HUMAN CORTEX

The concept of functional plasticity of the human cortex was introduced in the 1800's by the same workers who first reported evidence of lateralized cerebral specialization. Dax (1836) noted that aphasia seldom resulted from gradual destruction of left- hemispheric speech mechanisms but usually resulted from sudden destruction of those areas. He therefore posited that other intact cerebral structures were capable of maintaining normal language function. Broca (1865) reported that although motor speech was lateralized in the left frontal convolution in the adult brain (now termed Broca's area), redevelopment of normal speech following destruction of the area was enabled by the transfer of motor speech to the right frontal convolution.

Following those early reports, subsequent investigators noted that functional plasticity in the human brain decreases with maturation. Studies of language functioning following brain damage in infancy and childhood (e.g., Basser 1962; McFie 1961a, b; for reviews and critiques of those studies, see Dennis and Whitaker 1976; Hecaen 1976; Krashen 1972; Smith 1974) indicate that damage to either hemisphere in infants may disrupt language development, and that unilateral right-hemispheric damage produces transient language dysfunction more often in children than in adults. (Although unilateral damage to either hemisphere in infancy or early childhood rarely if ever causes gross permanent language dysfunction.) Thus, the immature brain appears to be able to compensate for local injury by atypical functioning (or recruitment) of other intact cortical structures (Bay 1975; Hecaen 1976; Zangwill 1975). That is, it seems that early brain damage to the left hemisphere's speech areas may result in the transfer of language functions, wholly or partially, to homologous areas in the right hemisphere. Rasmussen and Milner (1977) report, however, that if developing speech areas are damaged after age five, language functions, usually remain mediated by the remaining intact structures in the left hemisphere. (See Hillier 1954; Obrador, 1964; Van der Vlugt 1974; White 1961 for evidence that the right hemisphere may possibly take over language functions after age five.)

TIMELINE FOR THE DEVELOPMENT OF FUNCTIONAL LATERALIZATION

Evidence documenting the timeline in which these two processing systems attain adult specialized functioning is conflicting; the disagreements appear to depend on the population studied and the method of inferring lateralized functioning. Bay (1975) Krashen (1973a, b) Krashen and Harshman (1972) Lenneberg (1967) Smith (1974) and Zangwill (1960, 1975), who relied mainly on clinical data (see Kinsbourne and Hiscock 1978, for a critique of this literature), posit an equipotentiality of both hemispheres for language functioning at birth. Lenneberg (1967) argued that the period between age two and puberty is the critical period for language acquisition and the irreversible established of language in the left hemisphere. Since Lenneberg's statement, the upper limit for attainment of adult functional lateralization has been challenged. Krashen (1972) reanalyzed Lenneberg's data and stated that there was little evidence of complete linguistic recovery from lesions after five years of age. Citing additional auditory/perceptual studies (i.e., dichotic listening), he suggests that the two hemispheres are equipotent for language at birth, but that by five the left hemisphere attains the adult level of specialization for processing language (Krashen and Harshman 1972). Although considering available empirical data to be insufficient for a conclusive statement regarding the age at which stabilized functioning occurs, Bay (1975) posits two different timelines for lateralization of the motor or expressive speech area (e.g., Broca's area) and the sensory or receptive speech area (e.g., Wernicke's area). According to Bay's analysis the motor-speech area appears to specialize in conjunction with the appearance and stabilization of hand preference which occurs between two and ten years of age, whereas the temporal (receptive) speech area seems to specialize later, and more in correlation with acoustic and possibly cognitive and conceptual aspects of language, although stabilization is also terminated at approximately age ten.

However, as mentioned previously, there is evidence that the right hemisphere retains at least some receptive linguistic and speech-comprehension processing throughout life. Furthermore, in contrast to Bay, Brown and Jaffe (1975) hypothesize that the timeline for lateralization of receptive speech extends into senescence. From an extensive review of this literature, Searleman (1977) concludes that the left hemisphere for most adults is specialized for speech *production* but that the right hemisphere is also capable of at least some speech *comprehension*.

In addition, the age of onset of lateralization as well as the equipotentiality hypothesis have recently been questioned. Clinical, anatomic, experimental, and behavioral data suggests hemispheric differences may already exist in infancy and perhaps at birth or even prenatally.

Subtle deficits later in life have been associated with unilateral brain damage in patients as young as thirteen months old (Annett 1973; Dennis and Kohn 1975; Dennis and Whitaker 1976; Gardiner et al. 1955; Griffith and Davidson 1966; Kohn and Dennis 1974; Teuber 1967). Lesions of the right hemisphere have been associated with spatial and constructional difficulties, while diminished language competence, such as syntactical and abstract linguistic functioning, has been reported following left-hemispheric lesions. Moreover, during childhood left-sided lesions are associated with transient speech loss more frequently than are right-sided lesions, which suggests a left-hemispheric specialization for speech production during language acquisition (reviewed in Hecaen 1976; Witelson 1977c).

Although attempts to infer function from structure are hazardous, anatomical asymmetries have been reported at birth and prenatally. Geschwind (1974) and Geschwind and Levitsky (1968) first reported that the temporal plane (in the area of temporal speech cortex, or Wernicke's area) was larger on the left side of about 65 percent of adult brains, whereas only some 10 percent of the adult brains examined had a larger temporal plane of the right side (for a critique of those findings, see Whitaker and Ojemann 1977). Similar asymmetries have recently been reported in prenatal and neonatal brains (Wada, Clarke, and Hamme 1975; Witelson 1977a; Witelson and Pallie 1973). Wada and his colleagues state that these differences are found as early as the 29th week of gestation.

Electroencephalographic techniques, such as average evoked potential, on-going EEG frequency analysis, and photic driving, also suggests very early lateral differences in brain functioning (see Gardiner and Walter 1977; and Molfese 1976, for reviews). In fact, several workers present data indicating a greater asymmetric functioning in infants than in adults (Crowell et al. 1973; Molfese, Freeman and Palermo 1975). From brain functioning inferred from patterns of electrical activity recorded from leads attached to the scalp over the left and right hemisphere of infants, researchers have reported greater left hemispheric activity during linguistic (Gardiner et al. 1973; Molfese 1972; Molfese, Freeman and Palermo 1975) and mechanical-click stimuli (Davis and Wada 1977; versus Barnet, Vicentini and Campos 1974), and greater right-hemispheric activity during musical stimuli (Gardiner et al. 1973; Molfese 1972; Molfese et al. 1975), white noise (Molfese et al. 1975), and light flashes (Crowell et al. 1973; Davis and Wada 1977).

Behavioral data have also been cited as possible evidence of early asymmetrical brain functioning (for a review, see Turkewitz 1977a, b; Witelson 1977a). The majority of neonates, including premature infants and those born by caesarean section, exhibit a rightward-oriented asymmetric tonic neck reflex (Gesel and Ames 1947; Turkewitz, Gordon and Birch 1965); tend to turn their heads spontaneously to the right more often than the left; and also tend to turn preferentially to the right when bilaterally stimulated (Siqueland and Lipisitt 1966: Turkewitz, Gordon and Birch 1968). Infants during the first weeks of life exhibit this asymmetric responsiveness to tactile (Hammer and Turkewitz 1974; Siqueland, 1964; Turkewitz, Gordon and Birch 1965), visual (Wickelgren 1967), and auditory (Hammer and Turkewitz 1974; Turkewitz, Moreau and Birch 1966) stimuli when presented equally often from both sides.

In addition, there is evidence for early lateralization of motor control. Children as young as three years have been found to have greater strength in the right hand (Ingram 1975b), significantly faster right hand performance on a unimanual finger tapping task (Hiscock and Kinsbourne 1976, 1977, 1978; Ingram 1975b), significantly greater interference of finger tapping with the right hand while speaking concurrently (time-sharing task: Kinsbourne and Hiscock 1977a), and to make more gesturelike movements with the right hand while speaking (Ingram 1975b), Conversely, the left hand of three year-old children has been found to be superior to the right for drawing squares in a conflict drawing task (Buffery 1970, 1971; Buffery and Gray, 1972), copying hand postures (Ingram 1975b), and copying the finger spacing of a hand position (Ingram 1975b).

Further, asymmetries of response to auditory stimuli (dichotic listening) have been reported. In infants as young as one and one-half months old, measures of recovery from habituation indicate asymmetry (Entus 1977; Glanville, Best and Levenson 1977) and measures of overt behavioral responses in children as young as two and one-half to three years of age (Bever 1971; Gilbert 1976; Hiscock and Kinsbourne 1977; Kamptner, Kraft and Harper 1984; Kinsbourne and Hiscock 1977; Kraft 1982b; Nagafuchi 1970; Yeni-Komshian 1973; see Witelson 1977c, for a review and critique of this literature, and Berlin 1977, for a critique of the technique) also indicate hemispheric specialization for processing auditory input. A question currently studied and debated is whether the observed asymmetries increase until age five (Krashen 1973b, 1975, 1976b), age nine (Satz 1976; Satz et al., 1975), age ten (Bay 1974), puberty (Lenneberg 1967), or senescence (Brown and Jaffe 1975); or whether they decrease with age (Molfese et al., 1975); or do not change throughout life (Kinsbourne 1977a; Kinsbourne and Hiscock 1977, 1978).

The debate over timing may be artifactual because functional lateralization may not be a unitary process. For instance, some aspects of linguistic processing may become lateralized earlier than others (Krashen 1976b; Moscovitch 1977; Porter and Berlin 1975; Witelson 1977c). It is also quite possible that the more complex cognitive tasks (such as reading and problem-solving) may profit from complimentary or bilateral hemispheric functioning (Bogen 1969; Geschwind 1974; Kraft 1976; Languis and Kraft, this volume), or require bilateral processing during one stage of acquisition and become lateralized during later stages (Bakker 1973; Loeng 1976). This issue will be discussed further in another section.

ONTOGENETIC FUNCTIONAL REORGANIZATION OF THE BRAIN

In addition, there is some suggestion of ontogenetic functional reorganization of the brain (Brown 1976; Goldman 1975, 1976a; Hecaen 1976; Kraft 1984; Rudel 1978; Witelson 1977c, versus Kinsbourne and Hiscock 1977). Ablation studies on infant rhesus monkeys (Goldman et al., 1974; and Miller, Goldman and Rosvold 1973) indicate that at least some areas in the frontal cortex of these animals are not involved in mediating visual discrimination until adolescence (18 months to 2 years of age), which suggests that the neural substrates involved in these functions (discrimination-learning) may differ between infancy and maturity. In a similar vein, human neural mediation of any given cognitive function may also change with age, (Kraft 1984; Witelson 1977c;) a proposal which is consistent with Brown's (1976) hypothesis (based on human lesion studies) that there are predictable developmental stages through which language becomes increasingly lateralized in zones of the left limbic-cortical areas.

Several recent studies in this laboratory involving two and one-half to five and one-half year old children (Kamptner, Kraft, and Harper 1984; Kraft 1984), support this hypothesis. For example language development measured pscyhometrically (Verbal Expression subtest of the ITPA and Vocabulary subtest of the WPPSI) and by observations of the complexity and frequency of children's natural speech during free play was associated with an increase in right ear (left hemisphere) accuracy for dichotically presented verbal stimuli (digits) and a decrease in right ear and hand accuracy for nonverbal stimuli (environmental sounds and nonsense shapes). These findings were interpreted as evidence of a developmental functional reorganization of the left hemisphere during early language acquisition toward increasing mediation of verbal procession and decreasing involvement in nonverbal processing (Kraft 1982b).

Asymmetric Development of the Left and Right Hemispheres

Several theorists posit that the observed asymmetries result from a prepotency or earlier development of one hemispheric processing system over the other, although there is different interpretation over which hemisphere takes precedence. One group suggests that the left hemisphere may be activated earlier (Corballis and Beale 1976; Goldman 1972; Kinsbourne and Hiscock 1977; Moscovitch 1976; Steffen 1975; Turkewitz 1977 ab). From a series of frontal-lobe ablation studies in rhesus monkeys, Goldman (1972, 1976a) suggests that the ability of one hemisphere to assume the functional specialty of its mate depends on the maturation of its structures. If the structures are functionally immature (developing uncommitted), they will be free to assume the functions of other damaged areas. Once committed, however, cortical structures cannot assume other functions. Therefore, she reasons, the observed ability of the right hemisphere to assume linguistic functions following damage to the left hemisphere during childhood is indicative of the immaturity of the right relative to the left.

In a similar vein, on the basis of evidence that newborn babies orient more to the right than the left (e.g., Siqueland and Lipsitt 1966; Turkewitz, et al., 1968), Kinsbourne and Hiscock (1977) suggest that this inborn rightward orientation reflects an innate prepotency of the left hemisphere. Through mutually-inhibitory control centers in the brain (probably located in the brain-stem, although perhaps including interhemispheric commissures) attention is (disproportionally) directed to the left hemisphere, hence the infant assumes a rightward orientation in space. Although the two orientation-controlling systems become better balanced during infancy and childhood, the more powerful left hemisphere is still evident in adults as evidenced by the tendency to circle right when lost in a desert, to choose steps on the right when offered a choice, and underlies the observed hemi-inattention (ignoring one side of space including one's own body) that often follows right-hemisphere lesions but which is seldom observed following damage to the left hemisphere (Kinsbourne 1974a, b, 1975a, b; Kinsbourne and Hiscock 1977).

In contrast, others are positing that the right hemisphere is most active in early life (Brown and Jaffe 1975; Carmon et al. 1972; Fromkin et al. 1974; Harris 1975; Kraft and Languis 1977). Harris (1975) and Brown and Jaffe (1975) interpret the observed rightward orientation as indicative of selective right-hemispheric processing for incoming sensory information. They argue that if the infant's head is oriented to the right, the left eye and ear (right hemisphere) are selectively processing all incoming information. In addition, they cite research indicating that the visual cortex matures faster in the right hemisphere than the left (Crowell et al., 1973) and that high fevers, which produce greater brain damage in the more active hemisphere, cause more right-hemispheric damage in infants before the age of two (Taylor 1969). They suggest that the development of information processing in the right hemisphere precedes that of the left. This advanced right-hemispheric cognitive functioning is evidenced by the early ability to recognize and discriminate between faces (Ambrose 1961, 1973; Fitzgerald 1968; Kagen 1965) and the synthesizing of a multimodality space in early infancy (Aronson and Rosenbloom 1971 versus Lyons-Ruth 1975, and McGurk and Lewis 1974).

DEVELOPMENT OF NEURAL STRUCTURES

Thus far the nature of asymmetric functional specialization of the brain and the ontogeny of this asymmetry has been discussed, left to be discussed is the development of the neural structures themselves. Although many of the major findings concerning the workings of the human brain (e.g., identification of specific neurotransmitters and neuroreceptors and their interaction with dendritic spines) are left to be discovered. This section summarizes some of the theories, hypotheses, and speculation in the ontogeny of the human brain.

The cerebral hemispsheres develop their characteristic form during the first 16 weeks of fetal life. The commissures interconnecting the two hemispheres also first appear during this period. The anterior develops first, followed by the hippocampal commissure and finally the corpus callosum[2] (Trevarthen 1974). The fibers of the corpus callosum appear at about 11–12 weeks and cross the midline around 18–20 weeks (Rakic and

Yakovlev 1968) but may be fully developed at birth (Hewitt 1962). The postnatal production of new cortical cells consist mainly of microneurones of the cerebral hemispheres and cerebellum (Dobbing and Sands 1973) that are thought to have "a role in modification of circuits in later states of development" (see Cowan 1979a, b; Purpura 1981; Scheibel 1979; and Trevarthen 1974: 230 for reviews and discussions concerning brain development and see Goldman 1977; Jacobson 1975 and Milner 1976 for a discussion of brain development in relation to language). The main increase in brain growth after birth appears to be a function of increased extension and branching of axons and dendrites of the brain cell which form synaptic interconnections among the brain cells and the development of dendritic spines. Evidence is also accumulating that during normal development redundant brain cells and an overgrowth of neuronal branching decrease in number. The laying down of fatty insulation (Myelin sheath) of axons also occurs during development. A myelinated fiber has about 20 times the conduction velocity of an unmyelinated fiber of the same diameter. Yakovlev (1967) states that the cycle of myelination of a given fiber system is related directly to its functional maturation in that it "reflects and, in a sense defines the position of a fiber system or region in the hierarchy of functional organization of the developing nervous system . . . myelination of a fiber system indicates that this system has acquired definitive properties of conduction which cannot change. A fiber system, before it has become myelinated, may serve as a path of conduction for many different kinds of stimuli, however, once it has myelinated, it becomes exclusively a path only for the conduction of stimuli with specified characteristics ('parameters') . . . [myelination is] a morphological criterion of the functional maturity of a conduction path." (p. 68). Although that hypothesis has not been confirmed, it has received some support from a study investigating the firing latencies (or conduction velocity) of early-and late-maturing optic fibers projecting to the lateral geniculate nucleus in kittens. The authors report a correlation between the onset of myelination, synaptic formation, and functional maturation of the visual geniculo-cortical system (Norman, Pettigrew and Daniels 1977). Similar cell development has been reported in the human brain and has been posited to underlie a sensitive or critical period in the development of the visual system (Hickey 1977).

There have been several in-depth studies of myelin development in the human brain (e.g., Flechsig 1901; Langworthy 1933). A more recent study (Yakovlev and Lecours 1967) addresses the rate of myelination in the regional fiber systems as well as its onset and completion.[3] According to that study, the first system to start myelinating is the motor root system of the cerebral-spinal nerves projecting to the somatic musculature of the body. Its myelination cycle extends from around the fourth prenatal month to term or into the first postnatal month. The tempo of the myelogenetic cycle of the sensory roots, however, is slower and lasts longer than that of the motor root system. The sensory roots begin myelination in the fifth or sixth fetal month and complete it around the fifth postnatal month.

At the brain stem and midbrain level, those systems that mediate vestibular and cochlear sensory modalities myelinate rapidly before birth (the cycle lasts 6–9 months prenatally, possibly reflecting influences exerted by early gravitational stimuli), while the somatic systems (proprioceptive or muscle sense and exterceptive or tactile and pain) begin their cycle prenatally but myelinate more slowly, completing their cycle only after birth. The second relay in the acoustic system (fibers of the inferior colliculus to the medial geniculate nucleus) start myelinating in the ninth prenatal month and terminate around the third postnatal month. The projections from the medial geniculate acoustic relay in the paramedial thalamus to the cortical acoustic analyzer (transverse gyrus of Heshl) in the temporal lobe, however, have a protracted cycle lasting until the third or fourth year of life, which parallels the first stage of language acquisition. Conversely, while the acoustic modality evidences an early onset with a protracted termination, the optic modality evidences a short rapid cycle in which the entire afferent system (from retina through the lateral geniculate nucleus to the cortical visual analyzer surrounding the calcarine fissure in the occupital lobe) starts myelinating around the ninth fetal month and completes its cycle around the third postnatal month. This differential myelogenetic cycle may be correlated with the availability of early acoustic stimuli, such as mother's heartbeat and other sounds permeating the amniotic sac, which is not possible in the visual modality. In addition, the rapid myelination of the entire visual system (in comparison to the slow cycle of myelin development of the cortical acoustic fibers) may indicate a functional disposition during infancy for visual processing and a correlation of higher levels of acoustic processing with language development (see Kraft 1984, and Lecours 1975, for further discussion). The projections from the thalamic relay nuclei to the central lobe of Ecker in the postcentral gyrus (somesthetic and propriokinesthetic analyzer) myelinate relatively rapidly during the first year of life. However, the lateral-ventral complex projections to the precentral cortex of the temporal lobe (propriokinesthetic analyzer) exhibits a protracted cycle that may not be completed until about four years of age.

Other nonspecific thalamocortical projections exhibit a longer and more protracted cycle. Fibers from the medial dorsal and posterior (pulvinar) nuclei projecting through the dorsal, the anterior, and the posterior thalamic radiations to the frontal, parietal, temporal, and occipital areas surrounding the cortial analyzers do not complete their myelogenetic cycle until at least the middle of the first decade, and possibly later. This fiber system is thought to be involved in the brief "phasic" activation that directs momentary "attention" to particular sensory inputs (Sharpless and Jasper 1956), and, as stated previously, it may act as an asymmetric alerting system for verbal and nonverbal stimuli (Ojemann 1977), whereas the brain stem reticular formulation is thought to be involved in the prolonged "tonic" cortical activation that differentiates general wakefulness from sleep (Grossman 1973; Sharpless and Jasper 1956).

Although the fibers of the reticular formation start myelinating slowly after birth, little myelin is present by one year of age. The process continues in an increasing manner until puberty and continues slowly beyond the second decade and perhaps until senility.

The other systems evidencing protracted cycles of myelination were the intercortical commissural and intracortical association fiber systems and cortex of the supralimbic division of the cerebral hemispheres. The commissural fiber system that interconnects the two cerebral hemispheres starts myelinating around the second month of extrauterine life. The great cerebral commissure, the corpus callosum, and the anterior commissure also contain transcallousal fibers. These decussating fiber projections appear to myelinate before the onset of myelination of the intercortical fibers, and respectively terminate their cycles at around one year and at eight months of age. The callosal intercortical fibers appear to have a period of increased myelination from somewhere between one and two years of age until four years of age. Although the cycle may continue slowly beyond the first decade, the major myelogenesis of the commissural fibers is finished at about six to seven years of age (Yacolev and Lecours 1967: Figure 1, pp. 4–5. This fiber system has been found to have several potentially significantly functions: Inter-hemispheric communication and interhemispheric inhibition (see Selnes 1974 for further dicussion). Although there is evidence of effective transmission of impulses via the immature corpus callosum in mammals (Meyerson 1968; Seggie and Berry 1972; Ulett et al., 1974), these impulses should become more specific and efficient as the fibers become increasingly myelinated. Hence, as myelination progresses, interhemispheric communication should become increasingly efficient, and one might expect that the underlying substrates mediating cognitive functioning such as language should become more efficient as the more proficient functional areas in one hemispheric system become better able to inhibit less efficient areas in the other system and the two systems are capable of integrated processing which had not been previously possible.

Finally, a protracted developmental cycle through adulthood characterizes the maturation of supralimbic cortical and intrahemispheric association fibers that compose the bulk of the white matter in the cerebral cortex. The last to myelinate is a zone consisting of the nonspecific association cortices of the frontal, parietal, and temporal lobes and the intrahemispheric association fibers interconnecting them. Although the precise neuroanatomical substrates for higher cognitive processes, such as comprehension and production of meaningful language, are not known, the development of this zone probably corresponds with higher cognitive and social learning (see Geschwind 1968, and Lecours 1975, for discussion). In addition, these fibers appear to have inhibitory as well as excitatory (intrahemispheric communication) components. Therefore, with progressive myelination the neural substrates mediating cognitive functioning should become more focally represented (as Brown 1976, suggests) as functional areas acquire greater efficiency and specificity (becoming specifically committed) and inhibit less efficient systems intra- and interhemispherically

ONTOGENETIC MODEL OF BRAIN SPECIALIZATION AND COGNITIVE DEVELOPMENT

The research reviewed above suggests a model of the human brain as a neurochemical computer having two specialized, bilateral functional systems in an interactive but mutually inhibitory relationship. Each system includes a cerebral hemisphere with specific primary and secondary sensory analyzers, motor programmers, multimodality association areas and subcortical attentional and alerting mechanisms (e.g., ascending and descending reticular activating system fibers and thalamic connections). In addition, the intrahemispheric fibers interconnect areas within each system and the interhemispheric commissures connect each system with the other.[2]

At birth each system appears to be inherently predisposed to perceive and process certain kinds of information, with the left-hemispheric system having certain rapid sequential pattern analyzers, which may include specific speech detectors (Liberman 1975; Segalowitz and Gruber 1977c; also see Cole 1977) as well as superior abilities for rapid sequential fine-motor programming. These early language-specific pattern analyzers (and perhaps programmers) probably involve the lowest levels of linguistic processing, such as the phonetic level (Moscovitch 1977), which may be located in limbic or subcortical levels (Lecours 1975). Although less is known of the nature of the right-hemispheric system specialization, it is conceived as including certain gestalt pattern analyzers and motor-programming superiority. In addition, each system probably has its own functional alerting and additional mechanisms that orient it toward environmental stimuli of interest, and perhaps toward the contralateral side of space (Kinsbourne 1974 a, b, 1975b, 1977b; Kinsbourne and Hiscock, 1977, 1978). These potentials, however, probably need environmental stimuli for their development (Rudel 1978; Witelson 1977c).

As the neural systems underlying cognitive skills develop, those that require the processing of input in an analytic, temporal, and sequential modality will become lateralized to increasingly specific areas in the left hemisphere while those that require processing in a synthetic, gestalt, and holistic modality will become increasingly lateralized in the right. This increasing lateralization of specialized functions is presumably facilitated by the increasing efficiency of attentional and alerting mechanisms and the maturation of inhibitory mechanisms.

The development of lateral specialization, therefore, appears to be an interaction of endogenous and exogenous factors. In addition, the maturation of specific attentional and alerting mechanisms for perceiving and programming these patterns facilitate the development of greater efficiency, and perhaps specificity. Finally, more efficient inhibition of competing areas, both within and across the two systems, is developing as the interhemispheric commissures, association fibers, and other subcortical inhibitory systems mature.

Little is known about the cognitive precursor of the more complex linguistic skills, such as the semantic representational system, but they appear to have their origin in sensorimotor cognition (Moscovitch 1977;

Piaget 1970), and these sensorimotor schemas are probably represented in both hemispheric systems (see Moscovitch 1977, for a discussion of alternative hypotheses). Housing such a representational system in a single hemisphere would constitute a more efficient processing of such information[4] (Whitaker and Ojemann 1977). Even so, there may be stages during which these processes become lateralized. For example, during cognitive and language development certain concepts and skills might necessarily include a stage in which the right hemisphere is initially alerted to and involved in processing, and coding spatio-temporal patterns of input. This information is then transferred across the corpus callosum to the left hemisphere where it is processed and recoded in an analytic, temporal and verbal manner. As this input is used over and over in a linguistic analytic and sequential manner, the stimulus itself may become increasingly salient to the left-hemisphere system (i.e., it is now easy to verbalize); and the left hemisphere may now become the focus of perceptual alerting to the stimulus (i.e., the perception of the stimulus becomes lateralized to the left). In addition, some extremely complex cognitive processes, such as communicative and social competence, may be more efficient by continuing to utilize interhemispheric processing stages.[5] That is, where the task solution first requires a gestalt, analog-like processing of input which is then related via the inter-hemispheric connections for a second stage sequential, digital-like processing or vice versa.

Bakker (1973 and Bakker Teunissen and Bosch (1976) present data that they interpret as indicative of stages of lateralization underlying phases in the learning-to-read process. On the basis of evidence that proficient reading at a later stage of the learning-to-read process appears to be correlated with left-hemispheric verbal perceptual process (Bakker 1969; Bakker, Smink and Reitsma 1973; Satz and Sparrow 1970), they suggest that proficient reading in adults is related to left-hemispheric dominance. However, they cite additional evidence that proficiency during the early reading stage(s) may be correlated with right-hemispheric dominance. They speculate that some children may use left-hemispheric strategies in learning to read, while others use right-hemispheric strategies. The right-dominant readers are characterized as being more sensitive to the perceptual features of the stimuli. They explore the visual configurations carefully and would be relatively slow but accurate readers, while the left-dominant readers would be characterized by making guesses ("quickly comparing hypothetical word meaning with the words on the page"). These readers, like most fluent readers (Smith 1971), read rapidly but, because careful attention to the perceptual component is necessary at this stage, they risk making many errors.

The slow-but-accurate strategy would not be appropriate at later stages of the learning-to-read process and may indicate children who are stuck at an earlier stage. Citing research (Sparrow and Satz 1970; Witelson and Rabinovitch 1972; Zurif and Carson 1970) indicating a higher incidence of left-ear (right hemisphere) advantage to verbal stimuli in older retarded readers, they speculate that these readers may be still relying on right-hemispheric reading strategies. Leong (1976) also presents evidence which suggests that developmental lags in hemispheric lateralization may underlie retarded reading, while Witelson (1976a, 1977b) states that she has found evidence of reading retarded subjects who have atypical neural organizations, with both hemispheres involved in spatial, gestalt cognition (i.e., two right hemispheres functionally speaking).

These studies are based on correlations between subjects' verbal perceptual asymmetries and their reading ability. Reading ability, however, involves more than perceiving stimuli. After perception, the information perceived must be translated and converted into concepts that fit or interact with the individual's previous conceptual schemes. These concepts are then somehow stored in memory and finally retrieved when needed. It would be surprising if such complex cognitive processing involved only a single hemispheric system. In fact, there is some evidence that it does not.

In a recent experiment, Kraft (1976); Kraft, Mitchell, Languis and Wheatley 1980) monitored the electrical activity (EEG) of 18 right-handed children (mean age 8.09 years) while they performed reading-comprehension and Piagetian tasks.[6] The results indicated that, across subjects, silent reading of a passage elicited greater right-hemispheric activity than did the answering of questions concerning that passage. Subjects who missed the comprehension questions, however, evidenced greater left-hemispheric activity during the comprehension questioning period than did the better readers, although there were no statistical brain-wave differences between the groups during the silent-reading period. These results could be interpreted in several different ways, not all mutually exclusive. The observed shift from right-to left-hemispheric processing could indicate that these subjects were attending to the perceptual configurations of the words, which elicited right-hemispheric activity. It could also reflect greater right-hemispheric involvement during receptive language than during expressive-language functioning, as Searleman

(1977) posits. In addition, those who were better able to answer questions on the passage had greater right-hemispheric activity during questioning than did those who could not answer these questions. Since the shift from greater right-hemispheric functioning during the silent-reading period to greater left-hemispheric functioning during the questioning period was observed across subjects, at least some left-hemispheric functioning can be inferred across subjects during their response to questions. Therefore, the finding that the poorer readers evidenced more left-hemispheric activity than the better readers while responding to comprehension questions could be interpreted as indicating a positive relationship between bilateral or interhemispheric functioning and reading comprehension. In other words, the right hemisphere was active while processing the configural features of the prose and/or receptive linguistic information when all of the subjects were reading a passage silently, but efficient retrieval of information concerning the passage (semantic knowledge) involved processing in both hemispheres.

Furthermore, if Bakker and colleagues are correct about the developmental shift from "right dominance" in the learning-to-read process, the shift must be relative rather than absolute. For instance, underlying semantic knowledge of an abstract scientific article may have greater representation in the left-hemispheric system of most adults than would poetry or other prose involving imaginal or metaphoric passages (Ornstein 1977). It seems unlikely, however, that a single processing system would ever have exclusive representation of any complex knowledge, including abstract scientific concepts.

HYPOTHESIS OF ONTOGENETIC PARALLELISM BETWEEN PIAGETIAN THEORY AND ASYMMETRIC BRAIN-FUNCTIONING THEORY

The following discussion focuses on the similarities between Piagetian theory of cognitive development and asymmetric brain-functioning theory. Jean Piaget's (1970) hierarchic model of cognitive development traces children's progressive capability to perform logicomathematical operations. His paradigm for assessing a given child's level of development usually provides a visuo-spatial phenomenon that the child is asked to interpret. The criterion used to determine the level or stage of thinking is whether the subject can provide verbal/logical explanations of the phenomena. In his discussion of children's thinking processes (as revealed during these tasks), he includes two aspects of memory (abstract cognitive schemes and concrete imaginal schemata) and two parallel structures of knowledge (operative and figurative). The operative structures are the child's inventive constructions, either behavioral or symbolic and conceptual, while the figurative structures were the more passive perceptions and mental images. Both undergo development and both are important to the child (Furth 1972; Gruber and Voneche 1977; Piaget and Inhelder 1971, 1973). Although some figurative elements do not participate in the semiotic or symbolic function, the mental image is of equal importance with language as a symbolic representation (Oleron et al. 1977; Piaget 1969b). Defining the two, Piaget (1973) states " . . . these structures may be figurative, for example (static) perceptions and mental images, or operative, for example the structures of actions or of operations . . . [The image] serves on the par with language as a symbolic instrument to signify the content of cognitive significations; for spatial concepts the image is particularly evident" (356–357).

The development of hierarchic logico-mathematical oprations which Piaget assumes to underlie children's verbal responses reflects an increasing capability for logical/veral cognition, which has been described as a processing specialization of the left hemisphere, while the imaginal memory system and figurative structure of knowledge bear a remarkable resemblance to the description often attributed to the thinking processes of the right-hemispheric processing system, which has been described as an imaginal/spatial specialist.

In addition, Piaget's paradigm appears to have right- and left-hemispheric components: the visuo-spatial phenomenological stimuli (e.g., watching equivalent amounts of water being poured from identical containers into two containers of different sizes) should stimulate right-hemispheric functioning, and the required verbal-logical response (e.g., if there was the same amount to begin with and if no water was added or taken away during the pouring, then there is still the same amount) should stimulate left-hemispheric functioning. Exploring this hypothesis, Kraft (1976) and colleagues (Kraft et al. 1980) found that 6 to 8 year old subjects exhibited greater right- hemispheric activity during the visuo-spatial stimulus (or transformation) period which shifted to greater left-hemispheric activity during the response (or explanation) period, across subjects and Piagetian conservation tasks.[6]

Finally, reasoning that preoperational thinkers (those not recognizing conservation) could not answer the explanation question logically because they were attending to the misleading visuo-spatial perceptual cues (e.g., the taller and thinner container "looks" higher and therefore appears to contain more water), one would predict that, across tasks, they should have greater right-hemispheric activity than the concrete operational thinkers. However, Kraft (1976) found no statistical differences across tasks in the brain waves between subjects classified as preoperational and concrete operational, and no statistical differences in brain activity between subjects who recognized conservation and those who did not during the stimulus (transformation) period of individual tasks. Brain wave differences between groups, however, were apparent during the verbal response or questioning periods in three of six tasks. The subjects who could *not* logically answer the question had greater left-hemisphere activity than the conservors who successfully gave a logical explanation for their equivalent response. Since, across tasks and across subjects, the brain waves had shifted to greater left activity during the response period, these results seem to indicate that the conservers evidenced greater interhemispheric functioning (or both hemispheres functioning) than did the nonconservers. The results are certainly not conclusive and need further documenting, but they suggest that Piaget's conservation paradigm might be measuring an increasing capability of the verbal/logical left hemisphere to respond to visuo-spatial experiences (representations) to which the "spatial" right hemisphere was attending.

In other words, his paradigm may be measuring an expansion of the verbal representational system by an increasingly efficient interfacing with the visuo-spatial gestalt system. Over time, these two interacting systems also probably establish functional capabilities not possible for either processing system. As inhibitory mechanisms become more efficient, neural-chemical circuits become more specialized and more efficiently coordinated through mutual inhibition. In addition, it is quite possible that this larger system increasingly gained more and more complex processing capabilities by processing information in stages.

The myelogenetic cycle of the corpus callosum, which completes the major part of its cycle by 7 years of age, lends some support to that hypothesis. Citing the slow myelin development of the corpus callosum, Gazzaniga (1974) posits that the young child may be a "functional split-brain" up until two years of age. Exploring this possibility, Galin and colleagues (Galin et al. 1979) conducted a "blind" fabric matching test with children 3–5 years of age. First determining the set of fabric swatches that each individual child could successfully identify by touch with both hands, they presented the swatch to one hand and asked them to determine if a second swatch was the same or different using the other hand. Not surprisingly they found that the left and right hands of the three year old subjects could rarely identify what their mate had felt and that the ability for interhand and interhemispheric matching increased with age. They concluded that in young children the two hemispheres function relatively autonomously. The right hand seldom knows what the left hand is doing. Although, as mentioned previously, the unmyelinated corpus callosum has been found to transmit impulses in mammals, the transmission would not be as efficient as in myelinated fibers. In addition, the impulses transmitted across the human corpus callosum are mainly those that connect secondary or association areas with homologous areas in the other hemisphere (Fleschig 1901; Geschwind 1965; see footnote 2 for possible exceptions). In other words, most impulses transmitted across the corpus callosum appear to be processed and coded at least partially by the hemisphere initially attending to the stimuli. If that is the case, successful performance of Piagetian conservation tasks might require the development of some underlying processing system(s) in the right hemisphere that mediate certain required spatial gestalt skills, as well as efficient interhemispheric processing (communication integration and inhibition) and the development of the underlying processing system(s) in the left hemisphere that mediate the required verbal/logical thinking. In other words, Piaget's conservation paradigm may be measuring an expansion of the two representational systems both through learning and increasingly efficient processing within each system and by increasingly efficient interfacing between the two.

To carry the speculation one step further, the myelogenetic cycles of the brain appear to parallel the Piagetian stages of cognitive development. Piaget (1970) states that there are four qualitatively different stages in cognitive development (see Brainard 1978; Siegel and Brainard 1978 for critiques of his stage theory):

1. The Piagetian sensorimotor stages begins at birth and continues until the onset of the use of symbols at approximately 1½–2 years of age. This period is characterized by the growth of sensorimotor concepts and coordination and visuo-spatial relationships such as object permanence. Not surprisingly, this stage is the period during which the visual and primary sensorimotor cortices, their immediately adjacent regions as well as most limbic and subcortical structures are completing their monophasic myelogenetic cycle. (See Lamendella 1977

and Kraft 1984 for discussions of possible relationships between subcortical structures and developing sensorimotor skills.)

2. The preoperational stage, which lasts from about 2 until 7 years, is characterized primarily by the growth of the symbolic function; the capacity to construct and manipulate images, symbols, and concepts; manifested primarily in language development. During this period the major myelination of the auditory system and the interhemispheric commissures (e.g., the corpus callosum) is completed. The auditory system has a biphasic cycle. The acoustic fibres which are below the cortical level (from the cochlear nerve to the medial geniculate nucleus in thalamus) complete their myelin development shortly after birth. The projections from the medial geniculate nucleus to the cortical analyzer in the temporal lobe, however, have little myelin development until approximately 2 years of age. Starting at 2 years these fibers have a rapid myelogenetic cycle which terminates at approximately 4 years of age and parallels the first stage of language acquisition (see Lecours 1975 for further discussion of the correlates between myelin development in the acoustic system and language development and Kamptner, Kraft and Harper 1984; Kraft 1982b and Kraft 1984) for evidence that children's language acquisitions highly related left hemispheric auditory processing of verbal stimuli. The interhemispheric commissures have a prolonged monophasic cycle which lasts from approximately 2 until 7 or longer.
3. The concrete operational stage is evident in children between 7 and 11, and is characterized by the decline in perceptual centrations and the concommitant growth of logical, reflective thought. The content and application of this thought, however, is confined to concrete objects. During this period the thalamic and reticular fibers subserving attention are completing the major part of their myelogenetic cycle. In addition, the intrahemispheric association and supralimbic cortical fibers (intermodal and nonspecific analyzers) are maturing.
4. The formal operational stage, beginning at about 12 and continuing indefinitely, is the period of expanding logico-mathematical operations. The formal operational thinker can employ hypothetical propositions and simultaneously manipulate many alternative solutions to a problem, the supralimbic cortex, including the nonspecific association cortices and their interconnecting fibres, are completing their myelogenetic cycles. These systems are thought to mediate intermodal sensory integration and complex cognitive abilities (Yacovlev

and Lecours 1967; Lecours 1975; Geschwind 1968; Brodal 1969; Gazzaniga 1979; Gardner 1975; Schmidt 1975; Thompson 1975).

Thus, the advanced stages in Piaget's theory of cognitive development may be mediated by increased functional commitment of myelinated fibers within specific systems (in one or both hemispheres) as well as increasingly efficient interfacing of these programs. Further, mutual inhibition of competing areas, both within and across the two systems presumably increases as the interhemispheric commissures, attentional fibers and other subcortical inhibitory mechanisms mature. As inhibitory mechanisms become more efficient, programs within each system become more specialized by mutually inhibiting competing programs (Brown 1976; Kinsbourne 1974a, b; Levy 1968). The increasing specialization and functional commitment of fiber systems accompanied by the mutual inhibitation of other competing programs may result in periods of functional reorganization similar to the brain reorganization found in other primates (Goldman 1975; Goldman et al. 1974; Kraft 1984; Miller et al. 1973). As mentioned earlier, interacting systems should establish functional capabilities over time that are not possible for either processing system alone. This larger system probably becomes increasingly capable of more and more complex processing because it processes information in stages: beginning with one specialized program, which then sends the results to be processed by another specialized program, etc.

While maturation of brain areas appears to follow an invariant sequence (Conel, 1963; Yakolev and Lecours 1967), there is reason to suspect that there are individual and group brain organization differences (Kraft 1981b, 1983, 1984, forthcoming; Hacaen, DeAgostini and Monzon-Montes 1981; Alekoumbides 1978; Hecaen and Sauguet 1971) which may underlie differences in intellectual profiles (Kraft 1981, 1982b, 1983, 1984) school achievement (Kraft, forthcoming) and cognitive developmental patterns (Kamptner, Kraft and Harper 1984; Kraft 1982b, 1984). For instance, more males than females evidence specialization of the right hemisphere for spatial and nonverbal stimuli and are more likely than females to have high scores on tasks that require the mental manipulation of spatial concepts including some Piagetian formal operational tasks (Kraft 1982a; Maccoby and Jacklin 1974; see Harris 1978, for review and discussion).

In addition, both right- and left-handers, who have family histories of left-handedness, tend to have attenuated hemispheric specialization particularly for verbal processing (Hacaen, DeAgostini and Monzon-Montes

1981; Kraft 1981; 1983, 1984; Luria 1970) compared to subjects who have mainly right-handed biological relatives. There are also environmental (e.g., malnutrition and protein deficiency) and physiological (e.g., hormonal constraints which alter brain development (e.g., Dobbing 1971; Dobbing and Sands 1973; Norman et al. 1977; Reinisch 1974) and probably cognitive development.

Furthermore, both the hemispheric systems are capable mediating actions upon objects and dynamic problem solving (Levy et al. 1972; Levy-Argesti and Sperry 1971; Sperry 1969). That the figural-imaginal system assumes a subordinate role in Piaget's model is not surprising as his experimental method for assessing cognition usually involves providing visuo-spatial phenomena that the subject is asked to interpret. The criterion used to determine any given individual's level of cognition in the hierarchy is usually whether the subject can provide verbal-logical explanations for the phenomena. Although increasingly complex cognitive programs in both systems are probably necessary to solve these developmental tasks, Piaget insists that a verbal logical interpretation is both necessary and sufficient as the final processing step. The question he is asking in his quest to index advanced cognition is addressed to the left hemispheric processing system for a response. The left hemisphere is required to serve as the executive decision maker. Therefore, Piaget's logico-mathematical model of cognitive development, while including right hemispheric processing, appears to be biased toward left hemispheric processing. A question which may prove to be quite enlightening is: Would advanced levels of cognition be defined differently (1) if tasks were used which required that the right hemispheric processing system were the executive decision maker and/or (2) if the required right hemispheric processing were other than increasingly complex visuo-spatial relations among objects—e.g., increasingly complex relations among people and nonverbal communication.[5] In what mode would this system respond? Probably not in propositional language, but rather by painting, constructing, dancing, or composing music, poetry, or metaphysical passages.

FOOTNOTES

[1]Genie, discovered by authorities when 13 years and 7 months old, has a case history of severe sensory and social deprivation (Curtiss et al., 1976; Fromkin, et al., 1974). When discovered, she evidenced no receptive or expressive language, could not stand erect, and was malnourished but did appear to have average or above average spatial skills. She is now slow-

ly acquiring language, although with better receptive linguistic skills than expressive. Dichotic listening tests indicate that she has right-hemispheric laterality for speech perception and either bilateral or right-hemispheric laterality for stimuli normally perceived best by the right hemisphere. This indicates an atypical cerebral organization: either a nonfunctional left hemisphere or reversed language laterality with bilateral spatial representation.

[2]For many years the interhemispheric fibers of the corpus callosum were thought to connect only secondary or association areas with homologous areas in the other hemispheric (Fleschig 1901; Geschwind 1965). Recent research with rhesus monkeys (Karol and Pandya 1971), however, suggests that there are a relatively small number of projections interconnecting primary sensory (except visual) and motor areas representing the axis or midline of the body. In addition, the secondary sensory and motor interhemispheric homotopic fibers also appear to be those that represent the midline (reviewed in Selnes 1974). Those fibers have been found to pass through the corpus callosum in an orderly topographic manner (Panyda et al., 1971) and include heterotopic and transcallosal connections as well as the homotopic (Ironside and Guttmacher 1929).

[3]The sample included several hundred cerebra ranging in age from the fourth fetal month to one postnatal year, a large collection of cerebra from the third and older decade, and few cerebra in the age range of the first and second decade. The cerebra were prepared in whole-brain serial celloid in sections, cut at uniform thickness, stained by the Loyez method for myelin sheaths (Bertrand 1930), and compared with sections taken from the brain of a healthy 28-year-old male. Thus, the rate and termination of myelin development during the first and second decades was determined largely by charting the amount of infered myelin present in the infant and adult cerebra and then interpolating the probable course of development between infant and adult, placing the few known points of the cerebra from early and middle childhood on the graph.

[4]Whitaker and Ojemann (1977) review intercallosal reaction time studies and conclude that callosal transfer time of recognition, identification and same/different judgements adds approximately one to eleven percent more time to the task. In addition, they posit that transfer of more complex information particularly that which involved several interhemispheric transfers at different stages in processing would add considerably more time.

[5]For example, many aspects of nonverbal communication such as facial recognition and comprehension of emotional overtones in voice inflections and facial expression appears to be the specialty of the right-hemispheric system while linguistic and propositional skills appear to be the speciality of the left. The socially competent individual is proficient in nonverbal receptive and expressive skills as well as the linguistic and may or may not be competent in propositional thinking.

[6]This study measured brain activity by recording from homologous leads over the left and right parietal areas of the cortex (P3–P4) referenced to Cz (Jasper 1958). A polygraph (Grass 79D) recorded the individual electroencephalograms on two channels of four-track FM tape recorder (Hewlett-Packard 3960A). Recorded simultaneously on the third and fourth channels were DC codes marking the beginning and end of each segment of interest and an audio track. The taped data were sampled with a PDP-11/40 DECLAB computer, and 25 samples per second of each EEG channel were stored on RK05 disks. After editing for artifacts, a computer program performed a Fast Fourier Transform and power spectral calculation on each channel of EEG data in each 1/2 second segment. The spectral power values of all the segments in each task or subtask were then averaged together in five groups (1–3, 4–6, 7–12, 13–20, 21–30 Hz) corresponding to the normal bands of brain

waves adjusted for the age level of the group (Bungham, Godfrey and Tukey 1967; Lopes Da Silva 1976; Lairy, et al. 1969). Selected as measure of relative hemispheric activity was the ratio of the power in the alpha frequency band (7–12 Hz) in each channel (left/right alpha power ratio) (Butler and Glass 1974a, b; Donchin, Kutas and McCarthy 1977). The log of this ratio was used as the dependent variable giving a symmetrical swing from negative (more alpha from the right lead which infers greater processing activity in the left hemisphere) to positive (more alpha from the left lead which infers greater processing activity in the right hemisphere). The baseline used as a record of each subject's EEG when no "thinking" was taking place was an attention-to-breathing task in which the subject was instructed to relax, look at a sheet of white paper, try not to think of anything and concentrate on his/her breathing. To allow for the possibility of asymmetry in baseline alpha powers (Butler and Glass 1974a, b; also see Dunn, Chapter 5, this edition), baseline ratio was used to normalize the task ratios by subtracting it from each task ratio.

REFERENCES

Alekoumbides, A. 1978. Hemispheric dominance for language: Quantatative aspects. *Actaneurol. Scandinav.* 57:97–140.

Ambrose, J.A. 1961. The development of the smiling response in early infancy. *Determinants of infant behavior*, ed. B.M. Foss. New York: John Wiley.

Annett, M.A. 1973. Laterality of childhood hemiphegia and the growth of speech and intelligence. *Cortex* 8:4-33.

Aronson, E. and Rosenbloom, S. 1971. Space perception in early infancy: Perception within a common auditory-visual space. *Science* 172:1161–63.

Bakker, D.J. 1969. Ear asymmetry with monaural stimulation: Task influences. *Cortex* 5:36–42.

________. 1973. Hemispheric specialization and stages in the learning-to-read process. *Bulletin Orton Society* 23:15–27.

Bakker, D.J.; Smink, T.; and Reitsma, P. 1973. Ear dominance and reading ability. *Cortex* 9:301-312.

Bakker, D.J.; Teunissen, J.; and Bosch, J. 1976. Development of laterality-reading patterns. In *The neuropsychology of learning disorders: Theoretical approaches,* eds. R.M. Knights and D.J. Bakker. Baltimore: University Park Press.

Barnett, A.B.; Vicentini, M.; and Campos, M. 1974. EEG sensory evoked responses (ERIS) in early infancy malnutrition. *Neuroscience Abstracts* 43:130.

Basser, L.S. 1962. Hemiplegia of early onset and the faculty of speech with special reference to the effects of hemispherectomy. *Brain* 85:427–60.

Bay, E. 1975. Ontogeny of stable speech areas in the human brain. In *Foundations of language development*, eds. E.H. Lenneberg and E. Lenneberg. New York: Academic Press.

Benton, A.L. 1972. The 'minor' hemisphere. *Journal of History of Medicine and Allied Science* 27:5–14.

Berlin, C.I. 1977. Hemispheric asymmetry in auditory tasks. In *Lateralization in the nervous system*, eds. S. Harnad and R.W. Doty. New York: Academic Press.

Berry, M. 1976. Plasticity in the visual system and visually guided behavior. In *Advances in psychobiology*, Vol. 3, eds. A.H. Riesen and R.F. Thompson. New York: John Wiley.

Bertrand, I. 1930. *Techniques histologiques de neuropathologic.* Paris: Masson.
Bever, T.G. 1971. The nature of cerebral dominance in speech behavior of the child and adult. In *Language acquisition: Models and methods*, eds. R. Huxley and E. Ingram. New York: Academic Press.
________. 1975. Cerebral asymmetries in humans are due to the differentiation of two incompatible processes: Holistic and analytic. In *Developmental psycholinguistics and communication disorders*, eds. D. Aaronson and R.W. Riber. New York: New York Academy of Sciences.
Bogen, J.E. 1969. The other side of the brain: Parts I, II, III. *Bulletin of the Los Angeles Neurological Society* 34:73-105, 135-162, 191-203.
Brainard, C.J. 1978. The stage question in cognitive-developmental theory. *The Behavioral and Brain Sciences* 2:173-213.
Broca, P. 1863. Localisation des fonctions cerebrales siege du language articule. *Bulletin of Social Anthropology* 4:200-204.
________. 1865. Sur la faculte du language articule. *Bul Soc D'Anthropologie* 6:493-494. Cited in W.L. Smith, Dominant and nondominant hemispherectomy. In *Hemispheric disconnection and cerebral function*, eds. M. Kinsbourne and W.L. Smith. Springfield: Thomas.
Brown, J.W. 1976. The neural organization of language. *Brain and Language* 3:482-494.
Brown, J.W. and Jaffe, J. 1975. Hypothesis on cerebral dominance. *Neuropsychologia* 13:107-110.
Brodal, A. 1969. *Neurological anatomy*. New York: Oxford University Press.
Bryden, M.P. 1978. Strategy effects in the assessment of hemispheric asymmetry. In *Strategies in information processing*, ed. G. Underwood. New York: Academic Press.
________. 1979. Evidence for sex-related differences in cerebral organization. In *Sex-related differences in cognitive functioning: Developmental issues*, eds. M.A. Wittig and A.C. Peterson. New York: Academic Press.
Buffery, A.W.H. 1970. Sex differences in the development of hand preference, cerebral dominance for speech and cognitive skill. *Bulletin of British Psychological Society* 23:233.
________. 1971. Sex differences in the development of hemispheric asymmetry of function in the human brain. *Brain Research* 31:364-365.
Buffery, A.W.H. and Gray, J.A. 1972. Sex differences in the development of spatial and linguistic skills. In *Gender differences: Their ontogeny and significance*, eds. C. Ousted and D.C. Taylor. London: Churchill-Livingston.
Bungham, C.; Godfrey, M.D.; and Tukey, J.W. 1967. Modern techniques of power spectrum estimation. *IEEE Audio Electroacoustics* 15:53.
Butler, S. and Glass, A. 1974a. Asymmetries in the EEG associated with cerebral dominance. *EEG Clinical Neurophysiology* 36:481-491.
________. 1974b. EEG correlates of cerebral dominance. In *Advances in psychobiology*, Vol. 3A., eds. A.H. Reisen and R.F. Thompson. New York: John Wiley
Cameron, R.F.; Currier, R.D.; and Haerer, A.C. 1971. Aphasia and literacy. *British Journal of Disorders in Communication* 6:161-63.
Carmon, A. and Nachson, I. 1971. Effect of unilateral brain damage on perception of temporal order. *Cortex* 7:410-418.
Carmon, A.; Harishanu, Y.; Lowinger, E.; and Lavy, S. 1972. Asymmetries in hemispheric blood volume and cerebral dominance. *Behavioral Biology* 7:853-59.

Cohen, G. 1973. Hemispheric differences in serial versus parallel processing. *Journal of Experimental Psychology* 97:349-356.

Cole, R.A. 1977. Invarient features and feature detectors: Some developmental implications. In *Language development and neurological theory*, eds. S.J. Segalowitz and F.A. Gruber. New York: Academic Press.

Conel, J.L. 1963. *The postnatal development of the human cerebral cortex.* Vol. I–VII. Cambridge: Harvard University Press.

Corballis, M.C. and Beale, I.L. 1976. *The psychology of left and right.* Hillsdale: Earlbaum.

Corkin, S. 1965. Tactually-guided maze learning in man: Effects of unilateral cortical excisions and bilateral hippocampal lesions. *Neuropsychologia* 3:339–351.

Cowen, W.M. 1979a. The development of the brain. In D.H. Hubel, ed. *The brain.* San Francisco: Freeman.

________. 1979b. Selection and control in neurogenesis. In *The neurosciences: Fourth study program,* eds. F.O. Schmitt and F.G. Worden. Cambridge: MIT Press.

Crowell, D.H.; Jones, R.H.; and Kapunlai, L.E. 1973. Unilateral cortical activity in newborn humans: An early index of cerebral dominance. *Science* 180:205–08.

Curtis, S.; Fromkin, V.; Rigler, D.; Rigler, M.; and Krashen, S. 1976. An update on the linguistic development of Genie. In *Developmental psycholinguistics: Theory and applications*, ed. Dato. Washington, D.C.: Georgetown University Press.

Davis, A.E. and Wada, J.A. 1977. Hemispheric asymmetry in neonates: Spectral analysis of flash and click evoked potentials. *Brain and Language* 4:23–31.

Dax, G. 1836. Lesions de la moitie gauche de l'encephale coincident avec l'oubli des signes de la pensee. *Gas. Hebdom. Med. Chir.* 2:259–62. Cited in A. Smith Dominant and nondominate hemispherectomy. In *Hemispheric disconnection and cerebral function*, eds., M. Kinsbourne and W.L. Smith. Springfield: Thomas. 1974.

Dennis, M. and Kohn, B. 1975. Comprehension of syntax in infantile hemiplegics after cerebral hemidecortication: Left-hemisphere superiority. *Brain and Language* 2:472–82.

Dennis, M. and Whitaker, H.A. 1976. Language acquisition following hemidecortication: Linguistic superiority of the left over the right hemisphere. *Brain and Language* 3:404–33.

Dimond, S.J. 1972. *The double brain.* London: Churchill-Livingston.

Dimond, S.J. and Beaumont, J.G. 1974. *Hemispheric function in the human brain.* New York: John Wiley.

Dimond, S.J. and Blizard, D.A., eds. 1977. *Evolution and lateralization of the brain.* New York: N.Y. Academy of Sciences.

Dobbing, J. 1971. Undernutrition and the developing brain. In Stoelinga and Bosch, *Normal and abnormal development of brain and behavior.* Baltimore: Leiden University Press.

Dobbing, J. and Sands, J. 1973. Quantitative growth and development of the human brain. *Archives of Disease in Childhood* 48:757–67.

Donchin, E.; Kutas, M.; and McCarthy, G. 1977. Electrocortical indices of hemispheric specialization. In *Lateralization in the nervous system*, eds. S. Harnad: R.W. Doty; and L. Goldstein. New York: Academic Press.

Dorman, M.F. and Geffner, D.S. 1974. Hemispheric specialization for speech perception in six-year-old black and white children from low and middle socio-economic classes. *Cortex* 10:171–76.

Entus, A.K. 1977. Hemispheric asymmetry in processing of dichotically presented speech and nonspeech stimuli by infants. In *Language development and neurological theory*, eds. S.J. Segalowitz and F.A. Gruber. New York: Academic Press.

Fitzgerald, H.E. 1968. Autonomic pupillery reflex activity during early infancy and its relation to social and nonsocial stimuli. *Journal of Experimental Child Psychology* 6:470–82.

Flechsig, P. 1901. Developmental (myelogenetic) localization in the cerebral cortex in the human subject. *Lancet* 11:1027–29.

Fromkin, V.; Krashen, S.; Curtis, S.; Rigler, D.; and Rigler, M. 1974. The development of language in Genie: A case of language acquisition beyond the critical period. *Brain and Language* 1:81–107.

Furth, H.G. 1972. *Piaget and knowledge: Theoretical foundations.* Englewood Cliffs, NJ: Prentice-Hall.

Galin, D. and Ornstein, R. 1972. Lateral specialization of cognitive mode: An EEG study. *Psychophysiology* 9:412–18.

Galin, D.; Johnstone, J.; Nakell, L.; and Herron, J. 1979. Development of the capacity for tactile information transfer between hemispheres in normal children. *Science* 1330–1332.

Garai, J.E. and Scheinfeld, A. 1968. Sex differences in mental and behavioral traits. *Genetic Psychology Monographs* 77:169–299.

Gardiner, W.; Karnosh, L.; McClure, C.; and Gardiner, A. 1955. Residual function following hemispherectomy for tumor and infantile hemiplega. *Brain* 78:487–502.

Gardner, M.F.; Schulman, C.; and Walter, D. 1973. Facultative EEG asymmetries in babies and adults. *UCLA Brain Information Service Conference Report* 34.

Gardner, M.F. and Walter, D.O. 1977. Evidence of hemispheric specialization from infant EEG. In *Lateralization in the nervous system*, eds. S. Harnad and R.W. Doty. New York: Academic Press.

Gardner, R.F. *Fundamentals of neurology*. Philadelphia: Saunders.

Gazzaniga, M.S. 1974. Cerebral dominance viewed as a decision system. In *Hemisphere function in the human brain*, eds. S.J. Dimond and J.G. Beaumont. New York: John Wiley.

________, ed. 1979. *Handbook of behavioral neurobiology: Neuropsychology*, Vol. 2. New York: Plenum Press.

Gazzaniga, M.S. and Hillyard, S.A. 1971. Language and speech capacity of the right hemisphere. *Neuropsychologia* 9:273–80.

Geffner, D.W. and Dorman, M.F. 1976. Hemispheric specialization for speech perception in four-year-old children from low and middle socio-economic classes. *Cortex* 12:271–73.

Geffner, D. and Hochberg, I. 1971. Ear laterality performance of children from low and middle socioeconomic levels on a verbal dichotic listening task. *Cortex* 7:193–203.

Geschwind, N. 1965. Disconnection syndromes in animals and man. *Brain* 88:223–248.

________. 1968. Neurological foundations of language. In *Progress in learning disabilities*, Vol. 1., ed. H.R. Myklebust. New York: Grune and Stratton.

________. 1974. The anatomical basis of hemispheric differentiation. In *Hemisphere function in the human brain*, eds. S.J. Dimond and J.G. Beaumont. New York: John Wiley.

Geschwind, N. and Levitsky, W. 1968. Human brain: Left-right asymmetries in temporal speech region. *Science* 161:186–187.

Gesel, A. and Ames, L.B. 1947. The development of handedness. *Journal of Genetic Psychology* 70:155–175.

Gilbert, J.V.H. 1976. Dichotic listening in children 2-3 CA: A note. *Neuropsychologia.*

Glanville, B.B.; Best, C.T.; and Levenson, R. 1977. A cardiac measure of cerebral asymmetries in infant auditory perception. *Developmental Psychology* 13:55–59.

Goldman, P.S. 1972. Developmental determinants of plasticity. *Acta Neurobiologica Experimentalis* 32:495–511.

Goldman, P.S. 1975. Age, sex, and experience as related to the neural basis of cognitive development. In *Brain mechanisms in mental retardation*, eds. N. Buchwald and M.A.B. Brazier. New York: Academic Press.

________. 1976a. Maturation of the mammalian nervous system and the ontogeny of behavior. In *Advances in the study of behavior*, Vol. 7. New York: Academic Press.

________. 1976b. The role of experience in recovery of function following orbital prefrontal lesions in infant monkeys. *Neuropsychologia* 14:401–411.

________. 1977. The neurological bases of language disorder in children: Methods and directions for research. In NINCDS Monograph No. 22, eds. C.L. Ludlow and M.E. Doran-Quine. Bethesda: U.S. Department of Health, Education and Welfare.

Goldman, P.S.; Crawford, H.T.; Stokes, L.P.; Galkin, T.N.; and Rosvold, H.E. 1974. Sex-dependent behavioral effects of cerebral cortical lesions in the developing rhesus monkey. *Science* 186:540–542.

Griffith, H. and Davidson, M. 1966. Long-term changes in intellect and behavior after hemispherectomy. *Journal of Neurology, Neurosurgery, and Psychiatry* 29:571–576.

Grossman, S.P. 1973. *Essentials of physiological psychology*. New York: John Wiley.

Gruber, F.A. and Voneche, J.J., eds. 1977. *The essential Piaget*. New York: Basic Books.

Halperin, Y.; Nachson, I.; and Carmon, A. 1973. Shift of ear superiority in dichotic listening to temporally patterned nonverbal stimuli. *Journal of the Acoustic Society of America* 53:46–50.

Hammer, M. and Turkewitz, G. 1974. A sensory basis for the lateral difference in newborn infant's response to somesthetic stimulation. *Journal of Experimental Child Psychology* 18:304–312.

Hardyck, C. 1977. Individual differences in hemispheric functioning. In *Studies in neurolinguistics*, Vol. 3., eds. H. Whitaker and H.A. Whitaker. New York: Academic Press.

Harnad, S.; Doty, R.W.; Goldstein, L.; Jaynes, J.; and Krauthamer, G., eds. 1977. *Lateralization in the nervous system*. New York: Academic Press.

Harris, L.J. 1975. Neurophysiological factors in the development of spatial skills. In *Children's spatial development*, eds. J. Eliott and N.J. Salking. Springfield: Charles Thomas.

____________. 1977a. Sex differences in the growth and use of language. In *Women: A psychological perspective,* eds. E. Donelson and J.E. Gullahorn. New York: John Wiley.

________. 1977b. Sex differences in spatial ability: Possible environment, genetic, and neurological factors. *Asymmetrical functions of the brain*, ed. M. Kinsbourne. Cambridge: Cambridge University Press.

Hecaen, H. 1976. Acquired aphasia in children and the ontogenesis of hemispheric functional specialization. *Brain and Language* 3:114-134.

Hecaen, H.; DeAgostini, M.; and Monzon-Montes, A. 1981. Cerebral organization in left-handers. *Brain and Language* 12:261-284.

Hecaen, H. and Sauguet, J. 1971. Cerebral dominance in left-handed subjects. *Cortex* 7:19-48.

Hess, R.D. 1970. Social class and ethnic influences on socialization. *Carmichael's manual of child psychology*, ed., P.H. Mussen. New York: John Wiley.

Hewitt, W. 1962. The development of the corpus callosum. *Journal of Anatomy* 96:355-358.

Hickey, T.L. 1977. Postnatal development of the human lateral geniculate nucleus: Relationship to a critical period for the visual system. *Science* 198:836-839.

Hillier, W. 1954. Total left hemispherectomy for malignant glioma. *Neurology* 4:718-721.

Hirsch, H.V.B. and Spinilli, D.N. 1970. Visual experience modifies distribution of horizontally and vertically oriented receptive fields in cats. *Science* 168:869-887.

Hiscock, M. and Kinsbourne, M. 1976. Perceptual and motor measures of cerebral lateralization in children. Paper presented at the 37th annual meeting of the Canadian Psychological Association. Toronto. June.

________. 1977. Selective listening asymmetry in preschool children. *Developmental Psychology* 198:836-839.

________. 1978. Ontogeny of cerebral dominance: Evidence from time sharing in children. *Developmental Psychology* 14:321-329.

Hunt, J. McV. 1964. The psychological basis for using pre-school enrichment as an antidote for cultural deprivation. *Merrill-Palmer Quarterly* 10:209-284.

Ingram, D. 1975. Motor asymmetries in young children. *Neuropscyhologia* 13:95-102.

Ironside, R. and Guttmacher, M. 1929. Corpus callosum and its tumors. *Brain* 52:442-483.

Jacobson, M. 1975. Brain development in relation to language. *Foundations of language development*, Vol. 1., eds. E.H. Lenneberg and E. Lenneberg. New York: Academic Press.

Jasper, H.H. 1958. The ten-twenty electrode system of the International Federation of Societies for Electroencephalography. *EEG Clinical Neurophysiology* 10:371-375.

Kagen, J. 1965. The growth of the 'face' schema: Theoretical significance and methodological issues. Paper read at APA. Cited in L.J. Harris, Neuropsychological factors in the development of spatial skills. In *Children's spatial development*, eds. J. Elliot and N.J. Salkind. Springfield: Charles Thomas, 1975.

Kamptner, L.; Kraft, R.H.; and Harper, L.V. 1984. Lateral specialization and social-development in preschool children. *Brain and Cognition* 3:42-50.

Karol, E.A. and Pandya, D.N. 1971. The distribution of the corpus callosum in the rhesus monkey. *Brain* 94:471-86.

Khadem, F. 1977. Unpublished studies on illiteracy and cerebral dominance. Cited in S.F. Witelson, Early specialization and interhemispheric plasticity. In *Language development and neurological theory*, eds. S.J. Segalowitz and F.A. Gruber. New York: Academic Press.

Kimura, D. 1967. Functional asymmetry of the brain in dichotic listening. *Cortex* 3:163-78.

________. 1976. The neural basis of language qua gesture. In *Studies in neurolinguistics*, Vol. 2., eds. H. Whitaker and H. Whitaker. New York: Academic Press.

Kimura, D. and Vanderwolf, C.H. 1970. The relation between hand preference and the performance of individual finger movements by left and right hands. *Brain* 93:769–74.

Kinsbourne, M. 1974a. Lateral interactions in the brain. In *Hemispheric disconnection and cerebral function*, eds. M. Kinsbourne and W.L. Smith. Springfield: Thomas Books.

________. 1974b. Mechanisms of hemispheric interaction in man. In *Hemispheric disconnection and cerebral function*, eds. M. Kinsbourne and W.L. Smith. Springfield: Thomas Books.

________. 1975a. Minor hemisphere language and cerebral maturation. In *Foundations of language development: A multi-disciplinary approach*, Vol. 2., eds., E. Lenneberg and E. Lenneberg. New York: Academic Press.

________. 1975b. The ontogeny of cerebral dominance. *Annals of New York Academy of Sciences* 263:244–50.

________, ed. 1977a. *Asymmetrical functions of the brain*. Cambridge: Cambridge University Press.

________. 1977b. Hemi-neglect and hemisphere rivalry. In *Advances in neurology: Volume 18*, eds. E.A. Weinstein and R.P. Friedland. New York: Raven.

Kinsbourne, M. and Hiscock, M. 1977. Does cerebral dominance develop? In *Language development and neurological theory*. eds. S.J. Segalowitz and F.A. Gruber. New York: Academic Press.

________. 1978. Cerebral lateralization and cognitive development. In *Education and the brain,* eds. J.S. Chall and A.F. Mirsky. Chicago: University of Chicago Press.

________. 1984. Normal and deviant development of functional lateralization of the brain. In *Handbook of Child Psychology*. Fourth Ed. Vol. 2., ed., P. Mussen. New York: John Wiley.

Kinsbourne, M. and Smith, W.L., eds. 1974. *Hemispheric disconnection and cerebral function*. Springfield: Thomas Books.

Kohn, B. and Dennis, M. 1974. Selective impairments of visuo-spatial abilities in infantile paraplegics after right cerebral hemidecortication. *Neuropsychologia* 12:505–12.

Kraft, R.H. 1976. An EEG study: Hemispheric brain functioning of six to eight year old children during Piagetian and curriculum tasks with variation in presentation made. Doctoral dissertation. The Ohio State University.

________. 1981a. The relationship between family history and hand preference and the development of lateral specialization during middle childhood. Paper delivered at the Biannual Meeting of the Society for Research in Child Development, Boston, April.

________. 1981b. The relationship between right-handed children's assessed and familial handedness and lateral specialization. *Neuropsychologia* 19:697–705.

________. 1982a. Relationship of ear specialization to degree of task difficulty, sex, and lateral specialization. *Perceptual and Motor Skills* 54:703–14.

________. 1982b. Hemispheric specialization and integration and its relationship to stages of language and cognitive development. Paper delivered at the 5th International Conference in Child Neurology in Bratslava, Czechoslavakia, May 31.

________. 1983. The effect of sex, laterality and familial handedness on intellectual abilities. *Neuropsychologia* 21:79–89.

________. 1984. The development of lateral specialization and verbal/spatial abilities in pre-school children: Age, sex and familial handedness. *Neuropsychologia*, 22:319–335.

Kraft, R.H. and Kamptner, L. n.d. A longitudinal investigation of lateralization and verbal aptitude in preschool children: Sex and familial handedness differences. Forthcoming.

Kraft, R.H. and Languis, M.L. 1977. Dimensions of right and left brain learning in early childhood. In *Early childhood education*, eds. L.H. Golubchick and B. Persky. Newark: Avery Publishing.

Kraft, R.H.; Mitchell, O.R.; Languis, M.L.; and Wheatley, G.H. 1980. Hemispheric asymmetries during six- to eight-year-olds' performance of Piagetian conservation and reading tasks. *Neuropsychologia* 18:637–43.

Krashen, S.D. 1972. Language and the left hemisphere. *UCLA Working Papers in Phonetics* 24:1-72.

________. 1973a. Lateralization, language, learning, and the critical period. *Language Learning* 23:63-74.

________. 1973b. Mental abilities underlying linguistic and non-linguistic functions. *Linguistics* 115:39-55.

________. 1975. The critical period for language acquisition and its possible bases. In *Developmental Psycholinguistics and Communication Disorders: Annals of N.Y. Academy of Sciences*, eds. A. Aaronson and R.W. Rieber, 253:211-224.

________. 1976a. Cerebral asymmetry. In *Studies in neurolinguistics*, Vol. 2. eds. H. Whitaker and H.A. Whitaker. New York: Academic Press.

________. 1976b. The development of cerebral dominance and language learning: More new evidence. In *Developmental psycholinguistics: Theory and applications*, ed. Dato. Washington, D.C.: Georgetown University Press.

________. 1977. The left brain. *The human brain*, ed. M. Whittrock. Englewood Cliffs, New Jersey: Prentice-Hall.

Karshen, S.D. and Harshman, R. 1972. Lateralization and the critical period. *UCLA Working Papers in Phonetics* 23:13-21.

Lairy, G.C.; Remand, A.; Rieger, H.; and Leserve, N. 1969. The alpha average III: Clinical application in children. *Electroencephalography and Clinical Neurophysiology* 26:453–67.

Lamendella, J.T. 1977. The limbic system in human communication. In *Studies in neurolinguistics,* eds. H. Whitaker and H.A. Whitaker. New York: Academic Press.

Langworthy, O. 1933. Development of behavior patterns and myelination of the nervous system in the human fetus and infant. *Cont. Embryol.* 139:1-57.

Lecours, A.R. 1975. Myelogenetic correlates of the development of speech and language. In *Foundations of language development*, Vol. 1., eds. E.H. Lenneberg and E. Lenneberg. New York: Academic Press.

Lenneberg, E.H. 1967. *Biological foundations of language.* New York: John Wiley.

Leong, C.L. 1976. Lateralization in severely disabled readers in relation to functional cerebral development and synthesis of information. In *The neuropsychology of learning disorders: Theoretical approaches*, eds. R. Knights and D. Bakker. Baltimore: University Park Press.

Levy, J. 1968. Possible basis for the evolution of lateral specialization of the human brain. *Nature* 224:614-15.

Levy, J.; Trevarthen, C.; and Sperry, R.W. 1972. Perception of bilateral chimeric figures following hemispheric disconnection. *Brain* 95:61-78.

Levy-Argesti, J. and Sperry, R.W. 1968. Differential perceptual capacities in major and minor hemispheres. *Proceedings of the National Academy of Sciences* 61:115.

Liberman, A.M. 1975. The specialization of the language hemisphere. In *Hemispheric specialization and interaction*, ed. B. Milner. Cambridge: MIT Press.

Lopes Da Silva, F.H. 1976. Sampling, conversion and measurement of biolectrical phenomena. In *Handbook of electroencephalography*, Vol. 4A., ed. M.A.B. Brazier. Amsterdam: Elsevier.

Luria, A.R. 1970. *Traumatic aphasia: Its syndromes, psychology and treatment*. Mouton: The Hague.

Lyons-Ruth, K. 1975. Integration of auditory and visual spatial information during early infancy. Paper presented at the meeting of the SRCD, Denver, April.

McFie, J. 1961a. The effects of hemispherectomy on intellectual functioning in cases of infantile hemiplegia. *Journal of Neurology, Neurosurgery and Psychiatry* 24:240–49.

________. 1961b. Intellectual impairment in children with localized post-infantile cerebral lesions. *Journal of Neurology, Neurosurgery and Psychiatry* 24:361–65.

Meyerson, B.A. 1968. Ontogeny of hemispheric functions. An electrophysiological study in pre- and post-natal sleep. *Acta Physiologica Scandinavica* 312:1–108.

Miller, E.A.; Goldman, P.S.; and Rosvold, H.E. 1973. Delayed recovery function following orbital prefrontal lesion in infant monkeys. *Science* 182:304–306.

Milner, B. 1975. *Hemispheric specialization and interaction*. Cambridge: MIT Press.

________. 1976. CNS maturation and language acquisition. In *Studies in neurolinguistics*, eds. H. Whitaker and H.A. Whitaker. New York: Academic Press.

Molfese, D.L. 1972. Cerebral asymmetry in infants, children and adults: Auditory evoked responses to speech and music stimuli. Doctoral dissertation, Penn State University.

________. 1976. The ontogeny of cerebral asymmetry in man: Auditory evoked potentials to linguistic and non-linguistic stimuli. In *Recent developments in the psychobiology of language: The cerebral evoked potential approach*, ed. J.W. Desmedt. London: Oxford University Press.

Molfese, D.L.; Freeman, R.B.; and Palermo, D.S. 1975. *Brain and Language* 2:356–68.

Moscovitch, M. 1976. The representation of language in the right hemisphere of right handed people. *Brain and Language* 3:47–71.

________. 1977. The development of lateralization of language functions and its relation to cognitive and linguistic development: A review and some theoretical speculations. In *Language development and neurological theory*, eds. S.J. Segalowitz and F.A. Gruber. New York: Academic Press.

Mountcastle, V.B. 1962. *Interhemispheric relations and cerebral dominance*. Baltimore: Johns Hopkins Press.

Nagafuchi, M. 1970. Development of dichotic and monural hearing abilities in young children. *Acta Otolaryngologica* 69:409–14.

Norman, J.L.; Pettigrew, J.D.; and Daniels, J.D. 1977. Early development of x-cells in kitten lateral geniculate nucleus. *Science* 198:202–04.

Obrador, S. 1964. Nervous integration after hemispherectomy in man. In *Cerebral localization and organization*, eds. G. Schaltenbrand and C.N. Woolsey. Madison: University of Wisconsin Press.

Ojemann, G.A. 1977. Asymmetric function of the thalamus in man. In *Evolution and lateralization of the brain*, eds. S.J. Dimond and D.A. Blizzard. New York: New York Academy of Sciences.

Oleron, P.; Piaget, J.; Inhelder, B.; and Greco, P. 1977. Mental images. In *The essential Piaget*, eds. H.E. Gruber and J.J. Voneche. New York: Basic Books.

Ornstein, R., ed. 1972a. *Nature of consciousness.* San Francisco: W.H. Freedman.

________. 1972b. *Psychology of consciousness.* San Francisco: W.H. Freedman.

________. 1977. An EEG Study: Increasing right hemispheric functioning from technical material through prose to poetry. Cited in *Evolution and lateralization of the brain*, eds. S.J. Dimond and D.A. Blizzard. New York: New York Academy of Sciences.

Panyda, D.N.; Karol, E.A.; and Heilborn, D. 1971. The topographical distribution of interhemispheric projections in the corpus callosum in the monkey. *Brain Research* 532:31–43.

Papcun, G.; Krashen, S.; Terbeek, D.; Remington, R.; and Harshman, R. 1974. Is the left hemisphere specialized for speech, language and/or something else? *Journal of the Acoustic Society of America* 55:319-27.

Piaget, J. 1963. *On the development of memory and identity.* Barre, Massachusetts: Clark University Press.

________. 1969a. *The mechanisms of perception.* New York: Basic Books.

________. 1969b. *Psychology of the child.* New York: Basic Books.

________. 1970. Piaget's theory. In P.H. Mussen, ed. *Carmichael's manual of child psychology.* New York: John Wiley.

________. 1973. *Psychology of intelligence.* New Jersey: Little Field, Adams.

Piaget, J. and Inhelder, B. 1971. *Mental imagery and the child.* New York: Basic Books.

________. 1973. *Memory and intelligence.* New York: Basic Books.

Porter, R.J. and Berlin, C.I. 1975. On interpreting developmental changes in the dichotic right-ear advantage. *Brain and Language* 2:186–200.

Pribram, K.H. 1976. Hemispheric specialization: Evolution or revolution. In *Origins and evolution of language and speech*, eds. S.R. Harnad; H.D. Steklis; and J. Lancaster. New York: New York Academy of Sciences.

________. 1977. Hemispheric specialization: Evolution or revolution. In *Evolution and lateralization of the brain*, eds. S.J. Dimond and D.A. Blizard. New York: New York Academy of Sciences.

Purpura, D. 1981. Plasticity of the central nervous system. Invited address to the Biennial Meeting of the Society for Research in Child Development, Boston.

Rakic, P. and Yakovlev, P.I. 1968. Development of the corpus callosum and cavum septi in man. *Journal of Comparative Neurology* 132:45–72.

Rasmussen, R. and Milner, B. 1977. The role of early left-brain injury in determining lateralization of cerebral speech functions. In *Evolution and lateralization of the brain*, eds. S.J. Dimond and D.A. Blizard. New York: New York Academy of Sciences.

Reinisch, J. 1974. Fetal hormones, the brain and human sex differences: A heuristic, integrative review of the recent literature. *Archives of Sexual Behavior* 3:51–90.

Riklan, M. and Cooper, I.S. 1977. Thalamic lateralization of psychological functions: Psychometric studies. In *Lateralization in the nervous system*, eds. S. Harnad and R.W. Doty. New York: Academic Press.

Robinson, B.W. 1976. Limbic influences on human speech. In *Origins and evolution of language and speech*, eds. H.D. Steklis; S.R. Harnad; and J. Lancaster. New York: Academy of Sciences.

Rudel, R.G. 1978. Neuroplasticity: Implications for development and education. In *Education and the brain*, eds. J.S. Chall and A.F. Mirsky. Chicago: University of Chicago Press.

Sasanuma and Fujimura, 1971. Selective impairment of phonetic and non-phonetic transcriptions of words in Japanese aphasic patients. *Cortex 7:1-18.*

Satz, P. 1976. Cerebral dominance and reading disability: An old problem revisited. In *The neuropscyhology of learning disorders*, eds. R.M. Knights and D.J. Bakker. Baltimore: University Press.

Satz, P.; Bakker, D.J.; Teunissen, J.; Goebel, R.; and Van der Vlugt, H. Developmental parameters of ear asymmetry: A multivariate approach. *Brain and Language* 2:171-85.

Satz, P. and Sparrow, S. 1970. Specific developmental dyslexia: A theoretical formulation. In *Specific reading disability: Advances in theory and method*, eds. D.J. Bakker and P. Satz. Rotterdam: Rotterdam University Press.

Scheibel, A.B. 1979. Development of axonal and dendritic neuropil as a function of evolving behavior. In *The neurosciences: Fourth study program*, eds. F.O. Schmitt and F.G. Worden. Cambridge: MIT Press.

Schmidt, R.F. 1975. *Fundamentals of neurophysiology*. New York: Springer-Verlag.

Searleman, A. 1977. A review of right hemisphere linguistic capabilities. *Psychological Bulletin* 84:503-22.

Segalowitz, S.J. and Grubner, F.A. 1977a. The development of cerebral dominance. In *Language development and neurological theory*, eds. S.J. Segalowitz and F.A. Gruber. New York: Academic Press.

________. 1977b. Speech perception. In *Language development neurological theory*, eds. S.J. Segalowitz and F.A. Gruber. New York: Academic Press.

Seggie, J. and Berry, M. 1972. Ontogeny of interhemispheric evoked potentials in the rat: Significance of myelination of the corpus callosum. *Experimental Neurology* 35:215-32.

Selnes, O.A. 1974. The corpus callosum: Some anatomical and functional condiserations with special references to language. *Brain and Language* 1:111-139.

Semmes, J. 1968. Hemispheric specializations: A possible clue to mechanism. *Neuropsychologia* 6:11-26.

Sharpless, S. and Jasper, H.H. 1956. Habituation of the arousal reaction. *Brain* 79:655-80.

Siegel, L.S. and Brainard, C.J., eds. 1978. *Alternatives to Piaget: Critical essays on the theory*. New York: Academic Press.

Siqueland, E.R. and Lipsett, L.P. 1966. Conditioned head turning in human newborns. *Journal of Experimental Child Psychology* 4:356-57.

Smith, A. 1974. Dominant and nondominant hemispherectomy. In *Hemispheric disconnection and cerebral function*, eds. M. Knisbourne and W.L. Smith. Springfield: Charles Thomas.

Smith, F. 1971. *Understanding reading: A psycholinguistic analysis of reading and learning to read.* New York: Holt, Rinehart and Winston.

Sparrow, S. and Satz, P. 1970. Dyslexia, laterality and neuropsychological development.

In *Specific reading disability: Advances in theory and method*, eds. D.J. Bakker and P. Satz. Rotterdam: Rotterdam University Press.

Sperry, R.W. 1969. A modified concept of consciousness. *Psychological Review* 76:532–36.

________. 1974. Lateral specialization in the surgically separated hemispheres. In *The neurosciences: Third study program*, eds. F.O. Schmitt and F.G. Worden. Cambridge: MIT Press.

Springer, J. and Deutch, G. 1981. *Left brain, right brain.* San Francisco: Freeman Press.

Steffen, H. 1975. Cerebral dominance: The development of handedness and speech. *Acta Psychopediatrica* 41:223–35.

Sussman, H.M. 1971. The laterality effect in lingual-auditory tracking. *Journal of the Acoustical Society of America* 49:1874–80.

Sussman, H.M. and MacNeilage, P.F. 1975. Studies of hemispheric specialization for speech production. *Brain and Language* 2:131–51.

Taylor, D. 1969. Differential rates of cerebral maturation between sexes and between hemispheres. *Lancet* 2:140–42.

Teuber, H.L. 1967. Lacunae and research approaches to them. In *Brain mechanisms underlying speech and language*, eds. C.H. Millikan and F.L. Darley. New York: Grune and Stratton.

________. 1975. Effects of focal brain injury on the human brain. In *The animal neuroscience*, Vol. 2., ed. T. Chase. New York: Raven.

Thompson, R.F. 1975. *Introduction to physiological psychology.* New York: Harper and Row.

Trevarthen, C. 1974. Cerebral embryology and the split brain. In *Hemispheric disconnection and cerebral function*, eds. M. Knisbourne and W.L. Smith. Springfield: Charles Thomas.

Turkewitz, G. 1977a. The development of lateral differences in the human infant. In *Lateralization in the nervous system*, eds. S. Harnad and R.W. Doty, New York: Academic Press.

________. 1977b. The development of lateral differentiation in the human infant. In *Evolution and lateralization of the brain*, eds. S.J. Dimond and D.A. Blizard. New York: New York Academy of Sciences.

Turkewitz, G.; Gordon, E.; and Birch, H. 1965. Head turning in the human neonate: Spontaneous patterns. *Journal of Genetic Psychology* 107:143–58.

________. 1968. Head turning in the human neonate: Effect of prandial condition and lateral preference. *Journal of Comparative and Physiological Pscyhology* 59:189–92.

Turkewitz, G.; Moreau, T.; and Birch, H.G. 1966. Head position and receptor organization in the human neonate. *Journal of Experimental Psychology* 4:169–77.

Ulett, G.; Dow, R.S.; and Larsell, O. 1974. The inception of conductivity in the corpus callosum and the cortico-porto cerebellar pathway of young rabbits, with reference to myelination. *Journal of Comparative Neurology* 80:1–10.

Van der Vlugt, H. 1974. Dichotic listening. In *Lateralization of brain functions.* Boerhaavc Committee for Postgraduate Education. The Netherlands: University of Leiden Press.

Wechsler, A.F. 1976. Crossed aphasia in an illiterate dextral. *Brain and Language* 3:164–72.

Whitaker, H.A. and Ojemann, G.A. 1977. Lateralization of higher cortical functions: A critique. In *Evolution and lateralization of the brain*, eds. S.J. Dimond and D.A. Blizard. New York: New York Academy of Sciences.

White, H. 1961. Cerebral hemispherectomy in the treatment of infantile hemiplegia. *Confinie Neurologica* 21:1–50.

Wickelgren, L.W. 1967. Convergence in the human newborn. *Journal of Experimental Child Psychology* 5:74–85.

Wiesel, T.N. and Hubel, D.H. 1965. Extent of recovery from the effect of visual deprivation in kittens. *Journal of Neurophysiology* 28:1060–72.

Witelson, S.F. 1976a. Abnormal right hemisphere specializations in developmental dyslexia. In *The neuropsychology of learning disorders*, eds. R.M. Knight and D.J. Bakker. Baltimore: University Press.

________. 1976b. Sex and the single hemisphere. Specialization of the right hemisphere for spatial processing. *Science* 193:425–27.

________. 1977a. Anatomic asymmetry in the temporal lobes: Its documentation, phylogenesis, and relationship to functional asymmetry. In *Evolution and lateralization of the brain*, eds. S.J. Dimond and D.A. Blizard. New York: New York Academy of Science.

________. 1977b. Developmental dyslexia: Two right hemispheres and none left. *Science* 195:309–11.

________. 1977c. Early hemispheric specialization and interhemisphere plasticity. An empirical and theoretical review. In *Language development and neurological theory*, eds. S.J. Segalowitz and F.A. Gruber. New York: Academic Press.

Witelson, S.F. and Pallie, W. 1973. Left hemisphere specialization for language in the newborn: Neuroanatomical evidence of asymmetry. *Brain* 96:641–46.

Witelson, S.F. and Rabinovitch, M.S. 1972. Hemispheric lateralization in children with auditory-linguistic deficits. *Cortex* 8:412–26.

Worley, P. 1982. Hemispheric lateralization and preschool children's performance on creativity tasks. Unpublished master's thesis. University of California, Davis.

Yakovlev, P.I. and Lecours, A.R. 1967. Discussion of myelogenetic cycles of region maturation in the brain. In *Regional development of the brain in early life*, ed. A. Minkowski. Oxford: Blackwell.

Yamadori, A. 1975. Ideogram reading in Alexia. *Brain* 98:231–38.

Yeni-Komshian, G. 1973. Dichotic listening studies. Unpublished studies, cited in S.F. Witelson, Early hemispheric specialization and interhemisphere plasticity. In *Language development and neurological theory*, eds. S.J. Segalowitz and F.A. Gruber. New York: Academic Press.

Young, G. 1977. Manual specialization in infancy: Implications for lateralization of brain functioning. In *Language development and neurological theory*, eds. S.J. Segalowitz and F.A. Gruber. New York: Academic Press.

Zaidel, E. 1976. Auditory vocabulary of the right hemisphere following brain bisection or hemidecortication. *Cortex* 12:191–211.

________. 1977a. The split and half brains as models of congenital language disability. In

The neurological bases of language disorder in children: Methods and directions for research, eds. C.L. Ludlow and M.E. Doran-Quine. NINCDS Monograph No. 22. Bethesda: US Department of Health, Education and Welfare.

________. 1977b. Unilateral auditory language comprehension on the Token Test following cerebral commissurotomy and hemispherectomy. *Neuropsychologia* 15:1–18.

Zangwell, O.L. 1960. *Cerebral dominance and its relation to pscyhological function.* Springfield: Charles Thomas.

________. 1975. The ontogeny of cerebral dominance in man. In *Foundations of language development*, eds. E.H. Lenneberg and E. Lenneberg. New York: Academic Press.

Zurif, E.F. and Carson, G. 1970. Dyslexia in relation to cerebral dominance and temporal analysis. *Neuropyschologia* 8:351–361.

Chapter 7

A Metalanguage of Text

by Harold B. Pepinsky

PROLOGUE

In the world of words, the imagination is one of the forces of nature.
Wallace Stevens, *Opus Posthumous* (1957)

In current research on reading, investigators tend to emphasize the complex, cognitive processes by which people select, interpret, and subsequently retrieve information conveyed to them by texts. Underlying these diverse attempts to account for comprehension and recall is the idea that people make sense out of what they read and remember through hierarchically ordered schemata, developed out of prior experiences. A generic term for this conception is "schema theory," which Bruce Dunn examines elsewhere in this volume (cf. Freedle 1979, especially Adams and Collins 1979).

At the same time, Dunn offers new evidence that other variables play significant roles in determining a reader's comprehension of and memory for given texts. In experiments he describes, texts themselves were identified as a key variable, along with conditions under which they were read, and measurable attributes (Dunn used levels of cerebral activity) of the persons who read them. Moreover, there were significant interactions among these variables to account for differences in the performances of readers. On the one hand, his findings lend support to this chapter on text. On the other, they lend added weight to my belief that the analysis of information provided in text is a complicated skein to unravel. (Dunn's perspective on text itself further delineates the inquiry pursued in this chapter.)

Drawing on the concepts and methods of Bonnie Meyer (1975, 1977), Dunn argues that individual texts reflect the cognitive processes of their producers. Unlike the schemata imputed to the readers of texts, which must be inferred from their responses to a text or their reconstructions of it, texts themselves are posited to exist as records that can be analyzed directly by means of "semantic grammars." If we assume that texts have common formal properties, then common rubrics may be used to compare one text with another; in principle, across as much as within languages (Pepinsky 1974; cf. Meyer 1977).

According to Dunn, there are two primary levels of analysis currently employed by semantic grammarians in their work with texts. One level, which he identifies as "microanalysis," centers on sentence-by-sentence comparisons. The other level, of "macroanalysis," encompasses whole texts, which can also be decomposed into smaller component parts and interpreted accordingly, e.g., by reference to paragraphs, sentences, words. Using Meyer's (1975) system as a prototype, he shows how the analyst may identify in a given text various levels of "semantic organization" (akin to that of the interpreter's schemata), to portray the text's structural complexity (cf. Coulthard 1977; Crothers 1979; Halliday and Hasan 1976).

In this chapter, I shall be concerned more with microanalysis, but will demonstrate how one may bridge the gap between the two levels of analysis. What follows is expressly designed to contribute to a theory of text production and interpretation. But the argument to be presented has a broader import for the accumulation and use of knowledge. For example, although people trained in the behavioral and social sciences have conducted extensive research on communication (e.g., via text), their diverse professional languages are impediments to the collection and dissemination of information about communication or any other phenomenon.[1] In what follows, I hope to add modestly to a more usefully integrative language for the behavioral and social sciences to draw upon. A key ingredient, it seems to me, is our ability to make common property of the phenomena that we work with. An important means to this end, I further believe, is the development of a structural language that permits us meaningfully to identify things and relates them to each other.

To these ends, the remainder of the chapter introduces, discusses, and provides illustrative cases for an aggregate of definitions, axioms, and postulates to provide the reader with a basic conception of what it means to produce and interpret text. My distinction between axioms and postulates is simple-minded: the axioms are presented as truisms which readers in general would be expected to take for granted as what "anybody knows" to be the case. The postulates, by contrast, are statements of things I invite the reader to take for granted, but which I do not infer to be readily available truisms. In presenting these, I have attempted to proceed stepwise from more general and primitive concepts to ones that are both more particular and more complex. Before discussing the progression of individual concepts in detail, I have presented them in tabular form to introduce each of three clusters of topics: the first having to do with such things as meaning, information, communication, language, and text; the second, with the grammatical analysis of text; and the third, with derivative ideas of culture and policy. Beyond thus identifying these concepts, I intend to make evident their relevance to students of reading and other behavioral phenomena.

I. INTRODUCING A METALANGUAGE

Let me begin now with Figure 1. At the top of the figure is a line of text with which the chapter opens, a quotation from a poem by Wallace Stevens. Upon casual inspection, it appears to be in form a rather ordinary sentence. Those of us who read English can recognize and identify the contents—whether we agree with them or not—as a sensible message. At the second level the printed text, which has been analyzed grammatically by computer, is displayed, and at the third level a graphic reconstruction of the sentence is shown. Everything in the figure but the original text exemplifies metalanguage, as I shall be using the term. Identification of my remarks thus far as lines of printed words arranged on a white background also exemplifies metalanguage. People use it whenever they communicate about language, with each other or with non-persons like computers. In short, Metalanguage is whatever pertains to language, but is understood to be somehow peripheral to or outside of it. (*D*IA. 1).[2]

In Figure 1, the original sentence is analyzed by means of a more sophisticated metalanguage known as CALAS, an acronym for "a computer-assisted language analysis system." (Patton and Meara in press; Pepinsky 1974; Rush et al., 1974).

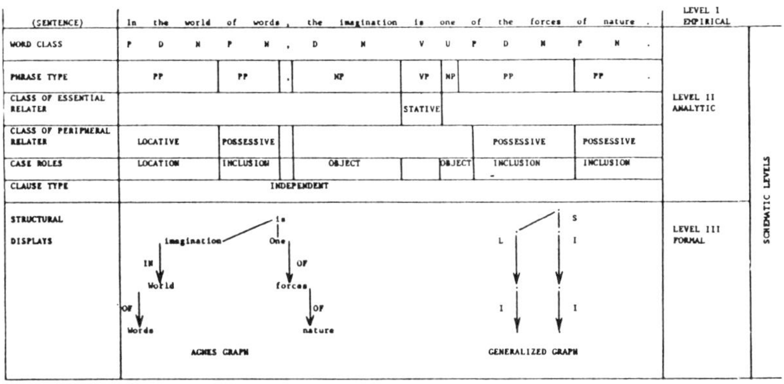

Figure 1. Schemapiric Representation of an English Language Text (after Hicks et al. 1977; Hurndon et al. 1979; Pepinsky 1974; S.S. Stevens 1969; Strong 1974; quotation from Wallace Stevens 1957). Word classes are P—preposition, D—determiner, N—noun, V—verb, U—pronoun. In the generalized graph, S—state, L—locative, I—inclusive. See text for explanation of formal graphs (Section V.A.2, after Strong 1974).

The body of this chapter provides a rationale for CALAS and, more broadly, for the analysis of text. CALAS as an operating system will be described briefly later (in Section V). Persons familiar with these things, will not be surprised to learn that the construction and the system and its rationale developed symbiotically. For instance, it was after several years of work on CALAS as an automated parser that James Rush, a leader in its initial construction, called attention to names and relations as essential components of the system (cf. Hicks et al. 1977). Figure 1 helps to illustrate his point by reference to the schema.

At levels 2 and 3 in Figure 1, named things—inferred to be counterparts of things in the text—are exhibited in relation to each other. The point will not be elaborated upon here; the idea to be conveyed for now is that the names and relations within and among levels define a particular kind of structure, graphic conceptions of which are displayed at level 3 (after Hicks et al. 1977; Strong 1974). At level 2, each event in the schema is also a category of named things; so is each row in the schema; so is each of the graphs at level 3; so, for that matter, is all of level 2 or level 3. By means of the metalanguage, then, events subsumed under any given category—e.g., communication, language, text, reading, culture, policy, etc.—would be further identified in terms of their common structural properties, and thus distinguished from events with dissimilar properties. As I shall be using the term, The defining attributes of a category are its structural properties, which take the forms of (a) any or all names for things postulated to exist as events subsumed by the category, and (b) relations postulated to exist between or among the named things (*D*I.A.2).

It is these two attributes, of names and relations, then, that constitute the vocabulary and rules of our metalanguage. If events subsumed "do not share a large proportion of their properties" (Sokal 1974), however, then the phenomenon itself cannot be inferred to exist as a single category; it would have to be reconstituted until that condition were satisfied. When that kind of structural analysis can be made directly from "raw" language texts describing a given phenomenon and events comprising it, an immediate check on the internal consistency of the descriptions is also provided for. When the metalanguage offers a common structural language for examining all such descriptions, apart from their classifications and the professional identification of the classifier, then we have a foundation for coherent discourse among the behavioral and social sciences.

As a metalanguage for use with English language texts, CALAS is designed to help build that kind of structural language. That is not so wild a dream. Pressures for large-scale and automated information storage and retrieval systems have increased with the burgeoning of scientific and technical activities; a structural language in which to encode and decode such information appears to be a necessity.

II. LANGUAGE AS MEANINGFUL STRUCTURE

In the preceding section, I introduced two propositions about language (Definitions I.A.1 and I.A.2). The first of these identifies as metalanguage all talk about language; the second identifies the focus of talk: the construction and use of a language about text, according to which linguistic phenomena can be meaningfully intended, aggregated, labeled, and otherwise related to each other. I offer in Sections II-IV a set of propositions about text. Table 1 exhibits in overview all of these propositions, culminating in definitions of language and text (*D*IV.C.1-2).

For now, Section II takes us into the worlds of meaning that language and communication make possible for humans to construct: i.e., to build

TABLE I

Some Propositions About Text: Definitions, Axioms, Postulates
(As they appear in Sections I–IV, this chapter)
D—Definition, *As*—Assumption, *Ax*—Axiom, *P*—Postulate;
roman and arabic numbers indicate major and minor sections;
e.g., *Ax*II.B.1—Axiom No. 1 in Section II.B.

(*D*I.A.1)
Metalanguage is whatever pertains to language, but is understood to be somehow peripheral to or outside of it.

(*D*I.A.2)
The defining attributes of a category are its structural properties, which take the form of (a) any or all names for things postulated to exist as events subsumed by the category, and (b) relations postulated to exist between or among named things.

(*D*II.B.1)
Signs are names, in the form of words or other symbolic representations, of things referred to.

(*D*II.B.2).
Significates are things referred to (things signified) by their signs.

(*Ax*II.B.1)
A language can have meaning if and only if the language includes names that refer to things.

(*P*II.B.1)
The triad, Delta_1, exists as a fundamental unit of meaning in language.

(*D*II.B.3)
The triad, Delta_1, is a unit of language comprised of sign, significate, and interpretant.

(*D*II.B.3a).
Intention is the identification and attribution of meaning to a thing.

(*D*II.B.4)
The triad, Delta_2, is a unit of language comprised of sign, sign, and interpretant.

(*P*II.B.2)
The triad, Delta_2, exists as a fundamental unit of meaning in language.

(*P*II.B.3)
Things exists apart from their intention by an interpretant.

(*P*II.B.4)
Meaning exists when at least one interpretant intends at least one thing.

Table I *Continued*

(*D*II.B.5)
Meaning is (a) the structuring of things by an interpretant, such that (b) things experienced by an interpretant are named and otherwise related to each other.

(*D*II.B.6)
The interpreter is a named thing (e.g., person or computer) that intends a relationship between or among named things.

(*D*II.B.7)
The interpretans, or non-intending interpreter, is a named thing (e.g., a verb) that is itself non-intending but that is intended by an interpreter as relating named things to each other. Henceforth, it will be referred to simply as "the relater."

(*P*II.B.1.1)
There exists in language a formulative dimension, Phi, such that the interpreters of a language use it to intend a variety of meanings in the process of naming things and relating them to each other.

(*Ax*III.A.I)
Any human language consists of statements that are meaningfully structured.

(*P*III.A.I.)
A statement may be postulated to exist as meaningfully structured if and if it is so intended by an interpreter, whether as the source or any subsequent interpreter of the statement.

(*D*III.A.1)
An instruction is a unit of meaning in a language, such that an interpreter intends it as stating (a) what its contents are in terms of their propositional form and (b) how its contents are to be interpreted in terms of what is to be done about them.

(*D*III.B.1)
A rule is (a) an instruction that is intended by an interpreter, in which (b) one or more relaters stipulate a categorizing of things such that (b_1) the members of any category are treated by a definitional procedure as if they were nominally equivalent and also that (b_2) there exists a relational procedure which treats the members as if they were variable.

(*Ax*III.C.1)
Any statement in a language is instructive and can be decomposed into units such that each unit is an instruction.

(*Ax*III.C.2)
There can exist in a language instructions of a particular kind, such that each instruction is a rule.

(*P*III.C.1)
A language and any or all of its constituent features (e.g., instructions, rules) exist if and only if they are so intended by an interpreter.

Table I *Continued*

(*D*III.C.1)
Formulating is any constructive activity by one or more interpreters, such that one or more interpreters intend a meaningful structuring of experience, the unit of which (by Definition III.A.1) is an instruction.

(*As*III.C.1)
Formulating consists of instructions, which one or more interpreters intend as a categorizing of experience that accords with rules of interpretation.

(*As*III.C.2)
The rules of interpretation either (a) presuppose or (b) are presupposed by the formulating of instructions.

(*P*IV.A.1)
Information and/or its communication exist if and only if one or both are intended by an interpreter.

(*D*IV.A.1)
Information is the occurrence of anything, which is intended by an interpreter and which is further intended to make a difference in something at a later time and/or another place.

(*D*IV.A.2)
Communication is any or all component parts of an activity that an interpreter intends as making information occur.

(*D*IV.B.1)
The informative display is a procedure or its resultant, which is intended by an interpreter as information that is communicated (a) in the form of an instruction or larger set of instructions and (b) according to interpretable rules.

(*P*IV.B.1)
The information display exists if and only if it is intended by an interpreter.

(*D*IV.B.2)
Formulative communication is any or all of the component parts of an activity that is intended by an interpreter as a collaboratively informative display.

(*D*IV.C.1)
Language is (1) a body of information, which is (2) intended by an interpreter as (3) a system of formulations (3.1) that people have recourse to (3.11) as common property (3.12) in constructing informative displays, and (3.2) that the people are able to use (3.21) in formulative communications (3.22) with each other and with non-persons.

(*D*IV.C.2)
Text is a collection of things that an interpreter intends as the record of a procedure, one that is further interpretable as the informative display of a language.

together. Two essential units of meaning (the Delta Phenomena) are presented as building blocks, together with a "formulative" ingredient (the Phi Phenomenon) that is at once ornamental and highly useful in providing for complexities and subtleties of meaning.

II. A. Language as Communicated Information

Among living organisms known to us, the human species is outstandingly—perhaps uniquely—capable of learning to produce and interpret complex patterns of speech sounds that take the form of "natural language." That term, in popular usage, designates any language employed spontaneously and routinely by a group of persons to communicate with each other in the conduct of their ordinary social activities. The ability of humans to communicate by means of language, presumably is the product of biosocial conditions, which are complex and interwoven. On the one hand, we cannot reject the premise that humans are biologically predisposed toward communicating with each other via what Searle (1969) calls "speech acts" (cf. Bickerton 1981; Chomsky 1965, 1968; Fraser 1975; Lenneberg 1967, 1969; Mattingly 1972). Nor can we reject the assumption of a "human capacity for culture" (cf. Spuhler 1959), which is evolving biologically with accompanying linguistic modifications (Fraser 1975; Malinowski 1923). On the other hand, human language communities are as diverse as they are numerous, and that these "district dialects" (Naroll 1968) tend to change over time. Hence, we cannot reject the idea that language usage is socially as well as biologically determined (cf. Berger and Luckmann 1966; Halliday 1973).

For reasons that are becoming clearer, however, humans in general are able to use sophisticated language systems to communicate with each other and to perform complex acts that accord with information thus communicated. Recent advances toward the automated analysis and synthesis of discourse, as humans use it in conversations as well as in the production and interpretation of text, have been impressive (cf. Abelson 1981). Current ideas and methods, however, are not yet adequate to simulate the acquisition of either complex sentences or imagery to be represented by them (Simon 1979, p. 382). Still, computers are enabled to act more and more like "intelligent" humans in conversing and in following linguistically conveyed instructions to solve assigned problems (Ableson and Dorfman 1982). By implication, if one can emulate in this fashion the human use of language, one can also understand it.

Winograd's (1972) dissertation on "understanding language" is often cited as a milestone in progress toward that goal. Though humans persist in being far more versatile and accomplished linguists than their emulators, the gap is narrowing between them (Hunt 1982).

Another avenue toward understanding the human use of language is through the study of its development in children, as compared to that in other living organisms. Although we still do not know why linguistic abilities manifest themselves, or fail to do so, a great deal of information has been collected to describe what does take place. Based on his extensive research and knowledge of what others have reported, Roger Brown (1973, pp. 38–39) postulates the existence of three attributes that distinguish human from nonhuman language in social communication. I shall try to restate them here. One is semanticity: the use of language to convey information whose substance and forms are richly meaningful. A second is productivity: a capacity to generate and interpret these linguistic constructions in seemingly endless variety. The third is displacement: the ability to convey by means of language information about things occurring at times and places other than those of its initiation or reception, e.g., something in another time or place may be alluded to metaphorically.[3]

II.B. Language as Meaningful Information

Those attributions underscore the difficulty of talking about language without reference to its users. A case in point is the attribution of meaningfulness. I should add that Brown himself has long recognized the key role of meaning in language usage. In a book appropriately titled *Words and Things* (Brown 1958), he earlier posited two basic abilities of language users: (a) to give names to things, and (b) to identify the names as signs for the things named.[4] Following Percy's (1972) nomenclature, I shall further assert that, by definition, Signs are names, in the form of words or other symbolic representations, of things referred to (*D*II.B.1), and that Significates are the things referred to (things signified) by their signs (*D*II.B.2). A requirement of meaningfulness, then, is the coupling of sign and significate, and A language can have meaning if and only if the language includes names that refer to things (*Ax*II.B.1).

However, the minimum essentials of meaningfulness in language have not yet been stated. You will remember my saying that Brown's attributions to language of semanticity, productivity, and displacement underscore the difficulty of talking about talk without reference to its

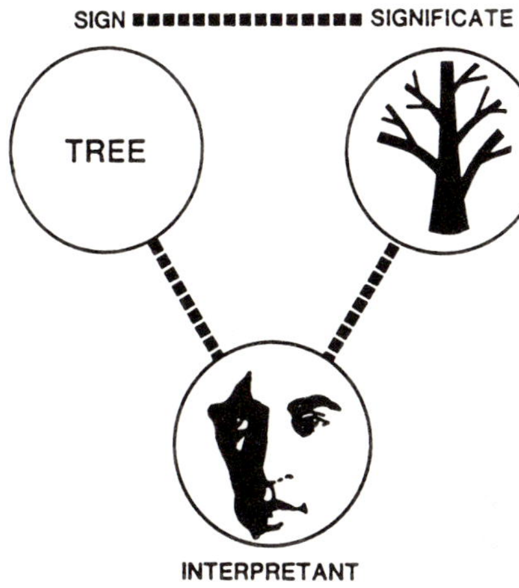

Figure 2.
The Delta$_1$ Phenomenon (after Percy, 1972, 1975)

users. The missing link in our coupling process is precisely to be found in the determination of who—or, as we shall see, what—does the coupling. Walker Percy (1972, 1975) is struck by the all-of-a-pieceness of sign, significate, and interpretant. This last ingredient, I gather, is who-ever—or whatever—provides the coupling by identifying and interpreting it as such. By implication, the interpretant thus gives meaning to sign and significate in the act of putting them together as one and the same thing. The result is an inseparable triad of sign, significate, and interpretant, and not alone the dyad of sign and significate; hence The triad, Delta$_1$, is a unit of language comprised of sign, significate, and interpretant (*D*II.B.3). Following Percy (1972, 1975), I shall postulate that The triad, Delta$_1$, exists as a fundamental unit of meaning in language (*P*II.B.1). Percy (1975) refers to this "irreducible" unit as the "Delta phenomenon,"[5] and considers it fundamental to a "triadic theory of meaning" (Percy 1972). Delta is schematized in Figure 2. Here, by way of illustration, the person as interpretant is depicted as linking the word "tree" with something identified as a tree.

What put him on to Delta, Percy (1975) tells us, was his rumination over a pivotal incident in the life of Helen Keller. It is described in her autobiography, *The Story of My Life*. The event occurred on a summer day in 1887 when she was eight years old. Her wonderful teacher, Anne

Sullivan, had taught Helen Keller to communicate simple words by means of taps on the hands, words put together from an alphabet of letters thus signaled. "Helen had learned to respond like any good animal," says Percy (1975), "When she wanted a piece of cake, she spelled the word in Miss Sullivan's hand, and Miss Sullivan fetched her the cake" (p. 55). Having done so on that day, Anne Sullivan next took her pupil to the well-house where someone was drawing water. Miss Sullivan put Helen's one hand in the water and in the other spelled out w-a-t-e-r. It was then the miracle of linkage occurred for Helen Keller: "Somehow the mystery of language was revealed to me. I knew then that "w-a-t-e-r" *meant* the wonderful cool something that was flowing over my hand . . . I left the well-house eager to *learn*." [From *The Story of My Life*, 1902, quoted in Percy 1975 56; italics added.]

What I am calling the $Delta_1$ phenomenon underlies Percy's "triadic theory of meaning" (1972). Its ingredient of sign, significate, and interpretant, Percy tells us further, were labeled as such by the 19th century philosopher, Charles Peirce. Peirce is credited with priority in identifying a concept of pragmatism in which the triad is a constituent feature.[6] However, his colleague, William James, was the clearer, more popular writer, and his view of pragmatism has prevailed. In his writings and those of later authorities such as Charles Morris (1946), the idea of the interpretant as a necessary pragmatic connector of sign and significant is not emphasized (after Percy 1972, 1975).

$Delta_1$ implies what Ernst Cassirer (1923) called attention to as "definitional" in thinking. In linguistic terms this is a process of interpretation by which things are named and, if assigned a common name, acquire a common identity. The process is one of abstracting from particular things that are named to a general category of named things, e.g., from "a tree" to "tree." By further abstraction, categories may become increasingly inclusive, e.g., "tree" becomes "plant" and "plant" becomes "living thing." Through a corollary process of linguistic definition, things that are not so-named also may be distinguished as such, e.g., anything that cannot be identified as "tree," "plant" or "living thing." Using senses other than those of sight and sound, for instance, Helen Keller came to discriminate *inter alia* between w-a-t-e-r and c-a-k-e things.

As a basis for abstraction and discrimination among things, therefore, $Delta_1$ is more than definitional; it is intentionally so. By that I mean to say, $Delta_1$ serves a purpose for its interpretant. As an "act of consciousness," in the words of Franz Brentano, the person "intends the object'' (i.e., of interpretation; Brentano 1972). In that sense, I may "intend'' something that impinges as an image on my retina, but if and only if in doing so I am aware of "it.'' The act is at least minimally intentional, therefore, if in the process I am aware of something, i.e., as a conscious experience. As interpretant, however, I give meaning to the act if and only if I can also label it, e.g., as "tree,'' and thus differentiate it from other things, e.g., "a tree'' from "a frog.'' The assumption that intention is purposive, of course, links it to much more complex phenomena, such as the "behavioral intention'' that one is inferred to have toward an "attitude object'' (cf. Fishbein and Ajzen 1972, pp. 495–496; Triandis et al. 1972, pp. 9–34.); the attributing of motive or "personal causation''—to oneself *or* other persons (as opposed to "impersonal causation,'' cf. Fauconnet 1929; Heider 1958; Jones et al. 1972) and to self *and* others in mundane encounters (e.g., your "in order to'' becomes my "because of,'' Schutz 1967, pp. 86–96); and the communication that one directs at another (others) for a reason (G.R. Miller 1966).[7] For our purpose here, it will suffice to say that Intention is the identification and attribution of meaning to a thing (*D*II.B.3a).

There is another ingredient of meaningfulness in language, which is implied by the Delta_1 phenomenon. Cassirer (1923) alludes to such a companion phenomenon in his concept of "relational'' thinking. Just as words or other signs in a language must necessarily refer to items of experience (things) if the language is to be meaningful, so there must exist a capability of relating the signs to each other. Indeed, the ability to engage in relational thinking and its expression in language are implicit in Roger Brown's (1973) attributions of productivity, semanticity, and displacement to human language.

The two kinds of linkage, sign-significate and sign-sign, are illustrated in the following sentences:

1. The *tree* has branches.
2. Did the dog *tree* the squirrel?

A sign-significate relationship, with "tree'' as referent (thing or things referred to), is implied in both sentences. In the first example, "tree'' itself is the name for a class of things; the sign refers to a member of that class. In the second example, "tree'' is the name for something attributed to other named things: here, the word implies something like "cause to get up in the tree'' and describes a relationship between "dog'' and "squirrel.'' The word "tree'' is used in the second sentence to mediate a sign-sign relationship. These relationships of sign to sign are given considerably greater emphasis in Brown's more recent book (1973) than in his earlier one (1958).[8] As was the case for relating sign to significate, though, I assume the linkage to be incomplete without reference to its interpretant. With apologies to Percy (1975), I shall identify the new triad as the "Delta$_2$ phenomenon," noting that The Triad, Delta$_2$, is a unit of language comprised of sign, sign, and interpretant (*D*II.B.4). Again, I postulate that The triad, Delta$_2$, exists as a fundamental unit of meaning in language (*P*II.B.2).

In Figure 3, both of the Delta phenomena are schematized. As shown in Figures 3.1 and 3.2, the conception of Delta has been altered slightly (cf. Percy 1972, 1975). The person as interpretant is now shown to link the sign "tree" with the tree as a thing intended by the interpretant. More properly, I think, we may regard that intended object—the "image" of something—as a cornerstone of Delta, rather than the thing itself (cf. Fisher 1976). The distinction is an important one. It is clearly implied in Daniel Weintraub's comprehensive review of publications on "perception": "Given that a physical world exists," he asks in conclusion, "What is the nature of the phenomenal world?" (Weintraub 1975, p. 281). I should express the belief somewhat differently, postulating that Things exist apart from their intention by an interpretant (*P*II.B.3), and that Meaning exists when at least one interpretant intends at least one thing (*P*II.B.4).

Illustratively, Figure 3.1 shows the image of an outside object to be impinging on a person's retina. What the person "sees" there, as suggested by the arrows from the eye to brain and brain to eye, is a complex perceptual phenomenon. How the object may be thus intended by the person is known to be affected, for example, by physical conditions under which the object is viewed, the neurophysiology of the viewing organism, and its prior experiences (Weintraub 1975; cf. Bock 1982). Prior experiences, demonstratively, are likewise affected by the physical and cultural circumstances of the person's development (Cole and Scribner 1974). In Figure 3.2 the person is depicted as having established a conceptual link between two sets of precepts: one is the intended object and the other is the word "tree," which names the object thus identified as a tree. That coupling by the person as an interpretant exemplifies Delta$_1$ as a unit of meaning.

The next figure, 3.3. displays an extension of the triadic idea. At the upper left, we now have represented a sentence produced by the person: e.g., "This thing is a tree," Here, "thing" and "tree" are seen to be ac-

Figure 3. The Delta Phenomena
(after Aid 1973; Cook 1979; Fisher; Percy 1972, 1975; Schank 1973)

(See text for elaboration upon these concepts; a fuller discussion of the verb types and case assignments to them is provided in Section V.B.2)

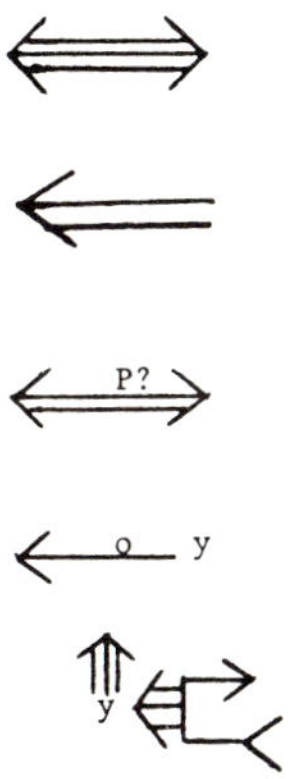

= mutual dependency = stative case;

= ownership = benefactive case;

= action-process case; past tense and interrogative mood;

= object, y, of intention;

= object, y, and how acted upon.

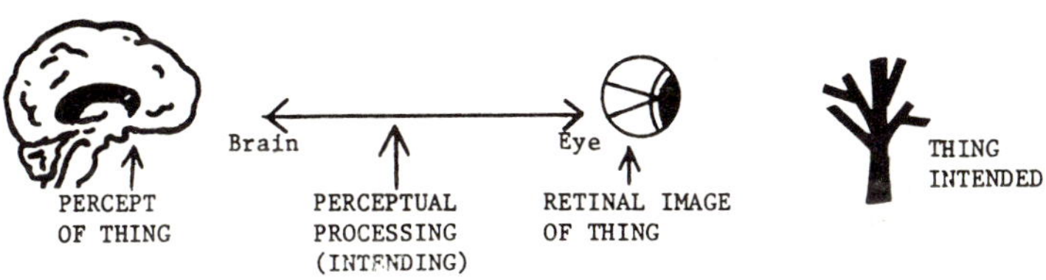

3.1. Intention of a Thing by a Person

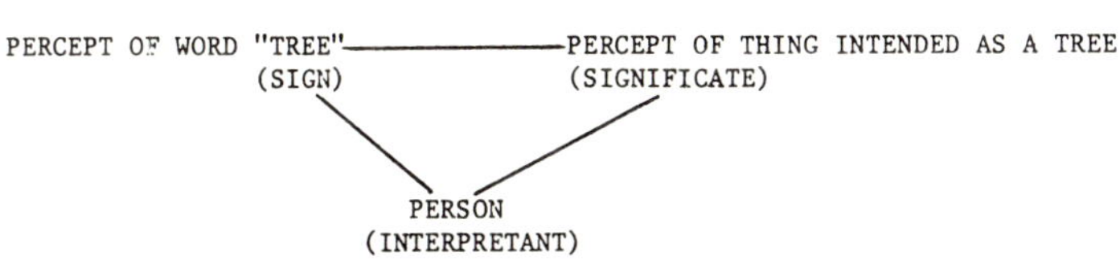

3.2. Delta$_1$, the Naming of a Thing: I. A Conceptual Link between Precepts

Figure 3 continued

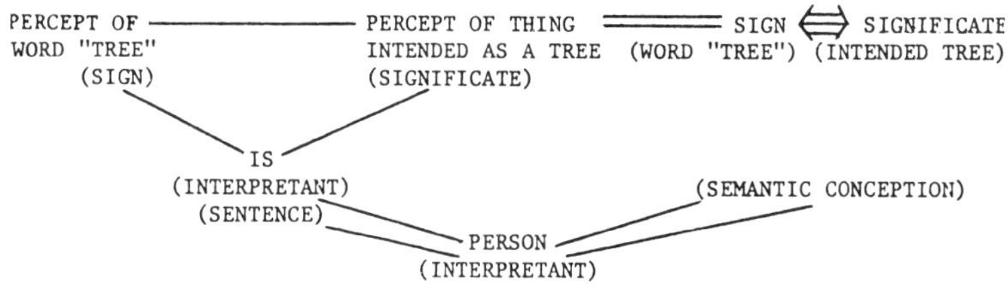

3.3. Delta$_1$, the Naming of a Thing: II. A Link between Language and Thought

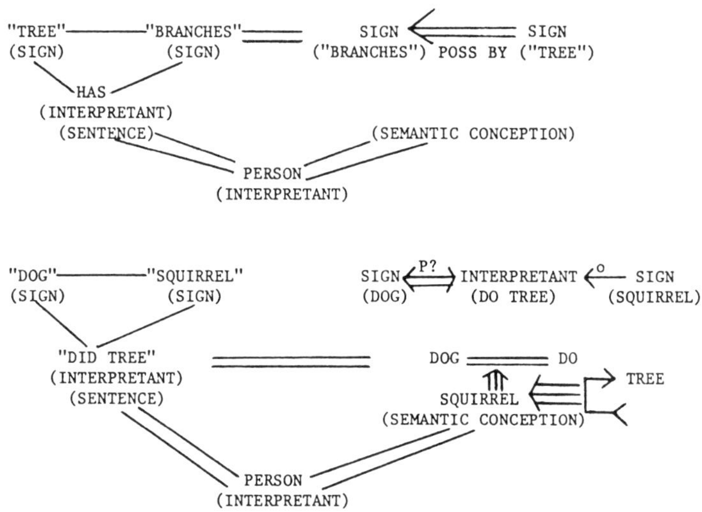

3.4. Delta$_2$, the Relating of Named Things: A Further Link between Language and Thought (top figure diagrams a person's interpretation of the sentence, "The tree has branches"; lower figure, "Did the dog tree the squirrel?")

companied by a non-person, the verb "is," which I have also identified as interpretant because it, too, serves to relate the word and the thing to each other. At the upper right of Figure 3.3, guided by an earlier model proposed by Roger Schank (1973), I have provided a semantic conception of the person's thought process. Some such process of cognition by the person is postulated to exist as an accompaniment to its linguistic expression. Again, what links the two is the person as interepretant. In this semantic conception of thought, sign and significate are connected by a symbol indicating their mutual dependency (by virtue of assigned roles defined by the "stative case frame" of the verb "to be"; see Section V.A.2 for a discussion of particular "case frames"). Although Schank does not emphasize the point, the semantic linkage "$\Leftrightarrow$" again implies an interpretant. And, critically, we must once more assume the person to be the interpretive link between his/her thought and the language that expresses it.

The two illustrative Delta_2 units in Figure 3.4 call attention to relations between named things as defined by their interpretive relaters. In the top illustration, a sentence, "The tree has branches," has been schematized according to imputed linguistic (upper left) and cognitive (upper right) features. In contrast to Figure 3.3, which depicts an interpretant's relating of sign and significate, Figure 3.4 exhibits how interpretants may serve to interconnect signs. The lower illustration schematizes the sentence, "Did the dog tree the squirrel?" in its putatively linguistic and cognitive forms. (Note that in the top illustration, the verb "has" is inferred to act as a "benefactive" interpretant; in the bottom illustration, the verb phrase "did tree" is said to denote an "action-process" relationship between the two signs; again, Section V.A.2 will contain a further discussion of these and other "case frames.")

The Delta phenomena, which have been identified as minimal essentials of meaning in language, also call attention to its structural properties. To imply or infer meaning is to categorize something, that is, by naming things that the category subsumes and by relating them to each other. We may impute a process of structuring by an interpretant to occur in the employment of ordinary language as much as the abstruse ones of chemistry, physics, or mathematics, asserting that Meaning is (a) the structuring of things by an interpretant, such that (b) things experienced by an interpretant are intended, named, and otherwise related to each other (*D*II.B.5). The structuring may be accomplished by a variety of interpretants—e.g., a person or a verb, as illustrated in Figure 3. However, meaningful structuring demands also an interpretant that intentionally aggregates, differentiates among, and otherwise relates to each other, named things in its experience. A person or a computer but not a verb, we assume, may structure things intentionally in that fashion. Let me clarify the distinction I am making by more explicit definitions. First, The interpreter is a named thing (e.g., person or computer) that intends a relationship between or among other things (*D*II.B.6). Second, The interpretans, or non-intending relater, is a named thing (e.g., a verb) that is itself nonintending but that is intended by an interpreter as relating named things to each other (*D*II.B.7). Henceforth, it will be referred to simply as "the related."

II.B.1 Meaning in Language: Related Concepts and a Third Dimension

There are many ways of talking about meaningfulness in language. For example, Frank Di Vesta (1974, pp. 69–73) reminds us of two qualifiers: the one having to do with affective meaning, the other with expressiveness. Roger Brown (1965, pp. 330–332) describes the latter as implicit meanings conveyed to us by the configurations of behavior accompanying the spoken language of other persons (speech intonations and stresses, activity/nonactivity patterns, gestures, postures, etc.). The former domain, of affective meaning, has been made operational for us by Charles Osgood's (e.g., Osgood, May and Miron 1975; Osgood, Suci and Tannenbaum 1957; Snider and Osgood 1969) extended inquiry into the "connotative" meanings people attach to particular words, especially qualifiers such as adjectives. As I shall indicate in discussing linguistic formulations the communication of affect and other subtleties of meaning may be treated as derivatives of the basic phenomena elaborated upon in this section. Di Vesta's attribution of expressive meaning implies a complex orchestration of events associated with the production and interpretation of language. The existence of such an orchestration cannot be negated, nor—as I have stated elsewhere (Pepinsky, 1974, p. 60, in press; cf. Liberman 1982)—can the phenomenon yet be easily affirmed, given present technology.

In explaining how persons communicate with one another so as to enact daily routines, Leonard Hawes (1973b, especially pp. 77–79 and 86–90) introduces additional concepts of meaning that are highly pertinent to this discussion. The first set has two major components: namely, the "meaning" that one person communicates to another and the latter's "understanding" of what is communicated. Here, he follows distinctions introduced by May Brodbeck (1968)—first, among meanings communicated: (1) "referential" (i.e., my sign-significate), (2) "signifying" (i.e., my sign-sign), (3) "intentional" (i.e., something is to follow, e.g., a handshaking ritual), and (4) "psychological" (i.e., how the communication is to be interpreted in a particular context of space-time, e.g., one depicting a football game vs. a brawl); and, second, among parallel and recipient categories of "understanding." Note that Brodbeck's two initial categories are equivalent to those specified by our own Delta phenomena; again, I assume the "intentional" and psychological" categories to be derivatives of the first two. Moreover, as I have defined the term "intentional," it encompasses both the productive and interpretive aspects of language usage, hence does not purport to differentiate between aspects of "meaning" and "understanding."[9]

However, Brodbeck's (1968) third and fourth categories of meaning, which Hawes (1973b) reviews, do suggest an important, additional dimension to be intended in language usage. Following Garfinkel and Sacks (1970), I shall identify the dimension as "formulative." The terms, as used here encompasses individual and aggregate Delta phenomena and much more. It encompasses Roger Brown's (1973) notions of productivity, semanticity, and displacement, but implies these attributes to be inseparable from their intention by human users of the language.

Linguistic formulation is implied by Brown's constructs in the following sense. Productivity indicates that Delta phenomena may be arranged and aggregated in infinite variety while semanticity implies an infinite variety of supplemental meanings about such matters as manner, purpose, cause, and the like. Likewise, displacement suggests that the capacity to reach through language beyond the here and now by referring to other places and times reflects the multiple shadings humans may assign to a communication, whether as participants or spectators in the process. Regardless of role, human perceptual capabilities are vastly enhanced by these alternative possibilities (Fraser 1975) and, as evidence suggests, the full capacity involves not just the present but retrospective revision and reinterpretation (Hawes 1973b; Garfinkle 1967; Merton 1957; Schutz 1967; Weick 1979). The idea of "formulativeness" in language thus connotes resourcefulness and creativity, exemplified by what already exists in language and what humans make of it (Garfinkle and Sacks 1970; Giles and St. Clair 1979). Thus There exists in language usage a formulative dimension, Phi, such that the interpreters of a language use it to intend a variety of meanings in the process of naming things and in relating them to each other (*P*II.B.1.1).

These notions take on new significance in light of concepts arising from an exotic hybrid known as cognitive science, which places less emphasis on the behavioral manifestations of both humans' and computers' linguistic actions and more on the complex cognitive processes involved in producing and interpreting such actions (Hunt 1982). Formulative activity, thus identified and defined, has been broadened and enhanced as a concept, and, in turn, has contributed significantly to a burgeoning computer science and technology (Abelson and Dorfman 1982). Numerous reports argue the role of formulative activity in the production and interpretation of oral and written language (for reviews, see Abelson 1981; Adams and Collins 1979; Anderson 1980; Bock 1982). The most fruitful applications of this new research on formulative activity have occurred in the field of "artificial intelligence." These developments, though impressive, are in their infancy. The eventual outcomes, however, envision computers that construct and use language as if they were, according to Kendig (1983, p. 28), "human conceptual mechanisms that deal with language . . . "

What is particularly significant with respect to the concept of "formulativeness" is that it represents a competence that is intentional, a competence that may be exercised by an interpreter such as a person or a computer but not by a non-intending relater such as a verb. The Phi phenomenon introduces the formulative dimension into language usage, by virtue of which an interpreter intends Delta phenomena to have variety of distinctive meanings, e.g., about time of occurrence, place, manner, purpose, cause, etc. With these two attributes in mind, let us now consider language as structure.

Currently, research and development of this kind has three other pertinent limitations for our purposes here. First, it does not yet afford us a structural language with which to describe and analyze the data of language usage and other kinds of behavior. Second, work in this area does not yet help the student of reading to differentiate among texts to be comprehended by their readers nor among the readers of texts (Pepinsky 1981, in press); see also Dunn this volume). Third, as a by-product of Reaganomics resulting in a drying up of federal funds for research and an encouragement to seek private sponsorship, those who engineer "artificial intelligence"—along with other technologists in an "age of computers and electronics"—are encouraged to market their wares. In consequence, one finds it necessary to consider buying the product of this work and without access to knowledge of how it works (Abelson and Dorfman 1982; Kendig 1983).

III. LINGUISTIC INSTRUCTIONS, RULES, AND FORMULATING

Charles Catania (1972) offers a useful distinction between structural and functional analyses of language. The latter is concerned with how language behavior comes to be emitted (e.g., the conditions of occurrence of a particular language utterance) and what its consequences may be (e.g., the increased frequency or amplitude of the utterance itself, or something more remotely consequential, say, earning for the person who produced it the higher esteem of his peers). In contrast, the structural analysis of language centers upon relations among the component parts of a language utterance, namely, its internal organization (e.g., what parts of speech immediately precede or follow a preposition, or what relations exist between noun phrases and verb phrases in a sentence). "Behaviorism" vs. "Mentalism" is not at issue, Catania (1972) writes; persons interested in cognitive events may be preoccupied as much with their functional as with their structural properties. Nor are the categories of structuralism and functionalism mutually exclusive; rather, functionalists like David Premack (1970) and B.F. Skinner (1957) and structuralists like Chomsky (Chomsky 1963; Chomsky and Miller 1963) have asked seemingly unrelated questions. Yet Catania (1972) makes it apparent that the two analytic modes are complementary. He also implies that, in one way or another, both modes are focused upon rules. From his arguments, indeed, we may infer that rules play an important part in human actions and their interpretation.

The belief that human action are rule-governed is a prevalent one.[10] In the realm of language, it is a corollary to the idea of meaningful structuring, which I have epitomized in Definition II.B.5. I shall next examine these assumptions with an eye toward the construction of language and its grammar.

III.A. From Meaning to Instructions

According to John Searle (1969, especially Chapter 2), language is composed of intentional "speech acts." These are characterized by (a) their performance as "utterances," (b) their propositional forms, and (c) indications of how they are to be interpreted. Utterances themselves are composed of such things as morphemes, words, sentences, and the like.[11] Propositional forms are essentially those of reference (cf. my Definition II.B.3) and predication (cf. my Definition II.B.4). Finally, utterances are variously interpretable, i.e., intended as assertions, questions, promises, commands, and so forth.

Searle's remarks are consistent with an axiom, which informs the previous discussion and what follows: namely, that Any human language consists of statements meaningfully structured (*Ax*III.A.1). As Definition

II.B.5 indicates, these are statements that interpreters intend, such that things are named and related to each other by interpreters. Any statement of this kind is also instructive because, as intended, it tells some interpreter(s) how the statement is to be intended as well as what is intended. In the sense of "what," the statement contains either reference to or predication about some thing(s), as Searle (1969) describes it. In the sense of "how," the statement indicates what is to be done about the information it contains; for example, an assertion may be intended to be accepted, a question to be answered, a promise to be believed, a command to be obeyed, etc. (Searle 1969). Recognizing the difference between a statement intended by an audience and by a source person, Searle (1969) refers to the original intent as an "illocutionary act" and to its subsequent interpretation by the audience as a "perlocutionary act." Note, however, my own presupposition about meaning (cf. Postulate II.B.4): namely, that A statement may be postulated to exist as meaningfully structured if and only if it is meaningfully intended by an interpreter, whether as the source or any subsequent interpreter of the statement (*P*.III.A.I) .[12]

Let us assume that text can be partitioned into a set of statements, and let us identify each of these as an instruction.[13] By definition, An instruction is a unit of meaning in a language, such that an interpreter intends it as stating (a) what its contents are in terms of their propositional form and (b) how its contents are to be interpreted in terms of what is to be done about them (*D*III.A.1). The propositional form of an instruction may be directly or indirectly apparent in a statement. For example, the upper half of Figure 3.4 (in Section II.B) diagrams an explicit assertion, "The tree has branches." This is a predication in which the sign "branches" is linked by a relater "has" to the sign "tree." In contrast, the lower half of Figure 3.4 exhibits a statement in the form of a question, "Did the dog tree the squirrel?" There is an implicit proposition in the question, i.e., "The dog did tree the squirrel." As it stands, however, there is no reason to affirm or deny or doubt the truth of the question. In other statements, the imputed propositional form may be more complex, as in an expressed desire, e.g., one which begins, "I wish that . . . " The concept of the instruction underlies our ideas about linguistic grammar. Before we examine these, however, we must understand what is intended by a derivative form of instruction, viz., the language "rule."

III. B. A Concept of "Rules" as Instructions

In beginning this discussion of linguistic rules, I cited the prevalent belief that the human use of language and related behavior is governed by rules. To further our understanding of this belief, and how it serves as a corollary to the idea of meaningful structuring and its manifestation in the form of instructive statements, I now turn for illustration to Stephen Toulmin (1974) who distinguishes among modes of inquiry by a cline of seven rules. At one extreme, rules explain the actions of others; at the other, rules are imputed to others as rational grounds upon which action is based.

The first of these defines a level of inquiry at which rules are imputed to natural phenomena. The observer "frames" rules to account for his observations, often through qualifiers such as "generally" or "as a rule." At the second level, an observer infers regularities in human conduct but does not impute reasons to them. At the third level, an observer invokes explanations such as "enculturation" to account for observations of group or social behavior, either on the basis of any number of reasons or for no apparent reasons at all. Then, at the fourth level, structural grounds are postulated for such "rule-governed" behavior. To this point, Toulmin assigns no rational bases to a level, but, for each remaining level of inquiry, rationality is assigned to observed actions. At level five, implicitly or explicitly constitutive rules are attributed to observed goal-directed activities such as problem-solving as opposed to activity in conformity with external demands. Level six characterizes unconscious application of these constitutive rules, which, in turn, has a determining effect on the activity. And, finally, at level seven, the observer interprets rational problem-solving to be premeditated and deliberate. Persons are understood to act both attentively and critically. Toulmin's distinctions capture the sense in which "rule" is intended here.

Segal and Stacey (1975) define "rule" as a "procedure applied to a variable" (p. 543). Events comprising the variable are assumed to be different from and distinguishable from one another, yet to exist as members of a set or category that are accorded some kind of equivalent treatment. Although these authors imply that categorization precedes treatment, the very act of placing things in a category treats them as if they were equivalent. That act does not preclude additional treatment to accord with a rule. For example, to assert that "a cat is a vertebrate mammal" is to invoke a rule; to add "At night all cats are gray!" is to state another.[14] What Segal and Stacey (1975) call "rule-governed behavior" thus implies a categorization of events and/or other procedures by which things in a category are to be treated equivalently. The sense of "rule" embodies the fuzzy nature of language categories (Lakoff 1972; Lofti 1971).

As stated earlier, the belief that humans are rule-governed in their linguistic and other activities is a prevalent one, and is a corollary to the idea of meaningful structuring. Beyond that, however, a rule denotes the relationship between or among named things: i.e., the relationship is both specified and stated as if it were—for whatever reason—a requirement. By Definition III.A.1, a rule is a form of instruction, a statement intended either by its source or by any subsequent interpreter. By Segal and Stacey's (1975) definition of rule, however, the instruction must be further qualified: A rule is (a) an instruction that is intended by an interpreter, in which (b) one or more relaters stipulate a categorizing of things such that (b_1) the members of any category are treated by a definitional procedure as if they were nominally equivalent and also that (b_2) there exists at least one relational procedure which treats the members as if they were variable (*D*III.B.1).

This rather formidable concept of rule merits further discussion. In the first place, as we have seen, an instruction is assumed to exist if and only if it is so intended by an interpreter producing or deciphering it (see Postulate III.A.1; also cf. Percy 1972, 1975; Toulmin 1974). As with meaningful structuring in general, a person or a computer may act as agent to intend the rule; a verb or other linguistic device (such as an adverb or preposition; see Section V), which an agent uses to relate named things to each other, may not. In the second place, we may assume the categorizing of things is made evident to an interpreter by named things that take the form of linguistic relaters; this is the stuff of a person's implicit grammar (again, see Section V) or of a computer's programs (e.g., Boolean algebra). In the third place, Attributes b_1 andb_2 in my definition reformulate slightly Segal and Stacey's (1975) original concept of rule as "procedure applied to a variable" (p. 543).

The relationship imputed to things by a rule has another attribute, one that is implicit in any instruction: a rule is also formulative (see Postulate II.B.1.1 and Section III.C.). Illustratively, harking back to Brown's (1973) identification of temporal displacement as a characteristic of language, we note that the imputed relationship may presuppose what can or will or might happen, or may be inferred from what is happening or has happened—during or after-the-fact of an experience. Thus, I may presume that $2 + 2 = 5$ or that wherever a sign says "Trespassers Will Be Prosecuted!" trespassers indeed will be prosecuted. However, on the basis of subsequent evidence, I may be led to infer rather that 2 + 2 = 4, or that to qualify legally as a trespasser a person must either admit to an offense of trespassing or be arrested, tried, and convicted of an offense.

Toulmin's (1974) conception, which introduces this section, captures the idea that rules exist for us because we impute them to things—including ourselves. Whether rules exist apart from our—or our computers'—intentions of them as such is a moot question. What I have alleged to be the case about the meanings we attach to things, including the intention of meanings (cf. Axiom III.A.1, Postulates II.B.4, III.A.1), thus applies to regulations as well as to any other instructions concerning them. Here, too, I may not deny the existence of things apart from our awareness of them; however, I may assert that Rules exist if and only if they are imputed to things by an interpreter (*P*III.B.1).[15] The "things" in question may be mundane, e.g., the desk at which I write or the chair upon which I sit, or abstract conceptions, e.g., the music of the spheres or anti-matter.

III.C. Formulating

Let me quickly summarize our progress toward a metalanguage of text by reference to a set of axioms, one of which has already been stated: Any human language consists of statements that are meaningfully structured (*Ax*III.A.1). By definition (*D*III.A.1), it follows that Any statement in a language is instructive, and can be decomposed into units such that each unit is an instruction (*Ax*III.C.1). By definition (*D*III.B.1), I may also allow for the existence of rules in a language: There can exist in a language instructions of a particular kind, such that each instruction is a rule (*Ax*III.C.2). According to my emergent meaning postulate (cf. *P*II.B.4, *P*III.A.1, *P*III.B.1), however, A language and any or all of its constituent features (e.g., instructions, rules) exist if and only if they are so intended by an interpreter (*P*III.C.1).

The requirement that a language be intended by interpreter—as instructive, for example—may seem to place undue restriction upon its employment. As implied by my formulativeness postulate (*P*II.B.1.1), such emphatically is not the case. Consider, again, for instance, Roger Brown's (1973) *ad hoc* attribution to language of the vaguely defined properties of productivity, semanticity, and displacement. It seems that these characterizations of language were necessary because of what grammarians could impute to it—and much more. Brown (1973) was attesting,

I think, to the inventiveness of even ordinary talk. Thus, to Brown, the grammarian, underlying rules of discourse were not fully understood nor specifiable but to Brown, the speaker of a language, the discourse was.

As I have said, many and diverse students of language have pointed out—in one way or another—that human language usage is rule-governed (see Introduction to Section III and Footnote 15; also Section III.B). Moreover, as Toulmin (1974) has indicated, the user of a language may have rules imputed to his/her/its behavior as a "natural" phenomenon at one extreme, or, at another, may be interpreted as rule-generating. That is what my formulative dimension speaks to; more accurately, to human talk as a rule-*engendering* activity. Let me now expand the idea. Harold Garfinkel and Harvey Sacks (1970) identify the latter kind of behavior as "formulating," which they assume to be a practical necessity whenever orderly, objective, or common sense is to be made out of anything. As they discuss it, formulating connotes rule-making as an artfully contrived, ingenious display of members' methods. Garfinkel and Sacks (1970) describe these methods as whatever displays [informatively] that communication is taking place with "cultural colleagues"—whether identified as lay persons or as fellow professionals studying lay persons. According to Garfinkel and Sacks (1970), we all necessarily engage in formulating to gloss over experiences that would otherwise have to remain untranslatable because of their uniqueness and indefiniteness. Formulation thus enables us to codify in language our individual experiences emancipated from personal constraints or those of particular times and places of occurrence. Illustratively, we may gloss over the problem of defining "member" by leaving the term in quotation marks; we may say "et cetera" or "and the like" to imply a category of things that we do not choose (or are unable) to identify further; we may partition such named things as "race" or "sex" without bothering to question the appropriateness of either the partition or what is included in it.

But, I am not inviting the reader to "garfinkel" a path toward enlightenment on the subject of language usage.[16] Rather, I want to indicate that even brilliant iconoclasts such as these[17] rely heavily on a conception of rules to suggest how people make their everyday worlds orderly and predictable. As Garfinkel and Sacks (1970) talk about formulating, people are predisposed to do so for the purposes of categorizing and publicizing their experiences, of avoiding situations in which interpretive rules are not applicable, and of creating situations that persons "in the know" can readily interpret as being enacted according to rules. Apparently, too, these situations are apt to be jointly, as much as individually, managed with considerable skill (cf. Patton 1984). Let me illustrate this with just one of several "glossing practices" that Garfinkel and Sacks (1970, pp. 362–366) describe. Suppose that I am talking to an audience, which laughs at something I say. I had not intended the statement as a joke but my audience is evidently treating it that way. Without dwelling upon the matter, I, too, am likely to act as if the joke had been intended all along. If I were to think about the matter afterward (most of the time, we don't bother), my reasoning might be as follows: (a) there is a rule that a joke is something intended to be laughed at; (b) the audience has laughed at my statement; therefore, (c) my remark must have been funny, and (d) I did tell a joke after all! (cf. Abelson, 1981).

There is ample warrant, I believe, for assuming the human use of language to be rule-governed (cf. references to supportive evidence from several disciplines and specialties cited in Footnote 15). In calling attention to formulativeness (the Phi phenomenon) as rule-*engendering*, however, I wish to emphasize that humans are likely to improvise (cf. Hawes 1973b, pp. 85–86) as well as be guided by rules in their language usage. As Garfinkel and Sacks (1970) define things (their own sources of evidence are cited on pp. 340–341n), people act as if impelled, individually and jointly, to construct situations that are interpretable by rule. This formulation begs the question of why people work so hard at formulating, as the authors imply that they do, and of why people do it much if not all of the time. One plausible inference is that Garfinkel and Sacks understand people to be doing these things—as Toulmin (1974) puts it elementally—"naturally," "as a rule," and pre-rationally (cf. summary of Toulmin's Rules 1–4, Section III.B.). A second plausible inference is that this kind of elemental predisposition is somehow "coded in the molecules" of all of us, however variously expressed from person to person, group to group, place to place, or time to time (cf. Fraser 1975). For language usage, I think, these inferences square with the postulated existence of structural properties common to all languages (cf. Pike 1967; Slobin 1969).[18]

Let me summarize these remarks about linguistic instruction, rules, and formulating by a definition and a brace of pertinent assumptions. First, by definition, Formulating is any constructive activity by one or more interpreters, such that one or more interpreters intend a meaningful structuring of experience, the unit of which (by Definition *III*.A.1) is an instruction (*D*III.C.1). The intention of linguistic activity as formulative, however, assumes that as a necessary condition of its occurrence Formulating consists of instructions that one or more interpreters intend as a categorizing of experiences, which accords with rules of interpretation (*As*III.C.1), and such that The rules of interpretation either (a) presuppose or (b) are presupposed by the formulating of instructions (*As*III.C.2). The latter assumption (III.C.2) has special import for language analysis: it further emphasizes that the use of language can be intended as rule-creating as well as rule-created—during and after-the-fact of its occurrence. Diverse sources offer warrant for this assumption (e.g., Bauer 1968; Bauer, de Sola Pool, and Dexter 1963; Fraser 1975; Garfinkel and Sacks 1970; Hawes 1973b; Kuhn 1970; Weick 1979; cf. Kelly 1955 on constructive activity). If one reads the word "categorizing" as "schematizing," the first assumption (III.C.1) becomes consistent with "schema theory" (see opening remarks, this chapter; cf. Freedle 1979).

IV. INFORMATIVE DISPLAY

The quotation from Wallace Stevens, with which this chapter opens, expresses in poetic metaphor something of what the formulative dimension of meaning (the Phi phenomenon) is intended to imply. I not only take it for granted that humans are biologically predisposed toward language, but am in accord with those who consider it likely that humans are genetically programmed to do so inventively. The idea can be extended to include reciprocated communications and language about language. These further implications of the Phi phenomenon will become more apparent, I think, as we proceed toward the analysis of text intended to be the contents of communications. In Section IV, en route, I want to develop a concept of text as the informative display of a language. Let me first briefly argue for some assumptions about information and its communication.

In a burst of enthusiasm about electronics engineering following World War II, the thermostat, the telephone, and the digital computer became popular referents for learned talk about communication as an information-processing system. Writings of the late Norbert Wiener (1948) on "control and communication in the animal and the machine" and of Shannon and Weaver (1949) on "a mathematical theory of communication" afforded prototypic examples for others to draw upon. By

1960, a number of diagrammed "general communication models" were available, most of them patterned after Shannon's while "making some clear place for human behavior" (Johnson and Klare 1961, 45). Despite repeated caveats (e.g. Cronbach 1955; Newman 1960; Schramm 1962; Tannenbaum and Greenberg 1968; Wiener 1948, pp. 34–35, 1950; Weiss 1971), the idea persists of analyzing human social behavior as if it were—or were part of—and information-processing system. Justifying the caveats, much of what has survived from the Wiener-Shannon prototype is little more than metaphor (cf. Watzlawick, Beavin, and Jackson 1967, on intra-group communication; Hill 1972, on intergroup communication within and among nations). However, recent advances in the mathematical or computer modeling of information-processing have departed from the earlier prototype. These do not appear to be inconsistent with my ideas about "formulating" and "formulative communication" (see next section IV.B.; cf. Simon 1979).

Elsewhere (H.B. Pepinsky 1974) I have restated the metaphor, identifying communication as:

A process, in which . . . (1) humans or non-humans act to send, receive, or exchange informative messages. (2) In the process, a display produced by one or more senders is noted and interpreted by one or more receivers. (3) Exchange occurs when at least one of the communicating parties receives a return message, i.e., informational feedback from at least one other party; the exchange is reciprocal when at least two of the parties send-and-receive messages to-and-from each other. (4) Original display of the message may take many forms (e.g., speech, writing, gestures, mechanical or electronic signals). (5) To provide a link between sender and receiver, the message must be transmitted, either through some medium (such as air, ether, a postal or telephone "system") or directly as in tactile stimulation. The message may be transmitted in its original state (e.g., as a written letter) or be transformed (e.g., into sound or light waves, electronic impulses). (6) In order to interpret a message, however transmitted, the receiver must become aware of ("sense") and decode (translate) it. (7) This implies, but does not ensure, that the sender's original display has encoded (somehow represented in symbolic form) an idea or ideas to be conveyed in the message. Attributes 3 and 7 are optional features of communication, thus defined.[19] (H.B. Pepinsky 1974, p. 59; footnote renumbered here).

An eighth attribute of communication, alluded to (cf. Attribute 3) but not specified, is that of feedback. Again, the Wiener-Shannon prototype has served as metaphor to define feedback as (8) a monitoring device by which some person(s) or non-person(s) receive(s), as inputs, return information about his/her/their/its outputs—about their occurrence and/or their effects. Ideally, feedback is supposed to correct subsequent outputs so as to achieve and maintain a desired state of affairs; in everyday life, it may not operate that way. For the sender of a message, feedback may occur at any phase of communication; for the receiver, feedback may act to relay information about how and with what effects a message is being noted and interpreted.

The important concept of biofeedback and the mounting evidence concerning it (e.g., Ornstein 1972; Schwartz 1975; Shapiro et al. 1972) support the idea of an intrapersonal communication equivalent to that between or among persons. Although these phenomena are said to differ in several respects (Barker and Wiseman 1973), both sets of events may be assumed to include any or all of the attributes described in the above paragraph.[20] Such equivalence is noteworthy in the case of "communication by spoken language," Fraser (1975) implies, because it always "presumes a source and a sink [i.e., a receptacle] equally adept in temporal structuring of sound" (p. 275). And because written language seems to have evolved from that produced and interpreted as vocal sounds (Mattingly 1972), we may postulate the existence of comparable events in communications that take the form of written text.

The following definitions, which are my attempted summary of these remarks, owe much to the contributions of Gregory Bateson (1972), George A. Miller (1973), and Marshall Yovits and Ronald Ernst (1970). Yet there is an important qualification. By reference to the Meaning Postulate (especially *P*II.B.4): Information and/or its communication exist if and only if one or both are intended by an interpreter (*P*IV.A.1). With that proviso, Information is the occurrence of anything (e.g., in a classroom, a student answers questions on a final examination for a course of study), which is intended by an interpreter and which is further intended to make a difference in something at a later time and/or another place (e.g., in her office, the course instructor subsequently checks answers on the student's paper and gives the paper a passing grade) (*D*IV.A.1). And Communication is any or all components parts of an activity that an interpreter intends as making information occur (*D*IV.A.2).

IV.B. Formulative Communication

Because this chapter is centered on the analysis and interpretation of text, I must touch lightly upon the processes by which linguistic messages are communicated. Conventional theories of information and communication, though, seem inadequate to explain what happens when persons are understood to be in communication with each other or with non-persons. Aaron Cicourel (1974) is in the vanguard of those who, alternatively, provide accounts of the "interpretive procedures" that people use, with the purported intent of achieving for themselves a sense of shared reality in which they hold a common membership. As Circourel (1974) discusses them, interpretive procedures are similar, if not equivalent, to those of formulating (see Section III.C.; Garfinkel and Sacks 1970). Hence, my conception of the Phi phenomenon (Postulate IIB.1.1) and the formulative activity it entails (Definition III.C.1 and Assumptions III.C.1-2) is also consistent with the alternative interpretation of events. A spate of publications during the 1970s describe, formulatively, interpretive procedures of that kind, attesting both to the formulativeness of their authors and to the vigor of their quest.[21]

Briefly stated, a rationale for much of this research is that people are able to collaborate in producing displays which enable them to know that they possess a common culture. By that means, people are able to construct and maintain for themselves a sense of objective reality, which they can assume to be common property (e.g., see Berger and Luckmann 1966; Cicourel 1974; Garfinkel 1967; "Theoretical Perspectives" in Rommetveit and Blakar 1979; Schutz 1962–1966, 1967; Schutz and Luckmann 1973; Turner 1974). Elsewhere, we have summarized these ideas in a schema that depicts how two parties (e.g., persons or groups) may thus establish for themselves a common understanding and the conjoint performance of daily routines (Patton in press; Patton, Fuhriman and Bieber 1977; Patton and Meara in press; Pepinsky 1974; Pepinsky and DeStefano 1983; Rush et al., 1974). The prototypic schema is exhibited in Figure 4. Here, beginning at the left of the figure, we allow for the existence, if any, of prior relationship between the parties; of prior experience[22] for (e.g., expectations held by) each; of initial "informative displays" by each (including non-activity, see footnote 19); of subsequent relationship between the parties; of some, if any, common understanding as a result; of coordinating actions (cf. Scheff 1967a, 1967b); of any changes in these actions over time. Note that the schema makes allowance for the occurrence of feedback at several points in the process of communication between the parties (see arrows labelled "data" and dotted arrows leading to them), with allowance for changes in expectations of the relationships (see inferred "transformations"). Michael Patton, Ad-

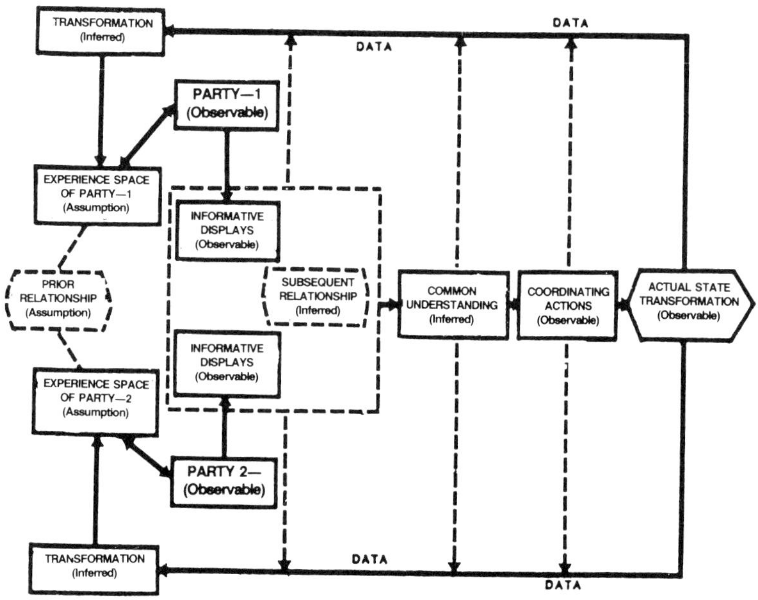

Figure 4.
A Spectator's View of Two-Party Communication via Informative Display (From Pepinsky 1974, p. 65; see also Patton, Fuhriman and Bieber 1977, and Rush et al. 1974; for relation to "schema theory": see Footnote 22, this chapter).

die Fuhriman, and Michael Bieber (1977) have adapted the schema to show how lingustic exchanges may take place between a counselor and his/her client and what these imply for change in their relationship. In discussing the schema, we have stressed that the conception of two-party interaction may be easily extended to include multi-person or multi-group relationships.

A feature of our conceptions and of research that accompanies it is something Michael Patton and I have identified as the "informative display" (Pepinsky 1974 65–66; Pepinsky and Patton 1971 1–30; in this chapter, see particularly Definitions III.A.1., II.B.1, IV.A.1–2; and the Meaning Postulate, e.g., *P*IV.A.1): The informative display is a procedure (e.g., neurophysiological activity; facial expression, body movement such as gesture or sign language; speech; writing or other use of materials) or its resultant (e.g., recording; typed or printed text or graphic display; blueprint; sketch or picture; sculpture; architecture), which is intended by an interpreter as information that is communicated (a) in the form of an instruction or larger set of instructions and (b) according to interpretable rules (*D*IV.B.1). Again, The informative display exists if and only if it is intended by an interpreter (*P*IV.B.1).

I want to emphasize three implications of the meaning postulate in this context: (a) that an interpreter must intend the display, of course, but also (b) that the display must be somehow evidential of an interpretable message and (c) that the display must be made evident on grounds acceptable to the interpreter.

The collaborative "negotiated" aspect of formulative/interpretive activity, has intrigued many investigators, in addition to those preoccupied with its social absurdity. Not only is such activity construed to be a necessity in "The social construction of reality" (Berger and Luckmann 1966); it has also come to be valued as socially useful. For example, a collaborative "social persuasion" (Frank 1973) or "biasing" (Pepinsky 1963, 1970) of this sort is described as essential to counseling or psychotherapy, if that process subsequently is to be evaluated as successful. In his "heavily evolutionary approach" (p. 281) to a human concept of time and communication about it, Fraser (1975, pp. 271–282) construes the development of oral and written language to be species-specific and hints at a biological basis for the collaborative use of talk—not the genetic programming of a universal set of grammatical rules, as such, but of a predisposition toward a collective as well as an individual engendering of rules. I have alluded to this in my discussion of formulating (Section III.C.), but wish to stress here its collaborative implications (cf. Goffman 1974). Whatever our views on the evolution of human capacity for culture (Spuhler 1959; see also Section II.A), we can but admire the ingenuity that people exercise in their social manufacture of realities. Given Definitions III.C.1, IV.A.1, and IV.B.1–2, we may say in partial summary of these remarks that Formulative communication is any or all component parts of communication that is intended by an interpreter as a collaboratively informative display (*D*.IV.B.2).

IV.C. The Informative Display of Language as Text

The kind of informative display that humans as a species use most conspicuously in their formulative communications is language, saliently, oral language. The word itself has come to us via the French *langue* from the Latin *lingua*, which denotes the tongue—hence connoting "use of the tongue" and by implication "the specific language of a people" (in modern Spanish *lengua* or tongue denotes also the language of a particular nation; *lenguaje* refers to language in general). Throughout this chapter, however, I have tried to convey the idea of language in many possible forms: e.g., speech, writing, pantomime, touch, odor, smoke signals, telegraphy, personal adornment, architecture, etc., and combinations thereof (e.g., in a ritual performance the movements, sounds, smells, dress, location, and type of decor and architecture involved). Benjamin Colby (1975) and Clifford Geertz (1972, 1975) have made explicit their conception of the diverse modes in which languages may be expressed, to be noted and interpreted by anthropologists in designating human cultures. Aaron Cicourel (1974), reporting upon his investigations of sign language used by deaf persons, hypothesizes that sign and spoken languages are markedly different from each other syntactically: i.e., spoken language is linear and sign language, non-linear. In his view, cross-modal research on language usage is all the more necessary because—as with those who speak and hear versus those who must resort to visual signing—the different modes of expression and interpretation may betoken dissimilar cultures for their users (see also Diaz-Guerrero and Salas 1975).

Others have demonstrated the utility of studying the multimodal expressions of a single language. For example, Leonore Love and Jacques Kaswan (1974) obtained videotapes of family interactions, from which separate visual, auditory, and typescripted records could be obtained. When judges rated separately these events of interaction, children could be differentiated on the basis of the greater or lesser internal consistency of messages received from their parents: children referred to a clinic as "troubled" by their public school teachers received more discrepant messages than a group of unreferred children who served as controls (Love and Kaswan 1974). Warrant for cross-modal analysis of this kind is provided in the research of Albert Mehrabian (1972). Moreover, on the basis of meticulous cross-cultural research, Paul Ekman (Ekman 1972; Ekman and Friesen 1974) argues for the existence of interpretable facial expressions, whose emotional import can be identified in the absence of accompanying speech utterances by their source persons.

One may liken the production of a language, it seems, to musical performance by an orchestra, in which for given compositions individual parts are played by members of the ensemble. For spoken language, the analogy may be applied to a single speaker, as in the Love and Kaswan (1974) research, to a dialogue between persons (cf. Figure 4), to larger groups of participants, and to intergroup communication. In all these instances, the informative displays may be intended by an interpreter and "read" as if they were a musical score with interwoven parts (cf. Section II.B.1, this chapter; Colby 1975; Geertz 1973; Pepinsky 1974; Pepinsky in press; Percy 1972). Relevantly, the English word "text" derives from the Latin *textus* or "woven" (from *texere*, "to weave"). Let me try to integrate this idea with that of language as a formulative communication: Language is (1) a body of information (Definition IV.A.1), which is (2) intended by an interpreter (Meaning Postulates and Definintion II.B.6) as (3) a system of formulations (Definition III.C.1–2), (3.1) that people have recourse to (3.11) as common property (3.12) in constructing informative displays (Definition IV.B.1), and (3.2) that the people are able to use (3.21) in formulative communications (Definition IV.B.2), (3.22) with each other and with non-persons (*D.IV*.C.1). Also, Text is a collection of things that an interpreter intends as the record of a procedure, one that the interpreter further intends as the informative display of a language (D.IV.C.2).

The line of printed words at the top of Figure 1, labeled there as a sentence, illustrates the kind of text that my colleagues and I have analyzed. Readers can identify the text further as a sentence couched in the English language, but are unlikely to know whether the words were produced originally in the form of speech or writing. Following a common pattern among human languages, written English evolved out of its spoken form, hence the two appear to have much in common structurally (Mattingly 1972). On the one hand, then, the conventional transcription of speech (as in a printed non-fictional or fictional account) can be expected to signal much of its meaningful implications to its readers. On the other hand, as indicated above, the conventional printing of a linguistic record offers but one—if a key—"melodic line" among the many possible facets of interpretative material that may be intended in a spoken utterance.

Recognizing the plausibility of alternative strategies, my colleagues and I have centered attention upon texts that are conventionally printed as our data base. For now, these are the texts of utterances in the English language; later, we hope to undertake comparable analyses of other language (see Section V.3). A disadvantage of that choice is the loss of information its use entails (e.g., as against the use of videotape records with accompanying transcripts of talk, cf. Love and Kaswan 1974, but cf. footnote 10 this chapter). An advantage that the choice affords is the opportunity to make use of computer-assisted procedures, in which (a) the computer can make a direct reading and interpreting of texts and (b) texts can be thus analyzed with demonstrable rapidity, reliability, and—against a criterion of informed human judgments—accuracy (cf. Rush et al. 1974; Young 1973). I have more to say about this strategy and its pay-off in the next section (also in Pepinsky in press).

V. TEXTUAL STRUCTURES

We have arrived at the point of focus in this chapter, " . . . the construction and use of a language about text, according to which linguistic phenomena may be meaningfully intended, aggregated, labeled, and otherwise related to each other" (from the introduction to Section II). My concerns in this portion of the chapter are, first, to offer a set of propositions to identify the ingredients of such language; second, to describe and discuss briefly the Computer-Assisted Language Analysis system (Calas), alluded to in the Prologue; finally, to indicate a promising extension of our metalanguage with a note on the intention of cultures and their underlying policies in textual materials.

V.A. Deriving a Language of Structural Surrogates

By definition (*D* 1.2 in Table 1), the initial task before us is one of deriving a language that will enable us to categorize the textual displays of a parent language according to their structural properties. Earlier Suzanne Strong (1974) identified the component parts and relations of our derived language as "structural surrogates" for phenomena that we, as interpreters, may intend in the text of a language such as English. Table 2 exhibits a set of propositions to introduce an exemplary language of structural surrogates. As clearly implied there, the specific contents of any surrogate language necessarily remain incomplete and "under construction." That is because parent languages, such as the English whence the Computer-Assisted Langauge Analysis System (CALAS) derives, are likely to be wantonly variable over times, places, constituencies, and individual users (cf., e.g., Naroll 1968; Shuy 1973). That variability is particularly to be expected with "natural language," as I have defined it in Table 2 (*D*V.A.4); by definition (*D*V.A.3), moreover, the elements of such a language are expected to vary over the occasions of their intention by any and all interpreters. Such variability may be less evident with a "semantically closed language," e.g., mathematics (cf. Thorson 1972); that kind of language, by definition (*D*IV.C.1 in Table 1), is also formulatively communicated in "situated talk" (the idea is that when people talk, particular talk—appropriate to the occasion—is made to happen; after Garfinkel and Sacks 1970; Zimmerman and Pollner 1970; cf. Leiter 1980), by its human users; hence—even if unnoticed by them—variable over occasions. Indeed, my postulate about a formulative dimension of meaning and its corollaries (see *P*11.B.1.1., *D*III.C.1, *As*III.C.1-2, *D*IV.B.2, in Table 1) take account of spatio-temporal irregularities in language usage, as do the propositions in Table 2.

TABLE 2
Some Propositions About a Surrogate Language of Text
(see legend for Table 1; *T*—theorem; *C*—corollary)

(*D*VA.1)
A grammar is (1) a system of rules (*D*III.C.1) with which (2) to interpret (2.1) the informative display (*D*IV.B.1) of (2.2) a language (*D*IV.C.1) (3) providing, in (3.1) its formulative communication (*D*IV.B.2), (3.2), a rationale for (3.21) identifying and otherwise relating to each other, i.e., (3.211) categorizing (*D*1.2), named things that (3.22) interpreters, as (3.221) parties to the communication, intend (*D*II.B.3a) in the language.

(*Ax*V.A.1)
A grammar is an essential feature of any language, even though one or more parties (e.g., people and/or computers) to the language in formulative communication may be unaware of or unable to articulate its grammar.

(*Ax*V.A.2)
Parties that an interpreter intends to be using a language in formulative communication with each other may also be intended to employ a common grammar for that language.

(*Ax*V.A.2a)
For parties that an interpreter intends to be using a language in formulative communication with each other, their common grammar defines the structural properties (*D*1.2., *D*V.B.1) of that language.

(*Ax*V.A.3)
For every category of named things in a language that is defined for its users by a

TABLE II *continued*

common grammar there exists in the grammar of that language a structural surrogate.

(*T*V.A.1)
Every member of a category of named things in a language that is defined for its users by a common grammar is isomorphic with every other member of the category by virtue of common structural properties imputed to members of that category.

(*T*V.A.2)
For every statement (*Ax*III.C.1) that is informatively displayed in a language that is defined for its users by a common grammar, there exists a structural surrogate such that statements thus displayed are intended by their interpreters to be equivalent to if not identical with, differentiated from, or otherwise related to each other.

(*C*V.A.1)
A common grammar that is articulated by the users of a language also exists for them as a surrogate language.

(*D*V.A.2)
A virtual representation of language is informative display that its interpreters can intend to have meaningful structures (*D*II.B.5) similar to, if not identical with those of statements originally produced.

(*Ax*V.A.4)
The informative display of text (*D*IV.C.2) either consists of statements originally produced in that form or as virtual representations of statements originally produced, e.g., in the spoken or written form of a language.

(*D*V.A.3)
A set-valued function is a set of elements such that the number of elements in the set is understood to vary over the occasions of their intention by any and all interpreters.

(*D*V.A.4)
A natural language is a set-valued function,[a] such that the element of the set is a sign (*D*II.B.1) used by a people in formulative communications with each other and that, in their communications, users of the language employ a common grammar; in the spoken or written form of a natural language, the element of the set is a sign called a word.[b]

(*A*xV.A.5)
There exist one and more spoken or written natural languages; English is such a language.

(*Ax*V.A.6)
For parties to formulative communication in the spoken or written form of a natural language, a common grammar exists as two set-valued functions of struc-

TABLE II *continued*

tural surrogates for significates (*D*II.B.2) intended in the language, such that the element of the first is a sign called a part of speech and that the element of the second is a sign called a relater.[b]

(*P*V.A.2)
For every part of speech that is an element in the common grammar of a spoken or written natural language, there exists in its text a significate called a word; likewise, a part of speech exists as a surrogate for aggregated subsets of words: i.e., a word compound represented by its structural surrogate, e.g., a phrase, a clause, or a sentence (say, as an aggregate of one or more clauses).

(*P*V.A.3)
In the common grammar of a spoken or written natural language, there exist two subsets of relaters: essential and peripheral, the first of which consists of verb phrases that link signs to signs or signs to significates and the second of which comprises all relaters other than verb phrases (e.g., prepositional or adverbial phrases indicative of time, manner, location, purpose, concomitance, etc.).

(*D*V.A.5)
A clause is a grammatical subset of parts of speech containing one and only one essential relater, i.e., predicate.

(*P*V.A.4)
The clause exists as a structural surrogate for the unit of meaning (*D*II.B.3–4) in each and every spoken or written natural language and its text.

(*T*V.A.3)
By virtue of the clause as a structural surrogate (a) every text of a spoken or written natural language is isomorphic with every other text in that language, and (b) the texts of that language are isomorphic with those of all natural language in spoken or written form.

---

[a]See the formulations of John Riner for precedence in applying a forerunner of this concept to people and their activities (in Pepinsky, Weick, and Riner 1965).

[b]Thus, the number of words in English usage can be expected to vary over the occasions of their intention by any and all interpreters. Also, their relations to things identified by the language and to each other can be expected to vary. We might have chosen the letter of the alphabet as our language element (cf. Thorson 1982, pp. 27–28), but that is not a requirement here.

"Sweet are the uses of adversity," as the banished Duke puts it (*As You Like It*, II, i, 12): hence, the propositions in Table 2 are stated to accord with the lack of spatio-temporal consistency attributed to language usage and its text. Nevertheless, our work with CALAS suggests that there is an orderliness that can be imputed to human uses of English and other languages, and that this orderliness has useful implications for the analysis and interpretation of text. Table 2 offers but partial elucidation of our experience with CALAS and is merely suggestive of its interpretive potential. A summary account of propositions in the table will preface the description of CALAS. Drawing upon a number of propositions about language, taken from Table 1, I define grammar as a system of rules for constructing an idea of language as classes of named things and relations implied in the language (Definition V.A.1). In that definition and a set of propositions related to it, an idea of grammar unfolds as two set-valued functions (Definitions V.A.3) whose elements are (a) parts of speech corresponding to words in a spoken or written natural language (Definition V.A.4) and (b) relaters corresponding to phrases that are inferred to link and/or to qualify words in the natural language (Axiom V.A.6). In that a grammar provides structural surrogates for named things categorized in the language it represents (Axiom V.A.3), the grammar, too, becomes a language for those who so intend and interpret the parent language (Corollary V.A.1). Building on the proposition that the clause as an essential relater (Definition V.A.5) exists as a structural surrogate for the unit of meaning in each and every spoken or written natural language and its text (Postulate V.A.4), I have theorized that the texts (a) within a spoken or written natural language and (b) among natural languages are isomorphic by virtue of the clause as a common structural property (Theorem V.A.3).

At this point, I have arrested my theorizing about the structural properties of text. To the extent that the clause as a theoretical construct enables us to identify and measure corresponding units of linguistic display, however, an important step has been taken in scientific and technical research on language, one that should help to reconcile structural and functional perspectives (Catania 1972). Endorsing that view of things, Walter Cook (1979) indicates how our own conceptual and empirical identification of the clause as an essential structural unit in language usage is supported by research on speech perception and semantic memory (cf. Bock 1982). Independently, Rom Harré and Thomas Secord (1973; Harré 1974) have identified the "episode" as a unit of social action intended by an interpreter. That and the "frame," a concept developed by Erving Goffman (1974), represent comparable attempts to partition mundane events into larger and more meaningful segments of experience. Proponents of "discourse analysis" (e.g., Halliday and Hasan 1976; Labov and Fanshel 1977) argue persuasively that only by focusing on these and even more inclusive "contexts" of utterances can we draw sensible inferences about what is communicated among the users of a natural language. As yet, however, the latter concepts remain less clearly and reliably identified in human discourse than that of "clause." Moreover, we may still infer the concept of clause to play a central role in helping us to locate and relate to each other things intended by an interpreter to occur within larger contexts, such as an account of "the funny thing that happened to me on the way to the forum" or a dinnertable conversation.

In pointing to the types and frequencies of clauses as indicators of stylistic complexity in texts, Cook (1979) also suggests how important the clause may be to the analyst of text. In the words of Robert Sokol (1974), the idea of the clause becomes a useful guide to the identification of "operational taxonomic units." My brief and simplified description of CALAS will show how such a unit can be made operational.

V.B. Calas

The discussion of text in this chapter necessarily reflects my experience in working with colleagues over the past fifteen years on the construction and use of CALAS, the Computer-Assisted Language Analysis System. Fuller descriptions of the system currently in use are available elsewhere (e.g., in DeStefano, Pepinsky and Sanders 1982 Appendix B; Gervasio, Pepinsky and Schwebel 1983; Meara et al. 1979; Patton and Meara in press; Pepinsky in press; Wycoff et al. 1982). Essentially CALAS includes (1) one or more persons who operate and monitor the system; (2) data in the form of English language texts, which have been selected as inputs to be analyzed by the system; (3) computer hardware and software with which to transform and process the data-inputs through the system in the form of information; and (4) outputs of the processed information to be further analyzed and interpreted by users of the system.

At present, CALAS's programs provide for three major stages of transformation.[24] First, a word-by-word parsing of the text into its grammatical components; second, an aggregating of the words and their grammatical equivalents into phrases; and third, an aggregation of phrases into clauses, such that each phrase within a clause may be assigned a case-role. In the third stage, moreover, clauses are arranged so as to indicate their level of embedding within a clause-block—i.e., the relative extent of

Column	1	2	3	4	5	6	7	8	9	10
Analytic Category	Body of Text	GC	CR	WF	CWF	PF	CPF	ClF	CClF	Emb
CALAS's	You	NP	Obj	1	1	1	1			
Output	may want	VP	SE(A)	2	3	1	2	1	1	1
at	to know	VP	SE(C)	2	5	1	3	1	2	2
Stage 3	that	Su		1	6	1	4			
	Stevens	NP	Agt	1	7	1	5			
	said	VP	AE	1	8	1	6	1	3	3
	quote		other							
	in the world	PrP	Loc	3	11	1	7			
	of words	PrP	Inc	2	13	1	8			
	the imagination	NP	Obj	2	15	1	9			
	is	VP	S	1	16	1	10	1	4	4
	one	NP	Obj	1	17	1	11			
	of the forces	PrP	Inc	3	20	1	12			
	of nature	PrP	Inc	2	22	1	13			
Total Frequencies				22	22	13	13	4	4	10

Figure 5.
Illustrative Display of CALAS's Output at Stage 3. (from a text: "You may want to know that Stevens said, 'In the world of words, imagination is one of the forces of natures' " [see Figure 1 for structural analysis of quotation from Stevens]. *Analytic Categories;* GC = Grammatical Category, CR = Case Role, WF = Word Frequency, CWF = Cumulative Word Frequency, PF = Phrase Frequency, CPF = Cumulative Phrase Fequency, ClF = Clause Frequency, CClF = Cumulative Clause Frequency, Emb = Embeddedness. *Grammatical Categories:* NP = Noun Phrase, VP = Verb Phrase, Su = Subordinator, PrP = Prepositional Phrase. *Case Roles:* Obj = Object, SE(A) = Stative-Experiential (Affective) Verb; SE(C) = Stative-Experiential (Cognitive) Verb; Aft = Agent, AE = Agentive-Experiential Verb; Loc = Location, Inc. = Inclusive. After DeStefano et al. 1982, Appendix B; Gervasio et al. 1983; Meara et al. 1981; Patton and Meara in press; all adapted from Cook's (1979) basic case grammar.

each clause's subordination to the one and only one independent clause in the block. That kind of output at Stage 3 is illustrated in Figure 5.

Figure 5 exhibits such a block of clauses in the compound sentence, "You may want to know that Stevens said 'In the world of words, the imagination is one of the forces of nature.' " That is the quotation whose structural properties are exhibited in Figure 1. The more inclusive sentence is now displayed in the left-hand Column of Figure 5, each line of which itself is a phrase. Note that Column 1 is indented for each dependent clause, to indicate its relative level of subordination from the main clause.

The next 2 columns further identify each phrase in terms of (Col. 2) its grammatical class and (Col. 3) its assigned case role within that class, Columns 4–10 provide frequency counts: of words (4) phrases (6), and clauses (8), of their cumulative frequencies (5, 7, 9), and of the weight assigned to each clause as an index of its level of subordination (embedding) in the block of clauses. In Column 8 of Figure 5, please note that a clause is marked every time that the occurrence of a verb phrase is identified in Column 2. That is because by definition a clause contains one and only one predicate (after Cook 1979). For "predicate" read "verb phrase," i.e., a part of speech that serves to relate named things to each other. Following Aid (1973), Anderson (1971), Chafe (1970) and especially Cook (1979), CALAS treats verb phrase as the essential, relational feature of a clause (Hicks et al. 1977; Rush et al. 1974): i.e., the verb phrase is assumed to act as the "essential relater" in any such linguistic proposition. Figure 5 identifies four verb phrases, hence 4 clauses.

Throughout Figure 5 there is implicit reference to Walter Cook's (1979) case grammar. Figure 1, which offers a schematic representation of the quotation from Stevens, makes some of these features more clearly evident. When we look below the listing of Phase Type in Figure 1, the further import of clause analysis becomes more apparent. In the row headed Class of Essential Relater, we find the verb phrase "is" identified there as "Stative." That kind of verb phrase implies nothing about action or change, rather it acts as a link between some named thing and a state or property attributed to it. "To be" and "to exist" are thought to be examples of relatively simple states; "to know" and "to own" exemplify more complicated ones: i.e., the first is assumed to exemplify an "experiential" and the second, a "benefactive" state. Thus, "I (the experiencer) can *know* something (the object of experience)" or "I (as beneficiary) can *own* something (the object of beneficence)." The above reference to simple and compound verbs that define the states or properties of named things is grounded in Cook's (1979) "case grammar matrix," which expands upon ideas of Wallace Chafe (1970) and Charles Fillmore (1968; see also John Anderson 1971).

Cook (1979) postulates the existence of four such verb types that he considers basic: (I) Stative (verbs that serve to identify named things as intended objects, such that action or change is assumed to be either nonexistent or suspended in the thing(s) named), (II) Action (verbs that describe activity performed by a named thing in the role of agent of action, e.g., "I *work, jump* or *run*"), (III) Process (verbs that are used to tell what is happening to a named thing—person or nonperson—as the object of action or change, e.g., "I *did*," "The cook *baked* the cake"). As implied above, Cook (1979) postulates additional verb types, which only exist interactively with each of the four basic verb types, forming compounds with them. The second category includes (a) Experiential (verbs that impute acts of consciousness to an experiencing person or thing), and (b) Benefactive (verbs that identify persons or things as beneficiaries of states or actions), and (c) Locative (verbs that indicate location or movement) verbs.

In all, then, there are 16 possible verb types: the basic 4 plus 12 compounds (i.e., categories I, II, III, IV, plus the compounds IA, 1B . . . IIIC, IVA, IVB, IVC). I have foreshortened and paraphrased Cook's (1979) descriptions (see charts 96, and Aid 1973 17, and their attendant discussions). Rush et al. (1974) and Young (1973) offer derivative systems of computer-assisted verb classification. On the basis of extensive experience in analyzing varieties of texts, we have further modified and redefined the verb types. At present there are 13 of these (Pepinsky, in press). Since my purpose here is merely to suggest how verb types might be classified once clause demarcations have been made, however, I shall not now pursue the matter. The important concept to be retained is that of the verb phrase as the "essential" or "central relater" in a clause.

I want now to call attention to the next line of Figure 1, labelled "Class of Peripheral Relater." Again, Walter Cook (1979) has followed Chafe (1970) and Anderson (1971) in identifying what he calls "modal relaters" that may be attached to a clause. These are nonpredicative phrases, optional features of a clause which point to additional properties of things named in the clause (e.g., Manner: We travelled *by car "; Concomitance:* "She is *with our group*"; Purpose: "I did it *for you*"; Time: "He will arrive *this afternoon*"). We call these "peripheral relaters," to indicate that they are not verbs and are nonessential to the clause as a unit of meaning, but are nonetheless important because they impute further relational attributes to things named in the clause. In Figure 1, I have identified the prepositional phrase "In the world" as "locative," and all the prepositional phrases beginning with "of" ("*of* words," "*of* the forces," "*of* nature") as "inclusive." Name these peripheral relaters what you will; more appropriate adjectives than "locative" or "inclusive" may come to mind. The important point here is that adverbial and prepositional phrases—among others—which are nonpredicative, may serve usefully as "peripheral relaters" of this sort in a text. Likewise, there is nothing sacred about the verb types listed above as "essential relaters"; these, too, may be reidentified, renamed, and redefined to suit a user's purposes.

Immediately below the Essential and Peripheral Relaters exhibited in Figure 1, we have the case roles assigned to noun phrases by virtue of relational features that we can now attribute to them in the clause. These new designations are more clearly revealed in Figure 5. At the top of Figure 5, we have a triadic unit of meaning, namely, Object (sign), and Object (sign) linked by a Stative Essential Relater. Immediately below, under each of the Objects, is a peripheral relation (i.e., Locative and Possessive, respectively) and immediately below each of these attributions is a case role (i.e., of Location and Inclusion) imputed to the embedded noun phrase (i.e., "the world" and "the forces"). The final two phrases (i.e., "of words" and "of nature") exhibit similar dependencies. These peripheral cases make clearer sense for us, evidently, when they help to explicate a unit of meaning ("the imagination is one . . . "), as shown in Figure 6.

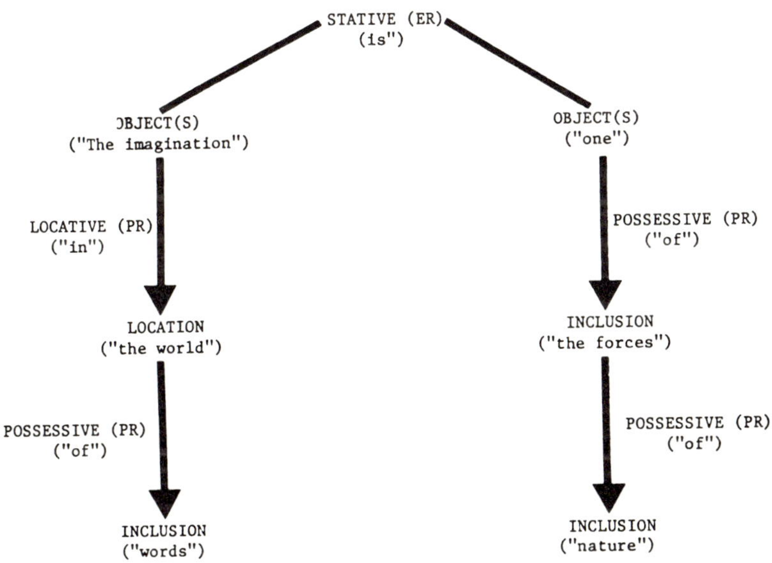

Figure 6.

Case Frames and Case Role Assignments Based on Text of Figure 1. (ER = Essential Relater, S = Sign, PR = Peripheral Relater)

Further illustrations of "case frames" associated with their relaters are provided by the sentences exhibited in Figure 3.4 (see above Section II.B.). For instance, "The tree has branches" exemplifies use of a Stative-Benefactive verb phrase ("has") and the Beneficiary ("The tree") and its Object ("branches"), related to each other by the verb phrase. In the question "Did the dog tree the squirrel?" an Action-Process verb phrase ("did tree") links an agent ("the dog") with an Object ("the squirrel").

The whole of Figure 1, as indicated on the bottom line of Level 2 (see "Clause Type"), is an Independent Clause. Again, that might have been otherwise; the "sentence" might have been a complicated affair, including one or more additional clause types, e.g., Dependent, Embedded, Partial, etc. Just as it makes sense to analyze text substantively in terms of its essential and peripheral relaters and their attendant case role assignments, so it makes sense to examine text in terms of its stylistic complexity by taking account of the relative frequencies and types of its clauses (cf. Cook 1979).

V.C.1. Agnes

In a prize-winning essay, Suzanne Strong (1974); also Hicks et al. (1977) demonstrated how one might extrapolate from CALAS to the schematic analysis of an entire text (cf. Adams and Collins 1979; Meyer 1977). Immediately, though, her work enables me to depict how CALAS may be used to represent formally the language in a text. That, too, is illustrated in Figure 1 at Level 3—with reference to the two graphs displayed there. Strong (1974) has developed an algorithm for this purpose: Algorithm for the Graphic Notation of English Sentences (or AGNES). At the left of Level 3 as an illustrative "structural display" we have an AGNES graph, which looks very much like the one depicted in Figure 6. At the right we have a "generalized graph," which is devoid of nearly everything but lines of varied slope, some of which have arrowheads attached to them and adjacent letter symbols, and all of which are connected by points to other lines.

Strong (1974 10) describes AGNES as "an algorithm which generates non-linear representations of English text," and in which the representations become "structural surrogates" for the text. A surrogate of this kind may be intended by its interpreter(s) to have the structural properties of a category, whose defining attributes are (a) any or all names for things postulated to exist [in texts written in English] as events subsumed by the category, and (b) relations postulated to exist between or among the named things (from the definition of a category, *D*I.A.2, Section I, this chapter). As we have seen, CALAS and AGNES, its derivative, provide in their initial phases instructions and rules for the linear representation of texts. It is in the third stage of analysis (see Figure 6) that the non-linear representations of text, dictated by a case grammar, are employed.

V.B.2 Applications of CALAS

Major and practical objectives of CALAS are (a) to furnish a means of storing and retrieving large amounts of information provided in text, (b) to do so with maximal rapidity and economy and minimal error, and (c) to analyze information so derived. The Case grammar analysis of English text points the way toward an extension of CALAS's programs so as to encompass texts in varied languages (see Pepinsky 1974; cf. Aid 1973).

At present, two major classes of measures are used to obtain scores within and among texts. One set measures "stylistic complexity." In Figure 6, for example, there is but one independent (or "main") clause. If all clauses were of this kind, the Average Block Length of all such clauses—the ratio of all clauses (N) to all independent clauses (n)—would be N/n or 1. Likewise, if all clauses were independent clauses, the Average Clause Embeddedness—the ratio of all clauses weighted by their level of subordination to a main clause (NxI) to all independent clauses (n, each with a weight of 1) would be N/n = 1 (after Cook 1979). We have derived other measures of stylistic complexity.

By reference to Figures 1 and 6, it will be noted that there are two essential cases ("the imagination" and "one") and four peripheral relaters (all prepositional phrases). Elsewhere in our research, with the number of independent clauses (defined here by "is" in Figure 6) as one variable, we have treated the total of all other phrases (here noun and prepositional phrases) as another variable, and computed a ratio for the two variables. Also, we have analyzed the ratios of essential cases (noun phrases) to main clauses, and of peripheral relaters (adverbial and prepositional phrases) to main clauses. Other such variables we have tapped include number of words, phrases, and clauses. One may identify scores thus derived as measures of "surface structure" (Meara et al. 1979).

A second class of measures is more explicitly semantic and relational, having to do with such things as the *kind* of essential relation defined by a verb phrase or of a peripheral relation defined by a prepositional or adverbial phrase. At present, we have not gone beyond the analysis of verb phrases. Here, the ratio consists of the frequency of mention of a particular type of verb phrase to the total number of verb phrases mentioned in a text. Scores thus derived may be identified as measures of "deeper structure" (Meara et al. 1981).

To date, both sets of measures are quite simple-minded, but they do make a difference—as revealed in the analyses of texts. (see references cited in DeStefano et al. 1982; Patton and Meara in press; Pepinsky in press). For results to date, indicative of "tracking," "convergence," or "divergence" in conversations over time (e.g., Bieber et al. 1977; Hurndon 1979; Meara et al. 1979; Patton et al. 1977) or in identifying to a surprising degree the varying "conceptual level" of texts by reference to their stylistic complexity (Hurndon et al. 1979). Even brief conversations, as in "spot" television interviews (McCarthy 1978) or "assertiveness" training (Gervasio et al. 1983), reveal significant differences among individuals or between groups.

V.D. Textual Structure in the Contexts of Policy and Culture

My colleagues, Johanna DeStefano, Tobie Sanders, and I (DeStefano et al. 1982; Pepinsky and DeStefano 1983) conducted a longitudinal study of discourse employed by pupils and their teacher during a classroom period devoted to "literacy learning." An important objective of this activity is for the pupils to learn how to read. The pupils were first-graders with culturally different backgrounds; their talk and that of the teacher was video- and audiotaped on several occasions during their first semester of enrollment in school. The setting was an elementary public school in a large Midwestern city and the timing of our research was fortuitous because the school system had just been desegregated under court order. Pre-existing educational policies had been modified in preparation for this event, which thus far has been accomplished peacefully. It is evident that further policy changes will be made *ad hoc* in response to conditions that no one can anticipate clearly. In the classroom we studied and over four and nine months, however, it was business as usual.

I mention our research and its context to illustrate (a) changing societal conditions that seem bound to affect the work of practitioners as much as investigators concerned with reading in this country and (b) how local conditions—as further illustrated by what our empirical research uncovered—can be highly resistant to change. Whether people read, what they read, and how they read are all related to cultures, subcultures, and the policies that emanate from them. One often sees and hears reference to the latter terms, yet with little more than transient attention to "culture" and "policy" as phenomena that have an important bearing on what people know and do (cf. Scribner 1979). What follows is an extension of our metalanguage to encompass these phenomena, especially as they may be revealed to us in the natural languages (Definition V.A..4) of people in societies. Table 3 introduces a set of relevant propositions.

TABLE 3
Some Propositions About Culture and Its Underlying Policies
(See Legend for Table 1)

(*D*V.C.1)
A system of languages is a set-valued function (Definition V.A.3) of languages, such that the element of the set is a language (Definition V.C.1) used by a people and that the language is defined for its users by a common grammar (Axioms V.A.2–2a).

(*D*V.C.2)
Culture is a system of languages that one or more interpreters (Definition II.B.6) intend (Definition II.B.3a) to be used distinctively by a people.

(*Ax*V.C.1)
The languages of a people exist in the form of texts (Definition IV.C.2) to be intended by one or more interpreters.

(*P*V.C.1)
Culture exists as one or more interpreters' orchestration of texts, such that these are informatively displayed (Definition IV.B.1) as a system of languages used distinctively by a people.

(*D*V.C.3)
Policy is (1) the "then" portion of an "if . . . then" proposition in a language, which one or more interpreters intend, such that (1.1) the "if" portion exists as a contingency to be modified (1.11) by reducing the discrepancy between what is intended to be an actual and a desired state-of-affairs, and that (1.2) policy rationalizes what is being done or ought to be done about it.

(*D*V.C.4)
A ground rule is any premise that one or more interpreters intend to underlie a category of social actions, either as a governing principle of action or as a justification for it.

(*Ax*V.C.2)
Policies exist in a culture to be intended by one or more interpreters as a set-valued function, such that the element of the set is a policy.

TABLE III *continued*

(*P*V.C.3)
Policy exists in the language of a people to be intended by one or more interpreters as a set-valued function such that the element of the set is a ground rule of actions.

(*As*V.C.2)
The ground rules of a policy either presuppose or are presupposed by a category of social actions.

It was Clifford Geertz who proposed that culture be studied as "an ensemble of texts" (Geertz 1972, p. 29; 1975). Benjamin Colby (1975) brought us closer to Sokol's (1975) ideal of "operational taxonomic units" for classifying phenomena indicative of culture. Colby (1975) also was concerned with textual structures: he envisaged culture as "an orchestration of many small systems" (p. 917), made evident to an investigator by the variegated texts of a people. In turn, these texts must be deciphered if the culture itself is to become evident. By reference to research that his colleagues and he have conducted, Colby (1975) demonstrated how one may proceed to assemble such evidence. I have intended the propositions in Table 3 to be consistent with this view of things; the propositions likewise derive from those about language, in Table 1, and its grammar, in Table 2. After defining "a system of languages" and then "culture" itself as a system of languages (Definitions V.C.1–2), I assert that (a) the languages of a people are to be made evidential by its texts (Axiom V.C.1) and (b) that culture exists for one or more interpreters as an orchestration of its texts (Postulate V.C.1).

Colby (1975) pointed to the study of "belief systems" as a place in which "to search for the elements and rules of culture (sic) grammars" and "as an area of convergence for linguists, psychologists . . . political scientists . . . and cultural anthropologists" (p. 917; cf. Diaz-Guerrero 1972, 1975; Diaz-Guerrero and Salas 1975; Holtzman, Diaz-Guerrero and Swartz 1975; Osgood et al. 1975). A quotation from Anthony Wallace (1970) helps to bridge the gap between culture, thus identified, and policy. For him, culture itself is "Policy, tacitly and gradually concocted by groups of people for the furtherance of their interests, and contract, established by practice, between and among individuals" (Wallace 1970, p. 28). He writes cryptically about "implicit contracts" (p. 36), but has nothing further to say about policy. As I identify the concept, policy—like culture—is an important theme to be identified in the texts of a people. Whereas culture is the ensemble/orchestration of texts (Colby 1975; Geertz 1972, 1975), however, policy is but one of a number of themes that may be revealed therein.

My initial proposition (Definition V.C.3) identifies policy more explicitly as the logical consequent in a proposition, which makes an assertion about an exigency of some sort to be rectified. By definition, policy thus rationalizes whatever is or ought to be done. For example in the U.S.A. since World War II, we seem to have lived through successive periods of "science policy" in which as a nation (a) we were to have bigger and better science and technology than those of any other nation in the world, then (b) we were to beat the Russians at this game, notably in the race for the moon, and now (c) confronted by scarce resources and enormous social problems to be resolved, we need to be doing more things that have immediate and practical applications.

As Raymond Bauer and his colleagues imply, though, public policies in the U.S.A. appear to occur more often as *post hoc* rationalizations, of things that have been or are being done, than of prior deliberation about what ought to be accomplished. A case in point is the foreign policy of American business (Bauer 1968; Bauer, de Sola Pool, and Dexter 1963). Curiously, reverse emphasis seems to occur in Scandinavia and certain other Western European nations, in which the public articulation of policy may well precede social planning and its implementation via social programs (cf. Crick 1971). Cameron Fincher (1974) has helpfully indicated the logical ordering in which policy is commonly supposed to occur, as indicated in the preceding sentence, but makes it clear that the observed temporal ordering of policy, plans, and programs is likely to be quite different. Because this variable ordering of events appears to be subject to empirical observation, I have treated the idea as an assumption, in principle, subject to empirical check by one and more interpreters (Assumption V.C.2; illustratively, see Meara et al. 1979; Pepinsky and DeStefano 1983; Pepinsky, Hill-Frederick, and Epperson 1978).

My definition of a ground rule as a component of policy identifies it as a premise underlying social actions (Definition V.C.4) and as an element of policy (Postulate V.C.2); also my definition anticipates what is assumed to be the case about policy as an accompaniment of social actions, i.e., by interpreting it as either a (prior) governing principle of or a (post hoc) justification for actions. In either event, it seems plausible to regard policies as derivative, if not a manifestation of a people's sociocultural premises (Diaz-Guuerrero 1972, 1975). Finally, in analyzing the texts of written and spoken languages, the identification of policies may provide yet another important clue to the existence of sensibly differentiated cultures (see Axiom V.C.2).

The construction of a bridge among disciplines concerned with the study of belief systems should become more evident if the structural properties of phenomena associated with such systems can be identified. In this note on culture and policy, I hope to have indicated that the study of language behavior and its structural properties can provide such a bridge. The newer "policy sciences," which provide a "contextual, problem-oriented, and multi-method" focus on "the social consequences and policy implications of knowledge" (Lasswell 1971, p. xiii), offer a rich source of subject matter. The late Harold Lasswell, who launched the hybrid discipline, also pioneered in the content analysis of texts (e.g., Lasswell, Leites et al. 1949). Lasswell (1971), like Rivlin (1971), was well aware of political constraints upon policy-making and its implications. For that reason, and because the policy-sciences are concerned to foster constructive social change, the policy sciences necessarily have ideological as well as theoretical implications (cf. Crick 1971).

Here, too, as Lindblom (1979) emphasizes, the identification and analysis of policy depends on who is conducting the analysis and who is interpreting its results. My propositions about policy *and* culture, by identifying these as the intentions of one or more interpreters, again take that important conceptual and methodological dictum into account.

The research that Johanna DeStefano and I directed took cognizance of these propositions. The act of reading was reported upon in the context of a classroom, and the larger context of events in which the teaching and learning of reading are expected to occur (DeStefano et al. 1982; Pepinsky and DeStefano 1983). Sinclair and Coulthard (1975) and Mehan (1979) demonstrate how the learning of discourse in the classroom is related to what goes on there. DeStefano's and my research relates this kind of activity in the classroom to what and how pupils learn to read.

EPILOGUE

Our metalanguage encompasses many things. In this chapter, it has been centered on the structural properties of language and their implications for the study of language behavior such as that involved in the reading of texts. A set of propositions about language and its communication were shown to have counterparts in a derived language of structural surrogates, as illustrated in the Computer-Assisted Language Analysis System (CALAS)

Identification of the clause as a structurally defined unit of meaning provides for the kind of "operational taxonomic unit" that Sokol (1975) considers to be an essential building block in the classification of humanly observed and recorded phenomena. A third set of propositions, which derive from those about language and about its grammar, center on cultures and their constituent policies as the kind of language phenomena that can be isolated and categorized in terms of their structural properties. As Sokol (1975), the mathematician, and Colby (1975), the anthropologist, both recognize, the problem of classification demands attention to conceptual and methodological rigor as well as to the idiosyncratic or more generally cultural dispositions of the analyst. The metalanguage of text, which this chapter propounds, attempts to convey both of these messages: on the one hand, the $Delta_1$ and $Delta_2$ phenomena have a comfortably discernible form and substance; on the other, the Phi phenomenon has comforting implications for human ingenuity and creativeness—exemplified by current efforts to simulate the processes by which people write and read and otherwise communicate with each other.

For the reading practitioner and researcher, there are numerous implications. One is that CALAS, as a means of analyzing and interpreting texts, provides concepts and methods for differentiating among them (Pepinsky 1981, in press). A second implication is that relatively simple, segmented analyses can provide useful information. A third is that microanalysis and macroanalysis are complementary rather than competitive modes of analyzing data (for example, DeStefano et al. 1982 found internal consistency among four sets of linguistic measures applied to the same data-base). A fourth is that reading, its teaching, and its assessment are shaped by the culture in which it occurs and by attendant policies about what is or ought to be done about reading. A corollary implication, provides a fitting close to this essay. It was nicely stated nearly one hundred fifty years ago by an extraordinary observer, reporting on an episode during his travels in a foreign land: "We must not judge others by rules known only to ourselves" (Stephens 1963 1:219). My note on culture and policy is to be read with that message in mind.

ENDNOTES

Based on research supported in part by NSF Grant No. 534.1 to The Ohio State University Computer and Information Science Research Center and by support from the Mershon Center at The Ohio State University. Work on this chapter was partially supported by the Mershon Center and NIE Grant No. G79-0032.

[1]For instance, Skinner (1974) complains that others' misunderstanding of his arguments about behavior stems *inter alia* from their failure to comprehend his use of language.

[2]Roman and arabic numerals in parentheses will be used throughout to identify theoretical constructions by chapter section and seriatim within a section. Preceding each set of numbers, italicized English letters will identify the class of construct, i.e., *D* for definition, *As* for Assumption, *Ax* for Axiom, *P* for Postulate, *T* for Theorem, *C* for Corollary. Here *D* I.A.1 identifies the first definition in the opening section of the chapter.

[3]Earlier, Brown (1958, sp. 139–154) elaborated upon the use of metaphor in language, a form of displacement in which words, a word, or part of a word may acquire a referent other than that originally intended, yet retain a quality attributed to the former. For instance, the idea of a steel girder or anything physically rigid, i.e., devoid of flexibility, may be invoked to designate an "inflexible" person as "rigid."

[4]Where Brown (1958) said "react to" (p. 109), I have substituted the term "identify."

[5]From this and other evidence in his writings, it may be surmised that Percy is also playing with words (and his audience): the Greek letter Δ, signifying a triadic unit, is also triangular; Percy himself grew up on the Mississippi Delta.

[6]Percy (1975) considers himself generous in according this priority: "Peirce's 'triad' . . . was rather part and parcel of a heavy metaphysic . . . hardly . . .something that happened among persons, words, and things" (p. 59).

[7]On the attribution of intent as a linguistic phenomenon, see especially Kanouse (1972). In his excellent review of ideas about intention, Sullivan (1968) indicates Brentano to have been concerned more with the conscious *act* of intention and less with its *content*; its *external referent* seems to have been ignored (however, cf. my meaning postulates, *P*II.B.3–4, below). As Roche (1973 7) points out, though, even Brentano recognized the complexity of the concept: he distinguished among representational, judgmental, and affective intentions; the first, as described above, a kind of "primitive awareness" of the object by the person, the second having to do with the truth or falsity of the intended object, and the third, with love or hate toward the object. Roche's (1973) own contemporary view of intention as a phenomenon is also nicely stated (pp. 297–301; for other current discussions of "intention" and "intentionality," cf. Harré 1974, and Mischel 1973).

[8]Brown's (1973) indebtedness to Noam Chomsky (1965) for his concept of "deep structure" and to the case grammarians (e.g., Chafe 1970; Fillmore 1968) is explicitly acknowledged. As will be made evident later in this chapter, case grammar does focus upon sign-sign relationships.

[9]This is not to be construed as invalidating the Brodback-Hawes (Hawes 1973b) distinctions. Rather, I want to argue on the one hand that the more subtle intention of meaning, as implied by their third and fourth categories, cannot occur without prior or concurrent intention of the first two kinds, i.e., of Delta phenomena. The point will be made clearer, I think, in discussion of the grammatical clause as an analogue to Percy's (1972, 1975) "irreducible" unit of meaning (see Section IV). On the other hand, I do not choose to neglect utterly the distinction between (the source's) "meaning" and (a receiver's) "understanding" (cf. my discussion of "Formulating" and "Formulative Communication" in Sections III.C and IV.A; also see Garfinkel and Sacks 1970, on "formulating" and Alfred Schutz 1967, spp. 86–96, on the "in order to" and "because of" motives in conversations).

[10]For example, among language philosophers, e.g., Harré (1974), Roche (1973), Searle (1969), Winch (1958), Wittgenstein (1963); among linguists, e.g., Chomsky (1965, 1968), Fries (1952), Langacker (1968), Pike (1967); among cognitive social psychologists,

sociologists, and anthropologists, e.g., Circourel (1974), B. Colby (1975), Goffman (e.g. 1974), Garfinkel (1967), Garfinkel and Sacks (1970), Harré and Secord (1973), Sudnow (1972), Turner (1974); among sociolinguists, e.g., Giglioli et al. (1972), Labov (1974), Shuy (1973); among psycholinguists, e.g., Brown (1973), Kanouse (1972), Segal and Stacey (1975); and among students of human communication, e.g.; Cronen and Davis (1978), Cushman and Pearce (1977), Cushman and Whiting (1972), Hawes (1973a), Nofsinger (1975), Pearce (1973), and Sanders (1973).

[11]Searle (1969) alludes to but does not elaborate upon the meaningful patterns of sound in speech; by implication, his argument pertains to written as well as oral discourse.

[12]Cf. my discussion in Section II.B of Figure 3 and of Definition II.B.5. Here and elsewhere in the chapter, I have sought to avoid the epistemological problem of claiming to have direct knowledge of another's meaningful structuring; rather, I can impute meaningful intentions to a specified interpreter and attempt to make evidential the consequences of doing so. The meaning postulate, stated immediately above, is reiterated in the chapter. Its implications, e.g., for hypothesizing and testing the relations of intended things and ideas to other events, will be discussed later.

[13]Use of the term "instruction" in this context was suggested by Miller, Galanter, and Pribram (1960; cf. Schank and Abelson 1977); its genesis as a pertinent concept here owes more to Pepinsky, Weick, and Riner (1965).

[14]Although one may dispute the veracity of this bit of folk wisdom, its status as a rule may not be contested.

[15]Erving Goffman, for instance, was a prolific and richly descriptive expositor of the idea that people's actions in everyday life are rule-governed. However, there is a tradition that on one occasion, when pressed to account for his recurrent allegations, he eventually replied, "Trust me!" Thomas Kuhn's (1970) message about the transience of scientific paradigms gives warrant for the assumption that scientists' rules generally, like those encountered elsewhere, are subject to revision and come to exist because scientists put them "out there," i.e., impute them to things. Lawyers' rules appear to be similarly factitious (cf. Meehl 1972).

[16]Rom Harré's delightfully outrageous phrase "to garfinkel" was coined to identify the "outrageous methods" of Harold Garfinkel and his fellow ethnomethodologists (Harré 1970, ix–x). The term will probably become a commonplace among sociologists who either can't or don't want to understand what Garfinkel is currently up to: it implies that one has to make trouble for people in order to find out how they try to avoid it in everyday life. Garfinkel changed his ways, however, guided by the belief that one doesn't have to upset "members" in order to discover how their methods work to "normalize" the "everyday world" for themselves and their "cultural colleagues" (cf. Garfinkel 1967; Garfinkel and Sacks 1970).

[17]See especially (a) the "phenomenology" of Alfred Schutz (1962–1966, 1967), also of Berger and Luckmann (1966) and Natanson (1970), and (b) the "ethnomethodology" of Harold Garfinkel (1967); also see, e.g., Cicourel 1974, spp. 99–140; Schenkein 1978; Turner 1974; and Zimmerman and Pollner 1970). Heap and Roth (1973) have attempted to distinguish between these two conceptions of things; moreover, Pauline Pepinsky's (1975) commentary suggests that *as method* ethnomethodology may have more in common with behavior modifications than with phenomenology.

[18]As Harré notes, Garfinkel and his fellow ethnomethodologists have chosen to ignore the biological implications of their research. At the same time, I think, Garfinkel and Sacks (1970) offer us a useful vision of structuring (constructive) activity that is common to human

societies, and expressed saliently in the form of human talk (cf. Berger and Luckmann 1966; Kelly 1955).

[19]Communication may, but does not necessarily, entail an exchange of information (Attribute 3); a "message" may be noted and interpreted when none was intended (Attribute 7). Thus, a receiver may interpret a sender's inactivity, such as silence, as informative (cf. Walzlawick, Beavin, and Jackson 1967, spp. 48–51).

[20]cf. Bateson (1972) and Watzlawick, Beavin, and Jackson (1967) on intrapersonal and interpersonal communication as cybernetic systems.

[21]Consider the following exemplary themes in the analysis of human conversations, supplementing those cited by Garfinkel and Sacks (1970): "negotiating status and role" (Cicourel 1970); "consensus on rules" (Cushman and Whiting 1972), "taking turns in conversations" (Duncan 1972; Wiemann and Knapp 1975); "the management of dissent" (Hall and Hewitt 1973); "interacts" (Hawes 1973a); "disclaimers" and other "aligning actions" (Hewitt and Stokes 1975); "the rhetoric of Good-bye" (Knapp, et al. 1973), "the demand ticket" (Nofsinger 1975); also see descriptive formulations, e.g., on "sequencing"; and "ritual insults" in Gumperz and Hymes 1972, and Sudnow 1972). It is gratifying to note that C. Wright Mills' (1940) seminal article on "situated actions," long overlooked (cf., e.g., Zimmerman and Pollner 1970, on "situated practices"), is now being cited in this connection.

[22]A line of reasoning that needs to be amplified may go something like this: any distinctive organization of names and relations is a category; any distinctive organization of categories is a schema; any distinctive organization of schemata becomes experience space (cf. Crothers 1979); also Figure 4, this chapter.

[23]Cf. my definition of language as "formulations . . . that people have recourse to . . . as common property" (*D*IV.C.1). Though I have treated this as axiomatic; others have legitimately concerned themselves with the problem of knowing whether anything is possessed as common knowledge (cf. Fraser 1975 75–76, and Schutz 1967, spp. 163–172, on the *Umwelt* as a world of things commonly perceived).

[24]Each of the three sets of programs for transformation includes an "editing" program to allow for human monitoring and correction of the computer's output. Recourse to this process also enables one to make reliability checks on human judgments as well as to detect and minimize redundant errors made by the computer.

REFERENCES

Abelson, P.H., and Dorfman, M., eds. 1982. Computers and electronics. *Science* 215: 749–873, 882.

Abelson, R.P. 1981. Psychological status of the script concept. *American Psychologist* 36:715–29.

Adams, M.J., and Collins, A. 1979. A schema-theoretic view of reading. In *New Directions in Discource Processing,* ed. R.O. Freedle. Norwood, NJ: Ablex.

Aid, F.M. 1973. *Semantic Structures in Spanish: A Proposal for Instructional Materials.* Washington, DC: Georgetown University.

Anderson, J.M. 1971. *The grammar of case, Towards a localistic theory.* Cambridge, England, Cambridge University Press.

Anderson, J.R. 1980. *Cognitive psychology and its implications.* San Francisco: Freeman.

Barker, L.L., and Wiseman, G. 1973. A model of intrapersonal communication. In *Exploration in speech communication*, ed. J.J. Makay. Columbus, Ohio: Charles Merrill.

Bateson, G. 1972. *Steps to an ecology of mind.* New York: Ballantine Books.

Bauer, R.A. 1968. The study of policy formation: An introduction. In *The study of policy formation*, eds. R.A. Bauer and K.J. Gergen. New York: Free Press.

Bauer, R.A.; de Sola Pool, I.; and Dexter, L.A. 1963. *American business and public policy.* New York: Atherton.

Berger, P.L., and Luckmann, T. 1966. *The social construction of reality.* Garden City, NY: Doubleday.

Bickerton, D. 1981. *Roots of language.* Ann Arbor: Karoma.

Bieber, M.R.; Patton, M.J.; and Fuhriman, A.J. 1977. A metalanguage analysis of counselor and client verb usage in counseling. *Journal of Counseling Psychology* 24:264–71.

Bock, J.K. 1982. Toward a cognitive psychology of syntax: Information processing contributions to sentence formulation. *Psychological Review* 89:1–47.

Brentano, F. 1972. *Psychology from an empirical standpoint.* London: Routledge and Kegan Paul. (Originally, 1874. *Psychologie vom empirischen Standpunkt.*).

Brodbeck, M. 1968. Meaning and action. In *Readings in the philosophy of the social sciences*, ed. M. Brodbeck. New York: Macmillan.

Brown, R. 1958. *Words and things.* Glencoe, Illinois: Free Press.

________. 1965. *Social psychology.* New York: Free Press.

________. 1973. *A first language.* Cambridge: Harvard University.

Cassirer, E. 1923. *Substance and function and Einstein's theory of relativity.* Chicago: Open Court.

Catania, A.C. 1972. Chomsky's formal analysis of natural languages: A behavioral translation. *Behaviorism* 1:1–15.

Chafe, W.L. 1970. *Meaning and the structure of language.* Chicago: University of Chicago.

Chomsky, N. 1963. Formal properties of language. In *Handbook of Mathematical Psychology*, Vol. 2, eds. R.D. Luce, R.R. Bush, and E. Galanter. New York: Wiley.

________. 1965. *Aspects of the theory of syntax.* Cambridge: M.I.T.

________. 1968. *Language and mind.* New York: Harcourt, Brace & World.

Chomsky, N., and Miller, G.A. 1963. Introduction to the formal analysis of natural languages. In *Handbook of mathematical psychology*, Vol. 2, eds. R.D. Luce, R.R. Bush, and E. Galanter. New York: Wiley.

Circourel, A. 1970. Basic and normative rules in the negotiation of status and role. In *Recent sociology*, ed. H.P. Dreitzel. New York: Macmillan.

________. 1974. *Cognitive sociology: Language and meaning in social interaction.* New York: Free Press.

Colby, B.N. 1975. Culture grammars. *Science* 184:913–19.

Cole, M., and Scribner, S. 1974. *Culture and thought: A psychological introduction.* New York: Wiley.

Cook, W.A. 1979. *Case grammar development of the matrix model (1970–1978).* Washington, DC: Georgetown University.

Coulthard, R.M. 1977. *An introduction to discourse analysis.* London: Longman Group.

Crick, F. 1971. On theory and practice. In *Theorie und Politik, Festschrift zum 70. Geburtstag für Carl Joachim Friederich*, ed. K. van Beyme. The Hague: Martinus Nijhoff.

Cronbach, L.J. 1955. The counselor's problems from the perspective of communication theory. In *New perspectives in counseling*, ed. V.H. Hewer. Minneapolis: University of Minnesota.

Cronen, V.E., and Davis, L.E. 1978. Alternative approaches for the communication theorist: Problems in the laws-rules-systems trichotomy. *Human Communication Research* 4:120–28.

Crothers, E.J. 1979. *Paragraph structure inference*. Norwood, NJ: Ablex.

Cushman, D.P., and Pearce, W.B. 1977. Generality and necessity in three types of theory about human communication, with special attention to rules theory. *Human Communication Research* 3:344–53.

Cushman, D., and Whiting, G.C. 1972. An approach to communication theory: Toward consensus on rules. *Journal of Communication* 22:217–38.

DeStefano, J.S.; Pepinksy, H.B.; and Sanders, T.S. 1982. Discourse rules for literacy learning in a classroom. In *Communicating in the clasroom*, ed. L.C. Wilkinson. New York: Academic Press.

Díaz-Guerrero, R. 1972. *Hacia una teoría historico-biopsico-socio-cultural del comportamiento humano*. Mexico City: Trillas.

________. 1975. *Psychology of the Mexican; culture and personality*. Austin, TX: University of Texas. (Originally, 1967. *Estúdios de psicología Mexicano*. Mexico City: Trillas.)

Díaz-Guerrero, R., and Salas, M. 1975. *El differencio semantico del idioma espanol*. Mexico: Trillas.

DiVesta, F.J. 1974. *Language, learning, and cognitive processes*. Monterey, CA: Brooks-Cole.

Duncan, S. 1972. Some signals for rules for taking speaking turns in conversations. *Journal of Personality and Social Psychology* 23:283–92.

Dunn, B.R. n.d. Bimodal processing and memory from text. In *Psychophysiological aspects of reading*, eds. V.M. Rentel, S. Corson, and B.R. Dunn. New York: Gordon and Breach. In press.

Ekman, P. 1972. Universals and cultural differences in facial expressions of emotion. In *Nebraska symposium on motivation: 1971*, ed. J.K. Cole. Lincoln: University of Nebraska.

Ekman, P., and Friesen, W.V. 1974. *Unmasking the face*. Englewood Cliffs, NJ: Prentice-Hall.

Fauconnet, P. 1928. *La responsibilité*. 2d. ed. Paris: Alcan.

Fillmore, C.J. 1968. The case for case. In *Universals in linguistic theory*, eds. E. Bach and R. Harms. New York: Holt, Rinehart & Winston.

Fincher, C.L. 1974. *The purpose and functions of policy*. Athens, GA: University of Georgia Institute for Higher Education.

Fishbein, M., and Ajzen, I. 1972. Attitudes and opinions. *Annual Review of Psychology* 23:487–544.

Fisher, H. 1976. The language and logic of forming an idea. *Journal for the Theory of Social Behaviour* 2:177–209.

Frank, J.D. 1973. *Persuasion and healing, a comparative study of psychotherapy*. rev. ed. Baltimore: Johns Hopkins University Press.
Fraser, J.T. 1975. *Of time, passion, and knowledge*. New York: Braziller.
Freedle, R.O., ed. 1979. *New directions in discourse processing*. Norwood, NJ: Ablex.
Fries, C.C. 1952. *The structure of English*. New York: Harcourt, Brace.
Garfinkel, H. 1967. *Studies in ethnomethodology*. Englewood Cliffs, NJ: Prentice-Hall.
Garfinkel, H., and Sacks, H. 1970. On formal structures of practical actions. In *Theoretical sociology: Perspectives and developments*, eds. J.C. McKinney and E.A. Tiryakian. New York: Appleton-Century-Crofts.
Geertz, C. 1972. Deep play: Notes on the Balinese cock-fight. *Daedalus* 101:1–37.
________. 1975. On the nature of anthropological understanding. *American Scientist* 63:47–63.
Gervasio, A.H.; Pepinsky, H.B.; and Schwebel, A.I. 1983. Stylistic complexity and verb usage in assertive and passive speech. *Journal of Counseling Psychology* 30:546–560.
Giglioli, P.P., ed. 1972. *Language and social context*. Middlesex, England: Penguin Education.
Giles, H., and St. Clair, R. 1979. *Language and social psychology*. Baltimore, MD: University Park.
Goffman, E. 1974. *Frame analysis*. Cambridge, MA: Harvard University.
Gumperz, J.H., and Hymes, D., eds. 1972. *Directions in sociolinguistics: The ethnography of communication*. New York: Holt, Rinehart & Winston.
Hall, P.M., and Hewitt, J.P. 1973. The quasi-theory of communication and the management of dissent. *Social Problems* 18:17–27.
Halliday, M.A.K. 1973. *Explorations in the functions of language*. London: Edward Arnold.
Halliday, M.A.K., and Hasan, R. 1976. *Cohesion in English*. London: Longman Group.
Harré, R. 1970. Foreword. In *A sociology of the absurd*, eds. S.M. Lyman and M.B. Scott . New York: Appleton-Century-Crofts.
________. 1974. Some remarks on "rule" as a scientific concept. In *Understanding other persons*, ed. T. Mischel. Oxford: Basil Blackwell.
Harré, R., and Secord, P.F. 1973. *The explanation of social behavior*. Totawa, NJ: Littlefield, Adams. (Originally, 1972. Oxford, England: Basil Blackwell.)
Hawes, L.C. 1973a. Elements of a model for communication process. *Quarterly Journal of Speech* 59:11–21.
________. 1973b. Interpersonal communication: The enactment of routines. In *Exploration in speech communication*, ed. J.J. Makay. Columbus, OH: Charles Merrill.
Heap, J.L., and Roth, P.A. 1973. On phenomenological sociology. *American Sociological Review* 38:354–67.
Heider, F. 1958. *The psychology of interpersonal relations*. New York: Wiley.
Hewitt, J.P., and Stokes. R. 1975. Disclaimers. *American Sociological Review* 40:1–11.
Hicks, C.E.; Rush, J.E.; and Strong, S.M. 1977. Content analysis. In *Encyclopedia of computer science and technology*, eds. J. Belzer, A.G. Holzman, and A. Kent. New York: Marcel Dekker.
Hill, L.B. 1972. International transfer of the Ombudsman. In *Communication in international politics*, ed. R.L. Merritt. Urbana, IL: University of Illinois.

Holtzman, W.; Díaz-Guerrero, R.; and Swartz, J.D. 1975. *Personality development in two cultures: A cross-cultural longitudinal study of school children in Mexico and the United States*. Austin, TX: University of Texas.

Hunt, M. 1982. *The universe within: A new science explores the human mind*. New York: Simon & Schuster.

Hurndon, C.J. 1979. Interpersonal styles of supervising and supervised counselors in a practicum setting: The language of interaction. Ph.D. diss., The Ohio State University, Columbus.

Hurndon, C.J.; Pepinsky, H.B.; and Meara, N.M. 1979. Conceptual level and structural complexity in language. *Journal of Counseling Psychology* 26:190–97.

Johnson, F.C., and Klare, G.R. 1961. General models of communication research: A survey of the deveopments of a decade. *Journal of Communication* 11:13–26, 45.

Jones, E.E.; Kanouse, D.; Kelley, H.; Nisbett, R.; Valins, S.; and Weiner, B. 1972. *Attribution: Perceiving the causes of behavior*. Morristown, NJ: General Learning.

Kanouse, D.E. 1972. Language, labeling, and attribution. In *Attribution: Perceiving the causes of behavior*, eds. E.E. Jones, D.E. Kanouse, H.E. Kelley, R.E. Nisbett, S. Valins, and B. Weiner. Morristown, NJ: General Learning.

Kelly, G.A. 1955. *The psychology of personal constructs*. 2 vols. New York: Norton.

Kendig, F. 1983. A conversation with Roger Schank. *Psychology Today* 17(4): 28–36.

Knapp, M.L.; Hart, R.P.; Friederich, G.W.; and Shulman, G.M. 1973. The rhetoric of goodbye: Verbal and non-verbal correlates of human leave-taking. *Speech Monographs* 40:182–98.

Kuhn, T.S. 1970. *The structure of scientific revolutions*. 2d ed., enlarged. Chicago: University of Chicago.

Labov, W. 1974. *Sociolinguistic patterns*. Philadelpha: University of Pennsylvania.

Labov, W., and Fanschel, D. 1977. *Therapeutic discourse*. New York: Academic.

Lakoff, G. 1972. Hedges: A study in meaning criteria and the logic of fuzzy concepts. In *Papers from the Eighth Regional Meeting of the Chicago Linguistic Society*, ed. P. Peranteau. Chicago: University of Chicago.

Langacker, R.W. 1968. *Language and its structure*. New York: Harcourt, Brace & World.

Lasswell, H.D. 1971. *A pre-view of policy sciences*. New York: American Elsevier.

Leiter, K. 1980. *A primer on ethnomethodology*. New York: Oxford University.

Lenneberg, E.H. 1967. *Biological foundations of language*. New York: Wiley.

________. 1969. On explaining language. *Science* 164:635–63.

Liberman, A.M. 1982. On finding that speech is special. *American Psychologist* 37:148–67

Lindblom, C.E. 1979. *The policy-making process*. 2d ed. Englewood Cliffs, NJ: Prentice-Hall.

Lofti, Z. 1971. Quantitative fuzzy semantics. *Information Sciences* 3:159–76.

Love, L.R., and Kaswan, J.W. 1974. *Troubled children: Their families, schools and treatments*. New York: Wiley.

Malinowski, B. 1923. The problem of meaning in primitive languages. Supplement 1 to Ogden, D.K., and Richards, I.A., *The meaning of meaning*. London: Routledge and Kegan Paul.

Mattingly, I.B. 1972. Speech cues and sign stimuli. *American Scientist* 60:327–37.

McCarthy, K.E. 1978. Sex-preferential differences in the language used by four interviewers on television. Ph.D. diss., The Ohio State University.

Meara, N.M.; Shannon, J.W.; and Pepinsky, H.B. 1979. Comparison of the stylistic complexity of the language of counselor and client across three theoretical orientations. *Journal of Counseling Psychology* 26:181–89.

Meehl, P.E. 1972. Law and fireside inductions: Some reflections of a clinical psychologist. *Journal of Social Issues* 27:65–100.

Mehan, H. 1979. *Learning lessons, social organization in the classroom*. Cambridge, MA: Harvard University Press.

Mehrabian, A. 1972. Nonverbal communication. In *Nebraska symposium on motivation: 1971,* ed. J.K. Cole. Lincoln: University of Nebraska.

Merton, R.K. 1957. *Social theory and social structure*. rev. ed. Glencoe, IL: Free Press.

Meyer, B.J.F. 1975. *The organization of prose and its effects on memory*. Amsterdam: North-Holland.

________. 1977. What is remembered from prose: A function of passage structure. In *Discourse production and comprehension*, ed. R.O. Freedle, Vol. 1 in the series *Discourse processes: Advances in research and theory*. Norwood, NJ: Ablex.

Miller, G.A.; Galanter, E.; and Pribram, K.H. 1960. *Plans and the structure of behavior*. New York: Holt, Rinehart & Winston.

Miller, G.R. 1966. On defining communication—another stab. *Journal of Communication* 16:88–98.

Mills, C.W. 1940. Situated actions and the vocabularies of motive. *American Sociological Review* 5:904–13.

Mischel, T. 1972. Understanding neurotic behavior: From "mechanism" to "intentionality." In *Understanding other persons*, ed. T. Mischel. Oxford: Basil Blackwell.

Morris, C. 1946. *Signs, language and behavior*. New York: Prentice-Hall.

Naroll, R. 1968. Some thoughts on comparative method in cultural anthropology. In *Methodology in social research*, eds. H.M. Blalock, Jr., and A.B. Blalock. New York: McGraw-Hill.

Natanson, M. 1970. *The journeying self: A study in philosophy and social role*. Reading, MA: Addison-Wesley.

Newman, J.B. 1960. A rationale for a defintion of communication. *Journal of Communication* 10:115–24.

Nofsinger, R.E. 1975. The demand ticket: A conversational device for getting the floor. *Speech Monographs* 42(1): 1–9.

Ornstein, R.E. 1972. *The pyschology of consciousness*. New York: Viking Press.

Osgood, C.E., May, W.H.; and Miron, M.S. 1975. *Cross-cultural universals of affective meaning*. Urbana, IL: University of Illinois Press.

Osgood, C.E.; Suci, G.J.; and Tannenbaum, P.H. 1957. *The measurement of meaning*. Urbana, IL: University of Illinois.

Patton, M.J. 1984. Managing social interaction in counseling. *Journal of Counseling Pyschology*. 31:442-56

Patton, M.J., and Meara, N.M. n.d. The analysis of natural language in psychological treatment. In *Spoken interaction in psychotherapy*, ed. R.J. Russell. New York: Plenum. In press.

Patton, M.J.; Fuhriman, A.J.; and Bieber, M.R. 1977. A model and a metalanguage for research on psychological counseling. *Journal of Counseling Psychology* 24:25–34.

Pearce, W.B. 1973. Consensual rules in interpersonal communication: A reply to Cushman and Whiting. *Journal of Communication* 23:160–68.

Pepinsky, H.B. 1963. On the utility of bias in treatment. *Journal of Counseling Psychology* 10:402–08.

________. 1970. Psychological help-giving as informed definition of the situation. In *People and information*, ed. H.B. Pepinsky. Elmsford, NY: Pergamon.

________. 1974. A metalanguage for systematic research on human communication via natural language. *Journal of the American Society for Information Science* 25:59–69.

________. 1981. Differentiating among texts to be comprehended. Eric Document Reproduction Service No. ED 195 934, Arlington, VA.

________. n.d. Language and the production and interpretation of social interactions. In *Language and logic in personality and society*, ed. H. Fisher. New York: Columbia University. In press

Pepinsky, H.B., and DeStefano, J.S. 1983. Interactive discourse in the classroom as organizational behavior. In *Advances in reading/language research*, ed. B.A. Hutson. Greenwich, CT: JAI.

Pepinsky, H.B., and Patton, M.J., eds. 1971. *The psychological experiment: A practical accomplishment.* Elmsford, NY: Pergamon.

Pepinsky, H.B.; Hill-Frederick, K.; and Epperson, D.L. 1978. *The Journal of Counseling Psychology* as a matter of policies. *Journal of Counseling Psychology* 25:483–98.

Pepinsky, H.B.; Weick, K.E.; and Riner, J.W. 1965. *Primer for productivity.* Columbus, OH: Ohio State University Research Foundation.

Pepinsky, P.N. 1975. Further thoughts on the Skinnerian connection: Ethnomethodology and behavior modification. *American Sociologist* 10:39–41.

Percy, W. 1972. Toward a triadic theory of meaning. *Psychiatry* 35:1–19.

________. 1975. The delta factor. *The Southern Review* 11:29–64. (Also published as introductory essay in *The message in the bottle.* New York: Farrar, Strauss & Geroux, 1975.)

Pike, K.L. 1967. *Language in relation to a unified theory of the structure of human behavior.* 2d, revised edition. The Hague: Mouton.

Premack, D.A. 1970. A functional analysis of language. *Journal of the Experimental Analysis of Behavior* 14:107–25.

Rivlin, A.M. 1971. *Systematic thinking for social action.* Washington, DC: Brookings Institution.

Roche, M. 1973. *Phenomenology, language and the social sciences.* London: Routledge and Kegan Paul.

Rommetveit, R., and Blakar, R.M. 1979. *Studies of language, thought and verbal communication.* New York: Academic Press.

Rush, J.E.; Pepinsky, H.B.; Meara, N.M.; Strong, S.M.; Valley, J.A.; and Young, C.E. 1974. *A computer assisted language analysis system.* Columbus, OH: Computer and Information Science Research Center, OSU-CISRC-TR-73-9, Ohio State University.

Sanders, R.E. 1973. The question of a paradigm for the study of speech-using behavior. *Quarterly Journal of Speech* 59:1–10.

Schank, R.C. 1973. Identification of conceptualizations underlying natural language. In *Computer models of thought and language*, eds. R.C. Schank and K.M. Colby. San Francisco: W.H. Freeman.

Schank, R.C., and Abelson, R.P. 1977. *Scripts, plans, goals, and understanding.* Hillsdale, NJ: Erlbaum.

Scheff, T.J. 1967a. A theory of social coordination applicable to mixed-motive games. *Sociometry* 30:215–34.

________. 1967b. Toward a sociological model of consensus. *American Sociological Review* 32:32–46.

Schenkein, J., ed. 1978. *Studies in the organization of conversational interaction.* New York: Academic Press.

Schramm, W. 1962. Mass communication. *Annual Review of Psychology* 13:251–84.

Schutz, A. 1962-1966. *Collected papers.* 3 vols. The Hague: Martinus Nijhoff.

________. 1967. *The phenomenology of the social world*, transl. G. Walsh and F. Lehnert. Evanston, IL: Northwestern University. (Originally, 1932. *Der sinnhafte Aufbau der sozialen Welt.* Vienna: Julius Springer.)

Schutz, and Luckmann, T. 1973. *The structures of the life-world*, transl. R.M. Zaner and H.T. Engelhardt, Jr. Evanston, IL: Northwestern University.

Schwartz, G.E. 1975. Biofeedback, self-regulation, and the patterning of physiological responses. *American Scientist* 63:314–24.

Scribner, S. 1979. Modes of thinking and ways of speaking: Culture and logic reconsidered. In *New directions in discourse processing*, ed. R.O. Freedle. Norwood, NJ: Ablex.

Searle, J.R. 1969. *Speech acts: An essay in the philosophy of language.* London: Cambridge University.

Segal, E.M., and Stacy, E.W., Jr. 1975. Rule-governed behavior as a psychological process. *American Psychologist* 30:541–52.

Shannon, C.E., and Weaver, W. 1949. *The mathematical theory of communication.* Urbana, IL: University of Illinois.

Shapiro, D.; Barber, T.X.; DiCara, L.V.; Kamiya, J.; Miller, N.E.; and Stoyva, H. 1972. *Biofeedback and self-control.* Chicago: Aldine.

Shuy, R., ed. 1973. *Georgetown university series in languages and linguistics, No. 25.* Washington, DC: Georgetown University.

Simon, H.A. 1979. Information Processing models of cognition. *Annual Review of Psychology* 30:363–96.

Sinclair, J.C.H., and Coulthard, R.M. 1975. *Towards an analysis of discourse.* London: Oxford University.

Skinner, B.F. 1957. *Verbal behavior.* New York: Appleton-Century-Crofts.

________. 1974. *About behaviorism.* New York: Knopf.

Slobin, D.T. 1969. Universals of grammatical development in children. Working paper No. 22, Language Research Laboratory, University of California, Berkeley.

Snider, J.G., and Osgood, C.E., eds. 1969. *Semantic differential techniques.* Chicago: Aldine.

Sokol, R.R. 1974. Classification: purpose, principles, progress, prospects. *Science* 185:1115–23.

Spuhler, J.N., ed. 1959. *The evolution of man's capacity for culture.* Detroit, MI: Wayne State University.

Stephens, J.C. 1963. *Incidents of travel in Yucatan*, 2 vols. New York: Dover. (Originally published in 1843.)

Stevens, S.S. 1968. Measurement, statistics, and the schemapiric view. *Science* 161:849–56.

Stevens, W. 1957. *Opus posthumous.* New York: Knopf.

Strong, S.M. 1974. An algorithm for generating structural surrogates of English text. *Journal of the American Society for Information Science* 25:10–24.

Sudnow, D., 1972. *Studies in social interaction.* New York: Free Press.

Sullivan, J.J. 1968. Franz Brentano and the problems of intentionality. In *Historical roots of contemporary psychology*, ed. B.B. Wolman. New York: Harper and Row.

Tannenbaum, P., and Greenberg, B.S. 1968. Mass communication. *Annual Review of Psychology* 19:351–86.

Thorson, S.J. 1972. Models, theories, and political theory. Polimetrics Laboratory, Ohio State University.

Toulmin, S. 1974. Rules and their relevance for understanding human behavior. In *Understanding other persons*, ed. T. Mischel. Oxford: Basil Blackwell.

Triandis, H.C.; Vassiliou, V.; Vassiliou, G.; Tanaka, Y.; and Shamugan, A.V. 1972. *The analysis of subjective culture.* New York: Holt, Rinehart & Winston.

Turner, R., ed. 1974. *Ethnomethodology: Selected readings.* Middlesex, England: Penguin Education.

Wallace, A.F.C. 1970. *Culture and personality.* 2d ed. New York: Random House.

Watzlawick, P.; Beavin, J.H.; and Jackson, D.D. 1967. *Pragmatics of human communication.* New York: Norton.

Weick, K.E. 1979. *The social psychology of organization.* 2d ed. Reading, MA: Addison-Wesley.

Weintraub, D.J. 1975. Perception. *Annual Review of Psychology* 26:234–89.

Weiss, W. 1971. Mass communication. *Annual Review of Psychology* 22:309–36.

Wiemann, J.M., and Knapp, J.L. 1975. Turn-taking in conversations. *Journal of Communication* 25:75–92.

Wiener, N. 1948. *Cybernetics, or control and communication in the animal and the machine.* New York: Wiley.

________. 1950. *The human use of human beings, cybernetics and society.* Boston: Houghton-Mifflin.

Winch, P. 1958. *The idea of a social science, and its relation to philosophy.* London: Routledge and Kegan Paul.

Winograd, T. 1972. Understanding natural language. *Cognitive Psychology* 3:1–191.

Wittgenstein, L. 1963. *Philosophical investigations.* Oxford: Basil Blackwell.

Wycoff, J.P.; Davis, K.L.; Hector, M.A.; and Meara, N.M. 1982. A language analysis of empathic responding to client anger. *Journal of Counseling Psychology* 29:462–67.

Young, C.E. 1973. *Development of language analysis procedure with application to automatic indexing.* Columbus: OH: Computer and Information Science Research Center, OSU-CISRC-TR-73-2, Ohio State University.

Yovits, M.C., and Ernst, R.L. 1970. Generalized information systems: Consequences for information transfer. In *People and information*, ed. H.B. Pepinsky. Elmsford, NY: Pergamon.

Zimmerman, D.H., and Pollner, M. 1970. The everyday world as a phenomenon. In *People and information*, ed. H.B. Pepinsky. Elmsford, NY: Pergamon.

Chapter 8

The Neuroscience and Educational Practice: Asking Better Questions

by Marlin L. Languis and R. Harter Kraft

OVERVIEW

Recent research in neuroscience offers the opportunity to apply understanding of the neural substrates of information processing and learning to significantly improve educational research and practice in the years ahead. The past focus in educational research has been on the influence of such factors as the various methods of teaching, teacher and pupil interaction, classroom environment, and instructional materials. We now recognize that what is happening physiologically within a child as processing takes place is an additional fundamental factor in understanding thinking, problem-solving, and learning. The purpose of this chapter is to redirect educational research to include questions that investigate educational implications of advances in neuroscience.

Two major benefits may accrue from including educators in a multidisciplinary team approach. First, educators may guide neuroscience researchers to address important questions that may affect educational practice. Second, a neurophysiological approach may add a new focus to educational research, traditionally focused on external factors. Judgments about the nature of cognition have been inferred from "external" observations of student behavior in response to "external" events. It has been largely a closed-box approach. Little attention has been given to what happens within the student during the processing of school tasks such as reading. Neurophysiological approaches to the study of cognitive processes provide a needed focus on the learning process through measurement of physiological indices while students interact with tasks. Applied to study of reading, this new focus of internal physiological indices, coupled with external observations of performance, provides a more vigorous research approach to evaluation of assumptions and inferences about the nature of the reading process.[1]

A major part of this new field is brain functioning. How the brain works has remained largely a mystery for thousands of years. Very recently there have been dramatic breakthroughs. Languis, Sanders and Tipps (1981) reviewed several conceptions of brain functioning that provide models for the study of learning. The evolutionary brain model and the hemispheric lateralization brain model are briefly discussed below.

EVOLUTIONARY BRAIN MODEL

Paul MacLean provided an evolutionary model of the brain called the "triune brain." In relating the old, middle, and new parts of the brain, he uses parallel evolutionary and developmental constructs of the increasing complexity of animal brains on the phylogenetic scale. As illustrated in the diagram below, MacLean pointed out that increasing complex behaviors in the animal kingdom resemble the abilities related to the three parts of the brain.

MacLEAN TRIUNE BRAIN MODEL

Structure	Function	Behaviors
Neocortex	Association Language Mediated Response	Learning Communication
Midbrain Limbic system	Emotions Sensory Relay	Survival responses based on emotions
Reptilian Complex	Survival	Feeding, Territoriality Sex, Routines, Instinctual Response

The neocortex, a convoluted mass of multiple cellular layers at the surface of the brain, is associated with rational behavior. The limbic system is a collection of small organs in the midbrain which control hormonal and chemical processes throughout the body and is especially associated with emotional aspects of response. The reticular formation at the bottom of the limbic midbrain also serves as a central relay point for sensory stimuli. Decisions about that to which we consciously attend are made there. One of the area's structures, the hippocampus, is important in memory (Milner 1959). Lastly, the reptilian complex is the oldest part of the brain. Instinctive behaviors, related to species survival emerge from predetermined programs in this part of the brain.

Carl Sagan's popular book *Dragons of Eden* (1977) built on MacLean's evolutionary model and hypothesized that the evolutionary development of the neocortex may signal the beginning of consciousness in man. Although the exact nature, cause, and progression of the brain's phylogenetic development is not fully known, the evolutionary model of the brain does not provide clues about behavior and learning.

There is increasing evidence from monkey studies that some skills are mediated by lower brain structures during early development with a functional shift to the neocortex as the organism matures (see Goldman 1977 for a discussion). Kraft (this volume) discusses evidence that lower levels of the human brain (reptilian complex and midbrain limbic) also mature earlier than the neocortex. The search for functional reorgnization in the human brain during development is an area which will receive much research attention in the near future (e.g., Kamptner, Kraft and Harper 1984; Kraft in press).

Lower brain levels, however, continue to be important cognitively throughout development. For example, Buck (1976) relates the role of emotion in learning to qualitative differences in cognitive outcomes. Direct and meaningful interactions exist between the functions of the limbic (autonomic) system of the brain via hormonal and axonal linkages and the rest of the central nervous system during learning. The role that these interconnecting structures can play in mediating cognition and learning through the life span should also receive much attention.

HEMISPHERIC LATERALIZATION BRAIN MODEL

Lateralization of brain structure and function is presently one of the most active areas of psychophysiologic research with substantive implications for learning. The human cerebral cortex is divided into two hemispheres which, to some extent, serve different cognitive functions. The left hemisphere has primary responsibility for processing visual and tactile information from the right side of space, and the control of movements of the right arm and leg. Conversely, the right hemisphere has primary responsibility for activities of the left side. In most people, the left hemisphere is dominant for language use (especially language production) while the right hemisphere is dominant for visual pattern recognition, some types of music processing, and spatial visualization and orientation. These hemispheric differences have emerged in studies using a wide variety of subjects—aphasics, split-brain patients, other brain-damaged subjects, and normals—as well as a variety of procedures—such as sodium amytal tests, dichotic listening, and visual hemifield presentations to a single hemisphere.

There are many important questions about hemisphere specialization that do not yet have firm answers. The basic division between the hemispheres may involve the type of input being processed, the type of mental processing applied to the input, or the type of representational code. It may also be that the main distinctions are centered on the type of responses the two hemispheres control. The large range of individual differences found in hemispheric organization make it unlikely that any simple theory will prove satisfactory.

Relevance for educational applications of this interactive dualism may be inferred from evidence accumulating from empirical neurological studies of the brain. The view we support, consistent with current insights on hemispheric brain function, is that the brain is viewed as a bilateral system in which the interplay of the differences in modality and function become of special interest. Dimond (1972) asserts that "while both hemispheres play a qualitative role, the contribution of one may be more important than the contribution of the other in respect to certain performances. At the same time weight must be given to the interplay between one hemisphere and the other and the integration of functions each within the performance of the other. This is envisaged largely as a cross-switching system by which the functions of each side of the body are able to gain access to the areas of specialization within each hemisphere." (p. 192).

Some investigations into hemispheric brain processes in normal persons are of particular relevance to education. These studies frequently have used three techniques: dichotic listening, tachistoscopic presentation, and electroencephalographic measurement of the brain's electrical activity, employing both frequency analysis and the event related potential. The research data thus accumulated are briefly discussed in the following section.

The dichotic-listening technique involves presenting subjects with simultaneous auditory stimuli (one in each ear) and then measuring performance differentials. Because each hemisphere receives information primarily, though not exclusively, from the contralateral ear, better left-ear perception indicates right hemisphere superiority, and vice versa (Kimura 1961). In addition, some researchers are positing that the ipsilateral input from the other ear may be suppressed (see Berlin and Cullen 1977 and Gruber and Segalowitz 1977b, for critique and discussion of this technique).

This technique used on normal right-handed adults has shown the left hemisphere (right ear) to be superior in perceiving and remembering digits (Kimura 1961, 1967), both meaningful words and nonsense words that are easily pronounced (Curry 1967), and syntactic structure (Zurif and Sact 1970); and in judging which of two stimuli came first and in making fine temporal-order judgments, i.e., Morse Code (Shankweiler and Studdert-Kennedy 1967); while the right hemisphere (left ear) is superior in perceiving and remembering melodies (Kimura 1964), pitch (Halperin, Nachson and Carmon 1973), environmental sounds (Curry 1967; Kraft 1981b, 1982a), vocal nonspeech sounds, i.e., coughing, laughing and crying (Knox and Kimura 1970; Kimura 1973; Kraft 1981a, 1982a), and intonation contours used to indicate commands, questions, and declarative sentences (Blumstein and Cooper 1974). The right-ear advantages for verbal stimuli (digit and nonsense syllables) has been found as young as 2.5 to 3 years of age (reviewed in Witelson 1977c; Kamptner, Kraft and Harper 1984; Kraft 1984a). Although not as robust as the right ear verbal relationship, the left ear advantage for environmental sounds and vocal nonspeech sounds has been reported in males by 6–7 years of age (Kraft 1982a).

The human visual system is structurally organized so that each hemisphere receives all the information from the contralateral visual hemifield. Therefore, a stimulus projected into one visual hemifield will be perceived first by the contralateral hemisphere before it is relayed across the corpus callosum to the other hemisphere. To control for eye movements, the presentation must be less than 100 msec. A large number of hemispheric specialization studies (for review see White 1969; Witelson review see White 1969; Witelson 1977c) have used a technique that employs a tachistoscope to project a stimulus to one visual hemifield or to project stimuli simultaneously to both visual hemifields (See Beaumont 1982 for a review and critique of the method).

Tachistoscopic studies also provide results which demonstrate left-hemisphere mediation in the processing of verbal information and right-hemisphere mediation of nonverbal information processing. Recognition of English words are more successful from tachistoscopic presentations to the right visual field (left hemisphere) than to the left. Kimura (1966) and White (1974) demonstrated this effect for letter identification, while Hines and Satz (1974) demonstrated that recall was superior for digits presented to the right visual field instead of the left. Mackavay, Curcie, and Rosen (1973) report results indicating right visual-field superiority in word recognition.

Although both habitual scanning patterns and relative hemisphere efficiency affect visual-field differences (Broadbent 1974; Hines 1972), right visual-field linguistic superiorities have been detected despite learned left-to-right reading habits of American students (Egoth 1971). Marcel, Katz and Smith (1974) extended the right visual-field evidence of superiority for single letter recognition to seven- and eight-year-old children.

In contrast to results from linguistic displays, Kimura (1966, 1969) reports a left-visual-field (right-hemisphere) superiority in dot-enumeration tasks. Utilizing dot stereograms, Kimura and Durnford (1974), and Durnford and Kimura (1971) determined that although binocular viewing was necessary in depth perception, the right hemisphere was superior. Yin (1970) suggests a right-hemisphere "predilection" for recognizing faces, and Gilbert and Bakan (1973) found that nonverbal material requiring spatial analysis, storage and recall, and gestalt synthesis, is processed by normal subjects more accurately in the right cerebral hemisphere.

Use of an electroencephalogram (EEG) to measure asymmetrical electrical activity in the cerebral hemispheres revealed lateralization of cortical function (See Butler and Glass 1974a, 1974b; Donchin et al. 1977 for reviews and critiques). Investigations have shown that the left hemisphere is more active when: 1) processing verbal material, including listening, reading, speaking, and writing (Buchsbaum and Fedio 1969; Doyle, Ornstein and Galin 1974; Galin and Ornstein 1974; Kraft et al. 1980; Mackavey, Curcie and Rosen 1973; McAdam and Whittaker 1971; McLeod and Peacock 1977; Mishkin and Forgays 1952; Morgan, McDonald and MacDonald 1971; Wood, Goft and Day 1971); 2) performing logical tasks (Butler and Glass 1974a; Dumas and Morgan 1975; Kraft et al. 1980; Morgan, McDonald and Hilgard 1974); and 3) making mathematical computations (Butler and Glass 1974b, 1976; Dumas and Morgan 1975; Morgan, McDonald and MacDonald 1971). The right hemisphere has been found to exhibit more activity during: 1) visuo-spatial tasks (Doyle, Ornstein and Galin 1974; Galin and Ornstein 1972, 1974; McLeon and Peacock 1977; Morrell and Salamy 1971); 2) processing of complicated visual stimuli (Buchsbaum and Fedio 1969; Dumas and Morgan 1975; Morell and Salamy 1971); 3) imaging various scenes (Morgan, McDonald and MacDonald 1971; Robbins and McAdam 1974); 4) watching a silent cartoon (Cole 1977); and 5) musical activity (Doyle, Ornstein and Galin 1974; McGee, Humphrey and McAdam 1973).

The timeline for attainment of adult functional aspecialization is currently under debate (Bay 1975; Brown and Jaffe 1975; Gardiner and Walter 1977; Kinsbourne and Hiscock 1977; Krashen 1975, 1976b, 1977; Lenneberg 1967) although there is evidence that structural (Geschwind 1974; Wada 1976; Witelson and Pallie 1973) and functional (Gardiner and Walter 1977; Turkewitz 1977a, 1977b; Wada 1976) asymmetries are present at birth or in utero. A clear consensus that adult patterns of brain functioning are clearly evident before puberty has not yet been reached (see Kraft this volume).

Much of the research described in the preceding paragraphs is oriented to a normative approach to neurological processing. There is some evidence, however, that there are group and individual differences in both degree and direction of functional lateralization in the adult population, and those differences have been posited to underlie performance differences. Current findings suggest that adult males tend to have lateralized functioning, whereas females are less lateralized (Bryden 1979; Harris 1975, 1978; Kraft 1982a; Lansdell 1964; McGlone and Kertesz 1973; Witelson 1976a) and have been hypothesized as having deficits in visuo-spatial skills, including some science and mathematical abilities (Garai and Scheinfield 1968; Harris 1978; Maccoby and Jacklin 1974).

Another group suspected of having atypical neural organization and atypical cognitive performance patterns is the left-handers (Alekoumbides 1978). Levy (Levy 1977; Levy and Reid 1976) suggests that backhand writing left-handers have language mediated by the left hemisphere (i.e., ipsilateral or same side hand-language hemisphere) and can be expected to have diffuse neural organization and either spatial or verbal deficits. Kershner (1974) reported that individuals with mixed hand-eye preference may have diffuse neural organization. Witelson (1976b) suggests that many children with reading disability have diffuse (or bilateral) spatial functioning, which she interprets as two of a single kind of processing system (i.e., two right brains).

Lake and Bryden (1976) report that handedness, sex, and familial history of sinistrality affect performance on verbal dichotic listening tasks e.g., a history of left-handedness increased the tendency for women to present atypical left-ear superiorities and superior spatial skills with the converse true for males. Other researchers also have posited a correlation with atypical neural organization and familial sinistrality (Hardyck 1977; Hecaen and Saugvet 1976; Hecaen, DeAgostini and Monzon-Montes 1981; Kocel 1977; Luria 1970).

In a series of studies designed to assess this hypothesis in children 2.5–15 years of age, Kraft found that regardless of their own degree of hand preference, right-handed and ambidextrous subjects who have left-handed biological relatives demonstrative attenuated lateral specialization (greater bilateral processing) for verbal (digits and nonsense syllables) and nonverbal (environmental sounds, nonsense shapes) stimuli (Kraft 1981b; Kraft in press; Kraft and Kamptner forthcoming). This relationship was evident by 2.5 years of age and predicted delays in language acquisition in the familial sinistral relative to the familial dextral children (Kraft in press; Kraft and Kamptner forthcoming). Bilateral processing of verbal information was associated with high Weschler verbal intelligence scores for right hand-eye preference familial sinistral preschool and adolescent children. Conversely, left hemispheric specialization for verbal processing was associated with higher verbal intelligence scores and right hemispheric specialization for nonverbal processing predicted higher spatial scores for right hand-eye preference familial dextral age mates (Kraft 1981b, 1983; Kraft and Kamptner forthcoming).

It is very possible that one's brain organization plays a large role in determining which information is most salient and the way in which this information is processed. For example, 6- to 12-year-old children's family handedness interacts with their own laterality to predict school achievement scores. A well-lateralized brain organization (in the expected direction) was associated with high reading, mathematics and spelling achievement for children with right-eye preference and mainly right-handed biological relatives. The mixed-eye familial handedness children, however, appeared to have a different pattern than the right-eye familial dextral children. Patterns of differential school achievement (e.g., high mathematics but low reading scores; high reading but low math scores, high reading but low spelling scores) was determined by specific hemispheric processing patterns within a given brain organization group (Kraft forthcoming). Thus, there is reason to suspect that brain organization differences underlie learning and processing-style differences and should provide a fruitful area of educational research in the future (Chall and Mirsky 1978; Kraft 1977; Snow, Federico and Montague 1980).

Evidence suggests that cultural differences in preferred cognitive style (Galin 1976) probably affects one's learning-processing style. Several studies (e.g., Cohen 1969; Marsh, Tenhauten and Bogen 1970) indicate that subcultures may be characterized by emphasized on a predominant cognitive mode. Middle-class subjects tend to employ a verbal-analytical mode while minority and lower class individuals such as the urban poor are more likely to utilize a spatial-synthetic mode. School related difficulties may arise from a mismatch between the instructional strategy used to teach certain skills and the learning-processing style of the learner, which appears to be determined by both environment and heredity.

These concepts suggested by research and theory in the brain-functioning literature can be summarized in the following five statements:

1. The two hemispheres of the brain process experience differently. The left hemisphere processes information sequentially and analytically, part by part. It focuses on and remembers verbal components of learning. The right hemisphere, in contrast, processes information from the same experience as a whole, simultaneously and synthetically, with a focus upon spatial components and remembers in images. Thus each child's brain has two very different but equally potent systems for thinking and learning which are interconnected.[3]

2. Developmental changes that occur in the brain seem clearly related to function. Some parts of the brain mature and become fully functional earlier than other parts. The brain has more adaptive plasticity in young children than in older persons (See Kraft this volume).

3. There are several sources of individual difference in brain functioning. In addition to developmental patterns, differential brain organization and preferred functioning patterns are being discovered.

4. Thus, differences between children in their characteristic approach to school tasks—frequently labeled cognitive styles or learning styles—may reflect the specialized processing of the brain's hemispheres.[4]

5. An individual's brain-processing patterns appear to be the result of neural organization that probably is based on heredity and is modified by chemical and environmental factors.

RECOMMENDED AREAS FOR EDUCATIONAL RESEARCH AND APPLICATION

Development of neurophysiological measures related to learning processes

Neurophysiological research designed for educational application is in an early stage of development. There is a need for development and validation of tasks and measures that will help delineate crucial characteristics of the learning process. More specifically, measurement involves defining things to be counted. Definition arises from perceiving attributes directly or from their effects. In education we characteristically assume the relationship between effects and attributes. Measurement error from these assumptions may be substantial. We need to utilize neurophysiological assessment to define with more precision and validity the attributes we claim to represent as basic and essential outcomes of educational practice. In this context, measurement of neural functioning correlated with learning should provide a more comprehensive and valid understanding of the nature of learning.

Such assessment will have to proceed through a series of development stages in which an important guideline for relevance, impact, and acceptance by educational practitioners will be the degree to which the experimental tasks reflect "real-world" classroom tasks. That is, neurophysiological assessment of subjects' momentary responses to clicks, flashes, or nonsense syllables may well be needed in building a research data base. Such tasks, however, are surely very different from comprehension tasks on passages of discourse. The latter will likely be viewed as more relevant for application by classroom practitioners. This recommendation simply points out the importance of having educators exercise initiative in guiding research efforts in this field. Of techniques available for the study of brain function, frequency-analysis EEG provides the opportunity to assess the child's neurophysiological interaction with reading tasks as the interaction occurs. Appropriate assessment is developing rapidly.

Curriculum and instruction

Curriculum denotes one of two basic elements defining the domain of education. At present, it seems likely that the major research operation of hemispheric function to school curriculum is task analysis. What are the neurophysiological parameters of learning tasks in the school curriculum? Curriculum task analysis potentially may be served through research that focuses upon the bilateral conception of brain function and the interaction of hemispheric modalities in task solutions.

It is also a possibility that curriculum research in reading, if designed around psychobiological dimensions of learning, would avoid the common tendency toward curricular compartmentalization. To illustrate, language and science competence in young children clearly appear to be related. In classrooms that use contemporary science curricula, not only does the science achievement of inner-city students (characteristically much lower in educational performance) equal that of their suburban peers, but they are also consistently more equally matched in language skills (Huff and Languis 1973; Rowe 1976).

Kraft (1976) analyzed EEG data from 18 first- and second-grade children while they performed Piagetian, reading, and other curriculum tasks. Subjects whose brain wave patterns suggested an integration of right and left hemispheric function demonstrated superiority in reading comprehension and Piagetian tasks. Kraft's data clearly suggest that it is not accurate to classify school subjects as right- or left-hemisphere areas of the curriculum. The nature of the learning process is better defined by considering other variables. For example, it appears that powerful external influences on how each child utilized brain hemispheres hinge on how tasks are presented to children, the nature of the response required of the child, and basic characteristics of the learning task. Also seeming to bear on brain functioning are such internal factors as the child's neural development and organization, pattern of experience, and cognitive-style preference. This array of factors provides a rich cluster of useful variables to assess problems in learning and to facilitate learning.

All the same, tasks with different basic characteristics do seem to have some influence on engaging the brain hemispheres differentially. Tasks with spatial characteristics, especially with three-dimensional dynamic qualities such as motion or novel interaction, frequently stimulate the right hemisphere. For example, as most children watch water running into a container or a silent cartoon movie, their right hemisphere "turns on." On the other hand, verbal tasks, especially those requiring a sequential or logical verbal answer, tend to engage the left hemisphere.

Analysis of curriculum in the expressive arts through hemispheric research paradigms is another area where the nature of the task probably does matter (Bogen 1975). For example, in children's literature, both brain modalities are probably significant: qualitative judgments clearly entail the integration of illustrations (visuo-spatial) with text (verbal). Moffett suggests that the integration of hemispheric modalities may be involved in the processing of visual metaphors in literature (John 1975). Zutell (this volume) has indirectly indicated several directions for task-analysis research in reading in his examination of the integrative hemispheric modality dimensions of syntax and semantics. In considering instructional aspects of curriculum assessment, this approach clearly relates to Paivio's (1974) and Wittrock's (1977) research on utilizing imagery in instruction. Many tasks such as Piagetian conservation tasks have both "spatial" right-hemisphere and "verbal" left-hemisphere components.

Instruction is the other basic area within the educational domain. Psychophysiological research in this area also may be very fruitful for education, for "hemispheric specialization tends to be process specific rather than material specific [which] suggests that subject matter may be less important than method of presentation" (Bogen 1975, p. 30).

The basic research problems in instruction are those encompassing instructional presentation mode by the teacher, response mode required of the student, and application of dual-trace theory in memory and instruction. There is evidence that learning and memory are enhanced by presenting subject matter in such a way that both hemispheres participate (Dimond 1972; Dimond and Beaumont 1974; Seaman 1974). Also it seems possible to challenge either hemisphere or both hemispheres by varying coding strategy (Seaman and Gazzaniga 1973). For example, children responded to repetition of the same task presented visuo-spatially in one instance and verbally in the other, Kraft (1976) noted a consistent change in most children from right-hemisphere activity to left-hemisphere activity.

Wittrock (1977) has suggested that the classroom teacher should first assess the individual's learning mode and then prescribe primary instruction techniques, those which would directly challenge the individual's preferred hemispheric mode, while supplementing this instruction with secondary instruction techniques designed to encourage the other hemisphere to participate in the activity. In addition, Sandman (1975 and this volume) has found significant differences in physiological responses and superiority in task performance when subjects have control of the initiation of learning tasks. It appears that control of beginning a task enables learners to establish an efficient "set." This concept suggests an extremely important notion for research on classroom and instructional organization, particularly with reading. Effective communication is the ultimate goal of reading and language arts. It involves interpersonal interaction that can be organized into verbal and nonverbal behavior. Elaborate coding mechanisms have been used for investigating verbal classroom interaction (Hough and Duncan 1975). Much attention has recently been given to the impact of non-verbal behavior in classroom communication. Galloway, (1968, 1971) who extensively analyzed nonverbal communication in the educational domain, argued that teaching is changed with nonverbal communication. Koch (1976) found that when verbal and nonverbal cues are not congruent, the nonverbal information is usually believed preferentially by the child. Woolfolk and Woolfolk (1974) supported that finding. It is well established that right-hemisphere modality is superior at facial recognition and general spatial nonverbal cues whereas left hemispheric process has the advantage in verbal communication. Rice and Languis (1979, 1980) tachistoscopically presented photos of a teacher of 60 fifth- and sixth-grade students after they had heard a statement by the teacher. Facial expression, content of the statement, and voice inflection varied from positive to negative. Subjects' response was to indicate a match of verbal (statement) and nonverbal (facial expression and voice interaction) cues. Responses were faster and more accurate to right-hemisphere presentations than to the left, and were especially superior when verbal and nonverbal cues mismatched. Galin (1974) has conceptualized and extensively documented the immediate and long-range psychiatric implications of congruence and conflict in verbal and non-verbal information fed to the two hemispheres. The implications for both adult and child are uncertain and capricious when a parent or reading teacher communicates verbally "I approve," but simultaneously communicates nonverbally, "I disapprove."

The importance to educators of verbal and nonverbal behavior with respect to brain hemispheres lies in the interaction of physiological mechanisms (including the autonomic nervous system and the brain hemispheres) that may indicate sources of stress and distress, or the reduction of stress and individual in stress responses (Corson and Corson 1975; Sandman 1975).

Bogen (1975) and Ornstein and Galin (1975) suggest that the entire school curriculum and indeed American culture may be inordinately skewed to reward left-hemisphere modality.

> . . . an elementary school program narrowly restricted to reading, writing and arithmetic will educate mainly one hemisphere leaving half of an individual's high level potential unschooled . . . Just as left hemisphere potential for propositionizing may be developed, so too should we expect that right hemisphere capacities can suffer from educational neglect . . . If our society has overemphasized propositionally at the expense of appositionality more is involved than the adjustment of isolated individuals. It means that the whole student body is being educated lopsidedly (Bogen 1975, 27–29).

Learning problems

As Geschwind (1982) pointed out, "one must remember that practically all of us have a significant number of learning disabilities . . . We happen to live in a society where the child who has trouble learning to read is in difficulty. Yet we have all seen dyslexic children who draw much better than 'normal children', i.e., who have either superior visual perception or visual-motor skills." In another setting, those same reading disabled children might excel. Therefore, as the demands of our society change, we may label a new group of persons "minimally brain-damaged." Guyer and Friendman (1975) found that learning-disabled children were not deficient in right-hemisphere skills or deficient in all aspects of verbal ability. They instead seemed to be attempting to use a nonverbal modality to solve many academic tasks. The lack of success we have with many children—frequently boys and children from lower-SES groups—in teaching the basic "verbal" skills of reading and writing (clearly the "passports" to success in American schools today) strongly suggests that we need to consider assessing nonverbal strategies and representational systems and their possible role in developing verbal skills. It is becoming increasingly evident that there are children who fit into a cluster of different neurological organizations[5]. There is continuing need to utilize the assessment of neurological brain-functioning patterns in diagnosing the learning problems of children in special and the normal classroom situations (Naour, Martin and Languis 1984).

Other parameters of individual variation have been related to brain function. These sources of variation include: gender (Languis and Naour in press), developmental level (Berlin and Languis 1980, 1981), handedness (Geschwind 1968, 1982), eye dominance, membership in American sub-cultures and socio-economic class, nutritional deficiencies, and environmental deprivation. Therefore, basic research questions relevant to learning problems should focus upon diagnosing the mismatch of the individual's neurological processing propensities with instructional and curricular expectations of parents and teachers, followed by attempts to facilitate adaptive behavior in the child and the school establishment (Languis 1983a, 1983d).

CHALLENGES TO EDUCATION

While these patterns that are emerging are tentative beginnings, not conclusions, they do strongly suggest several basic challenges to education:

1. The first challenge is for educational researchers to accept the initiative and launch efforts to build interdisciplinary research with neuroscientists' efforts (Languis 1983c; Languis et al. in press). Teachers may know from first-hand experience what the important problems of learning are. But solutions will not be found by working alone. Our experience demonstrates that specialists in the academic sciences are genuinely concerned and ready to cooperate in educational research.

2. The second challenge is to rethink the questions we have typically asked about the educational enterprise. It is very clear that approaches are now available to study basic problems in learning by investigating the learning process as it occurs within the child (Buck 1976). Perhaps this suggests a new model for educational research and may offer an explanation of why so little real progress has resulted from the traditional research emphasis of the past.

3. A third challenge is to work toward balance in the entire school program. Clearly our schools today emphasize verbal left-hemisphere processing. Such misplaced emphasis should be corrected because the right hemisphere's cognitive potential is as important for high-level problem solving as well as for complex language tasks, and it is necessary, though probably not sufficient, for creative thinking (Bogen 1969).

4. A final challenge from brain research emerges from expanded evidence of individual differences. It is possible that many children who drop out of school and the many more who "turn-off" school do so because of serious mismatches between their individual learning patterns and school expectations.

We may be able to ameliorate these deficiencies in education. For example, Wittrock (1977) suggests that we may be able to provide for individual differences in hemispheric functioning patterns, and ultimately in learning styles, by determining the child's preferred modality and then designing instructional strategies and materials that will directly challenge the preferred hemisphere first and provide secondary instructional experiences that encourage the other hemisphere to participate in the activity.

We may also be able to help children through mechanisms such as biofeedback. Eventually, the day may come when children will exercise voluntary control of self-development and the self-control of biological mechanisms that enhance learning potency.

Evidence provided from research of neurophysiological indices of cognitive processes strongly suggests that the puzzle of children's successes and failures in learning may be soluble after all (Languis 1983b, 1983c; Torello, Languis and Naour 1984). A new direction has been established. Opportunity and challenge await those willing to accept them.

ENDNOTES

[1]Past attempts to educe man's ways of knowing have been basically a closed-box approach, with inferences drawn from behavioral outputs associated with specific inputs. By contrast, insight into hemispheric brain-processing modalities has resulted from a stronger open-box approach, in which, for example, study has been made of the consequences of surgically disconnecting the hemispheres of epileptic patients and of anesthetizing a hemisphere in normal subjects. The degree of congruence between current brain-research findings and the wisdom of the centuries supports continued exploration of educational applications of hemispheric brain process.

[2]Comprehensive reviews of this research and its implications are found in Chall and Mirsky (1978), Dimond and Beaumont (1974), Kinsbourne and Hiscock (1983), Kraft and Languis (1977), Springer and Deutch (1981), and Wittrock (1977).

[3]In 1861, Paul Broca reported functional asymmetry between the two cerebral hemispheres. Broca (cited in Milner 1975) postulated that articulated speech was a function of the left cerebral hemisphere. In 1874, Hughlings Jackson (cited in Benton 1962), a British neurologist, reported that damage in the right cerebral hemisphere was associated with loss in visuo-spatial recognition and memory, resulting in visuo-spatial disorientation, failure to recognize faces, and inability to dress.

Those reports were later confirmed and extended. Observations of patients with hemispheric lesions have indicated an association of the left hemisphere with reading, writing, speaking, understanding the spoken word, calculation, and analytical tasks, and an association of the right hemisphere with visuo-spatial performance such as visual-pattern identification, visual closure, spatial orientation, musical pattern, and Gestalt synthesis (Benton 1976; Corkin 1965; Milner 1975a, 1975b). The significance of the functional asymmetry was not understood, however, until the later 1960's, when R.W. Sperry and his associates began publishing the results of tests performed by "split-brain" patients. Those patients had undergone surgical sectioning of the major commissures connecting the two cerebral hemispheres in order to prevent the interhemispheric spread of epileptic seizures (Bogen, Fisher and Vogel 1965).

The hemispheres in the "split-brain" patients functioned independently, yet had specialization of function. The right hemisphere had few words but had little or no impairment in visual discrimination tasks and spatial orientation, whereas the left hemisphere had visual discrimination and spatial impairment but scored well on the verbal subtests of the Weschler and was able to calculate (Bogen 1969; Bogen and Gazzaniga 1965; Gazzaniga, Bogen and Sperry 1967; Levy 1974; Sperry 1968, 1969, 1974; Sperry, Gazzaniga and Bogen 1969). "Thus began the theory of two states of consciousness, two personalities within one brain. Each was conceived as having its own system of processing sensory information as well as its own cognitive mode. The role of the commissures then was viewed as that of unifying the two into a single personality, the self (Kraft 1976, 14)."

Following Sperry's discovery, a growing body of literature has confirmed that the functional asymmetry reported in lesioned and split-brain patients is evident also in "normal" people with intact commissures and no history of brain damage or neurosurgery.

[4]Case histories have shown that very early brain damage usually results in functional recovery. The degree of recovery usually depends on the locus of the brain injury and the age of the patients, indicating functional plasticity of the brain in infancy. The chance for recovery is often improved when the injured area is removed suggesting that the injured brain structure that subserves a function competes with uninjured structures that could take over the function (Rasmussen and Milner 1977). From case histories indicating full recovery of language facilities in infancy and early childhood, some researchers are speculating that adult-like degree of lateralization of function is either present at birth (Kinsbourne and Hiscock 1977, 1983) or occurs between the ages of five to twelve (Dorman and Geffner 1974; Krashen and Harshman 1972), whereas Brown and Jaffee (1975) suggest that lateralization extends into senescence.

[5]At least three organization patterns have been defined: 1) lateralized functioning (individuals having most of their language functioning housed in one hemisphere and most of their spatial functioning in the other hemisphere); 2) diffuse language functioning (individuals having language representation in both hemispheres, which results in spatial deficits); and 3) diffuse spatial functioning (individuals having spatial representation in both hemispheres, which results in language deficits) (Kraft and Languis 1977).

Current research findings suggest that males tend to have lateralized functioning, while females tend to have diffuse language representation in both hemispheres (summarized in Harris 1978). Those findings may partially explain the well documented differences between the sexes in spatial and language tasks (Maccoby and Jacklin 1974).

Left-handers also often have a greater discrepancy between language and spatial skills than right-handers do (Levy 1974). Levy and Reid (1976) found that left-handers who use inverted hand posturing (i.e., write backhanded or in a hooked position) have either a diffuse language functioning (resulting in either superior language performance and poor spatial performance) or diffuse spatial functioning (resulting in superior spatial but inferior language performance.) They further suggest that right-handers who use inverted hand posturing also have diffuse neural organizational patterns. Furthermore, Kershner (1974) citing research on men and women with mixed hand-eye dominance, states that mixed dominance patterns might be a function of diffuse organization.

[6]The distinctive and different ways of knowing that characterize an individual's cognitive or learning style have been recognized for hundreds of years. These ways of knowing have frequently been expressed as dichotomous pairs: analytical-holistic (Ornstein 1977), rational-metaphoric (Bruner 1965), operative-figurative (Piaget 1973). Cognitive style is viewed as a

pervasive, rather stable, superordinate system that characterizes the individual's approach to learning tasks. Historical insight and current research investigating differences in style of learning and cognition bear marked similarities to the recently discovered information-processing styles of the right and left hemispheres (Languis and Kraft 1976). Several views of cognitive style have been suggested. Among those views is Witkin's (Witkin et al. 1977) psychological differentiation model, which is represented in the concept of field dependence-independence. In measures of GFDI, field-dependent inviduals have difficulty separating out an element from the total context, whereas field-independent persons are more competent in focusing attention on a part of the whole while ignoring the Gestalt of the "field." Research is under way to assess the relative involvement of the hemispheres in tasks requiring the contrasting components of various models of cognitive style.

From the models and theories of brain function, several implications may be drawn. Wittrock (1977) stated that there is a clear connection between brain research and generative cognitive processes. Brain programs are built from external information and internal elaboration. Second, the importance of emotional climate in learning is supported. The vital role of the limbic system as a cognitive relay and processing point is confounded by its emotional role. Third, brain research strongly supports the validity of multiple ways of learning, thinking, and knowing. Effective coordination of all these may be the definition of individual intelligence. Finally, knowledge of the brain justifies the educational emphasis on awareness and acceptance of the wide range of individual differences among children. Differences need not be deficits if strengths rather than weaknesses become the basis for teaching.

In many ways, the most striking impression from more than twenty years of brain research is the validation of individual differences. Evidence of anatomical, organizational and functional differences in the brain leads one to conclude that each human brain is custom-made, not turned out on some genetic or cultural assembly line. This consistent finding is all the more convincing because most brain researchers work from the empirical point of view in which the approach is to demonstrate differences between defined groups of people.

To the experienced teacher, individual variability in the brain is a validation of deeply rooted educational values in the primacy of the individual and at the same time is a salient challenge to characteristic educational practice which tends to ignore individual differences and attempts, instead, to mold the learning of every child in essentially the same way at the same time to tenets of behaviorism.

REFERENCES

Alekoumbides, A. 1978. Hemispheric dominance for language: Quantitative aspects. *Acta Neurologica Scandinavia* 57:97–140.

Bay, E. 1975. Ontogeny of stable speech areass in the human brain. In *Foundations of language development*, eds. E.H. Lenneberg and E. Lenneberg. New York: Academic Press.

Beaumont, J.E., ed. 1982. *Divided visual field studies of cerebral organization*. New York: Academic Press.

Benton, A.L. 1962. Clinical symptomatology in right- and left-hemisphere lesions. In *Interhemispheric relations and cerebral dominance*, ed. V.B. Mountcastle. Baltimore: Johns Hopkins Press.

Berlin, C.A., and Cullen, J.K. 1977. Acoustic problems in dichotic listening tasks. In *Language development and neurological theory*, eds. S.J. Segalowitz and F.A. Gruber. New York: Academic Press.

Berlin, D., and Languis, M.L. 1980. Measures of age and sex differences in brain lateralization. *Perceptual and Motor Skills* 50:959-967.

________. 1981. Hemispheric correlates of the rod and frame test. *Perceptual and Motor Skills* 52:35-41.

Blumstein, S., and Cooper, W. 1974. Hemispheric processing of intonation contours. *Cortex* 10:146-158.

Bogen, J.E. 1969. The other side of the brain: Parts I, II, III. *Bulletin of the Los Angeles Neurological Society* 34:73-105, 135-162, 191-203.

Bogen, J.E. 1975. Educational aspects of hemispheric specialization. *UCLA Educator* 17:24-33.

Bogen, J.E., and Gazzaniga, N.S. 1965. Cerebral commissurotomy in man. *Journal of Neurosurgery* 23:394-399.

Bogen, J.E.; Fisher, D.; and Vogel, W. 1965. Cerebral commissurotomy. *Journal of the American Medical Association* 194:1328-1329.

Broadbent, D.E. 1974. Division of function and integration of behavior. *The neurosciences: Third study program*. Cambridge MIT Press.

Brown, J.W., and Jaffe, J. 1975. Hypothesis on cerebral dominance. *Neuropsychologia* 13:107-110.

Bruner, J.S. 1965. *On knowing—Essays for the left hand.* Cambridge: Harvard University Press.

Bryden, M.P. 1979. Evidence for sex-related differences in cerebral organization. In *Sex-related differences in cognitive functioning: Developmental issues*, eds. M.A. Wittig and A.C. Peterson. New York: Academic Press.

Buck, R. 1976. *Human motivation and emotion*. New York: Wiley & Sons.

Buschsbaum, H., and Fedio, P. 1969. Visual information and evoked responses from the left and right hemispheres. *EEG Clinical Neurophysiology* 26:266-272.

Butler, S., and Glass, A. 1974a. Asymmetries in the EEG associated with cerebral dominance. *EEG Clinical Neurophysiology* 36:481-491.

________. 1974b. EEG correlates of cerebral dominance. In *Advances in psychobiology*, Vol. 3A, eds. A.H. Reisen and R.F. Thompson. New York: Wiley & Sons.

Chall, J.S., and Mirsky, A.F. 1978. *Education and the brain*. Chicago: University of Chicago Press.

Cohen, H.A. 1969. Conceptual styles, culture conflict and non-verbal tests of intelligence. *American Anthropologist* 71:826-856.

Cole, R.A. 1977. Invariant features and feature detectors: Some developmental implications. In *Language development and neurological theory*, eds. S.J. Segalowitz and F.A. Gruber. New York: Academic Press.

Corkin, S. 1965. Tactually-guided maze learning in man: Effects on unilateral cortical excession and bilateral hippocampal lesions. *Neuropsychologia* 3:339-351.

Corson, S., and Corson, O. 1975. *Constitutional differences in physiological adaptation to stress and distress in certain psychopathology of human adaptation*. New York: Plenum Press.

Curry, F.K.W. 1967. A comparison of left-handed and right-handed subjects on verbal and nonverbal dichotic listening tasks. *Cortex* 3:343–352.

Dimond, S.J. 1972. *The double brain*. London: Churchill Livingston.

Dimond, S.J., and Beaumont, J.G., eds. 1974. *Hemispheric function in the human brain*. New York: John H. Wiley.

Donchin, E.; Kutas, M.; and McCarthy, G. 1977. Electrocortical indices of hemispheric utilization. In *Lateralization in the nervous system*. eds. S. Harnad, R.W. Doty, L. Goldstein, J. Jaynes, and G. Krauthamer. New York: Academic Press.

Dorman, M.F., and Geffner, D.S. 1974. Hemispheric specialization for speech perception on six-year-old black and white children from low and middle socioeconomic classes. *Cortex* 10:171–176.

Doyle, J.C.; Ornstein, R.; and Galin, D. 1974. Lateral specialization of cognitive mode: II. EEG frequency analysis. *Psychophysiology*.

Dumas, R., and Morgan, A. 1975. EEG asymmetry as a function of occupation, task and task difficulty. *Neuropsychologia* 13:219–228.

Durnford, M., and Kimura, D. 1971. Right hemisphere specialization for depth perception reflected in visual field differences. *Nature* 231:394–395.

Egoth, H. 1971. Laterality effects in perceptual matching. *Perception and Psychophysics* 9:375–376.

Galin, D. 1976. Two modes of consciousness and the two halves of the brain. In *Symposium on consciousness*, ed. R.E. Ornstein. New York: Viking Press.

————. 1974. Implications for psychiatry of left and right cerebral specialization. *Archives of General Psychiatry* 31:572–583.

Galin, D., and Ornstein, E. 1972. Lateral specialization of cognitive mode: An EEG study. *Psychophysiology* 9:412–418.

————. 1974. Individual differences in cognitive style: Reflective eye movements. *Neuropsychologia* 4:291–294.

Galloway, C.M. 1968. Nonverbal communication. *Theory into Practice* 7:172–175.

————, ed. 1971. The challenge of nonverbal awareness. *Theory into Practice* 10:4.

Garai, J.E., and Scheinfeld, A. 1968. Sex differences in mental and behavioral traits. *Genetic Psychology Monographs* Genetic Psychology Monographs 77:169–299.

Gardiner, M.F., and Walter, D.O. 1977. Evidence of hemispheric specialization from infant EEG. In *Lateralization in the nervous system*, eds. S. Harnad and R.W. Doty. New York: Academic Press.

Gazzaniga, M.S.; Bogen, J.; and Sperry, R.W. 1967. Dyspraxia following division of the cerebral commissures. *Archives of Neurology* 16:606–612.

Geschwind, N. 1974. The anatomical basis of hemispheric differentiation. In *Hemisphere function in the human brain*, eds. S.J. Dimond and J.G. Beaumont. New York: John H. Wiley.

Geschwind, N., and Behan, P. 1982. Left-handedness: Association with immune disease, migraine and developmental learning disorders. *Proc. Natl. Acad. Sci.* 79:5907–5100.

Geschwind, N., and Levitsky, W. 1968. Human brain: Left-right asymmetries in temporal speech region. *Science* 161:186–187.

Gilbert, C., and Bakan, P. 1973. Visual asymmetry in perception of paces. *Neuropsychologia* 11:335–361.

Goldman, P. 1977. In *The neurological bases of language disorder in children: Methods and directions for research*, eds. C.L. Ludlow and M.E. Doran-Quine. NINCDS Monograph No. 22. Bethesda, MD: U.S. Department of Health, Education, and Welfare.

Gruber, F.A., and Segalowitz, S.J. 1977. Some issues and methods in neuropsychology of language. In *Language development and neurological theory*, eds. S.J. Segalowitz and F.A. Gruber. New York: Academic Press.

Guyer, B.L., and Friedman, M.P. 1975. Hemispheric processing and cognitive styles in learning disabled and normal children. *Child development* 46:658–668.

Halperin, Y.; Nachson, I.; and Carmon, A. 1973. Shift of superiority in dichotic listening to temporally patterned nonverbal stimuli. *Journal of the Acoustical Society of America* 53:46–50.

Hardyck, C. 1977. A model of individual differences in hemispheric functioning. In *Studies in neurolinguistics*, Vol. 3, eds. H. Whitaker and H. Whitaker. New York: Academic Press.

Harris, L.J. 1975. Neuropsychological factors in the development of spatial skills. In *Children's spatial development*, eds. J. Elliot and N.J. Salkind. Springfield, IL: Thomas.

________. 1978. Sex differences in spatial ability: Possible environmental, genetic, and neurological factors. In *Asymmetrical function of the brain*, ed. M. Kinsbourne. London: Cambridge University Press.

Hecaen, H.; DeAgostini, M.; and Monzon-Montes, A. 1981. Cerebral organization in left-handers. *Brain and Language* 12:261–284.

Hecaen, H., and Sauguet, J. 1971. Cerebral dominance in left-handed subjects. *Cortex* 7:19–48.

Hines, D. 1972. Bilateral tachistoscopic recognition of verbal and nonverbal stimuli. *Cortex* 8:315–322.

Hines, D., and Satz, P. 1974. Cross-modal asymmetries in perception related to asymmetry in cerebral function. *Neuropsychologia* 12:239–247.

Huff, P., and Languis, M.L. 1973. The effects of the use of SAPA activities on the oral communication skills of disadvantaged kindergarten children. *Journal of Research in Science Teaching* 10:165–173.

John, E.R. 1977. *Foundations of cognitive process.* Hillsdale, NJ: Lawrence Erlbaum Associates.

Kamptner, L.; Kraft, R.H.; and Harper, L.V. 1984. Hemispheric specialization and social-verbal development in preschool children. *Brain and Cognition* 3:42–50.

Kershner, J. 1974. Ocular-manual laterality and dual hemisphere specialization. *Cortex* 10:293–302.

Kimura, D. 1961. Some effects of temporal lobe damage on auditory perception. *Canadian Journal of Psychology* 15:156–165.

________. 1964. Left-right differences in the perception of melodies. *Quarterly Journal of Experimental Psychology* 16:355–358.

________. 1966. Dual functioning asymmetry of the brain in visual perception. *Neuropsychologia* 4:275–286.

________. 1967. Functional asymmetry of the brain in dichotic listening. *Cortex* 3:163–178.

________. 1969. Spatial localization in left and right visual fields. *Canadian Journal of Psychology* 23:445–458.

———. 1973. The asymmetry of the human brain. *Scientific America* 238:70–78.

Kimura, D., and Durnford, M. 1974. Normal studies on the function of the right hemisphere in vision. In *Hemispheric function in the human brain*, eds. S.J. Dimond and J.G. Beaumont. New York: Academic Press.

Kinsbourne, M., and Hiscock, M. 1977. Does cerebral dominance develop? In *Language development and neurological theory*, eds. S.J. Segalowitz and F.A. Gruber. New York: Academic Press.

———. 1983. The normal and deviant development of functional lateralization of the brain. In *Carmichael's manual of child psychology*, Vol. 2. 4th ed. New York: John H. Wiley.

Knox, C., and Kimura, D. 1970. Cerebral processing of verbal and nonverbal sounds. *Neuropsychologia* 8:22–25.

Kocel, K.M. 1977. Cognitive abilities: Handedness, familiar sinistrality and sex. In *Evolution and lateralization of the brain*, eds. S.J. Dimond and D.S. Blizzard. New York: Academy of Science.

Koch, R. 1976. Nonverbal observables. *Theory into Practice* 10:4.

Kraft, R.H. 1976. An EEG study: Hemispheric brain functioning of six to eight year old children during Piagetian and curriculum tasks with variation in presentation made. Ph.D. diss., The Ohio State University.

———. 1977. Cognitive processing underlying junior high concept learning. Paper presented to the Child Development Graduate Group, University of California at Davis, May.

———. 1981a. The relationship between family history and degree of hand preference and the development of lateral specialization during middle childhood. Paper delivered at the Biannual Meeting of the Society for Research in Child Development in Boston, April.

———. 1981b. The relationship between right-handed children's assessed and familial handedness and lateral specialization. *Neuropsychologia* 19:697–705.

———. 1982a. Relationship of ear specialization to degree of task difficulty, sex, and lateral specialization. *Perceptual and Motor Skills* 54:704–714.

———. 1982b. Hemispheric specialization and integration and its relationship to stages of language and cognitive development. Paper delivered at the 5th International Conference in Child Neurology in Bratislava, Czechoslovakia, May 31.

———. 1983. The effect of sex, laterality and familial handedness on intellectual abilities. *Neuropsychologia* 21:79–89.

———. n.d. Lateral specialization and verbal/spatial abilities in preschool children: Age, sex, and familial handedness differences. *Neuropsychologia.* In press.

———. n.d. Hemispheric specialization and school achievement. Forthcoming.

Kraft, R.H., and Kamptner, L. n.d. A longitudinal investigation of lateral specialization and verbal ability: Sex and familial handedness differences. Forthcoming.

Kraft, R.H., and Languis, M.L. 1977. Dimensions of right and left brain learning in early childhood. In *Early childhood education*, eds. L.H. Golubchick and B. Persky. New York: Avery Publishing.

Kraft, R.H.; Mitchell, O.R.; Languis, M.L.; and Wheatley, G.H. 1980. Hemispheric asymmetries during six- to eight-year-olds' performance of Piagetian conservation and reading tasks. *Neuropsychologia* 18:637–643.

Krashen, S.D. 1975. The critical period for language acquisition and its possible bases. In *Developmental Psycholinguistics and Communication Disorders: Annals of N.Y. Academy of Sciences.* eds. A. Aaronson and R.W. Rieber 253:211–224.

________. 1976a. Cerebral asymmetry. In *Studies in neurolinguistics*, Vol. 2, eds. H. Whitaker and H.A. Whitaker. New York: Academic Press.

________. 1976b. The development of cerebral dominance and language learning: More new evidence. In *Developmental psycholinguistics: Theory and applications*, ed. Dato. Washington, DC: Georgetown University Press.

________. 1977. The left brain. In *The human brain*, ed. M. Whittrock. Englewood Cliffs, NJ: Prentice-Hall.

Krashen, S.D., and Harshman, R. 1972. Lateralization and the critical period. *UCLA Working Papers in Phonetics* 23:13–21.

Lake, D.A., and Bryden, M.P. 1976. Handedness and sex differences in hemispheric asymmetry. *Brain and Language* 3:266–282.

Languis, M.L. 1983a. Cognitive dimensions of spatial learning with the personal computer. Paper presented at Ohio Academy of Science, Bowling Green, Ohio.

________. 1983b. Learning style: A point of view for valuing young learners. ERIC Publication No. ED 23518.

________. 1983c. A model of learning style in professional development programs for physicians. In *Learning style in continuing medical education*, ed. L. Curry. Ottawa, Canada: Canadian Medical Assn.

________. 1983d. Neurocognitive substraits of learning style. Paper presented at National Association for Engineering in Medicine and Biology, Columbus, Ohio.

Languis, M.L., and Kraft, R.H. 1976. Hemispheric brain functioning: What it means for you. *OCESS Journal* 7:14–18.

________. 1978. An educational perspective on the hemispheric process of the brain. ERIC Document No. ED 151 748.

Languis, M.L., and Naour, P.J. n.d. Sex difference in neurological functions: A vector model. In *The neuropsychology of individual differences*, eds. L.C. Hartlage and C.F. Telzrow. New York: Plenum. In press.

Languis, M.L., and Wilcox, J. 1981. Learning: A life span human development model for early childhood education. In *Theory into practice*, eds. C.R. Williams and C.R. May.

Languis, M.L.; Naour, P.; Martin, D.; and Buffer, J., eds. n.d. *Cognitive science: Contributions to education.* Washington, DC: ERIC Publications. In press.

Languis, M.L.; Sanders, T.; and Tipps, S. 1980. *Brain and learning: Directions in early childhood education.* Washington: National Association for the Education of Young Children.

________. 1982. Brain functioning models for learning. ERIC Publication Nos. ED 212 373; PS 012 638.

Lansdell, H. 1964. A sex difference in effect of temporal-lobe neurosurgery or design performance. *Nature* 194:852–854.

Lenneberg, E.H. 1967. *Biological foundations of language.* New York: John H. Wiley.

Levy, J. 1973. Lateral specialization of the human brain: Behavioral manifestations and possible evolutionary basis. In *The biology of behavior,* ed. J. Rigen. Eugene, Oregon: Oregon University Press.

________. 1974. Psychobiology implications of bilateral asymmetry. In *Hemispheric function in the human brain*, eds. S. Dimond and J. Beaumont. New York: John H. Wiley.

________. 1977. Manifestations and implications of shifting hemi-inattention in commisuratory pateitns. In *Advances in neurology*, Vol. 18, eds. E.A. Weinstein and R.P. Friedland. New York: Raven.

Levy, J., and Reid, M. 1976. Variations in writing posture and cerebral organization. *Science* 194:337-339.

Luria, A.R. 1970. *Traumatic aphasia: Its syndromes, psychology and treatment.* Mouton: The Hague.

Maccoby, E.E., and Jacklin, C. 1974. *The psychology of sex differences.* Stanford: Stanford University Press.

Mackavay, W.; Curcie, F.; and Rosen, T. 1973. Tachistoscopic word recognition performance under conditions of simultaneous bilateral presentation. *Neuropsychologia* 13:27-33.

Marcel, T.; Katz, L.; and Smith, M. 1974. Laterality and reading proficiency. *Neuropsychologia* 12:131-139.

Marsh, J.F.; Tenhauten, W.D.; and Bogen, J.E. 1970. A theory of cognitive functioning and social stratification. Progress report, O.E.O. Contract, Department of Sociology, University of California, Riverside.

McAdam, D.W., and Whittaker, H.A. 1971. Language production: Electroencephalographic localization in the normal human brain. *Science* 172:499-502.

McGee, G.; Humphrey, B.; and McAdam, D. 1973. Scaled laterality of alpha activity during linguistic and musical tasks. *Psychophysiology* 10:441-443.

McGlone, J., and Kertesz, A. 1973. Sex differences in cerebral processing of visuospatial tasks. *Cortex* 9:313-320.

McLeod, S.S., and Peacock, L.J. 1977. Task-related EEG asymmetry: Effects of age and ability. *Psychophysiology* 14:308-311.

Milner, B. 1958. The memory defect in bilateral hippocampal lesions. *Psychiatric Research Reports* 11:43-58.

________. 1975a. Hemisphere specialization: Scope and limits. In *The neurosciences: Third study program*, eds. E.O. Schmitt and F.G. Worden. Cambridge: MIT Press.

________. 1975b. *Hemispheric specialization and interaction.* Cambridge: MIT Press.

Mishkin, M., and Forgays, D. 1952. Word recognition as a function of temporal focus. *Journal of Experimental Psychology* 43:43-48.

Morgan, A.H.; McDonald, P.J.; and MacDonald, H. 1971. Differences in bilateral alpha as a function of experimental task with a note on lateral eye movement and hypnotizability. *Neuropsychologia* 9:459-469.

Morrell, L., and Salamy, J. 1971. Hemispheric asymmetry of electrocortical response to speech stimuli. *Science* 174:164-166.

Naour, P.J.; Martin, D.J.; and Languis, M.L. 1984. Electrophysiological evidence for a predominantly visuospatial processing style in learning disability students. Paper presented at the American Education Research Association in New Orleans.

Ornstein, R.E. 1977. *The psychology of consciousness.* 2nd ed. San Francisco: W.H. Freeman.

Paivio, A. 1974. *Imagery and verbal processes.* New York: Holt, Rinehart, & Winston.

Piaget, J. 1973. *The psychology of intelligence.* New York: Littlefield Adams.

Rasmussen, R., and Milner, B. 1977. The role of early left-brain injury in determining lateralization of cerebral speech functions. In *Evolution and lateralization of the brain*, eds. S.J. Dimond and D.A. Blizard. New York: New York Academy of Sciences.

Rentel, V. 1975. The utility of physiological measures in reading and language acquisition. Research paper presented to Ohio State University Interdisciplinary Research Group.

Rice, D., and Languis, M.L. 1979. What is for real in communication: Your right left brain decides. *Reading Improvement* 16(1): 50–55.

________. 1980. Hemispheric brain responses of children to verbal and nonverbal cues. *Alberta Science Education Journal* 18(1): 24–32.

Robbins, K.I., and McAdam, D.W. 1974. Interhemispheric alpha asymmetry and imagery mode. *Brain and Language* 1:189–193.

Rowe, M.B. 1976. *Teaching science as continuous inquiry.* New York: McGraw-Hill.

Sagan, C. 1977. *The dragons of Eden.* New York: Ballantine Books.

Sandman, C.A. 1975. Physiological responses during escape and non-escape from stress. *Biological Psychology* 2:202–216.

Seaman, J.G. 1974. Coding and retrieval processes and the hemispheres of the brain. In *Hemisphere function in the human brain*, eds. S.J. Dimond and J.G. Beaumont. New York: Wiley & Sons.

Seaman, J.G., and Gazzaniga, A. 1973. Coding strategies and cerebral laterality effects. *Cognitive Psychology* 5:8–15.

Shankweiler, D., and Studdert-Kennedy, M. 1967. Identification of consonants and vowels presented to the left and right ears. *Quarterly Journal of Experimental Psychology* 10:239–241.

Snow, R.E.; Federico, P.; and Montague, W.E. 1980. *Aptitude, learning and instruction,* Vols. 1 and 2. Hillsdale, NJ: Lawrence Erlbaum Associates.

Sperry, R.W. 1968. Hemisphere deconnection and unity in conscious awareness. *American Psychologist* 23:723–733.

________. 1969. A modified concept of consciousness. *Psychological Review* 76:532–536.

________. 1974. Lateral specialization of cerebral function in the surgically separated hemisphere. In *The neurosciences: Third study program*, eds. F.O. Schmitt and F.G. Worder. Cambridge: MIT Press.

Sperry, R.W.; Gazzaniga, M.S.; and Bogen, J.E. 1969. Interhemispheric relationship: The neurocortical commissures. In *Handbook of clinical neurology*. Amsterdam: North Holland Publishing.

Springer, S., and Deutch, G. 1981. *Left brain, right brain.* San Francisco: Freeman Press.

Torello, M.; Languis, M.; and Naour, P. 1984. The use of event related potentials to measure cognitive processing in the head injured. Paper presented at American Educational Research Association in New Orleans.

Turkewitz, G. 1977. The development of lateral differences in the human infant. In *Lateralization in the nervous system,* eds. S. Harnad and R.W. Doty. New York: Academic Press.

________. 1977b. The development of lateral differentiation in the human infant. In *Evolution and lateralization of the brain*, eds. S.G. Dimond and D.W. Blizard. New York: New York Academy of Sciences.

Wada, J.A. 1976. Pre-language and fundamental asymmetry of the infant brain. Paper presented to the New York Academy of Science Conference on the Evolution and Lateralization of the Brain in New York, October.

White, M.J. 1969. Laterality on differences in perception. *Psychological Bulletin* 72:387–405.

________. 1974. Visual hemifield differences in the perception of letters and contour orientation. *Canadian Journal of Psychology* 25:207–212.

Witelson, S.F. 1976a. Abnormal right hemisphere specialization in developmental dyslexia. In *The neuropsychology of learning disorders*, eds. R.M. Knight and D.J. Bakker. Baltimore: University Press.

________. 1976b. Sex and the single hemisphere: Specialization of the right hemisphere spatial processing. *Science* 193:425–427.

________. 1977a. Anatomic asymmetry in the temporal lobes: Its documentation, phylogenesis, and relationship to functional asymmetry. In *Evolution and lateralization of the brain*, eds. S.J. Dimond and D.A. Blizard. New York: New York Academy of Sciences.

________. 1977b. Developmental dyslexia: Two right hemispheres and none left. *Science* 195:309–311.

________. 1977c. Early hemisphere specialization and interhemisphere plasticity: An empirical and theoretical review. In *Language development and neurological theory*, eds. S.J. Segalowitz and F.A. Gruber. New York: Academic Press.

Witelson, S.F., and Pallie, W. 1973. Left hemisphere specialization for language in the newborn: Neuroanatomical evidence of asymmetry. *Brain* 96:641–646.

Witkin, H.A.; Moore, C.A.; Goodenough, D.R.; and Cox, P.W. 1977. Field-dependent and field-independent cognitive styles and their educational implications. *Review of Educational Research* 47:1–64.

Wittrock, M.C. 1977. Education and hemispheric process of the brain. In *The human brain*, ed. M.C. Wittrock. New York: Prentice Hall.

________. 1980. *The brain and psychology*. New York: Academic Press.

Wood, C.C.; Goft, W.R.; and Day, R.S. 1971. Auditory evoked potentials during speech perception. *Science* 174:1248–1261.

Woolfolk, R.L., and Woolfolk, A.E. 1974. The effects of teacher verbal and nonverbal behaviors on student perceptions and attitudes. *AERA Journal* 11:297–303.

Yin, R.K. 1970. Face recognition by brain injured patients. *Neuropsychologia* 8:239–243.

Zurif, E.B., and Sact, P.E. 1970. The role of syntax in dichotic listening. *Neuropsychologia* 8:239–243.